Federalism and Decentralization in European Health and Social Care

Federalism and Decentralization in European Health and Social Care

Edited by

Joan Costa-Font

Reader in Political Economy, London School of Economics and Political Science, United Kingdom

and

Scott L. Greer

Associate Professor, Department of Health Management and Policy, University of Michigan, USA

First published 2013 by
PALGRAVE MACMILLAN

Palgrave Macmillan in the UK is an imprint of Macmillan Publishers Limited, registered in England, company number 785998, of Houndmills, Basingstoke, Hampshire RG21 6XS.

Palgrave Macmillan in the US is a division of St Martin's Press LLC, 175 Fifth Avenue, New York, NY 10010.

Palgrave Macmillan is the global academic imprint of the above companies and has companies and representatives throughout the world.

Palgrave® and Macmillan® are registered trademarks in the United States, the United Kingdom, Europe and other countries.

ISBN 978–0–230–28524–8

This book is printed on paper suitable for recycling and made from fully managed and sustained forest sources. Logging, pulping and manufacturing processes are expected to conform to the environmental regulations of the country of origin.

A catalogue record for this book is available from the British Library.

A catalog record for this book is available from the Library of Congress.

10   9   8   7   6   5   4   3   2   1
22 21 20 19 18 17 16 15 14 13

Printed and bound in Great Britain by
CPI Antony Rowe, Chippenham and Eastbourne

Contents

Tables and Figures

Tables

Figures

Acknowledgments

This book is the result of a joint undertaking between Joan Costa-Font and Scott L. Greer, working together at the London School of Economics and Political Science. We are grateful to David K. Jones for his comments, Connie Rockman for administrative assistance, and Liz Blackmore for her patience while waiting for the manuscript to be fully edited.

Contributors

Joan Costa-Font, London School of Economics and Political Science, London, England

Thomas Czypionka, Institute for Advanced Studies, Vienna

Berit Gerritzen, University of St Gallen, St Gallen, Switzerland

Scott L. Greer, University of Michigan, Ann Arbor, Michigan, United States

David K. Jones, University of Michigan, Ann Arbor, Michigan, United States

Gebhard Kirchgässner, University of St Gallen, St Gallen, Switzerland

Katarzyna A. Kuć-Czajkowska, Maria Curie Skłodowska University, Lublin, Poland

Janet Laible, Lehigh University, Bethlehem, Pennsylvania, United States

Jon Magnussen, Norwegian University of Science and Technology, Trondheim

Pål E. Martinussen, SINTEF Technology and Society, Department of Health Research, Trondheim

Margitta Mätzke, Johannes Kepler University Linz, Austria

Małgorzata Rabczewska, Maria Curie Skłodowska University, Lublin, Poland

Ulrike Schneider, WU Vienna – Vienna University of Economics and Business, Vienna, Austria

Birgit Trukeschitz, WU Vienna – Vienna University of Economics and Business, Vienna, Austria

Gilberto Turati, Department of Economics and Public Finance "G. Prato" University of Torino, Italy

1

Health System Federalism and Decentralization: What Is It, Why Does It Happen, and What Does It Do?

Joan Costa-Font and Scott L. Greer

1. Introduction

Discussions of decentralization in health systems are ubiquitous, in politics and political economy, in economics, in health services, and in public policy. So is decentralization or territorial complexity in health policy and other areas of welfare responsibility, such as education and social care. It seems no country's policy elites or scholars can quite stop debating the territorial organization of their government, public administration, and health services. They also decentralized more, starting in the 1970s in most cases. Its causes are much discussed, with diversity, democracy, and nationalism all playing clear roles (Hooghe et al. 2010; Loughlin et al. 2011; McEwen and Moreno 2005).

The rising tide of decentralization has major consequences for at least some health and social care systems (Saltman et al. 2007). Symbolically, it undermines the link between health, social citizenship, and the state (Greer 2009; Ferrera 2005). There is a strong tradition of thought that associates the state with citizenship, and which assumes that as both a practical and ethical matter, social citizenship rights such as health should be a national responsibility. From that point of view, any fragmentation of health services would be seen as privileging some at the expense of the rest, and hence would be unfair and unequal. However, the development of European integration and deepening of democracy unveiled differences in preferences and need, and the increasing perception of government inefficiency acted as a trigger for decentralization reforms; health care was a key one among them both in budget magnitude and strategic importance. More specifically, Besley and Kudamatsu (2006) argue that the correlation between health and

1

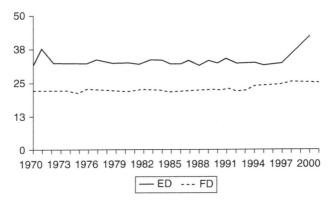

Figure 1.1 Expenditure and fiscal decentralization in the OECD (1970–2001)
Source: Stegarescu, 2005.

democracy can be explained because they contend that democracies demand accountability to a broad set of citizens at regular intervals.

These patterns are complex; to speak of decentralization as if it were simple is to create confusion. Figure 1.1 shows that decentralization of expenditures (ED) is more prevalent than decentralization of fiscal revenues (FD), but looking at patterns there is a clear decentralization of patterns in OECD countries after the mid-1990s. More and more countries have been entrusting at least the management of health systems, if not their revenue raising, to regional and local governments (also Hooghe et al. 2010; Adolph et al. 2012).

Decentralization promises all sorts of things: to permit diversity and experimentation; to encourage learning and competition; to bring policymakers closer to the people so they are more informed and accountable; to coordinate and delegate; to get the central government out of the details of local policy; to engage people in decisions affecting their lives; to reflect territorial differentiation and afford stateless nations some self-determination. It is no wonder that it has appeared as a solution to all sorts of problems and it has been associated with all sorts of democratizing, modernizing, and budget-cutting policies. It can, in particular, be a way to rejuvenate and defend welfare states. Some economists have presented it as an alternative to privatization (Tanzi 2008). Unlike the privatization strategy that would lead to making use of market to complement or supplement what public healthcare systems provide, the decentralization strategy attempts to transfer health care and other responsibilities to subnational levels of government, creating as a result further veto power to attempts to wipe out public healthcare provision at a country level. This argument is consistent with evidence that decentralization does not lead to a "race to the bottom" (Costa-Font and Rico 2006) and if public entrepreneurs are scattered through the territory, decentralization can further public healthcare development (Costa-Font 2010a; Costa-Font et al. 2011). Political scientists are less likely to approach the choice of political institution as an optimization problem, but their many case studies of decentralization driven by an effort to enhance or defend welfare provision are consonant with this idea.

For all the importance of decentralization as a phenomenon, inquiry reveals that as a concept it is much too broad. It has almost no meaning on its own or that it can be invoked for almost anything, up to and including obviously centralizing policies within certain regional territories. More generally, decentralization proxies variables are as diverse as "regional autonomy", "regional and local democracy", and "veto points".

2. The book's mission

This publication both integrates and, we hope, clarifies this practically and theoretically confusing realm. It integrates across three divides: between economics and political science, between "federal" and other kinds of country, and between health and social care. It musters two disciplines – economics and political science – to map the past, present, and future of the territorial allocation of authority in the decentralized and big countries of Western Europe. It bridges between the different categories of state and terms such as "federal" or "devolution" that often obscure the interesting similarities and differences between Austria, Belgium, France, Germany, Italy, Poland, Spain, Switzerland, Nordic countries, and the UK. It thereby shows the ubiquity of territorial politics and the necessarily territorial nature of many health and social care policies. Finally, it incorporates social care as well as health. Social care is not just an understudied sibling of the healthcare system; it is also a key determinant of the workings of health care because its success or failure influences both the composition of need for health care and the fate of patients after their treatment is over. In ageing societies with increasing incidence of non-communicable and chronic diseases, the distinction between health and social care is increasingly difficult to maintain as a policy or an intellectual stance.

It clarifies, we hope, by stripping out assumptions that economists, political scientists, and practitioners have too often introduced into their analyses of decentralization and the allocation of authority in health. All too often, intriguing hypotheses with a germ of truth have been given more credit and power than they deserve, whether it is the old Jacobin hypothesis that centralized states deliver equality and prevent corruption or the Tiebout hypothesis that decentralization forces local governments to compete away their services (Chapter 2). Instead, it brings to the fore both theoretical discussion from second-generation fiscal federalism and new politics of the welfare state, alongside empirical evidence both quantitative and qualitative of different European countries that differ widely in institutional design and historical inertias.

This introduction frames the theoretical and empirical chapters by stating the key questions that are often begged or ignored: what does decentralization mean, why does it happen, and what are its effects? It then briefly reviews the book, highlighting lessons from the theories reviewed in Chapter 2 and the country studies.

3. The allocation of authority in health care

There is a great deal of received wisdom about decentralization, much of it the half-remembered remains of debates about the territorial organization of one country or another, or overenthusiastic application of intuitive but limited hypotheses. Unfortunately, much of it is contradictory, dated, limited, or even possibly wrong and often does a disservice to the authors who formulated the original ideas. The second chapter shows how both economics and political science have handled the causes and effects of decentralization. The territorial politics of health is a terminologically and intellectually complicated area hosting multiple disciplines, approaches, and nationally specific discourses. "Decentralization" can be a slippery topic that encompasses topics as diverse as constitutional change in the UK and re-centralization of planning in Norway (see relevant chapters in the book). This chapter presents our shared questions.

We define decentralization as a change in the allocation of authority in which powers shift to smaller territorial units of government. We argue for agnosticism about the causes and consequences of decentralization. There are plenty of explanations and intuitions, and functionalist interpretations, but many go beyond their data. This book, starting with a clear focus on the territorial allocation of authority, helps bring out the plausibility and limits of different causes and consequences.

3.1. What does decentralization mean?

As mentioned above, the very meaning of decentralization is a cause of no little confusion. Much of the problem lies in the continuing use of a framework developed by a World Bank economist in the early 1980s that incorporated almost every form of administrative change into the definition of "decentralization" including, most notably, privatization as well as more conventional territorial definitions (Rondinelli 1981, 1983). This definition creates a remarkable level of confusion: simply put, creating a Scottish Parliament, selling British Telecom, and moving the drivers' license agency out of London are three profoundly different kinds of actions, and lumping them together does not make them easier to understand (Lemieux 2001). Only in the crude perspective of early-1980s neoliberal economics could they be seen as meaningfully similar in causes, mechanisms, or consequences (Exworthy and Greener 2008; Peckham et al. 2007).

It is not hard to define decentralization more meaningfully. The first important statement about decentralization is that it is *territorial*. It means shifting the territorial level of organization of some power or another, altering the allocation of territorial authority by giving rise to some expansion of regional autonomy, and more specifically a regional political agency (Besley 2006). This means that it excludes de-concentration (moving government offices around) as well as other kinds of administrative reform, such as privatization or New Public Management. Governments committed to such other reforms have sometimes also embraced decentralization, but there is no necessary link between decentralization and any other kind of reform. For every case of decentralization coupled with neoliberal management reforms in this book, there is one in which it went with expansion of the welfare state (e.g. Spain) or an effort to democratize public administration (e.g. France), and the epitome of new public management, the UK under Thatcher and Major, was also the epitome of territorial and political centralization (Bulpitt 1983). The territorial allocation of authority is the object of study here.

The key subordinate distinction for many purposes is that between elected and unelected general governments. Territorial politics and territorial issues are ubiquitous, of course. Population characteristics including demographics, economies, and health needs all vary territorially. As a consequence every government policy has some territories that get more than others: money spent on teaching hospitals rewards areas with those (usually big old cities), while money spent on rural primary care does nothing for cities. This automatically means that territorial politics always has a distributive component: taxpayers are funding programs and policies that have different effects in different places. But those distributive decisions can be made more or less visible and political. Heterogeneity can be accommodated rather than set aside. Greater visibility for territorial differences, in the case of health and social care, can have many effects. It can trigger further healthcare development and innovation if political credit can be traced to regional incumbents. But, as Chapter 2 explains, soft budget constraints can be particularly pervasive in the case of health care because it is unlikely that the central government will not bail out regions that fail to meet their budgetary commitments (Crivelli et al. 2010).

Chapter 2 presents the work of economists and political scientists on the conditions for the various outcomes, stressing how institutional design can shape them. But one finding that is rare in territorial politics literature shapes the data, health systems, and health policies of the countries we study. That is the distinction between National Health Service systems, where taxation finances a state-dominated system, and social insurance systems where legislation shapes semi-public insurance carriers. National Health Service systems in decentralized countries, such as Italy, Spain, Norway, and the UK, tend to be decentralized to the major level of local or regional government (e.g. regions in Italy, Spain, and the UK, or local government in Scandinavia). In social insurance systems, whether centralized or decentralized, the health finance system and the organization of health care are separated from regional governments, as in France where the state's use of regional health agencies is quite separate from elected regional governments, or in federal Germany, whose constitutional court went so far as to declare the logic of territory alien to the logic of social insurance (see the chapter by Mätzke). The reasons for this difference – the apparent propensity to decentralize National Health Service systems – remain as unexplored as the difference is unremarked. It could be a strategy to democratize, to harness competition, to spread blame, or just a response to the expectations and veto players found in social insurance systems.

3.2. Why do countries decentralize?

For all the debates about decentralization and the allocation of authority, there is remarkably little structured attention to territorial politics and territorial political change: it can be extraordinarily difficult to identify the responsibilities of tiers of government within a country, let alone to explain how they got that way.

The dominant mode of discussing centralization and decentralization in health is technocratic. It argues the costs and benefits of a particular allocation of authority: will services be more efficient, innovative or responsive, or cheaper if they are run by a particular level of government? We see it in every article about centralization or decentralization that simply takes governments at their word about the functional benefits of a particular allocation of authority (Costa-Font 2010b), or that argue for one change or another on grounds of good health services.

The problem is when these functional justifications are taken as explanations of the decision. Decentralization might produce better health policies in the UK or Spain, but a cursory look at those countries' histories suggests that health policy did not motivate devolution or furthering regional autonomy, but the demands lie in the political arena instead. At most, it was one of many issues that contributed to a sense among leaders of the stateless nations that they should have more autonomy (Greer 2007; Tanzi 2008; Costa-Font 2009). In general, it is a methodological failing to assume that a given allocation of authority is explained either by its practical effects or by statements of policy justification. As some of the following chapters reveal, decentralization might or might not be efficiency-enhancing overall. It depends on the underlying incentives of the institutional design of the health system.

The association between decentralization and other political events further muddies the waters. There have been cases in which territorial decentralization was a technique to cut back the state. There have been cases in which it seemed like an idea to do more with less in an era of cutbacks (as in the French cases discussed by Jones in his chapter). There have also been cases where all of these explanations were at work at once: in Spain in the 1990s, regional politicians wanted health systems and the central government was increasingly interested in shedding expensive, inflationary welfare services. Many of the regions then adopted various forms of public–private health systems management. New public management, states shedding responsibilities, and regional pressure for more power were all at work in Spain, and there is no reason to associate the Spanish or any other decentralization decisions exclusively with nationalism, neoliberalism, democratization, or new public management. All these explanations are hypotheses. Their actual value remains to be discovered.

The literature explaining territorial political choice and change, moreover, tends to concentrate on the politics of multinationalism in a few states such as Canada, Spain, and the UK that decentralized as a way to stay together (Stepan 2004). This is a useful complement to older studies that focused on the voluntarily created federations such as Australia and the USA, but it still leaves the territorial politics of less ethnonationally complex states under-researched (for a few works that start to remedy this problem by studying the complexity of government in less ethnonationally diverse states, see Baldersheim and Rose 2010; O'Dwyer 2006; Jeffery 2003).

Neither the review in Chapter 2 by Costa-Font and Greer nor the country chapters should give much comfort to those who would adopt a priori assumptions or functionalist explanations for decentralization. Efficiency and better government are essentially contested concepts and their explanatory power may vary. So are stateless nationalism, partisanship, localism, or any other value. There is a tremendous amount of variation that should be explored, rather than assumed, if we are to understand or contribute to debates about decentralization in health policy.

3.3. What are the effects of decentralization?

While decentralization is not always a health policy (health can be caught up in broader political changes) it makes sense to evaluate it for its effects on health policy. Does multiplying smaller governments produce greater or lesser efficiency? What kinds of divergence do we see, and do we see diffusion and learning of good ideas?

The next chapter will make the case that this question, while useful, must be posed with care. The particular form of decentralization shapes the incentives and democratic accountability, as well as the effective political power, of each government. This is a question that puts the emphasis on institutional changes and the design of different governments as well as their interactions with pre-existing health systems and territorial heterogeneity of all sorts. So while we ask this question, our answer is framed in terms of what institutional frameworks, under what conditions, appear to trigger beneficial effects for health systems and health.

4. Conclusion

Government decentralization of health policy responsibilities is a common feature throughout Europe, which has not received an adequate level of attention in the literature. This book attempts to bridge the literature gap and offer an interdisciplinary answer to the questions that government decentralization encompass. Health is a fruitful area to examine for scholars of federalism if they are to better understand the effect of a territorial distribution of power and government resources over the vertical levels of government.

The next chapter reviews and synthesizes the state of the art in economics and political science. Both disciplines have long traditions of discussing federalism and strong, applied research agendas. More recently, both disciplines have seen new developments and a degree of convergence as qualitative evidence, quantitative research, studies of institutions, and studies of political decision-makers produce similar arguments and evidence. The subsequent chapters discuss the allocation of authority and territorial politics of health in Europe, covering all the countries with substantial regional power as well as Scandinavian states with strong local and regional governments, and the French and Polish systems, where regional elected governments are weaker and which are accordingly interesting for their illumination of the ways that decentralization and territorial politics work when elected regional governments are not major parts of government. They show how ostensible decentralization can actually be a form of more effective central control, as in France for example. Collectively, the chapters fill gaps in our understanding of how territory really works in health policy.

References

Adolph, C., da Fonseca, E.M. and Greer, S.L., 2012, Allocation of authority in European health systems. Forthcoming, *Social Science and Medicine*.

Baldersheim, H. and Rose, L.E., 2010, *Territorial Choice: The Politics of Boundaries and Borders*, Palgrave Macmillan, New York.

Besley, Y., 2006, *Principled Agents?* Oxford University Press, UK.

Besley, T. and Kudamastsu, M., 2006, Health and democracy, *American Economic Review*, 96 (2), pp. 313–318.

Bulpitt, J., 1983, *Territory and Power in the United Kingdom: An Interpretation*, Manchester University Press, Manchester.

Costa-Font, Joan, 2009, Simultaneity, asymmetric devolution and economic incentives in Spanish regional elections, *Regional and Federal Studies*, 19 (1), pp. 165–184.

Costa-Font, Joan, 2010a, Devolution, diversity and welfare reform: long-term care in the "Latin Rim", *Social Policy & Administration*, 44 (4), pp. 481–494. ISSN 0144-5596.

Costa-Font, Joan, 2010b, Does devolution lead to regional inequalities in welfare activity? *Environment and Planning C: Government and Policy*, 28 (3), pp. 435–44.

Costa-Font, Joan and Rico, A., 2006, Vertical competition in the Spanish National Health System (NHS), *Public Choice*, 128 (3–4), pp. 477–498.

Costa-Font, Joan, Salvador-Carulla, Luis, Cabases, Juan, Alonso, Jordi and McDaid, David, 2011, Tackling neglect and mental health reform in a devolved system of welfare governance, *Journal of Social Policy*, 40, pp. 295–312.

Crivelli, E., Leive, A. and Stratmann, T., 2010, Subnational health spending and soft budget constraints in OECD countries. IMF Working Paper, 10/147.

Exworthy, Mark and Greener, Ian, 2008, Decentralization as a means to reorganize health-care in England: From theory to practice? in L. McKee, E. Ferlie and P. Hyde (eds), *Organizing and Reorganizing: Power and Change in Health Care Organizations*, Palgrave Macmillan, Basingstoke, pp. 46–58.

Ferrera, Maurizio, 2005, *The Boundaries of Welfare: European Integration and the New Spatial Politics of Social Protection*, Oxford University Press, Oxford.

Greer, S.L., 2007, *Nationalism and Self-Government: The Politics of Autonomy in Scotland and Catalonia*, State University of New York Press, Albany.

Greer, S.L. (Ed.), 2009, *Devolution and Social Citizenship in the United Kingdom*, Policy, Bristol.

Hazel, R., 2006, *The English Question*, Manchester University Press, Manchester.

Hooghe, Liesbet, Marks, Gary and Schakel, Arjan, 2010, *The Rise of Regional Authority: A Comparative Study of 42 Democracies*, Routledge, London.

Jeffery, C., 2003, The German Laender: from milieu-shaping to territorial politics, in K. Dyson and K. Goesz (eds), *Germany, Europe and the Politics of Constraint*, Oxford University Press for the British Academy, Oxford, pp. 97–108.

Lemieux, V., 2001, *Décentralisation, politiques publiques, et relations de pouvoir*, Presses de l'Université de Montreal, Montreal.

Loughlin, J., Hendriks, F., and Lidström, A., 2011, *The Oxford Handbook of Local and Regional Democracy in Europe*, Oxford University Press, Oxford.

McEwen, Nicola and Moreno, Luis, 2005, *The Territorial Politics of Welfare*, Routledge, London.

O'Dwyer, C., 2006, *Runaway State-Building: Patronage Politics and Democratic Development*, Johns Hopkins University Press, Baltimore.

Peckham, S., Exworthy, M., Powell, M. and Greener, I., 2007, Decentralizing health services in the UK: a new conceptual framework, *Public Administration*, 86 (2), pp. 559–580.

Rondinelli, D.A., 1981, Government decentralization in comparative theory and practice in developing countries, *International Review of Administrative Sciences*, 47, pp. 133–145.

Rondinelli, D.A., 1983, Decentralization in developing countries, *World Bank Staff Working Papers* (581), World Bank, Washington, D.C.

Saltman, R.B., Bankauskaite, V., and Vrangbæk, K. (Eds.), 2007, *Decentralization in Health Care: Analysis and Outcome*, Open University Press/McGraw-Hill Education, London.

Stegarescu, D., 2005, Public sector decentralization: measurement concepts and recent international trends, *Fiscal Studies*, 26 (3), pp. 301–333.

Stepan, A., 2004, Federalism and democracy: beyond the U.S. Model, in U.M. Amoretti and N. Gina Bermeo (eds), *Federalism and Territorial Cleavages*, Johns Hopkins University Press, Baltimore, pp. 441–456.

Tanzi, V., 2008, The future of fiscal federalism, *European Journal of Political Economy*, 24, pp. 705–712.

Part I
Background

2
Territory and Health: Perspectives from Economics and Political Science

Joan Costa-Font and Scott L. Greer

1. Introduction

It is tempting to talk about "decentralization" as if it were simple: a technical decision to grant more authority to regional or local governments, with the objective of aligning incentives, power, and information a bit more efficiently. But decentralization is far from simple. In fact, it is not a policy, it is not just a technocratic decision, and it does not have reliable and easily predictable effects. In effect, one of the reasons why health policy specialists, economists, and political scientists have had such difficulty with the effects of decentralization on health policy and, more generally, on the welfare state is that they have paid too little attention to the specific institutional pathways in which decentralization does and does not matter.

This chapter reviews the dominant discussions of economics and political science. It brings together findings and debates from two literatures, which substantially overlap and complement each other – where one is quiet and makes assumptions, the other tends to be more theoretically elaborate and debated. Joined, research and theories from the two fields shed much light on the political economy of decentralization and health. Section 2 defines decentralization with special reference to health systems. Section 3 reviews the reasons that political scientists and economists have identified for decentralization, without passing judgment on their often functionalist logic. Section 4 addresses the debates associated with decentralization, such as the race to the bottom, and sketches the logic of each debate. Section 5 then changes direction from these systemic, institutional and incentive-focused debates, to focus on the complex internal politics of regional governments – all too often forgotten in stylized accounts focused on architecture, incentives, and competition. Section 6 concludes by reviewing the answers of these literatures to the questions of the introduction: what does decentralization mean, why is it adopted, and what are its effects? The juxtaposition of those theoretical answers with the empirical chapters that follow shows the scale of the possible future research on the topic. The section, and the chapter, ends by highlighting the importance of this kind of research in the current fiscal and policy straits of Europe.

Tritely, the territorial politics of health are about unity and diversity. The allocation of authority between different levels of government reflects and shapes the balance between territorial differentiation and the advantages of risk pooling. In Europe, health care is typically financed through statewide insurance schemes either through taxes or social insurance contributions. Public healthcare financing takes advantage of pooling and single-payer welfare gains to counteract heterogeneity of insurance pooling and information asymmetry. This is consistent with the fact that in the majority of European countries, healthcare financing is a publicly financed package, but there is often at least a level of decentralization within the system. While 75% of total healthcare expenditures are publicly financed in Organisation for Economic Cooperation and Development (OECD) countries (OECD 2009), both needs and politics within health insurance pools differ dramatically between and within countries. One of the most obvious ways of improving health systems' accountability and efficiency in territorially differentiated societies is through allocating tasks, resources, and responsibilities to different levels of government, moulding health systems by allocating responsibilities to the "relatively more efficient" level of government and harnessing intergovernmental competition (Breton 1996).

The economics of fiscal federalism gives quite clear instructions as to how this should be done. The classical principle put forth to guide decentralization processes (Oates 1972) is that "each public service is provided by the jurisdiction having control over the minimum geographic area that would internalise benefits and costs of such provision". In theory, for fiscal decentralization to take its full effects, fiscal responsibilities in the form of taxes and subsidies alongside political responsibilities should be allocated to subcentral governments.[1]

Traditional economics of fiscal federalism tend to model governments as firms competing for taxpayers by selling services. This argument relies on mobility. There is, however, an increasing amount of interest in arguments that rely on other kinds of competition – electoral competition between governments to be seen as better in the eyes of their citizens. Mobility is not irrelevant but nor is it the main mechanism that defines the decentralization of health systems in Europe. Rather, the most powerful mechanism is that of political and fiscal accountability, and more specifically yardstick competition. The latter is in many ways a return to the classical claim that a representative government works best, the closer it is to the people (Stigler 1957).

Political science historically has been a good deal less prescriptive, in part because there is less clarity about the normative objectives of federalism, the actual reliability of the mechanisms that would produced the desired aims, and the actual desirability and simplicity of the normative goals. Political scientists note that the purpose of a given allocation of authority is often unclear; most federations are products of either compromises intended to hold a country together for some other purpose such as military victory (Riker 1964), or for the purpose of maintaining the borders of a multinational state (which, as Stepan 2001 noted, is far more common). The normative case for federalism might be unclear, and its contribution to democracy or regime stability has never been seen as clear in political studies (Levy 2007). An allocation of authority created by the need to unite under military threat, or the need to satisfy stateless nations' elites, or to serve given economic interests, might be stable and successful on its terms but a failure by the standards of fiscal federalism. Likewise, the mechanisms of decentralization are poorly understood and little researched; recent research in political science has found that decentralization is indeterminate and underspecified as a variable and disappointing as a policy (Treisman 2007; Lane and Ersson 2005). Decentralized states seem to underperform centralized states in multiple ways, including procedural democracy (Gerring and Thacker 2008). In the last decade political scientists, seeking to add some specificity to "decentralization", have turned their attention to institutional mechanisms that make some states' allocations of authority more or less equitable, sustainable, and democratic, and found a huge field of complex institutional interactions in which details matter (Bednar 2011). Moving power "closer" to people, as Stigler (1957) suggests in a reprise of the classical republican tradition, turns out not to be much of a guarantee of responsiveness or democracy, and the principal–agent relationships that underpin so many economic models turn out to be easier to impute than to actually find. Finally, the normative objectives of centralization or decentralization are hardly simple in themselves. The *Federalist Papers* make a compelling and influential argument that smaller polities are less democratic, and democracy in itself contains complexities ranging from the threat of majority tyranny, to imbalances of power among citizens, to the problem of salience (it is by no means clear that it is bad when a few people who care win against many who do not). Likewise, redistribution among citizens is hardly unproblematic when there is no single national community associated with a given state (Banting and Corbett 2002; Banting 2006). The upshot is that political science, while less theoretically and practically ambitious than economics, has a stock of critical perspectives on the often uncritical arguments for and against any given allocation of authority.

2. What is healthcare decentralization?

Every country has a certain level of decentralized allocation of authority over health policy (Adolph et al. 2012). Decentralization means the power and autonomy of subcentral governments (Oates 1986), identifiable in the strength and decision space (Bossert 1998) of subnational power in the form of resources, lawmaking and taxation powers. It is part of the general allocation of political authority in a society, and subsumes the formal legal category of federalism, which maps only poorly onto the actual degree of regional or local autonomy (our chapters suggest that federal Austria and Germany are more centralized than non-federal Spain and the UK).

At a minimum, decentralization involves legal or financial mechanisms that give units of government a greater role in a policy area such as health (see the Introduction, Chapter 1, for more definitional detail). The first categorical division, before any further discussion, is that between elected and unelected governments. An elected government, particularly one with a broad range of policy responsibilities, is a very different creature from a branch or field office of a central government. Put simply, the formal and informal hierarchy that keeps a field office in check does not work as well, if at all, with an elected regional government that has its own electoral mandate, electoral accountability, and leaders with their own partisan and personal ambitions and political strategies. The leaders of the unelected Polish and French agencies (see chapters 7 and 10) responsible for healthcare services can be coordinated, commanded, and fired by their superiors in the health ministries; the health ministries in the other states enjoy few or no such powers. Central–local relations tend to be much more about bargaining when central and local governments are both elected, and the resulting interactions are both complicated and distinct (Trench 2006). Power and money are crucial, and their distribution is the focus of territorial politics and the main determinant of what decentralization does.

2.1. Law

Law means the legal powers of the regions. What do they control, and what can they do? Law partly means the overall structural features of the state: the constitutional provisions governing regions, the extent and contents of the legislative framework governing regional powers, the independence and structure of the judiciary, and the status and number of intergovernmental agencies and formal arrangements. It shows up in all sorts of ways – both the broad allocation of authority (such as the one that gives social insurance to the federal government and hospital policy to the states in Germany) and in details (such as the endless bureaucratic coordination problems between different governments doing different things). The central state does often exert an active role in invading state powers and repossession can be legally possible (Costa-Font 2005). Courts are also capable of intervening in the distribution of powers, frequently to the benefit of the central state and not necessarily solidaristic and territorially bounded health systems at the regional level (Fierlbeck 2011).

Understanding the role of law in healthcare policymaking involves understanding the overall territorial structure of the state, and then the specific provisions in law. So the health powers of regional governments tend to be set within a broader framework governing regional governments' powers and are framed in a language of political generalists (e.g. distinguishing between primary and secondary legislation in the UK, or between framework, state, and regional laws in Spain) (Greer 2006; Poirier 2001). This reflects the fact that most regional governments' creation and shape is due to much bigger political issues than the quality of health policymaking.

2.2. Money

As undergraduates learn in public policy classes, no money equates to no policy. The power to act in a given area is not significant without the money to do something. Without money, most policy can affect neither lives nor votes nor careers. Thus, finance is as important to understanding the politic of decentralized health care as law. There are a wide range of financial mechanisms in European states, and it is common for multiple mechanisms to coexist in the same country (Boadway and Shah 2009).

Both expenditure decentralization and tax revenue decentralization are imperfect measures of autonomy because not all amounts are truly expended by subcentral governments, or decisions on expenditure taken at a subcentral level. The latter is particularly the case when subcentral governments are funded by block grants, as in the UK and Spain. In those cases, finance is centrally controlled or shared, but the content of policy is largely determined by regional governments.[2]

More specifically, decentralization's success depends on the extent to which it manages to align the political credit and fiscal blame for each policy within the health system. If the central government does not decentralize the "blame" of public policy action (taxation) and only decentralizes mechanisms of credit claiming (expenditure), it is likely that decentralization will bring an expansion of government expenditure with limited effects on efficiency (Costa-Font 2010b). The latter is commonly known as a soft budget constraint – budget constraints that lack credibility can be surpassed without real threat of consequences. Similarly, lack of subnational financial autonomy and more specifically limits to the expansion of financial resources to pay for health services can be a strategy for cost containment employed frequently to impede an expansion of health expenditure (Lopez-Casasnovas et al. 2005), and increased diversity in the system. In such cases, one might not observe a generalized efficiency outcome from government decentralization.

2.3. Resources

Finally, there are resources: the staff, infrastructure, knowledge, and equipment that any organization acquires in the course of doing its work. Resources are a lagged effect of expenditure (training staff turns money into the resource of expertise), but cannot always be built quickly. It means that governments are not all interchangeable; local knowledge is valuable and encoded in certain organizations, as is technical skill or highly educated specialists. The distribution of resources means that intergovernmental cooperation is frequently critical – and that governments given new tasks and money might not deliver well at first.

2.4. Health systems under decentralization

Institutional factors such as political and social, legal and historical constraints play a role in constraining the efficiency of fiscal decentralization even when it does not always model them more formally. Figure 2.1 plots the patterns of public health-expenditure variation relative to the gross domestic product (GDP) of each of the countries considered in this study. It shows no clear relationship between allocation of authority and expenditure. Indeed, social insurance systems such as in France, Germany, Austria, and Belgium exhibit high levels of expenditure, with the exception of veto-ridden Switzerland, where federalism as well as a more intense use of private providers explains lower levels of expenditure (Immergut 1992).

Figure 2.2 plots patterns of relative public health expenditure of health systems organized under the umbrella of a federal state against expenditure

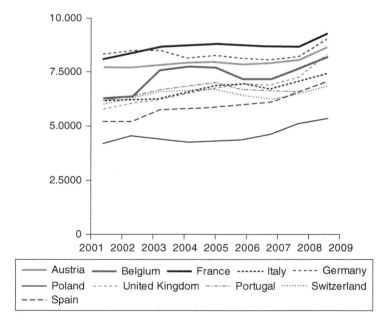

Figure 2.1   Relative public health expenditure to GDP in Europe
Source: OECD, 2001.

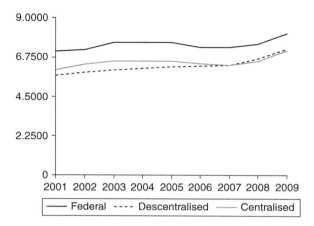

Figure 2.2 Relative public health expenditure by healthcare constitutional form
Source: OECD, 2011.

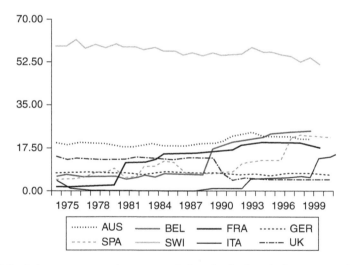

Figure 2.3 Autonomous own-tax revenue in hands of subcentral governments
Source: Stegarescu, 2005.

of countries that do not but have or have not decentralized the provision of health care to subcentral governments. Importantly, evidence on unadjusted relative health expenditure suggests that decentralized health systems do not exhibit significantly different levels of relative expenditure, but that countries that are organized as federal states have traditionally exhibited about 1% larger relative health expenditure than the rest, though expenditure patterns seem to reveal a similar evolution over time, which indicates that the difference might well carry a historical weight.

This framework can seem strangely besides the point in social insurance systems, since most of the health spending and practically all of the political, policy, and academic debate focuses on the money that flows through the social insurance system (a point that Mätzke makes in her chapter on Germany in this book). Who cares how Laender are financed in Germany if the real money and action is in the interaction of social funds, professions, and the federal state that regulates them?[3] Interregional inequalities, should they exist, should be studied not through the lens of intergovernmental relations but rather through the politics of the social insurance system. This is true (and an interesting research agenda), but for current purposes there are two answers. First, there is a noticeable amount of regional government health spending in many systems, often focused on hospitals (e.g. in Belgium; see Figure 2.3 and Germany). Its disposition matters, even if it is not salient in public and political debates. Second, social insurance funds and providers are hardly creatures found in the state of nature. They are methods for gathering and allocating money that were generalized and are increasingly tightly regulated by states. Their room for maneuver is set by the governments that constitute and regulate them – no matter their history, they are an allocative tool of the government that structures their framework.

Financial frameworks are impressively intricate, as every country chapter in this book will show. The important aspect for our purposes is that they shape the extent of possible policy divergence, and the extent to which there is "coercive isomorphism" (i.e. the adoption of the same structures and policies because a superior level of government imposed them).[4] That is usually easy to see when discussing law, but more difficult in terms of finance. Crudely, the more untied funding a region has, the more autonomy it has to make specific health policies (as with Scotland in its first 11 years, when it had a large block grant and could focus on spending it better or worse on health, education, and local government). The more it controls its own taxes, the more autonomy it has to have a distinctive political economy (the European record here is probably the highly autonomous Basque Country). The more tied funding, the more the priorities of the central government will affect it, and the less money it has overall, the less it probably matters. It is no surprise that the block-funded Spanish, Italian, and UK regional governments are the dominant players in their healthcare systems and are recognized as such. The fiscal framework, like the legal framework, shapes the extent to which regional governments can diverge – meaning adapt, innovate, compete, or drag state average outcomes up or down.

3. Reasons for health system decentralization

There are a variety of reasons for decentralization, all of them found frequently and all of them appealing to different normative bases and theories of territorial politics. Despite the diversity of territorial politics and demands for a different allocation of authority, it is possible to construct a basic list of the reasons that economists and political scientists have identified, with overlapping concerns expressed in different language.

3.1. Efficiency: preference heterogeneity and mobility

Decentralization is naturally an institutional device to embrace heterogeneity and overcome the uniformity by granting regional autonomy to region states to shape policies to their preferences; hence it stands as a mechanism through which a welfare state can be made consistent with the existence of heterogeneity among voter and interest groups across territory. From this perspective, common in economics, the desirability of decentralization boils down to whether the gains from addressing regional heterogeneity overcome lower scale economies and higher transaction costs that a centralized health system would avoid.

The key underlying normative proposition of the theory of fiscal federalism (Oates 1972, Weingast 2006) is that decentralization is an institutional reform that provides incentives for subcentral governments to spend to attain consumption efficiency, which would not be achieved under a centralized institutional organization. The latter will be the case of so called "subnational public goods", namely goods where the state level allows social marginal benefit and the social marginal cost to match, and hence maximize efficiency. Many healthcare services, with the exception of communicable disease control, qualify as regional public (or publicly managed) goods; that is, goods whose optimal scale is at the central level to respond to territorially scattered needs and preferences. More generally health needs tend to be far from homogenous; hence the identification of potential (often unobserved) marginal benefits and true marginal costs tend to be more efficient at a subnational level. In other words, under or overprovision of public services under a centralized allocation of regional public goods would come with a cost to taxpayers that would not exist under a decentralized government with hard budgets (Bordignon and Turati 2009).

If preferences and willingness to pay for different health programs differ throughout the territory, individuals could sort themselves, voting with their feet and either choose health care out of their state or reside in the area where their preferences for health care match the existing supply. Examples explain why there is evidence of internal patient mobility based on the existence of observable quality differences across the territory (Levaggi and Zanola 2007). Nonetheless, skeptics might have a point in arguing that it is difficult for the average citizen to identity a regional or an area where quality of care is higher (it is certainly difficult for health policy scholars to identify good health care, given the state of indicators and data; consider the resources that have to be invested to get beyond life expectancy). The costs of mobility within a given territory might wipe out the benefits, and the most specialized procedures where excellence might be clearest are also the ones that most systems find a way to provide to all citizens equally (as with Norway's national hospitals in Chapter 6).

Another criticism points out that an argument against one given territorial allocation of authority presupposes that another one would be better. It would more generally challenge the benefit of decentralization against a uniform central state when scale economies are lost. Decentralization brings complexity, and in some institutional settings gridlock, to the system, and especially in the transition leads to duplicities and potential sunk costs, and politically gives rise to veto points to central-level legislation. However, the question is whether complexities are a one-off event or whether they endure over time, and lead to cost savings as some studies identify (Costa-Font and Moscone 2008).

3.2. Accountability and scale

Possibly one of the most important benefits of government decentralization lies in the associated effect of competition between constituent governments, and hence tightens the so-called political agency. This argument relies on the "exit option", using mobility to discipline governments and make them offer a good balance of services and taxes (Tiebout 1956).[5]

While intergovernmental competition is important, it is too limiting to confine it to horizontal competition theories that model governments as firms and taxpayers as consumers. There are other types of competition between governments because citizens have a "voice" as well as an exit option (Hirschman 1970). Rather than moving, citizens can reward or punish their governments for performance relative to neighboring jurisdictions and other governments on other levels. A resident of Upper Austria can compare that state's services with those of neighboring states, and its government with the Austrian federal government, and reward or punish as she chooses, in what economists call "yardstick competition."

Clearly decentralized forms of taxation and governance lead to diversity in services and prices for such services (taxes) and therefore citizens' capacity to form the so-called wicksellian connections (that is to associate expenditures action and taxes) under decentralization. However, any but the most centralized allocation of authority implies the introduction of another level of government in the provision of health care, which can blur the lines of accountability. It is generally true that comparing health-system performance is a complicated task for individuals. The latter has to do with the information imperfections and the trust relationship in many healthcare services, and hence the difficulty in observing important dimensions of quality. However, there are salient features such as coverage, waiting times and waiting list that can, with more or less caution and political effectiveness, be used as proxies.

More local accountability must be balanced, however, against economies of scale and externalities. One of the main reasons to keep some health services centralized lies in the existence of optimal scales for global public goods. This is the case of the management of epidemics for instance. In addition to scale benefits of centralization, it is important to mention externalities or interjurisdictional spillovers both positive and negative that can in turn lead to an under- or over-provision of public goods. Indeed, if spillovers in one specific government responsibility are high enough then the utility of decentralization diminishes (though some theory contends that if spillovers are high enough, decentralized expenditures are welfare-enhancing (Koethenbuerger 2008)).

3.3. History and politics

Nor are all decentralization processes technocratic enough to describe in the language of fiscal federalism. Anybody who wishes to enter such normatively tinged discussions must remember that territorial politics is more than health politics. For example, Spain, Belgium, and the UK decentralized because the alternative was (and remains) the breakup of the entire country.[6] Health is a single policy area, and it is more often acted upon in these debates than it is the cause of the debates; even if it is a dispute about allocating money that is driven by health care, the politics are fundamentally those of governments arguing about money rather than debates about good health policy. In countries without such important territorial politics, the allocation of powers is more likely to be driven by partisan and political issues than by any theory of federalism, which means that the strictures of federal design matter less than politicians' efforts to assign policies to the levels of government most likely to carry them out in accordance with the politicians' desires. In only a few countries, most of them highly unitary jurisdictions such as England or Sweden, are discussions of decentralization at all technocratic.[7]

There is nothing wrong with discussing the costs and benefits of decentralization, but it is worth remembering that the terms of the trade are more often about the politics of multinational states and partisan advantage than they are about the quality of health policy. Even in states such as Poland and France, where elected regional governments are not a factor in healthcare policy, the decision to decentralize or not decentralize is a deeply political one. Formal centralization by no means eliminates territorial political contestation. An ahistorical explanation of a state's allocation of authority is going to go nowhere in most countries, and evaluations of its policy consequences should be mindful of the world beyond policy consequences.

3.4. Experimentation

The link between decentralization and experimentation has been an old argument that dates back to Hayek (1937) and his argument that decentralization, by increasing experimentation, produced more information on how to run a government. The Affordable Care Act of 2010, in the USA, was a nice example of this Hayekian dynamic, with the plan of Republican Governor Mitt Romney, adopted in Massachusetts, lifted to the national level by Barack Obama and the Democrats.

Evidence from different countries reveals that experimentation does take place. First, regional governments tend to legitimize themselves by introducing innovation in the way they run the health system (Greer 2004). Second, decentralization can help to provide voice to the opposition party or regional minorities that they would lack under a decentralized system. The latter nurtures some degree of vertical competition with the central government that can provide additional political incentives for innovation (Costa-Font and Rico 2006b). Finally, if soft budget constraints are corrected, decentralization can provide fiscal incentives for innovation, especially if innovation encompasses costs savings. Some evidence of the latter is found in some European countries (Costa-Font and Moscone 2008). In contrast, if states are dissimilar, decentralization allows experimentation at a lower scale and, as some scholars argue, enhances the credibility of the fiscal contract due to the lower cost of letting a small state go bust.[8] In general, experimentation might be a reason to decentralize, but neither discipline nor the chapters in this book have found much evidence that it, rather than concerns about representing territorial variation, is a reason that has actually caused countries to adopt a decentralized allocation of authority. Like many functionalist explanations, it makes more sense as an advantage of a system than as its explanation.

4. Challenges

The potential disadvantages and unexpected effects of decentralization are various; careful studies of decentralization and territorial politics have found them as often as they have found advantages (e.g. Grindle 2009; Treisman 2007), and a massive literature review found little or no democratic case for decentralized as against accountable and focused government (Gerring and Thacker 2008). There are a variety of reasons why decentralization might not produce the desired results. This section reviews the debates that appear in economics and political science.

4.1. Race to the bottom? Under-provision and over-provision

One of the reason decentralization is either advocated, or subject to criticism has been labeled as the "Leviathan hypothesis" put forward by Brenan and Buchanan (1980). It is essentially an efficiency argument for decentralization following classical Bertrand price-competition games where governments are seen as agents competing on taxes. According to this hypothesis, decentralization stands out as a pro-competitive mechanism to tame Leviathan as follows:

Total government intrusion into the economy should be smaller, *ceteris paribus* the greater the extent to which taxes and expenditure are decentralised.

Hence, government intervention would be expected to decline with decentralization, and one would expect a waning down of unnecessary expenditures and red tape as a result. Alternatively, Oates (1985) suggests a counterbalancing argument, namely that while decentralization is more efficient by tailoring programs to heterogeneous preferences, it implies a loss of some scale economics that alone can be large enough to trigger expenditure to increase. In the case of health care, empirical evidence is suggestive of the second effect. As Figure 2.1 shows, the argument does not receive empirical confirmation in the case of health care (see also Hansen 2006).

Different explanations have been put forward to explain why public expenditure increases after decentralization:

- Short-term scale loss versus long-term efficiency gains. Health expenditure might increase but the total welfare expenditure in the long run would not increase due to the longer-term savings that come from allocative efficiency gains from decentralization in those administrations that have more experience in managing their budgets in comparison with centrally managed models. This is the evidence that Costa-Font and Moscone (2008) find in the Spanish system of regional healthcare services. Their findings suggest that experience in managing healthcare responsibilities come with a lower expenditure per capita.
- Collusion (Brenan and Buchanan 1980), due to horizontal cooperation or vertical coordination, which typically takes place when there are fiscal imbalances resulting from expenditures being decentralized but a higher level of government collects taxes and assigns them through block transfers to the states. This is the case in the UK with the Barnett formula or in Spain for ordinary regions subject to common financing (see the chapters 4 and 5 on Spain and the UK, in this volume). Alternatively, one can imagine the influence of the central state through framework laws that set out framework packages. Examples from Italy show that regulation has managed to reduce the extent of diversity, which might explain a moderate inter-regional competition.
- Vertical competition and policy innovation can explain to an extent why a standard race to the bottom does not take place. Vertical competition, as we explain below, refers to competition for underfunded policy responsibilities when there are opportunities for credit claiming. Costa-Font and Rico (2006b) argue that the rationale of vertical competition in health care is to expand rather than reduce healthcare expenditure. An important consequence of vertical competition is the development of

policy innovation at the subcentral level to differentiate themselves from other region states, and avoid competition. Evidence of this effect on pharmaceuticals regulation explains significant policy innovation that, when successful, tends to be diffused (Costa-Font and Puig Junoy 2007). An alternative explanation for expenditure rise is based on the existence of government differentiation, which is consistent with the findings suggesting that the policy innovation is boosted to keep the cannibalization effects of competition under control.

4.2. Exacerbating regional inequalities?

One of the oldest arguments against institutional decentralization is that decentralization creates or exacerbates regional inequalities. It stands to reason: if there is policy divergence, then some polities will end up choosing policies that impoverish or enrich them, and people will end up having different qualities of life.

In fact, regional inequalities in health expenditure per capita (a measure of unadjusted output) appear to decline with decentralization. Dupuy and Le Galès (2006) and Greer (2010a) found that decentralizing provision to democratic governments made inequalities visible and gave politicians incentive to highlight and fix them. Similarly, Costa-Font (2010b) and Costa-Font and Rico (2006a) find that regional inequalities in health, education, and social care have declined. Why is that? One explanation lies in the effects of equalization mechanisms and the use of block grants as a funding mechanism. A second explanation is the one put forward in Costa-Font (2010a; Costa-Font and Rico 2006a) that uses policy diffusion as a mechanism to externalize the innovations in one state thanks to devolution. These mechanisms would not exist in more centralized health systems. Hence, although decentralization does indeed give rise to diversity, in the long run, diversity declines if there is policy diffusion. The mechanisms for policy diffusion are primarily those associated with political accountability, and more generally credit-claiming by innovative governments.

4.3. Misaligned incentives: strategic interaction between governments

Incentives and imbalances preoccupy both the economists of fiscal federalism and political scientists interested in institutional interactions. The problem with the extremely common horizontal competition models that model governments as firms is that Tiebout's logic is clear, but by the time we are done with the scope conditions it works in relatively few cases. Fundamentally, its applicability depends on the extent to which local governments benefit from competition and have incentive to compete for tax revenues.

If they do not draw their revenue from the relevant tax bases, or are big enough to avoid such competition, or enjoy natural advantages, then the logic is quite weak. Political responsibility also matters.

In designing a system of incentives that attains diversity and competition, which is precisely what decentralization is ultimately about, responsibilities should be clearly allocated to each level of government. In doing so there are a set of features that should be taken into account, including the following.

First, decentralized budget constraints are not necessarily soft. That is, the existence of common pool and moral hazard effects in designing the decentralization of health systems should be one that does not give rise to bailout expectations. If the latter is the case, then the perverse incentives are to expand expenditure and overlook efficiency. Fiscal federalism theory predicts that allocative efficiency improvements follow from states self-financing, and hence own-taxes should be the primary revenue source. Soft budget constraints in health care are specifically problematic; the central government cannot credibly allow subnational government to go under in proving highly visible services, such as health care.

Second, good economics suggests that subnational governments must have adequate resources to pursue their activities, and include a certain level of own resources so that they can sacrifice income or allocation to other public expenditure to improve the health system. If revenues of local or regional government do not equal or exceed their expenditures, then vertical fiscal imbalances arise, with some levels of government better funded relative to their expenditures than others. Fiscal imbalances are common. They can be corrected through the use of transfers, which can be discretionary – and hence politically manipulated – or based on an allocation formula to adjust by difference in needs and risk across subnational governments.[9] However, countries differ in whether health care receives a specific allocation formula, or instead is part of the general funds that are allocated to subnational governments. Overall, the more transparent and general the financing of subnational governments, the system encourages financial planning and efficiency.

Third, together with vertical imbalances, one can identify the effects of externalities or spillovers between regional governments, or that respond to a phenomenon that exceeds that jurisdictional domain of the regional government. Another parallel effect is that of the existence of significant disparities in the size and capacity of regional governments; the latter require either adjustments for population or risk in the allocation, and are generally known as horizontal imbalances.

These three principles emerge from long debates about the incentive effects of different forms of intergovernmental finance. In all countries that have decentralized their health system, transfers represent a large proportion of subnational governments' revenues (OECD 2009), the share of own-taxes revenue with respect to transfers differs from country to country, and the specific transfer design. Intergovernmental transfers are viewed as a supplementary means of finance to tackle the existence of externalities, and to deal with vertical and horizontal imbalances. Transfers act as a form of redistribution as well as a source of insurance against region-specific shocks, horizontal imbalances between richer and poorer regions, and to promote innovation when there are limits in the capacity of region states to invest in innovation, and more generally they are employed to use the central state economies of scale in tax collection. The obvious downside is that unless transfers contain fiscal effort corrections they can lead to soft budget constraints and more generally moral hazard problems.

Intergovernmental transfers can cause their own problems. The most assertive group of scholars pointing this out, branded as students of "second generation fiscal federalism" by Barry Weingast in his manifesto (Weingast 2009), distinguish themselves from "first generation" fiscal federalists by their focus on the incentives facing politicians and the extent to which they have incentives to defect from federal settlements through bad behavior, such as excessive debt. So far, this tradition of work quickly narrows down to analyzing defections from federal arrangements such as excessive regional government debt. Finally, one of the most-cited potential costs of a decentralized polity lies in the capacity of the central government to enhance fiscal responsibility which demands no expectations of bailouts (Rodden 2005; Bordignon and Turati 2009; Crivelli et al. 2010). If subnational governments expect to receive additional funds in the events of financial need, this expectation weakens the budget constraint of subnational governments that instead behave strategically. Its key point is that "decentralization" might encourage debt, government growth, and misbehavior just as easily as parsimony and competition (Rodden 2005). Much lies in the institutions (Bednar 2009), a point also made by previous scholars (Watts 2000, 2006).

One of the most-documented empirical regularities in the fiscal federalism literature is the so-called flypaper effect (Gamkhar and Shah 2007). This refers to the observation, stressed by economists, that increases in grants produce larger increases in local or regional government expenditure than increases in the regional or local government's income. It further produces the problem, stressed by political scientists, that the central government can make grants that induce smaller governments to take on spending obligations, but then reduce its transfers and leave the smaller governments with a larger share of the cost. Similarly, if the allocation of political and fiscal responsibilities is poorly defined, then it will be difficult to trace the political credit for health policy decisions, and hence one might expect region states to invest only in credit-claiming projects and not in welfare-improving ones more generally.

Another feature that can redress horizontal inequality but enable poor financial management is direct fiscal equalization (direct equalizing grants to regions). Fiscal equalization schemes exist in almost all decentralized countries and range from 3% of the GDP in Switzerland, Finland and Spain to 1% in Greece and 2% in Germany (OECD 2009).

4.4. Intergovernmental political competition

As noted above, governments do not just compete horizontally for mobile factors of production; they also compete with each other for political credit. For obvious reasons, mobility is less of an issue in Europe compared with the USA. In the United States, 40% of the population lives in a different state than that of birth, and the percentage increases to 50% if we look at college graduates (Baicker and Skinner 2010). Similarly, 2.5% of US residents change state every year. Nonetheless, mobility is far more limited in Europe for a variety of reasons, including the fact that individuals build significant regional attachments and networks, as well as other social barriers such as language that reduce mobility within countries such as Belgium, Spain, and Switzerland.

For decentralization mechanisms to enhance welfare, appropriate democratic accountability is necessary. That is, decision-makers are supposed to be responsive to the demands of their constituents. The most obvious way for this to take place is through regional or statewide electoral processes so that officials in subnational government align citizens' interests in improving their own lives with that of their constituents. To gain these benefits, elections should be such that are based on region- or state-specific affairs and not intertwined with other countrywide matters as for instance is the case for many Spanish regions (Costa-Font 2009).

The fiscal federalism literature (Breton 1996) contends that governments compete. However, in understanding the wide range of competitive relationships one must distinguish between vertical and horizontal forms of competition – between governments on different (vertical) and the same (horizontal) levels. The most obvious form of competition comes out of tournaments theory whereby citizens of one jurisdiction evaluate the performance of their own constituency relative to other jurisdictions' performance (Salmon 1987). The only inconvenience of this mechanism is that performance is not easily observable, especially with quality dimensions, which could be the main elements motivating citizens to either move or use the political agency to punish or reward the incumbent party ruling the health system. Nonetheless, even if citizens can evaluate the performance of the health system, there is no way to only vote on the health system, because elections are not functionally specific.

Intergovernmental, vertical, competition and market, horizontal, discipline are empirical determinations rather than valid assumptions. Governments' exposure to markets, and the impact on their economies, varies and is determined largely by institutions – in the UK, for example, the UK government (rather than any devolved government) is responsible for overall fiscal performance.

4.5. Capture and procedural democracy

One of the common concerns in writing about the effect of decentralization on health policy is that of capture, leading to policy failure (Costa-Font and Puig-Junoy 2007). Capture means that specific interests gain control over a government or agency and use it to their own ends, typically at the expense of others' interests (Laffont 2000). On the other hand, it is well documented that decentralization increases the transaction costs of capture on a country level. Hence, whether decentralization gives rise or serves as an incentive to contain the effects of regulatory capture of European health systems depends generally on the effects it has on transparency and corruption in general, and/or whether the welfare loss from regional capture exceeds that of lesser captures resulting from higher transaction costs in a decentralized health system.

"Capture" is a vastly oversimplifying concept that frequently just expresses academics' irritation at real-world actors whose behavior diverges from a preferred model. In terms of democratic theory, it is not clear why it is bad if a few people who care deeply about a topic overwhelm many who do not care much. Some theories, and historical and contemporary political practice, assume that it is good for one social group or another to capture a polity – most notably the propertied or those of a given race or ethnicity. In terms of empirical analysis, the problem with capture is that it only makes sense when contrasted to a normative ideal of how the institution ought to work. This is a difficult if not impossible task for a democratic government. It might make more sense to pay attention to the democratic credentials and processes that legitimate governments, such as freedom of the press and assembly (legal and real), the relationship between economic and political power, and electoral turnover.

Procedural democracy does not necessarily improve with decentralization. Decentralization can permit the creation of corrupt local empires – "authoritarian enclaves" in which local elites can control politics, administration, and the public debate in a way that could not happen in national politics (Gibson 2005; O'Dwyer and Ziblatt 2006). A focus on information and accountability has some prima facia problems when applied to much larger regions; the eight million people of Andalucia or the far-flung five millions of Scots are not the citizens of democratic Athens or a New England town hall (Stepan 2001). Local and regional politics and policy tend to be low salience and under-reported; it is unreasonable to assume that citizens can attribute responsibility correctly in multi-level regimes, or that they will be informed about what a given level of government is doing.

In fact, there is a good chance that they will be less informed about their local and regional governments than they are about national politics; press attention tends to focus on national politics, leaving smaller governments in the shadows.[10]

4.6. Veto points and welfare state development

The macrosociological literature on decentralization, health, and the welfare state in general starts from different premises and arrives in a very different place. It generally tries to explain the size, nature, and benefits of the welfare state (with a focus on transfers and income replacement, rather than the presumably tricky area of health). It has given us one major contention and an abundant amount of supporting research (Castles 1999; Hicks 1999; Huber and Stephens 2001; Huber et al. 1993; Lancaster and Hicks 2000; Schneider 2006; Swank 2001, 2002). Federal and decentralized states have smaller and stingier welfare states. They might be slower to retrench their welfare states, but the same constraints that led them to smaller and slower development also means that they are less able to update their welfare provision in response to new challenges (Hacker 2004), such as that of an ageing population with multiple chronic conditions.

These authors basically all pursue the same approach. Eschewing the prescriptive policy focus and strong assumptions of the others, they usually opt for large-scale quantitative comparisons of program expenditure or entitlements in the OECD states, backed up by more or less intensive case studies. In other words, the units are states, and territorial decentralization is like union density, age structure or GDP: a property of the state that might or might not explain its welfare choices. Differences between regional governments, or different parts of the countries, are averaged out in a case of what Richard Snyder calls "mean-spirited" analysis, thereby disguising valuable information about both policy divergence and the effects of a given country's decentralized political institutions (Snyder 2001). In some cases, territorial decentralization is part of a larger composite variable called "fragmentation", incorporating federalism, bicameralism, and referenda. The causal processes that are supposed to link "fragmentation" to an aggregate welfare state outcome are not clarified by the leading works using that variable (Huber and Stephens 2001).

Such a literature, with doubtful aggregate variables and few convincing causal stories, is obviously open to attack by those with policy and country-specific expertise (e.g. Obinger et al. 2005). As with the technocratic literature, it turns out that clear statements rely on knowledge of a host of factors, including details about institutional framework, that are still often confined to case studies. This is a pity, since many of those variables are susceptible to comparative analysis. Macrosociological approaches, meanwhile, have a different problem: even if we grant the value of statewide expenditure averages or eligibility data for statewide programs as our measure of the welfare state, their handling of decentralization generally conflates it with all the other veto points in a polity. Making different political institutions into a single "fragmentation" variable is tendentious, and using it to explain country averages needlessly destroys data.

Furthermore, the case studies underlying the notion of general "fragmentation" often fail to bear it out, because not all forms of fragmentation are correlated. Some institutionalist, veto-focused accounts of welfare state politics in federal countries make their argument with variables such as separation of powers and do not even mention federalism (Bonoli 2000, pp. 38–51). Even Huber and Stephens, for example, tend to use Australian examples to make the point that federalism slows welfare state development – but in reading their account, it looks like bicameralism is the culprit behind federal incapacity (Huber and Stephens 2001, pp. 172–177).[11]

Public choice scholars, ever worried about big government, combine this argument with a competitive horizontal claim and consequently advocate for federalism on the grounds that veto points are a good thing. They are more prone to focus on the ways in which decentralization constrains government. They tend to focus on the ways that federalism limits government by allowing citizens both political and economic exit options; governments that become predatory will lose population, while the federal institutions might prevent such predation (Riker 1982; Weingast 1995). Or, in Hayek's version, federations will be less likely to pass sectionally preferred laws (von Hayek 1992, pp. 264–266).[12] The problem is that if horizontal mobility is not that important, and veto points are not necessarily connected with federalism (as we have argued), then the case for federalism as a weapon against the welfare state remains as weak in their hands as in the hands of macrosociologists.

Veto points are also logically and empirically double-edged: some studies reveal that decentralization can actually help to water down the blame and hence give rise to reform (Costa-Font 2010a). It might provide an opportunity to overcome a central level veto or policy neglect, as for instance is traditionally the case of mental health care in Spain, where decentralization has allowed experimentation and reform at a regional level and overcome lack of sufficient consensus (Costa-Font et al. 2011). American fondness for federalism is partly due to the greater chances that some state, somewhere, solves a problem that Washington could solve were it not gridlocked (Greer and Jacobson 2010).

5. Politics and policy divergence

Legal and fiscal structures shape the space within which regional governments can diverge, and thereby the extent to which they can influence a country's health policy outcomes. Understanding the likelihood and effects of divergence, good, or bad regional policies depends on understanding what regional governments do with their agency. They are easily studied political units, rather than the black-box forms of many deductive theories, and we can supplement theories focused on their constraints with theories focused on their agency. Within their permitted space, what do they do? Following on the issues highlighted by the well-established "multiple streams" perspective in political science (Kingdon 1995), this section reviews important systematic empirical regularities in the behavior of regional governments that are not attributable to the institutional architecture and incentive that take up so much attention; it sorts them by the origin of policies, the structure of politics, and agenda-setting, since those are the ingredients of policy (Greer 2006).

5.1. Policy

Policy ideas tend to live independently of any need. They are often answers without questions; whether they survive in political discourse is not a test of whether they are needed. Rather, it is a test of whether people can muster the financial support, credibility, and stamina to keep propounding and "selling" an idea. Definitions of policy communities (and associated terms such as networks) are complex (Jordan and Richardson 1982; Rhodes 1981; Richardson 2000; Walker 1989), but the basic concept is clear: "a shared-knowledge group having to do with some aspect ... of public policy" (Heclo 1978, p. 103). These people are policy advocates, and they can range from lobbyists to academics, to journalists to entrepreneurial bureaucrats. Collectively, these people make up a policy community – the group of people with the collective expertise to pass judgment on policy and suggest credible ideas. The makeup of the policy community is crucial to understanding the kinds of ideas it produces. The existence of distinctive policy communities, which are a result of webs of regional organizations, varies. We can analyze the institutional locations where policy advocates can lodge: think tanks, universities, certain kinds of private sector firms, major health institutions such as hospitals, foundations, and government itself. Insofar as those bases of support differ – with fewer or more universities, different numbers and kinds of think tanks, and so forth – they will produce different policy debates (Greer 2004).

Sometimes ideas will jump from system to system with little involvement of the policy experts (politicians are not inert), but those ideas will typically be the simplest and cheapest (Boushey 2010). It is more likely that some combination of cross-border interest groups, professional networks, experts, civil servants, or ideologically motivated activists will be discussing ideas with each other and be poised to propose their idea to a politician when a likely problem emerges.

5.2. Politics

Policy ideas only matter if they are heard out, and adopted, by a politician. In the case of the countries we study here, that means the parliamentary governments. They are the ones who can read politics in such a way as to decide that a given policy is a good idea. While their personal objectives can be diverse and personal, they generally involve making a mark. But life in competitive electoral democracies means that they must also take the broad strategy and position of their party as the main goal – office usually trumps other goals, because few goals can be effectively pursued when out of office. Just as we look at the nature and culture of the policy community to see what ideas will be put forth, we look at the nature and strategies of party competition, and party leaderships' take on them, to see what political functions a policy idea must fulfill (Hough and Jeffery 2006).

Party systems and competition structure the incentives of party leaderships as well as individual politicians. In multilevel politics, they can give politicians of the same party incentives to pursue different policies defending territorial interests and trying to deny ethnoregionalist challengers a "monopoly" of concern for a territory (van Biezen and Hopkin 2006, pp. 17–18). Under these circumstances, a theoretically unified statewide party must adapt to different party systems. This has been the lot of the Spanish Socialists since the transition, and there is considerable evidence that this disaggregation and reorientation is taking place within the UK's Labour Party (Hopkin and Bradbury 2006; Laffin 2007).

Party systems are more consistently important than parties (Trench 2006). Winning is what matters in politics, and the structure of party competition is the single most important fact for any politician. This means that the role of statewide parties as ideological enforcers is a distant third to their position in the various party systems that exist for various elections and to their role as coordinating devices for politicians on various levels. The result is that there is no particularly good reason to look to parties as causes of horizontal isomorphism; they are likely to appear, rather, as actors in crucially important party systems and as crucial coordinating networks across government.[13]

5.3. Problems

What creates a problem? Much of the answer is the media. Outside the smallest, simplest, and least relevant jurisdictions, people depend on the media to tell them what has been happening. Even in the age of social media and rapidly evolving search technologies, the people who generate content and their gatekeepers are very powerful – in fact, the declining numbers of reporters in most countries might make them more powerful. The different structure of the media, and variation in data collection and releases, should help to shape agendas and deserve attention – for a nice example, the Scottish press has traditionally driven a more distinctive agenda than the Welsh press because most of the Welsh read English newspapers and watch English TV. Governments' agenda-setting mechanisms will, we should assume, be loosely linked, but in all sorts of ways, and the linkages will be highly imperfect (Baumgartner and Jones 1993; Boushey 2010).

5.4. Models?

We should therefore expect some variation simply because the agenda-setting mechanisms will be different in each jurisdiction. But the policy communities, political systems, and problems streams in some places are more distinctive than in others. Start with media: some regions have largely autonomous media (e.g. the Belgian regions, Scotland, and Catalonia). They raise different problems according to their different debates, ownership, and interests.

Behind this lie the politics of stateless nations. The most distinctive party systems, policy communities, and problems are found in the most-studied cases of regionalization: Scotland, Catalonia, and the Basque Country. Some observers take the presence of a distinctive social model as a nebulous sign of the "success" of a stateless nation. Using autonomy to choose broadly similar policies, which might be taken as a sign of maturity and self-confidence, tends to be taken as the opposite. So while we can enumerate the ways in which distinctive party systems, policy communities and problem-creating mechanisms produce distinctive policies, at the top end, in the most distinctive regions, that diversity reflects what made them stateless nations (Hopkin 2009; Greer 2007).

Notably, there is no necessary reason to expect that a stateless nation will have some sort of identifiable national model; rather, policies should emerge, probably unplanned, out of the decisions made by politicians dealing with distinct problems in distinct partisan environments and receiving distinct advice. Only later will it be celebrated for the pragmatism, admirable ethical nature, or other virtues that it shows the stateless nation to possess, and a few lucky intellectuals will gain credit for enunciating it.

6. Conclusion

This chapter, in synthesizing political scientists' and economists' work on the causes and consequences of a given allocation of authority, has shown the extent of overlap between the two disciplines. Both find that horizontal competitive mechanisms have limited influence on regional or local politics – and that the scale of that influence depends on the financial and legal institutional structures. Both find that vertical competition between levels of government is underrated as a cause of policy change. Both find that institutional design is crucial, for institutions can produce misaligned incentives that lead regions to overspend or central governments to offload expenditure and blame, or bad conflict-management problems that create or exacerbate political conflict. The language and focus is often different; economists are more prone to use median voter approaches and political scientists more likely to focus on strategic interaction within fixed political institutions. More political scientists view regional autonomy and welfare states as obviously good things; more economists focus on allocative efficiency and budget constraints. These are differences of emphasis and language, not theory. Both give students of health policy a similar task.

What, then, do the two disciplines suggest about the three questions we posed in the introduction?

6.1. What is decentralization?

The literature in this chapter directs our attention to the vertical and horizontal links that create and shape a particular government's decisions. The vertical ones are:

- What laws allocate regional health policy responsibilities?
- What mechanisms finance each government, and its health policy activities?
- What, if any, influence do regional governments have on central government decisions?

The horizontal ones are:

- What is the structure of problem definition, and to what extent does it vary between different regions?
- What is the structure of the health policy community in each region, and how distinctive and interlinked are the health policy communities of different regions?

What is the structure of party politics in each region:

- What distinctive problems does it set for politicians in each region?
- How distinctive are different party systems within a country?
- How interconnected are politicians of the same party in different governments?

6.2. Why do governments opt for decentralization?

Clearly, decentralization is in vogue. There are a variety of reasons that we have canvassed:

- It might be an alternative to privatization.
- It might reflect changing concepts of nationhood and social citizenship as the territorial politics of social citizenship evolve (Greer 2008; Banting and Costa-Font 2010).
- It might reflect the challenges of multinational states such as Belgium, Spain, and the UK that opted for decentralization because the alternative was to break up into their component nationalities (Stepan 2001).
- It might improve the democratic accountability of public services, a value in itself since at least the 1960s, when government responses to the disturbances of the 1960s included efforts to incorporate more local accountability in government.

- It might improve the quality of services – a reason consistent with the increase in fiscally decentralized expenditure noted in Figures 2.1 and 2.2, and with the merits of transparency, closeness, and electoral accountability that decentralization can bring under the right circumstances.
- It might shuffle blame and credit in a way strategic politicians appreciate.
- It might thereby open the way to increased welfare expenditures (Costa-Font and Rico 2006a).
- Finally, it might improve some aspects of efficiency by responding to heterogeneity, allowing and giving policymakers incentive to respond to different local conditions and tastes.

6.3. Third, what are the effects on health systems?

There are two broad conclusions from the literature review. First, "decentralization" in itself can produce just about any effect, or no effect. It can democratize by producing a government that is more accountable to local voters who in turn are better informed – or it can entrench corrupt local elites. As Treisman noted in his extensive review of the political decentralization literature, "some of the conditions required for successful decentralization are actually benefits that decentralization is supposed to produce", while others, such as fiscal arrangements, are actually endogenous to decentralization (Treisman 2007, p. 280). That is why a general recommendation for "decentralization" or "recentralization" is dangerously vague.

Second, there is consensus among scholars that the key to the success of decentralization boils down to its institutional design (Bednar 2009). The virtues of transparency, responsiveness, innovation, and competition are all contingent on institutional and local political factors that might or might not hold (Beramendi 2007, p. 775). Any allocation of authority is intricate, with the interactions of laws, money, political incentives and underlying territorial and cultural differences producing results that are not always what policymakers expect (e.g. Greer 2010b). Particularly important design features include addressing fiscal imbalances, promoting competition, policy innovation, and making sure that political democracy works so that representatives represent and are accountable to free voters. Limits to the success of decentralized health systems at achieving any of the possible ends include the alignment of fiscal and political accountability, the design of resource allocation mechanisms and more generally the development of incentives to policy diffusion and horizontal equity that can, if successful, reduce health inequalities between and within regions.

6.4. The political economy of territory

Joining the two disciplines makes it inescapable: policymaking is political. Politics filters and channels economic and institutional constraints and opportunities. The hazard of imputing interests and incentives is that the unit of analysis might be wrong: a theory that assumes regional politicians want autonomy for their region can go wrong if it turns out they want personal political advancement in the central government, just like a theory that assumes business executives want the best for their firm goes wrong if it turns out they want to maximize their personal wealth at their firm's expense. Starting with the positions, interests, incentives, and ideas of the actual actors, such as politicians and policy advocates, allows us to both spell out generalizable statements about health policy and avoid the fundamentally apolitical formalism that so often leads us astray. Otherwise, when deductive theories on the wrong level of analysis match wits with real practitioners, the practitioners will win.

The "policymakers" of whom so many analysts speak are political creatures: elected politicians and highly political civil servants and policy experts. Their careers depend on understanding politics, relationships, and chance. If we are to understand how decentralized health institutions shape what they do, we had better understand what they want and how they operate.

Notes

1. The latter includes borrowing powers and the capacity to collect new taxes and expand or reduce the tax base and the tax rate. See also Mellett (2009).
2. Conditional grants are typically used to internalize externalities between jurisdictions following a form of Pigouvian subsidy.
3. It was noticeable, assembling this book, that the social insurance countries were far less likely to publish useful regional spending data – including even data on health spending by regional governments.
4. For isomorphism and federalism, an underused perspective, see Miller and Banaszak-Holl (2005). For the original sociological framework in the background, see DiMaggio and Powell (1991).
5. Paul Peterson has made the argument that American local (Peterson 1981) and state (Peterson 1995) governments are also subjected to the Tiebout logics, though he found fairly small effects and had to assume that education is not part of the welfare state.
6. And decentralization has been named as a precipitating factor in the breakup of countries; Cornell (2002) is a nice example of the argument.
7. As the English experience suggests, technocratic debates need not be any more rational for that (e.g. Greer (2008)).
8. A theory that several states, as well as the Eurozone, tested to destruction in 2012.
9. It can also be partially compensated by transfer payments to individuals, such as social insurance.
10. Knowing that, it should be no surprise that there seems to be a relationship between corruption and the isolation of US state capitals (Campante and Do 2012).
11. The obvious counterfactual is Canada, where the upper house is weak and represents nothing, and the provinces were not able to formally intervene in federal legislation. Unsurprisingly, the effectively unicameral Canadian federal

government passed a much more inclusive and sensible healthcare finance system. See, for example, Maioni (1998).

12. "This readiness to have no legislation at all on some subjects rather than state legislation will be the acid test of whether we are intellectually mature for the achievement of suprastate organization" (p. 266).

13. The American literature on parties, has a single-country focus on a country with an unruly and transactional legislature. This has been an unexpected blessing, giving it some applicability in increasingly complex systems because it means it need not shed a legacy of theories that worked best in unitary states with well-organized parties. The question of whether parties will reward core supporters or swing districts – a key issue in territorial politics – is aired from an American perspective by Cox (2009).

References

Adolph, C., da Fonseca, E. M. and Greer, S. L. (2012). Allocation of Authority in European Health Policy. *Social Science and Medicine* 75 (9), pp. 1595–1603.

Baicker, K. and Skinner, J. (2010). Health care spending growth and the future Of U.S. tax rates. Prepared for the tax policy and the economy conference, 23 September 2010.

Banting, Keith G. (2006). Social citizenship and federalism: Is the federal welfare state a contradiction in terms. In Scott L. Greer (Ed.) *Territory, Democracy, and Justice* (pp. 44–66). Basingstoke: Palgrave Macmillan.

Banting, Keith G. and Corbett, Stan (2002). Health policy and federalism: An introduction. In Keith G. Banting and Stan Corbett (Eds.) *Health Policy and Federalism: A Comparative Perspective on Multi-Level Governance* (pp. 1–37). Montreal and Kingston: McGill-Queens University Press.

Banting, Keith and Costa-Font, Joan (2010). Decentralization, welfare, and social citizenship in contemporary democracies. *Environment and Planning C: Government and Policy*, 28 (3), pp. 381–38.

Baumgartner, F. R. and Jones, B. D. (1993). *Agendas and Instability in American Politics*. Chicago: University of Chicago Press.

Bednar, J. (2009). *The Robust Federation: Principles of Design*. Cambridge, MA: Cambridge University Press.

Bednar, J. (2011). The political science of federalism. *Annual Review of Law and Social Science*, 7 (1), pp. 269–288.

Beramendi, P. (2007). Federalism. In C. Boix and S. C. Stokes (Eds.) *The Oxford Handbook of Comparative Politics* (pp. 752–781). Oxford: Oxford University Press.

Boadway, R. and Shah, A. (2009). *Fiscal Federalism: Principles and Practice of Multi-Order Governance*. Cambridge: Cambridge University Press.

Bonoli, G. (2000). *The Politics of Pension Reform: Institutions and Policy Change in Western Europe*. Cambridge: Cambridge University Press.

Bordignon, M. and Turati, G. (2009). Bailing out expectations and public health expenditure, *Journal of Health Economics, Elsevier*, 28 (2), pp. 305–321.

Bossert, T. (1998). Analyzing the decentralization of health systems in developing countries: Decision space, innovation and performance. *Social Science and Medicine*, 47 (10), pp. 1513–1527.

Boushey, G. (2010). *Policy Diffusion Dynamics in America*. Cambridge: Cambridge University Press.

Brenan, G. and Buchanan, J. (1980). *Power to Tax: Analytical Foundations of a Fiscal Constitution*, New York: Cambridge University Press.

Breton, A. (1996). *Competitive Governments: An Economic Theory of Politics and Public Finance*. New York: Cambridge University Press.

Campante, F. R. and Do, Q. A. (2012). *Isolated Capital Cities, Accountability and Corruption: Evidence from US States*. Cambridge, MA: Harvard Kennedy School of Government.

Castles, F. G. (1999). Decentralization and the post-war political economy. *European Journal of Political Research*, 36 (1), pp. 27–53.

Cornell, S. E. (2002). Autonomy as a source of ethnic conflict: Caucasian conflicts in theoretical perspective. *World Politics*, 54 (2), pp. 245–276.

Costa-Font, J. (2005). Inequalities in self-reported health within Spanish regional health services: devolution re-examined? *International Journal of Health Planning and Management*, 20 (1), pp. 41–52.

Costa-Font, J. (2009). Simultaneity, asymmetric devolution and economic incentives in Spanish regional elections. *Regional and Federal Studies*, 19 (1), pp. 165–184.

Costa-Font, J. (2010a). Devolution, diversity and welfare reform: long-term care in the 'Latin Rim'. *Social Policy & Administration*, 44 (4), pp. 481–494.

Costa-Font, J. (2010b). Does devolution lead to regional inequalities in welfare activity? *Environment and Planning C: Government and Policy*, 28 (3), pp. 435–449.

Costa-Font, J. and Moscone, F. (2008). The impact of decentralization and interterritorial interactions on Spanish health expenditure. *Empirical Economics*, 34 (1), pp. 167–184.

Costa-Font, J. and Puig-Junoy, J. (2007). Institutional change, innovation and regulation failure: evidence from the Spanish drug market. *Policy and politics*, 35 (4), pp. 701–718.

Costa-Font, J. and Rico, A. (2006a). Devolution and the interregional inequalities in health and healthcare in Spain. *Regional Studies*, 40 (8), pp. 1–13.

Costa-Font, J. and Rico, A. (2006b). Vertical competition in the Spanish National Health System (NHS). *Public Choice*, 128 (3–4), pp. 477–498.

Costa-Font, J., Salvador-Carulla, L., Cabases, J., Alonso, J. and McDaid, D. (2011). Tackling neglect and mental health reform in a devolved system of welfare governance. *Journal of Social Policy*, 40, pp. 295–312.

Cox, G. W. (2009). Swing voters, core voters, and distributive politics. In I. Shapiro, S. C. Stokes, E. J. Wood, and A. S. Kirshner (Eds.), *Political Representation* (pp. 342–57). Cambridge, MA: Cambridge University Press.

Crivelli, E., Leive, A. and Stratmann, T. (2010). Subnational health spending and soft budget constraints in OECD countries. IMF Working Paper, 10/147.

DiMaggio, P. J. and Powell, W. W. (1991). The iron cage revisited: Institutional isomorphism and collective rationality in organization fields. In W. W. Powell and P. J. DiMaggio (Eds.), *The New Institutionalism in Organizational Analysis* (pp. 63–82). Chicago: University of Chicago Press.

Fierbeck, Katherine (2011). The dialectics of law and policy: Federal health policy in Canada and the EU. In Finn Laursen (Ed.), *The EU and Federalism* (pp. 133–154). Farnham: Ashgate.

Gerring, J. and Thacker, S. C. (2008). *A Centripetal Theory of Democratic Governance*. Cambridge: Cambridge University Press.

Gibson, E. L. (2005). Boundary control: Subnational authoritarianism in democracy countries. *World Politics*, 58, pp. 101–132.

Greer, S. L. (2004). *Territorial Politics and Health Policy: UK Health Policy in Comparative Perspective*. Manchester: Manchester University Press.

Greer, S. L. (2006). The politics of divergent policy. In S. L. Greer (Ed.), *Territory, Democracy, and Justice: Regionalism and Federalism in Western Democracies* (pp. 157–74). Basingstoke: Palgrave Macmillan.

Greer, S. L. (2007). *Nationalism and Self-Government: The Politics of Autonomy in Scotland and Catalonia*. Albany: State University of New York Press.

Greer, S. L. (2008). A very English institution: Central and local in the English NHS. In R. Hazell (Ed.) *The English Question*. (pp. 194–219). Manchester: Manchester University Press

Greer, S. L. (2010a). Devolution and Health: Structure, Process and Outcome since 1998. In G. Lodge and K. Schmuecker (Eds.) *Devolution in Practice* 3. (pp. 141–165). London: IPPR.

Greer, S. L. (2010b). Territorial Politics in Hard Times: The Welfare State Under Pressure in Germany, Spain and the United Kingdom. *Environment and Planning* (C), 28 (3), pp. 405–419.

Greer, S. L. and Jacobson, P. D. (2010). Health policy and federalism. *Journal of Health Politics, Policy and Law*, 35 (2), pp. 203–226.

Grindle, M. S. (2009). *Going Local: Decentralization, Democratization, and the Promise of Good Governance*. Princeton: Princeton University Press.

Hacker, J. S. (2004). Reform without change, change without reform: The politics of U.S. Health policy reform in cross-national perspective. In M. A. Levin and M. Shapiro (Eds.), *Transatlantic Policymaking in an Age of Austerity: Diversity and Drift* (pp. 13–63). Washington, DC: Georgetown University Press.

Hansen, Susan B. (2006). *Globalization and the Politics of Pay*. Washington, DC: Georgetown University Press.

Hayek, F. (1937). Economics and knowledge. *Economica*, 4, pp. 33–54.

Heclo, H. (1978). Issue networks and the executive establishment. In A. King (Ed.), *The New American Political System* (pp. 87–124). Washington, DC: American Enterprise Institute.

Hicks, A. (1999). *Social Democracy and Welfare Capitalism: A Century of Income Security Politics*. Ithaca: Cornell University Press.

Hirschman, Albert. 1970. *Exit, Voice and Loyalty: Responses to Decline in Firms, Organizations and States*. Cambridge, MA: Harvard University Press.

Hopkin, J (2009). Party matters: Devolution and party politics in Britain and Spain. *Party Politics*, 15, pp. 179–198.

Hopkin, J. and Bradbury, J. (2006). British statewide parties and multilevel politics. *Publius*, 36 (1), pp. 135–152.

Huber, E. and Stephens, J. D. (2001). *Development and Crisis of the Welfare State: Parties and Policies in Global Markets*. Chicago: University of Chicago Press.

Huber, E., Ragin, C. and Stephens, J. D. (1993). Social democracy, Christian democracy, constitutional structure, and the welfare state. *American Journal of Sociology*, 99 (3), pp. 711–749.

Immergut, Ellen M. (1992). The rules of the game: The logic of health policy-making in France, Switzerland, and Sweden. In Sven Steinmo, Kathleen Thelen and Frank Longstreth (Eds.) *Structuring Politics: Historical Institutionalism in Comparative Analysis* (pp. 57–89). Cambridge: Cambridge University Press.

Jordan, G. and Richardson, J. J. (1982). The British policy style or logic of negotiation? In J. J. Richardson (Ed.), *Policy Styles in Western Europe* (pp. 80–110). London: George Allen & Unwin.

Kingdon, J. W. (1995). *Agendas, Alternatives, and Public Policies.* New York: HarperCollins.

Koethenbuerger, M. (2008). Revisiting the "Decentralization Theorem" – On the role of externalities. *Journal of Urban Economics*, 64, pp. 116–122.

Laffin, M. (2007). Comparative British central–local relations: Regional centralism, governance and intergovernmental relations. *Public Policy and Administration*, 22 (1), pp. 74–91.

Laffont, J. J. (2000). *Incentives and Political Economy.* Oxford: Oxford University Press.

Lancaster, T. D. and Hicks, A. M. (2000). The impact of federalism and neo-corporatism on economic performance: An analysis of eighteen OECD countries. In U. Wachendorfer-Schmidt (Ed.), *Federalism and Political Performance* (pp. 228–241). Abingdon: Routledge.

Lane, J. E. and Ersson, S. (2005). The riddle of federalism: Does federalism impact on democracy? *Democratisation*, 12, pp. 163–182.

Levaggi, R. and Zanola, R. (2007). Patients' migration across regions: The case of Italy. *Applied Economics*, 36 (16). 1751–1757.

Levy, Jacob T. (2007). Federalism, liberalism, and the separation of loyalties. *American Political Science Review*, 101, pp. 459–477.

Lopez-Casasnovas, Guillem, Costa-i-Font, Joan and Planas, Ivan (2005). Diversity and regional inequalities in the Spanish system of health care services. *Health Economics*, 14 (S1), pp. 221–235.

Maioni, A. (1998). *Parting at the Crossroads: The Emergence of Health Insurance in the United States and Canada.* Princeton: Princeton University Press.

Mellett, R. (2009). A Principles-Based Approach to the Barnett Formula. *Political Quarterly*, 80(1), pp. 76–83.

Miller, E. A. and Banaszak-Holl, J. (2005). Cognitive and normative determinants of state policymaking behavior: Lessons from the sociological institutionalism. *Publius*, 35 (2), pp. 191–216.

Oates, W. E. (1972). Fiscal Federalism. New York: Harcourt Brace Jovanovich.

Oates, W. E. (1985). Searching for the Leviathan: An empirical study. *American Economic Review*, 75, pp. 748–757.

Obinger, H., Leibfried, S. and Castles, F. G. (2005). *Federalism and the Welfare State: New World and European Experiences.* Cambridge: Cambridge University Press.

O'Dwyer, C. and Ziblatt, D. (2006). Does decentralisation make government more efficient and effective? *Commonwealth and Comparative Politics*, 44 (3), pp. 326–343.

OECD (2009). Explaining The Sub-National Tax-Grants Balance In OECD Countries. OECD Network on Fiscal Relations Across Levels of Government.

Peterson, P. (1981). *City Limits.* Chicago: University of Chicago Press.

Peterson, P. (1995). *The Price of Federalism.* Washington, DC: Brookings Institution.

Pettit, P. (1997). *Republicanism: A Theory of Freedom and Governance.* Oxford: Oxford University Press.

Piperno, S. (2000). *Fiscal Decentralisation in Italy: Some Lessons,* mimeo.

Poirier, J. (2001). Pouvoir normatif et protection sociale dans les fédérations multinationales. *Canadian Journal of Law and Society/Revue Canadienne Droit Et Societé*, 16 (2), pp. 137–171.

Rhodes, R. A. W. (1981). *Control and Power in Central-Local Government Relations.* Westmead: Gower/Social Sciences Research Council.

Richardson, J. J. (2000). Government, interest groups and policy change. *Political Studies*, 48, pp. 1006–1025.

Riker, W. (1964). *Federalism: Origins, Operation, Significance.* Boston: Little, Brown.

Riker, W. (1982). *Liberalism Against Populism: A Confrontation Between the Theory of Democracy and the Theory of Social Choice.* Prospect Heights, IL: Waveland.

Rodden, J. A. (2005). *Hamilton's Paradox: The Promise and Peril of Fiscal Federalism.* Cambridge: Cambridge University Press.

Salmon, P. (1987). Decentralisation as an Incentive Scheme. *Oxford Review of Economic Policy*, 3 (2), pp. 24–43.

Schneider, A. (2006). Who gets what from whom: The impact of decentralisation on tax capacity and social spending. *Commonwealth and Comparative Politics*, 44 (3), pp. 344–369.

Snyder, R. (2001). Scaling down: The subnational comparative method. *Studies in Comparative International Development*, 36 (1), pp. 93–110.

Stegarescu, D. (2005). Public sector decentralisation: Measurement concepts and recent international trends. *Fiscal Studies*, 26 (3), pp. 301–333.

Stepan, A. (2001). *Arguing Comparative Politics.* Oxford: Oxford University Press.

Stigler, G. (1957). Tenable range of functions of local government. In *Federal Expenditure Policy for Economic Growth and Stability* (pp. 213–219). US Congress (ed) Washington, DC: Joint Economic Committee, Subcommittee on Fiscal Policy.

Swank, D. (2001). Political institutions and welfare state restructuring: The impact of institutions on social policy change in developed democracies. In P. Pierson (Ed.), *The New Politics of the Welfare State* (pp. 197–236). Oxford: Oxford University Press.

Swank, D. (2002). *Global Capital, Political Institutions, and Policy Change in developed Welfare States.* Cambridge: Cambridge University Press.

Tiebout, C. M. (1956). A Pure Theory of Local Expenditure. *Journal of Political Economy*, 64, pp. 416–424.

Treisman, Daniel S. (2007). *The Architecture of Government: Rethinking Political Decentralization.* Cambridge: Cambridge University Press.

Trench, A. (2006). Intergovernmental relations: In search of a theory. In S. L. Greer (Ed.), *Territory, Democracy and Justice: Regionalism and Federalism in Western Democracies* (pp. 224–256). Basingstoke: Palgrave Macmillan.

van Biezen, I. and Hopkin, J. (2006). Party organisation in multi-level contexts. In D. Hough and C. Jeffery (Eds.), *Devolution and Electoral Politics* (pp. 14–36). Manchester: Manchester University Press.

von Hayek, F. A. (1992). *Individualism and Economic Order.* Chicago: University of Chicago Press.

Walker, J. L. J. (1989). Policy communities as global phenomena. *Governance*, 2, pp. 1–5.

Watts, R. L. (2000). *The Spending Power in Federal Systems: A Comparative Analysis.* Kingston, ON: Queens University Institute of Intergovernmental Relations.

Watts, R. L. (2006). Origins of cooperative and competitive federalism. In S. L. Greer (Ed.), *Territory, Democracy and Justice* (pp. 201–224). Basingstoke: Palgrave Macmillan.

Weingast, B. (1995). The economic role of political institutions: Market-Preserving federalism and economic development. *Journal of Law, Economics and Organization*, 11 (1), pp. 1–31.

Weingast, B. (2009). "Second Generation Fiscal Federalism: The Implications of Fiscal Incentives". *Journal of Urban Economics*, 65 (3), pp. 279–293.

Part II

Cross-Country Evidence in Tax-Funded Health Systems

3
The Italian *Servizio Sanitario Nazionale*: A Renewing Tale of Lost Promises

Gilberto Turati

1. Introduction

According to the Italian Constitution, art. 32, "the Republic protects health as a fundamental individual right and in the public interest. It guarantees free of charge healthcare services to the poor". It is in the light of this constitutional provision, with a strong flavor in terms of equity, that one needs to begin the journey through the evolution of the Italian healthcare system, from its creation at the end of the 1970s up to now. To present the road ahead, I will first concentrate on presenting the evolution of the system in Section 1. I will then discuss the results of about 30 years of the Italian *Servizio Sanitario Nazionale* (SSN) – both in terms of efficiency and equity – in Section 2. I leave to Section 3 some thoughts on the future problems to be solved, including the current policy discussion and the long-run impact of population-ageing.

2. A brief (institutional) history of the Italian SSN

2.1. From the creation of the SSN to European constraints on public finances

There are three fundamental reforms that structured the Italian SSN: the Law 833/1978; the Legislative Decrees 502/1992 and 517/1993; and the Legislative Decree 229/1999. The first of these laws basically created the SSN by substituting more than 100 health insurance funds – largely a reflection of the corporative nature of the Italian welfare state – with a single universal and comprehensive public fund. The second and the third reforms were instead implemented during the 1990s, an era of extensive reforms and counter-reforms pushed forward in an effort to reach a new equilibrium for Italian public finances, plagued by a huge stock of debt.

2.1.1. *The creation of a National Health Service (NHS)*

The Law 23 December 1978 n. 833 – mainly due to the Christian Democrat Tina Anselmi, the Health Minister in the government guided by Giulio
Andreotti – gave substance after 30 years, to art. 32 of the Italian 1948 Constitution, by stating that "the Republic protects health as a fundamental
individual right and in the public interest by means of the *Servizio Sanitario
Nazionale* (National Health Service)" (art. 1). The NHS is defined by the same
law as "the complex of functions, structures, services, and activities directed
to the promotion, maintenance, and recovery of physical and mental health
of the whole population, without any differences of individual and social
conditions, assuring equalities of all citizens with respect to the Service".
Not surprisingly, given the fragmentation and the inequalities created by
the previous system of health insurance funds, the goals established in the
law are markedly related to extending coverage to a comprehensive set of
services and to improve equity in health.[1] Section 3 of Law 833/78 contains
a detailed description of all services to be provided by the SSN: preventive
care, services to guarantee health and safety at work, GPs and specialist care
services, hospital care, and access to medicines.

Provision has to be guaranteed by a multilayered organization involving
the central government, the regional governments, and a number of local
health units. The central government is in charge only of defining, together
with regional governments, the goals to be pursued by the NHS and the levels of healthcare services to be guaranteed all over the country. The main
characters in the organization designed by the 1978 law are surely the *Unità
Sanitarie Locali* (USL, literally Local Health Units (LHUs)), newly created public bodies to pursue the goals of the SSN. These are complex organizations
combining administrative and care services, including producers like public
hospitals, and involving one or more municipalities, that can freely contract
also with private producers for the provision of care.

The idea of involving municipalities in the management of health care
was basically to guarantee participation of citizens in the process of planning. While probably correct in principle, this involvement resulted in a
strong political control at the local level of a politically hot issue. This,
in turn, contributed to create large inefficiencies and a large growth in
expenditure, with massive deficits generated every year (see Figures 3.1a
and 3.1b).

Planning at the central level was to be based on the National Health Plan
(NHP), ideally a three-year program defining the amount of financing of
the National Health Fund (NHF), the criteria for apportioning the NHF to
regions, and the goals to be pursued by the SSN. Starting from the NHP,
regional governments had to define their own regional health plans, sharing
common goals but with freedom of choice as for the organization of services
(e.g. the hospital network, the role of private providers, etc.).

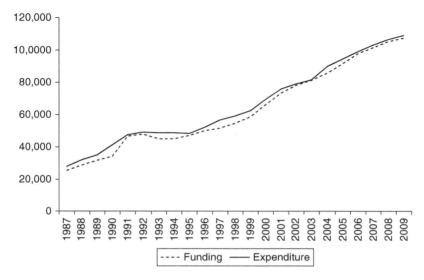

Figure 3.1a Current expenditure and funding in the NHS (1987–2009, million euro)

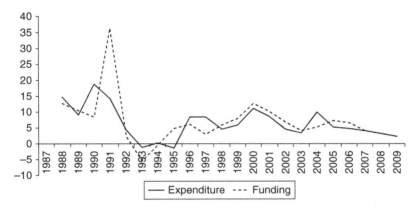

Figure 3.1b Current expenditure and funding year-to-year annual growth rates (1987–2009, %)

Source: Relazione Generale sulla Situazione Economica del Paese.

The total amount of funding was (and still is) defined by the central government in accordance – at least in principle – with regional governments, distinguishing between funds for current expenditures and for investments. Allocation of funds to each region was a task assigned to the *Comitato Interministeriale per la Programmazione Economica* (CIPE, literally an Interministerial Committee for Economic Planning) on the basis of indices and standards to be chosen to guarantee territorial equity in the provision of services (art. 51, Law 833/78). In turn, regional governments need to allocate funds to their LHUs in accordance with municipalities. Again, the parameters for the apportionment formula have to be chosen so as to assure uniform services in each LHU.

The NHF was financed (up to 1992) by two basic sources: sickness contributions (to be levied on the gross wages or pensions, adding to social security contributions) and central government funds. Sickness contributions were guaranteed by making mandatory the enrollment to the public health insurance for all citizens starting from 1 January 1980. Certainly, for a universal public health insurance scheme with a strong equity flavor, like the newly created SSN, these different sources of funds generated some confusion, resulting in a mix between a "corporative" and a "social-democratic" welfare model.

This was not, however, the main problem plaguing the SSN. The most important issues were the inabilities to plan and define goals by the central government, as well as the allocation of responsibilities across different layers of governments, resulting in a misalignment between expenditure and funding. As for the planning at the national level, even though art. 54 of Law 833/78 established that the first plan for the 1980–1982 period was to be presented in Parliament on 30 April 1979, the first NHP was presented in 1994, after 16 years and a new reform of the SSN. As for the spread of responsibilities across different layers of governments, this surely contributed (and still continues to contribute, at least to some extent) to create inefficiencies, corruption, and a waste of resources. This is because of the opportunistic behavior of local governments in the presence of the central government footing their bill; and a strict political control of USL, which guaranteed local politicians great power and – consequently – a number of votes, but left citizens with worse-than-expected services given expenditure, especially in some areas of the country. The reforms put forward during the 1990s tried to tackle exactly these shortcomings of the original design of the SSN. I examine each in turn.

2.1.2. *The 1992–1993 wave of reforms*

Public healthcare expenditure was out of control during the 1980s, with double-digit annual growth rates, and ex-ante funding always inferior to ex-post expenditure (Figures 3.1a and 3.1b). Despite taking contrary stands, during the whole period the central government stepped in and bailed out regional deficits on an almost regular basis of two to three years, probably recognizing some degree of under-funding (which was motivated by the short lives of governments). But the political landscape was on the eve of a critical change for the Italian public finance. In 1992, after a severe political and financial crisis that basically destroyed the old system of political parties and brought the country close to default, the central government defined one of the most impressive fiscal crunches of the Italian history, making the first painful steps on the way to meeting the Maastricht Treaty constraints. The ratification of the Treaty is a landmark in the management of post-war public finance in Italy: it made clear that the huge deficits of the past were unsustainable, and opened the door to a number of reforms aiming at controlling expenditure in a "structural" way. These winds of change touched, among other issues, electoral rules (to strengthen governments in power at all levels), pensions, and – of course – health care.

The 1992–1993 reforms due to a center-left governing coalition guided by Giuliano Amato tried to address all the problems afflicting the SSN. As for the inefficiencies in the provision of services, and the political control of USL, the reforms were inspired by the introduction of quasi-markets in the British NHS in 1990. Basically, the idea behind quasi-markets was to split providers from purchaser of services, to obtain – via competition for patients – a boost in efficiency, without any changes in the equity to be guaranteed in a universal public health insurance scheme. This was exactly the objective pursued by central government. However, well-known potential drawbacks in the quasi-markets organization are the increase in the volume of services, the lack of competition in some areas of the country, and the cream-skimming of patients by certain types of providers. Of course, given these drawbacks, at this stage there was no empirical evidence on the effectiveness of this mechanism in curbing expenditure, which was a second main goal to be pursued with the reforms.

The move toward quasi-markets required several different changes. First, USL were transformed into *Aziende Sanitarie Locali* (ASL, literally Local Health Firms), independent public bodies with their own organization, budget, and management. In essence, the law designed a new type of publicly owned firm, with a strong focus – at least in the aim of its proponents – on the efficient management of the budget. This is why the 1992–1993 reforms are often identified in Italy as the "business-transformation" of the SSN. The transformation in ASL had at least two important implications: first, any links with municipalities were cut, with the balance of power now in favor of regional governments; and this would have helped in eliminating political control by local politicians. Second, it required a new internal organization, quite close to that of a private firm: a board of directors and a chief executive officer, to be appointed by regional governments; a board of statutory auditors for internal audits, with up to five members appointed by regional governments (two members), the municipal governments (one member), and the Ministry of the Economy (two members). As we will see below, however, the political control came back through the window of regional governments. Moreover, despite the design of an efficient internal organization, ASL were (and still are in some cases) far away from managing funds efficiently: managers appointed by politicians sometimes rely more on political pressures than on market forces in allocating funds; the internal auditors sometimes do not audit much.

A second change required by the move toward the quasi-market model was to separate producers from purchasers of services. The basic implication here was for ASL to hive off hospitals, and create the so-called *Aziende Ospedaliere* (AO, literally Hospital Firms). ASL were supposed to retain mostly administrative services (including the definition of needs at the local level), and then contract with different producers (from GPs to newborn AO) services for their policyholders (i.e. all residents in their jurisdiction). Again, this fundamental change had different implications: since the ASL had to contract with producers, they also needed to define a price for the services to be purchased. The solution proposed was to introduce a prospective payment system (PPS) based on Diagnosis Related Groups (DRG) – created in the USA at the beginning of the 1980s and experimented with in the US Medicare – which basically replaced per-day fees for private providers and full ex-post payment for public hospitals.[2] In turn, this solution implied a change in hospital management, imposing an administrative burden on nurses and physicians: the *Scheda di Dimissione Ospedaliera* (SDO, literally Discharge Form) had to be filled out to require payment from the ASL of the hospital services provided. Of course, the SDO was useful to identify for each patient the DRG and the corresponding tariff; but the tariffs still had to be defined. After the initial proposal of a national listing of charges, regional governments were set free to adopt their own. In any case, the new PPS had to be started between 1995 and 1997; in the absence of regional tariffs, regions should then adopt the national ones. Again, these changes were more promised than realized: only one region (Lombardy) separated all providers from purchasers. Moreover, after the initial years following the reform, also the PPS–DRG system was partly abandoned in favor of a budget-based approach, especially with private producers.

As for the SSN funding, the 1992–1993 reforms emphasized the change in the balance of power in favor of regional governments, by explicitly assigning sickness contributions to regional budgets. Together with the introduction of a property tax to finance municipalities in the same year, this was the first fundamental move towards the introduction of some degree of fiscal decentralization in the Italian context. The move has to be interpreted as a first trial to explicitly solve the misalignment between expenditure and funding responsibilities, to make more-accountable local governments. It was inspired both by the pressures exercised by new political parties combating against corruption and inefficiencies that rapidly gained votes in northern regions (especially the *Lega Nord*, literally North Alliance), and by the precepts of second-generation fiscal federalism theories, rapidly evolving those same years (e.g. Oates, 2005; Weingast, 2009). To emphasize that the devolution of own resources to regional governments was aimed at increasing their accountability, the Legislative Decree 502/92 explicitly excluded that the central government would take care of any future deficits (art. 13). Unfortunately, this is another unfulfilled promise.

Given the introduction of a seminal form of fiscal federalism, the apportionment of the NHF slightly changed. The major change was not in the apportionment formula itself (still based on some parameters identifying needs), but in the logic behind the working of the NHF. After devolution of sickness contributions, the role of general taxation was to *top-up* regional resources to cover regional financial requirements. The huge territorial differences in the tax bases caused (and still cause) very different vertical imbalances for each region: in particular, southern regions need to receive more funds from central government than center-northern regions. The equalization role played by the NHF was then magnified in this new context. This presumably propelled the tensions among regions, and further strengthened the idea to move toward a more mature form of fiscal federalism.

2.1.3. *The 1999 reform*

The call for fiscal federalism received another boost after the substitution of sickness contributions with both a newly created regional tax, the *Imposta Regionale sulle Attività Produttive* (IRAP, literally Regional Tax on Productive Activities), and a Surcharge on Personal Income Tax (*Addizionale* IRPEF), proposed by the center-left coalition guided by Romano Prodi in 1997.

Despite this trend, however, which should have increased regional responsibilities, deficits were more the rule rather than the exception despite some years of retrenchment (see Figure 3.1a). Moreover, the quasi-market model and the role of competition in improving efficiency was contested by the Health Minister Rosy Bindi, who pushed more on equity as for the role assigned to the SSN, getting back with the 1999 reform to the original spirit of the 1978 law.

The Legislative Decree 229/99 introduced the notion of *Livelli Essenziali di Assistenza* (LEA, literally Essential Levels of Care), that is to say mandatory and uniform services to be guaranteed in all regions. At present, the only definition of LEA consists of a positive list of all services to be included in the public insurance scheme and a negative list of all services excluded, defined with the agreement between central and regional governments of 8 August 2001. The choice of what services are included and what services are excluded is based on their effectiveness. Besides fixing this principle, however, the notion of LEA has an operational content, which is difficult to grasp.

Given that some services are explicitly excluded from those provided by the SSN, the Legislative Decree 229/99 introduced also Supplementary Funds of the SSN (art. 9). These are thought of as public or private insurance schemes that cannot select risks and can offer coverage for (1) all the services excluded from SSN; and (2) the co-payments required for some of the services included in the LEA. At present, they play a very minor role in the Italian landscape: not surprisingly, private healthcare spending in Italy is almost entirely out-of-pocket.

As already discussed, the Legislative Decree 229/99 also reneged on the quasi-market model just introduced, and called for more "co-operation" between ASL and providers, particularly private providers. In essence, this meant that ASL should contract with private providers assigning them a given budget and a given role in the provision of services.

The 1999 reform also pushed for more integration between healthcare and social care policies, again stressing the role of the SSN in combating inequities, deprivation, and social exclusion (art. 3 – *septies*). Integration involved the responsibility of municipalities in providing social services to disadvantaged people, like the elderly. Included are services like those provided by nursing homes, for example.

Finally, the 1999 reform made it definitely clear that the management of healthcare services was a responsibility of regional governments. In the light of these changes, it was more a reform setting principles than a reform aimed at solving the structural problems of the SSN. Despite the effectiveness implicit in the definition of the LEA, these principles were those characterizing the original design of the SSN: a clear emphasis on equity and much less focus on efficiency.

2.2. The dawn of the new century in the Italian SSN

The Italian SSN stemming from reforms implemented during the 1990s appears to be different from the original design of the Law 833/78, even though – at the beginning of the new century – the shape of the new project was (and still is) unclear. The conflict between reforms and counter-reforms that characterized the first 20 years of the SSN are most likely deriving from an apparent tension between efficiency and equity, which characterized also the first ten years of the new century.

Despite the difficulties in identifying the whole picture, there are then few important pieces of the puzzle that can help in clearing potential developments. A first undisputed piece of evidence is that the regions are the layer of government in charge of managing health care. This has been sanctioned both by reforms implemented during the 1990s, and by the recent Constitutional Law n. 3, 18 October 2001. Article 117 of the newly reformed Constitution defines competencies for the different levels of government. In particular, art. 117 comma 1 letter (m) assigns to the central government the *exclusive* right to only "define the Essential Levels of Services linked to civil and social rights to be guaranteed in the whole country". Healthcare services are of course included, so that only the central government can identify the mandatory level of care to be assured in all regions, and has the exclusive right to define the framework legislation. However, art. 117 comma

2 states that the "protection of health" is a shared responsibility between the central government and the regional governments. The common interpretation of this statement is that the management of the healthcare systems at the local level is the responsibility of regional governments that have to exercise their freedom within the framework legislation established by the central government.

Hence, the organization of the SSN is essentially unchanged from the 229/99 reform. Basically every region can choose how to organize the provision of services, and the role of the central government is only to define the framework. This includes, for instance, the list of essential services, but also the main directions to be pursued by regional governments. For example, assigning more resources to territorial care and reducing the role played by acute care hospitals are two trends inspired by policies at the national levels that (should) direct regional choices.

A second undisputed stylized fact is the difficulty in implementing a new system of funding, with the aim of making regional governments more accountable. Clearly enough, the involvement of different layers of governments in health care makes the issue of funding the SSN intertwined with the introduction of fiscal federalism in the Italian system of governments. As the story goes, there have been many different attempts to implement a fundamental form of fiscal decentralization in the country, proposed by both center-left and center-right governing coalitions, but none have been successful so far. The Legislative Decree n. 56, 18 February 2000, is the first comprehensive law aimed at changing regional funding in Italy, by eliminating earmarked transfers and reducing vertical imbalance. It was implemented by the center-left governing coalition guided by Massimo D'Alema, a representative of the former Italian Communist Party. In particular, the Legislative Decree 56/2000: (a) identifies a set of rules to define the annual funding for health care and other minor spending categories at the regional level; (b) identifies a set of taxes to fund these expenditures; (c) identifies a set of rules to equalize resources taking into account differences in both regional fiscal capacities and regional needs. Differing from the past, the evolution of regional spending (of which health care represents about four-fifths) has been thought to be consistent with the evolution of the main taxes on which funding was based. These were the IRAP and *Addizionale* IRPEF, introduced in 1997, plus the increase in revenues' sharing on the Specific Tax on Gasoline and – more importantly – the introduction of revenues' sharing on the Value Added Tax (IVA).

The philosophy inspiring the project was to increase regional accountability by both increasing regions' fiscal autonomy and – contemporaneously – the freedom to manage their budget within the limits of the framework legislation defined at the central level (removing earmarked transfers). In this perspective, the "solidarity coefficient" in the equalization formula was fixed at 90% to guarantee an "incomplete" equalization. In other words, part of the own revenues was excluded from equalization to provide appropriate incentives to regional governments to correctly manage their revenues. Not surprisingly, this mechanism would have favored regions with a larger fiscal capacity (i.e. mostly northern regions).

Apportionment of resources in 2001 did not provoke any reaction by the regions, simply because this was based on past expenditures. In 2002, however, 5% of the resources were to be shared according to the new criteria (fiscal capacity and needs), while the remaining 95% on the basis of past expenditures. This was established by the Decree 56/2000 to allow regional governments to adjust slowly (in 13 years) to the new rules. In fact, in 2013 all resources would have been apportioned according to the new criteria fixed by the Decree. But the new criteria were never applied: as soon as it has become clear that some regions lost part of their funds, regional governments blocked the Decree. In particular, Campania and Puglia – two southern regions – appealed to the Constitutional Court by exploiting the basic principle of the SSN, that views health as a "fundamental individual right" to be protected by the republic. The central government was then forced to "suspend" the Decree.

The following years were characterized by a large uncertainty surrounding the allocation of funds to regions, that end up in a new agreement signed by the central and the regional governments, translated into law with the Budget Law for the year 2006 (Law 266/2005, art. 1, comma 320 and following). As of 2006, however, the Decree 56/2000 is substantially dead.

New proposals on how to reform funding of lower tiers of governments (including regional governments) came up from both the central government and one of the leading regional governments (the *Regione Lombardia*), but none has been ever translated into law. It was not until the Law 42/2009 proposed by the center-right governing coalition led by Silvio Berlusconi that fiscal federalism took a center role in Italian politics. The principle fixed by this new law is that of "standard costs"; but nobody knows exactly what the law means by "standard costs". The recent Legislative Decree 68/2011 (aimed at translating the Law 42/2009 into practice) defines the criteria to compute "standard costs", and – in particular – the Regional Health Services (RHS) to be used as benchmarks. However, how the "standard costs" will influence the allocation of funds is still unclear. The apportionment of funds is still based on a measure of needs as in the past, while the total amount of resources is defined according to macroeconomic constraints on public budget. The agreement for 2010 confirms this view, postponing the complete implementation of the new mechanism (e.g. Muraro 2011).

3. An overall evaluation of the Italian SSN: where do we stand?

In this section of the essay, I discuss the impact of these regulations on efficiency and equity in the provision of healthcare services in Italy.[3] I start by considering the country as a whole, comparing the performance of the Italian SSN with the performance of healthcare systems in other similar European countries. I then move to the analysis of regional differences.

Taken together, the Italian SSN performs fairly well with respect to other spending categories (for instance, education). Following a pattern similar to most Western countries, healthcare expenditure reached 7.1% of GDP in 2009, with an increase in the last year mainly due to the fall in the denominator than to an increase in spending (Figure 3.2). However, compared with other countries, like France, Germany, and Sweden, the *level* of spending is lower. Italians spent less during the whole first decade of the twenty-first century; only Spain spent a bit less during the same period. Also the recent dynamics is relatively slow: differently from the past, when – especially at the end of the 1980s – the rate of growth was worrisome, being well above 10% each year, the rate of growth is recently under control and further slowing down (see Figure 3.1b). According to Joumard et al. (2010), in real terms the average rate of growth of per capita healthcare spending in Italy was 2.5% in the period 1995–2007, while the average for the OECD countries was 4.1%.

Despite spending less, results obtained in terms of population health are even better than in other countries. Considering again Joumard et al. (2010), if we look at average life expectancy at birth as an indicator of population health, Italy obtained a gain of 3.1 years over the period 1995–2007, which is the average gain obtained in the OECD countries. Similar conclusions are obtained by looking at average life expectancies at different ages, but also at infant mortality rate, which dropped massively from 81 to 37 per 10,000 births during the 1990s. The same figure dropped from 68 to 47 per 10,000

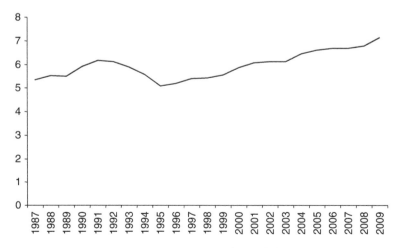

Figure 3.2   Healthcare spending in percentage of GDP (1987–2009)
Source: Relazione Generale sulla Situazione Economica del Paese.

births in the EU's 16 countries over the same period. Given these figures, it does not come as a surprise that the benchmarking exercise conducted by Joumard et al. (2010) suggests that Italy is doing quite well in the group of "heavily regulated public systems and with a stringent budget constraint", which includes countries like the UK.

If we consider more complete evaluation exercises, these conclusions do not change very much. For instance, in one of the benchmarking exercises carried out across countries, the World Health Organization (WHO) ranked healthcare systems according to three goals that they should pursue: the level and the distribution of health, the level and the distribution of responsiveness, and fairness in financial contribution (WHO, 2000). Ranking 11th in terms of per capita total health spending, the Italian SSN ranked second taking into account all the three goals, just behind the French system, which is however the fourth in terms of spending. Germany, ranking third for spending, performs poorly compared with Italy, since it is only 25th in terms of overall evaluation.

But this fairly nice picture at the country level hides unacceptable differences at the regional level, and generalized problems in terms of governance and control of regional healthcare systems. Average per capita spending totaled about 1800 euro in 2009 (Ministero dell'Economia e delle Finanze, 2010), with a maximum of 2170 euro in the Autonomous Province of Bolzano and a minimum of 1671 in Sicilia, another Special Statute Region. If we restrict the attention to Ordinary Statute Regions, Molise spent 2080 euro (the maximum) while Calabria 1732 euro (the minimum), a sum which is quite close to per capita spending in Lombardia (1763 euro). Given large differences in terms of fiscal capacity, it is clear that the SSN operated important *ex ante* redistribution in favor of less endowed regions (i.e. the southern regions). This is clear when looking at the share of own resources out of the total funding for health care, which is about half for center-north regions and less than 20% for southern regions (Table 3.1).

However, regional governments spoil this *ex ante* redistribution when managing the funds they receive; and, unfortunately, this is especially true for southern regions. Considering "ex-post redistribution", i.e. redistribution evaluated by taking into account services *effectively* consumed by citizens, requires spending levels to be corrected for a number of factors, such as population age, patients mobility, and complexity of services, to be somewhat comparable across regions. Conducting a similar exercise, researchers at the Bank of Italy suggest that – 100 being the per capita spending at the national level – southern regions spend 104, center regions 101.9, while northern regions only 96 (Alampi et al. 2010). In other words, northern regions contribute heavily to transfer resources to southern regions, and spend better and more efficiently the resources they retain. Evidence on this point is widespread, and can be grasped by looking at official data on the perceived quality of services (Figure 3.3), patient mobility, and inappropriateness.

Table 3.1 The structure of healthcare funding (Ordinary Statute Regions only, 2009, %)

	Own resources			Transfers from central government			
	IRAP – IRPEF surcharge	ASL own revenues	Extraordinary revenues	Ex-D.Lgs-56/00	Additional transfers	Earmarked transfers (ex National Health Fund)	Total
North	47.8	4.6	0.5	43.2	2.0	1.8	100
Center	44.5	4.3	0.8	47.7	0.9	1.9	100
South	15.3	2.2	0.5	79.4	0.8	1.9	100
Italy	38.4	3.9	0.5	53.9	1.4	1.9	100

Source: Ministero dell'Economia e delle Finanze (2010).

All indicators point in the same direction: southern regions are the worst performers at the country level (Piacenza and Turati 2010; Francese and Romanelli 2010; Francese et al. 2010).

One important question is why southern regions spend more. According to Alampi et al. (2010), this is for a number of reasons: (a) because pharmaceutical and hospital expenditures are higher than in other regions, and these categories are more costly; (b) because the hospital network is badly managed: there are too many small-sized hospitals where people obtain inappropriate services of low quality; and (c) because there are too many prescriptions by GPs of inappropriate drugs, and of more costly drugs by given active ingredient. Of course, this does not solve the problem, and one may still ask why pharmaceutical and hospital expenditures are higher or why there are too many prescriptions by GPs in southern regions. There are not, however, easy answers here.

One possible explanation is related to the lack of planning. For instance, Pelliccia and Trimaglio (2009) show that regions in the center-north started the practice of Regional Health Plans well ahead of the first NHP presented in 1994, as envisaged by the Law 833/78. On the contrary, southern regions started planning their RHS only at the end of the 1990s, after the central government approved the first NHP. Not surprisingly, inefficiencies are common in all areas of the country, but are highest in southern regions. For instance, Piacenza and Turati (2010) estimate that – between 1993 and 2006 – average inefficiencies in southern (Ordinary Statute) regions were almost double inefficiencies in the center-north ones. Inefficiencies take many different forms: apart from those already mentioned above for the abnormal role assigned to hospitals, the report of the Carella Parliamentary Commission (from the name of its president) suggests other types. To list a few: hospitals in the south are characterized by structural deficiencies, like the absence of minimal security standards and "elementary" hygienic conditions; a greater

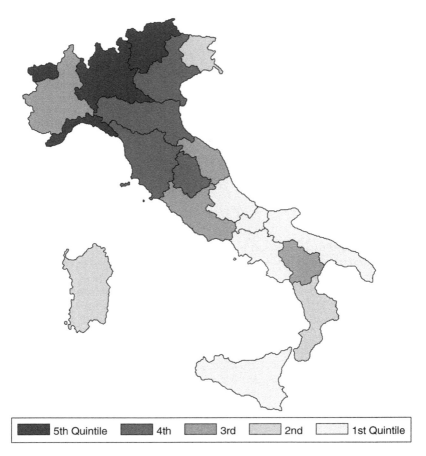

Figure 3.3 People very satisfied with medical assistance in hospitals (2006)
Source: ISTAT – Health for All.

inertia in the use of funds for healthcare facilities[4]; and connected problem of still unfinished or finished-but-never-used healthcare facilities (e.g.
Caroppo and Turati 2007).

Inefficiency however is not the sole explanation, because inefficiency
sometimes is the result of corruption. Indeed, a second important explanation for the inferior performance of southern regions is the presence in these
areas of criminal organizations. Public health care is in some regions the
largest industry in terms of GDP, and this allures criminals and creates – in
the absence of financial responsibility – a perverse mechanism. To clarify this
point, the "exchange" is structured as follows: criminal organizations gather
votes for regional politicians, and politicians guarantee jobs and monies. Not

surprisingly, then, in these realities the RHS is not thought of primarily as providing services, but rather is regarded as providing a job to some and monies to others in exchange for votes, with somebody else footing the bills (e.g. Lane (2009)).

The presence of corruption is likely to fuel also regional deficits, which in the last few years have shown the tendency to strongly concentrate in a small subset of southern regions (particularly Lazio, Campania, Puglia, Calabria, and Sicilia). Notice that – while the mechanism for obtaining additional funds is less "automatic" than in the past – the central government is likely to step in and bail out past debts should the regional governments become unable to guarantee their financial stability (e.g. Bordignon and Turati (2008)).

In summary, despite the nice picture of the Italian SSN at the aggregate level, the situation at the regional level shows large differences, all pointing in a clear direction: southern regions perform worse than center-north ones. According to the available evidence, the main problem is not the lack of funds, but how (mostly) transferred funds are managed at the local level. In other words redistribution ex-ante (i.e. the equalization of fiscal capacities) is not matched by ex-post redistribution (i.e. the equalization of services for citizens). It is this mismatch that creates the tensions that will drive the likely changes in the near future.

4. Winds of change?

Given the good standing at the aggregate level, and the regional differences outlined in the previous section, it is not surprising that there are tensions, which are expected to characterize the future evolution of the Italian SSN. As already emphasized, in my view these tensions find their fundamental origin in the lack of correlation between ex-ante and ex-post redistribution. Center-north regions focus on the massive ex-ante redistribution, which occurred in the past and it is still occurring today in the country, but which generated inefficiencies and corruption instead of services ex-post. According to this view, the SSN is plagued by an *efficiency* problem, which is related to the issue of soft budget constraints, originating from the misalignment in responsibilities of spending and funding. We have evidence that the expectations of future bailouts negatively influenced expenditure, and propelled inefficiencies (Bordignon and Turati 2009; Piacenza and Turati 2010). On the contrary, southern regions focus on the large differences in terms of availability and quality of services, which is a problem of *equity* in the access to health care (that can also generate a problem of equity in health). The difficulties in implementing some form of fiscal federalism clearly originate from this clash between efficiency and equity. The agreement on regional federalism shows that the apportionment formula can be probably improved, but the structural problem of equalizing resources to guarantee mandatory levels of care across the whole country cannot find an easy solution. Southern regions will also need to receive funds from other regions in the future and this will continue to reduce their accountability from the financial side.[5] What can we do then?

The policy discussion in the country focuses on two main interrelated types of mechanisms: on the one hand, the improvement of the "identification strategies" of inefficiencies and corruption; on the other hand, the improvement in the accountability of local politicians to be obtained by developing new and alternative political institutions (given that fiscal federalism cannot work for southern regions). As for the first mechanism, one needs to recognize that the 1992–1993 reform package introduced a board of internal auditors in each ASL, with the task of auditing the budget, and reporting to regional governments in case of irregularities and waste in the management of public monies. Clearly enough, auditors can control the budget if there is one; but in several cases, Local Health Firms did not even present their budgets, or presented budgets that were evidently faked. One striking example of this practice is the *Regione Lazio*, where undisclosed past debts in 2007 amounted to 10 billion euros (Bordignon and Turati 2008). One may ask why the regional government did not intervene before the debt was too out of control to solve the problem. One piece of the answer is probably related to the bailout received from the central government by the *Regione Lazio* in the same year, which covered the surfaced debts almost completely.

If internal audits do not work, a solution could be to recur to external audits. The Italian Constitution envisages the *Corte dei Conti* (Court of Auditors), to which it assigns the task – among others – of controlling ex-post the management of public funds. The Court has a specific Section (*Sezione delle Autonomie*) dedicated to the audit of lower-tier governments' budgets. And the reports and the deliberations of the Court of Auditors are full of warnings on the management of healthcare funds at the regional level, especially related to southern regions with the highest levels of debt.[6] Despite these recommendations, however, the central government and the Parliament simply "shut their eyes": most reasonably, because the careers of politicians at the regional level are too closely intertwined with the careers of politicians at the central level, for the latter being available to effectively sanction the former (Merlo et al. 2009). In a sense, Italian politicians have become a "caste" of untouchables (Stella and Rizzo 2007).

Another mechanism to improve external audit, which suffers from this same drawback, is to improve the benchmarking of Regional Health Care services. This is the implicit aim of the original Law 42/2009, the Legislative Decree 68/2011, and the reference therein to "standard costs". Differently from other sectors, the availability of data is quite substantial in the case of health care. It does not come as a surprise, then, that some benchmarking exercises are already available, and others will surely follow (e.g. Piacenza and Turati 2010; Francese and Romanelli 2010; Pammolli et al. 2009). There is also a first report produced by the Ministry of Health on the benchmarking of regional healthcare systems (Ministero della Salute 2010). But, again, after producing the evidence of inefficiencies and corruptions – substantially the same in all the benchmarking exercises – the game ends there, without any effects on the apportionment of resources. And the suspicion that "rogue" regional governments to continue managing public monies badly is still alive.

These difficulties bring us to the second group of mechanisms that is new institutions to improve the accountability of local politicians. A first example, already implemented but not formalized in any specific law, is the so-called *Piano di Rientro* (literally, a repayment plan), which is a formal agreement between the central government and one specific regional government that accumulated past deficits. Most of the southern regions already signed repayment plans, which typically include measures like the restructuring of the public hospitals network (on the expenditures side) and the (automatic) increase of the local tax rates at their maximum level (on the revenues side). But while the Minister of the Economy seems particularly happy with the experience of these plans for the future financial stability of these regions, the Court of Auditors appears rather sceptical (see Resolution n. 22/2009/G). In any case, it would be important to translate this practice into a proper provision by the law, creating a framework legislation for the default of regional and local governments (at present, we have only bankruptcy legislation for provinces and municipalities), that formalizes the automatic mechanism of increasing local tax rates.

A second institution that characterizes the recent policy discussion is the so-called "political failure", which is a system of perverse incentives for local politicians. At present, only citizens of indebted regions (and, more generally, all Italian citizens) pay more local taxes as a "punishment" for having elected inept representatives. However, to better control moral hazard by politicians, one should create a system of disincentives also for them. This should include banning local administrators who created a deficit from being commissioners charged with fixing it. At present, though incredible, the practice for regional governments in financial difficulties is to assign *additional* powers to governors in office, (i.e. governors that presumably contributed to create the problem: that is, to use a "carrot" in place of a "stick"). A second provision should be an economic "punishment" for local politicians, for instance by stopping remunerating the governor and all the member of the regional council, but also public funding for political parties sustaining the regional government (Bordignon and Brusco 2010). A third provision is the "end-of-mandate certificate" envisaged in the recent report by the ministerial Commission for the implementation of fiscal federalism (see *Relazione sul Federalismo Fiscale*, 30 June 2010, Rome). At the end of each mandate, six months before new elections will take place, the governors should basically provide a certificate (for which they are made accountable) that the budgets they signed are representing the true and fair view of the state of affairs in their region, so as to avoid undisclosed debts.

Despite the charm of these new ideas, I find that they suffer from the same problem discussed before: why should (Italian) politicians implement a set of rules that can considerably worsen their payoffs? That is why I still believe that the most important institutions are those implemented at the European level: this is the only way the Italian government can "tie its hands" and renege any ex-post bailouts of regional debts, so to prevent the occurrence of any financial difficulties. European rules worked apparently well in curbing bailout expectations of regional governments in Italy during the painful adjustment to reach the goals provided by the Maastricht Treaty, wiping out deficits almost entirely (Bordignon and Turati 2009). The provisions of the Amsterdam Treaty worked relatively less well (e.g. Piacenza and Turati 2010): the successive crises of the Stability and Growth Pact opened the door to new problems of financial stability at the country level, which can exacerbate stability problems also at the local level, via the expectations' mechanism. I am not sure the recent European Financial Stability Facility will work. But I am sure that Europe can impose external constraints to countries with fragile political institutions, and help them to maintain financial rigidity in public finances.

Besides this "short run" standpoint, it appears important to emphasize one final point on the future of the Italian SSN. In terms of spending, since expenditure is clearly age-related, rapid population ageing is potentially a problem for expected spending growth. A large share of inpatients and of pharmaceutical expenditure are due to people over 65 years of age, which now accounts for 20% of the total population, but this percentage is projected to grow swiftly in the next decades, more than in other countries. The picture is even worse if we consider that – for a given individual – a large share of the lifetime health spending is concentrated in the year immediately before death. Given that life expectancy at birth is now a few years above 80, one can consider the share of people over 80 years out of the total population as a more precise indicator of expected growth in spending. This share, which is now about 6% for Italy, is expected to more than double by 2050 (Eurostat). Over the same period, the EU 27 average will rise from 4.6 to 11%. Notice that the problem that population-ageing poses is not only in terms of rising expenditure, but also in terms of GDP growth: an older country will grow less, further reinforcing worries about how to finance expected increase in spending. The easy solution will be to recur to private insurance markets; and some hints in this direction have been already advanced in the policy discussion. But recurring to a "second pillar" also for health care can be troublesome. The pension reform implemented in 1995 will drastically cut pensions for future retirees, and reducing health care services will impose a double-burden on these generations. On the one hand, they are now contributing heavily to sustain a generous welfare system for their parents, without receiving much in exchange, for instance in terms of schooling for their children. On the other hand, they will receive less in the future, because current constraints on public finances impose to restructure the public welfare system to make these financially sustainable. How all this will impact on the Italian society is difficult to forecast. But, apparently, there is not good news.

Acknowledgments

I am indebted to Massimo Bordignon, Nerina Dirindin, Massimiliano Piacenza, and Franco Reviglio for the ongoing discussions on the Italian healthcare system and its future. Needless to say, I am the sole person responsible for any errors and the opinions expressed here.

Notes

1. For instance, art. 2 states – among other issues – that the NHS aims at overtaking territorial imbalances in the social and health conditions of the country; art. 4 assigns central government the task to guarantee uniform conditions in some of the determinants of citizens' health (e.g. pollution, safety at work, food safety).
2. Of course, the DRG-PPS system also has its pros in the fact that – being a fixed-price mechanism – it should boost efficiency. But it also has its own cons, like up-coding, cream-skimming, skimping, dumping, ...
3. This section draws on a speech (joint with Massimo Bordignon) before the Scientific Committee of Confindustria, the Italian organization of manufacturing and services companies, in July 2010.
4. This is true also for structural European funds. Again, lack of planning seems to be one of the most important reasons to explain why regions with high needs of infrastructures are not able to spend available monies.
5. Unless, of course, we reduce mandatory levels of care up to a point where all regions can finance their services with their own funds. However, since services should be cut back heavily to allow also the poorest region to finance its own services, this is politically unsustainable at the current stage of development of the SSN.
6. The most recent example is the Resolution n. 22/2009/G on the management of additional resources made available by the central government for the reduction of structural deficits in the SSN. The evaluation of the Court advances serious doubts on the idea that financial responsibility for southern regions is improving.

References

Alampi D., Iuzzolino G., Lozzi M., Schiavone A. (2010), La sanità, in Atti del Convegno "Il Mezzogiorno e la Politica Economica dell'Italia", Roma: Banca d'Italia.

Bordignon M., Brusco S. (2010), Una penitenza per chi manda la sanità in rosso, *Lavoce.info*.

Bordignon M., Turati G. (2008), Health, fiscal federalism, and local public services, in M. Donovan, P. Onofri (eds.), *Italian Politics: Frustrated Aspirations for Change*, New York: Berghahn Books.

Bordignon M., Turati G. (2009), Bailing out expectations and public health expenditure, *Journal of Health Economics*, 28, 305–321.

Caroppo M. S., Turati G. (2007), *I sistemi sanitari regionali in Italia. Riflessioni in una prospettiva di lungo periodo*, Milano: Vita e Pensiero.

Francese M., Romanelli M. (2010), Health care in Italy: expenditure determinants and regional differentials, in A. Testi et al. (eds.), *Proceedings of the XXXVI International ORHAS Conference – Operations Research for Patient-Centred Health Care Delivery*, Milano: Franco Angeli.

Francese M., Piacenza M., Romanelli M., Turati G. (2010), Understanding inappropriateness in health treatments: The case of caesarean deliveries across Italian regions, Banca d'Italia, Roma, *mimeo*.

Joumard I., André C., Nicq C. (2010), *Health Care Systems: Efficiency and Institutions*, OECD Economics Department Working Papers, No. 769, OECD Publishing, doi: 10.1787/5kmfp51f5f9t-en.

Lane D. (2009), *Into the Heart of the Mafia. A Journey Through the Italian South*, London: Profile Books.

Merlo A., Galasso V., Landi M., Mattozzi A. (2009), The labour market of Italian politicians, PIER Working Paper, n. 24, Department of Economics, University of Pennsylvania.

Ministero della Salute (2010), *Il sistema di valutazione della performance dei sistemi sanitari regionali*, Roma.

Ministero dell'Economia e delle Finanze (2010), *Relazione generale sulla situazione economica del Paese*, Roma.

Muraro G. (2011), Federalismo regionale: la rivoluzione può attendere, *Lavoce.info*.

Oates, W.E. (2005), Toward a second-generation theory of fiscal federalism, *International Tax and Public Finance*, 12, 349–373.

Pammolli F., Papa G., Salerno N. C. (2009), La spesa sanitaria pubblica in Italia: dentro la "scatola nera" delle differenze regionali, Quaderno Cerm, n. 2.

Pelliccia L., Trimaglio F. (2009), I Piani sanitari regionali: aspetti metodologici, contenuto e funzione, in P. Bosi, N. Dirindin, G. Turati (eds.), *Decentramento fiscale, riorganizzazione interna e integrazione socio-sanitaria*, Milano: Vita e Pensiero.

Piacenza M., Turati G. (2010), Does Fiscal Discipline towards Sub-national Governments Affect Citizens' Well-being? Evidence on Health, Working Paper n. 56, IEB – Institut d'Economia de Barcelona, Universitat de Barcelona.

Stella G. A., Rizzo S. (2007), *La casta*, Milano: Rizzoli.

Weingast, B.R. (2009), Second Generation Fiscal Federalism: the implication of fiscal incentives, *Journal of Urban Economics*, 65, 279–293.

World Health Organization (2000), *The World Health Report 2000: Health Systems: Improving Performance*, Geneva: WHO.

4
Decentralization and the Spanish Health System: Soft Budget Constraint Modernization?

Joan Costa-Font

1. Introduction

Spain is a country of paramount importance for healthcare decentralization scholars given its deep process of devolution of health and education to region states. Such a process dates back to a strategy of democratization of a centralistic state as well as a modernization mechanism to improvising the efficiency in the delivery of public services. However, there is an unintended agenda. More precisely, by creating different regional health services, a health system takes advantage of welfare gains associated with interjurisdictional competition and innovation and at the same time encourages local healthcare preference matching. These can take place if citizens exert the so-called "vote with one's feet" exit option. Or, under restricted mobility but visible political and fiscal accountability it can open up political mechanisms of the political action to exercise voice, and more generally electorally reward regional incumbents benchmarked against those of similar jurisdictions (Besley and Case 1995; Revelli 2002). As discussed in Chapter 2 on fiscal federalism, both mechanisms are important to incentivize incumbents to improve the performance of public services, and are generally absent in centralized health system.

The Spanish case study as I argue in this chapter is a paradigmatic example of a health system that managed to significantly devolve healthcare responsibilities to relatively junior governments, mostly newly created region states and a few historical regional states that were vocal enough to put forward self-government claims. Overall, I argue that the Spanish case exhibits evidence of success although structural vertical imbalances in the system remain unaddressed. The latter has to do with a significant mismatch between tax and expenditure autonomy resulting from limited tax autonomy, that has led to the expansion of health-related deficits and debt.

Another important noteworthy result that can inform federalism scholars is the evidence that the Spanish case is an example of a process of decentralization with important effects on reducing enduring inequalities (Costa-Font 2010b; Costa-Font and Rico 2006b). As we explain latter, part of this effect results from the existence of policy diffusion exerting a marked influence in exporting innovations throughout the territory (Costa-Font and Rico 2006a), which explains that healthcare mobility from more- to less-affluent region states, if anything, it appears to decline overtime. In contrast, an important mechanism that explains inter-jurisdictional interactions in health care is the fact that it is a heavily politicized policy area, regardless of its lesser visibility of healthcare quality. Indeed, constituents and region state incumbents have access to some information on their neighboring jurisdiction health policies, which allows voters in one jurisdiction to use some of this information to evaluate neighboring government's performance as a yardstick to evaluate their own government (Salmon 1987).

Nonetheless, objections to devolution processes include potential externalities taking the form of informal regional competition (or cooperation) among region states, which might produce policy diffusion of successful experimentation. However, the Spanish case study reveals evidence on the former but very limited evidence of the latter, as we explain below.

A key argument in the devolution debate refers to how the incentive design (see chapter on fiscal federalism) determines the success of devolution in achieving desirable goals such as social and regional cohesion, innovation and efficiency primarily. The developments of the Spanish territorial organization after the constitutional arrangements in the late 1970s provide a particularly interesting example where to examine the qualitative and quantitative evidence on the outcomes of devolution structures, given that Spain currently stands as one of the EU countries where region states (so-called autonomous communities, AC in Spain) exercise a superior level of expenditure responsibilities in certain areas such as health care and education.

The devolved nature of Spanish healthcare system lies in several reasons. First, some of the key Spanish region states exhibit significant differences in institutional development of health-related civil society and management practices, and this has important ramifications for the organization of the market for healthcare provision. The latter is the case of Catalonia where two-thirds of the healthcare providers are privately owned and where public–private sector collaboration has always been the norm, and hence a one-model-fits-all based on public provision as in the rest of the country, including the capital Madrid, would be inefficient. In other words, there are differences in regional preferences for healthcare delivery through the territory. Second, leading hospitals and health professionals were not based in the country capital at the time that the Constitution was elaborated, but in other areas. Hence, a central control of the health system would be inefficient form a simple view of use of resources.

Third, a country of more than 40 million people exhibits dramatic differences in health needs that might not be managed centrally without a significant loss of information and capacity. Fourth (as above mentioned), some regional responsibilities would have to be devolved as part of a strategy of democratization as well as a way to come to terms with the over-centralization of a dictatorial Spain.

The decentralization of health care in Spain was consensually agreed as part of the pre-constitutional political pacts but formally began during the early 1980s and staggered over almost 13 years. It took place in two steps, or so-called "decentralization waves." The first was a wave of asymmetric federalism where only a few region states were managed regionally and the rest were run through a centrally managed agency INSALUD. The second wave cleared existing asymmetries and dismantled INSALUD, which was defined by a form of homogeneous federalism as all regions were invested with the same level of healthcare responsibilities. The first wave began with the transfer of healthcare responsibilities to the following set of regional states: Catalonia (1981), followed by Andalucía (1984), the Basque Country and Valencia (1988), Galicia and Navarra (1991), and ending with the transfer of healthcare responsibilities to the Canary Islands (1994). In contrast, the second wave was a one-shot event where the remaining ten regions that were centrally managed finally obtained healthcare responsibilities in 2002, so that healthcare responsibilities were finally transferred to the remaining region states.

This chapter deals with examining the most important features of the design of a decentralized healthcare system in Spain. We describe the rationale for the specific institutional design, as well as its limitations and expected outcomes. The chapter examines the impact that the specific type of devolution that has been taking place in the Spanish National Health System (NHS) over the last decade has had on health policy outcomes. More generally, we examine the patterns of health expenditure, inequalities, policy innovation, and more qualitative evidence on the limitations of decision-making in a decentralized setting. The relevance of the Spanish example lies in the fact that the NHS has been devolved by progressively creating a number of politically (though not fully fiscally) accountable regional health services in a context of weak central state regulation as well as insignificant patient mobility. Therefore, the territorial design has fostered political interactions between regional states (so-called Autonomous Communities, AC) (Costa-Font and Pons-Novell 2007; Costa-Font and Moscone 2008). The effect of political interactions across regions has shaped the nature of the political agency relationship whereby incumbents in some ACs – although legally are representatives of the Spanish state – become "region-specific political agents", more sensitive to their constituents demands. The latter explains, as described below, that no evidence of "race to the bottom", or contraction of health expenditure is observed in Spain. Section 2 describes the institutional background of the decentralization process that has taken place in the Spanish NHS. Section 3 examines inter-jurisdictional competition in such a setting. Section 4 reports evidence on outcomes and innovation, and Section 5 concludes.

2. Designing a decentralized health system

2.1. Basic health systems patterns

The Spanish health system is almost fully financed by general taxes – with user co-payments having a markedly restricted role. The population is entitled to free access to services and benefits are comprehensive. Funds to finance health care have been centrally collected with the exception of Navarra and the Basque Country. Once Parliament determines the amount of healthcare expenditure in the National General Budget, expenditure is allocated to region by means of a block central grant according to a capitation formula (Rico and Costa-Font 2005; Lopez-Casasnovas et al. 2005) that only takes insularity and demographics into consideration. There are important differences in healthcare delivery across the territory. While in Catalonia about two-thirds of the inpatient centers are private, healthcare delivery in other Spanish region states is mainly undertaken through a network of publicly owned centers.

Healthcare expenditure has expanded in both total and relative terms; the percentage of public expenditure appears to remains relatively constant with only small increasing patterns after 2005 all the way to 2009 as shown in Table 4.1. Public expenditure has increased almost 1% of the GDP overall in part as a contraction and in part because some components of health expenditure have been expanding at a faster pace. This is especially true for pharmaceuticals, which are still a heavily centralized responsibility. This pattern not only compares to other countries of the OECD, but actually exhibits a lower expenditure rise in relative terms. In contrast, private health expenditure exhibits similar patterns over time and has remained at around 2% of the GDP throughout the period examined. Total health expenditure appears to have risen from 7.6% of the GDP in 1995 to 8.7% in 2009. If long-term care (LTC) expenditure is included, it rises from 8.3 in 2005 before the LTC reform was incepted to 9.5% of the GDP in 2009 once some of the provisions of the LTC reform were put in place (Costa-Font 2010a). Similarly, this evidence contradicts some of the classical "race to the bottom" criticism to devolution processes, as devolution if anything, appears to maintain health system structures under some level of inertia, and hence protects it from a potential dismantling agenda (Costa-Font and Rico 2006a).

Table 4.1 Health expenditure in Spain (1995–2009)

	1995	2000	2005	2009
Public health expenditure				
%	72%	72%	71%	75%
% GDP	5.5	5.4	5.4	6.5
Private health expenditure				
%	28%	28%	29%	25%
% GDP	2.1	2.1	2.2	2.2
Total health expenditure				
% GDP	7.6	7.5	7.6	8.7

Source: Ministerio de Sanidad, Política Social e Igualdad, 2011.

2.2. The allocation on healthcare powers

Health care, together with education, ranks first in the responsibilities of region states and it is the first government priority of Spanish citizens (Lopez Casasnovas et al. 2005). Health care accounts for about 40% of regional public expenditure, and regional parliaments have exerted a significant legislative capacity, which has only been limited by framework central state legislation. Hence, as a devolved responsibility it offers significant opportunities of credit-claiming because it appears as an attractive responsibility for junior governments to legitimize themselves, but at the same time if the process backfires, it can delegitimize the whole decentralization process. This explains in part the gradual process of decentralization where region states that were perceived as exhibiting a better fit were given priority in the decentralization process. From the central levels perspective, devolving responsibilities can be seen as a way of sharing or even shifting the blame of critical policy responsibilities (Costa-Font 2010a). This motivates the development of decentralization processes whereby regional jurisdictions become key political actors, especially in those health systems that operate along the lines of an NHS.

In contrast to other southern European health systems with the exception of Italy, the Spanish model has succeeded in transferring healthcare powers to regions, although this was undertaken in a rather unplanned way leading to vertical competition (Costa-Font and Rico 2006). Indeed, due to the lack of an entrenched division of responsibilities, the central state has played both a weak coordination role and has left certain areas under blurred central-state control, which has in turn stimulated the regional legislative action. This is a similar pattern found in the post-devolution UK. The Ministry of Health (MoH) in conjunction with the Inter-territorial Committee of regional states has been responsible for central coordination, although in some critical healthcare domains the Ministry of Social Security and the

Ministry of Finance exercise important unconstrained powers, such as the fixing of drug prices.

2.3. Regional resource allocation and "soft budget constraints"

With the exception of the so-called "foral region states" (Basque Country and Navarra), all the other so-called "common region states" are financed through block grants allocated centrally and have only been mildly modified, as explained below. This creates higher vertical imbalances in those regions as the degree of autonomy in expenditures and revenues do not generally coincide, hence giving rise to potential soft budget constrains (and ex-ante moral hazard more specifically). This in turn is consistent with an expected overspending pattern. Since the inception of decentralization, fiscal autonomy has been increased in several occasions, including the 1992 regional participation of 15% of the personal income tax revenues, a percentage later raised to 30% and recently 40%, and includes VAT. In 1994, the government made a firm commitment to put into force a regionally homogenous non-weighted capitation system for a four-year period, where it linked expenditure growth rates to GDP and imposed tighter conditions on the recourse to extraordinary resources. Originally, resource allocation barely took into account demography, population density, or morbidity and mortality. Only in 1997, the principle of capitation was expanded to include population, partly due to the political pressures of the Catalan executive. By 2002, a deeper structural reform was accomplished, ending with the inclusion of healthcare funding in the general regional resource allocation system.

Even if revised financial settings provide wider options for revenue raising (e.g. surcharges on petrol taxes to pay for health care – so-called "health cents"), the extent of fiscal autonomy in most Spanish region states is limited. Similarly, reforms in 1997 and 2001 have provided more leeway on own taxes such as inheritance tax as well as tax revenue sharing on general taxes. This includes 33% of income tax and 40% of VAT, though with a very restricted capacity to raise the tax base and tax rate. The funds are allocated on a per capita basis rather than to cover the cost of the health services transferred. The operation of that model was a constant source of conflict between the central government and the ACs, which almost permanently claimed they were under-funded. After 2001, healthcare financing was integrated into the general regional financial system, which meant that region states can decide the share of resource to devote to health vis-à-vis other public responsibilities. This ends the untransparent political negotiation of the past in allocating healthcare funds. Finally, a cohesion fund was created as an equalization fund to correct for horizontal imbalances.

On the other hand, the central state has systematically "under budgeted" health care as an informal mechanism to halt expenditure expansion as well as a bargaining asset. But it has regularly and unilaterally expanded the reimbursement of high-cost medicines (which remains a central-level responsibility) with limited regional say on it. Given that regional government could obtain external financing from financial markets, the traditional way out for region states has to make use of an expanding debt as a funding source, which has increased systematically around 10% per annum on average and is generally between 10% and 15% of total budgeted expenditure.[1]

Importantly, regional fiscal deficits have boosted when regional incumbents are run by the opposition party at the central level, which is consistent with the soft budget constraint incentives (moral hazard) to expand expenditure to increase chances of re-election. It is not infrequent that regional incumbents become members of the central cabinet after the old opposition government recovers the mandate at the central level. However, the mounting healthcare debt cannot be attributed to decentralization as when health care was centrally run under INSALUD debt increased at a similar or even faster rate than that of regionally run health services. Overall, the finances of region states have run a deficit over time, unveiling the unbinding nature of soft budget constraints whereby region states prefer to expand their deficit rather than use their tax power to increase revenues, which similarly to Italy, can be explained by the existence of bailout expectations (see Turati in this book). The ultimate consequence of these mechanisms is the generation of a significant mounting debt. Finally, and as a last resort, the state can appeal against regional legislation and to the Constitutional Court.

To curve the existing vertical fiscal imbalances and introduce harder budget constraints, one can envisage two lines of thought. On one hand, proponents stress territorial inequities and advocate for tighter central controls, though without much evidence that this would actually reduce the level of mounting debt. Alternatively proponents of furthering fiscal autonomy by tightening fiscal constraints suggest it would stimulate efficiency and cost-containment. To do so, resource allocation should expand its criteria to measure differences in "health need", and more generally, region states should have an increasing number of tax autonomy to expand to contract their health expenditure in accordance to regional preferences. The latter implies that universality encompasses a common package, but it allows diversity to match regional-specific media voter preferences.

3. Inter-jurisdictional interactions

3.1. Strategic interactions

Strategic interaction might take place among regional governments on setting their taxes and expenditures so that some welfare competition has been suggested to take place. Citizens of one jurisdiction might look at neighboring jurisdictions' benefits levels in judging their own performance. Accordingly, incumbents at the regional level might react to this effect by both reducing taxes and benefits (healthcare coverage) if they are fiscally accountable governments and the other way around if they are not. On the other hand, equilibrium might take place through the so-called "welfare migration". Under welfare migration, welfare "generosity" leads to tax increases in more generous regions to fund new recipients of welfare. However, when welfare migration is limited – as is the case in Spain (less than 1% of patients are treated in hospitals of different AC) and in most European countries – then a separate equilibrium can take place while regional incumbents might have incentives to increase coverage. When coordination by the central state is weak, there are incentives for regional incumbents to compete with the central state. The latter is catalogued as vertical competition and takes place together with yardstick competition mechanisms whereby political accountability allows constituents in one region to benchmark their demand on the basis of other regions' performance.

In the Spanish NHS, incentives are not to reduce taxes, insofar as taxes are uniformly defined with the exception of two ACs, but to increase expenditure. This might potentially take place in the political arena, whereby regional and national incumbents might not be willing to cut expenditure in certain areas, and welfare benefits in one region are likely to exhibit a so-called race to the top rather than a race to the bottom. If this is the case, we should expect some strategic interaction whereby welfare coverage of some ACs is likely to depend on the coverage of neighboring regions. The Spanish Constitution and the statutory laws of each AC region define the shape of a genuine political agency where ACs are subject to both constituents preferences and central-state coordination.

Importantly, patient mobility has declined from 2001 where 60,500 patients were seeking care in another region's state, to 58,000 patients in 2005. The region-specific flow of patients travelling has also generally declined. This stands as a relief from region states such as Catalonia and Madrid that were traditionally receiving high demand from other regions. Given the insignificant geographical mobility of the Spanish population – at least under the period examined – regional political power does not equilibrate through welfare migration (Tiebout 1956). Following Salmon (1987), under lack of welfare migration and imperfect information, constituents of one jurisdiction are able to evaluate the performance of similar jurisdictions. Hence, instead of voting with their feet, citizens use the mechanisms of electoral competition to induce their own government to do as well as its neighbor region. Indeed, some studies suggest that the equilibrium mechanisms of the political agency place their effects though numerous examples of spatial interactions defined by vertical competition mechanism (Costa-Font 2006).

3.2. The conflict of being under two principles

Regional incumbents can be conceived of as following the command of their own constituents, as well as that of central-level principles. The latter refers to the extent to which a regional government follows policies established by the central government, through central state coordination. Normally, both types of accountability operate independently; however in implementing new programs, regional governments arguably might have to trade off policy goals set by the two principles (e.g. a new regional health program might lead to expenditure rises, which conflicts with central government fiscal-discipline goals), and thus are compelled to balance in favor of one of them (e.g. regional constituents or central government). Examples of agencies that depend mainly on central government are those regions under the coordination of the central state. Examples of double agencies are region states with healthcare responsibilities; in other words, when coordination mechanisms fail to take place.

Double agencies might be regarded as an "unstable equilibrium" when regions trade off vertical and horizontal accountability. In the Spanish case, an important limitation to the stability of double agencies is that – with the exception of Navarra and the Basque Country – the other AC with devolved healthcare responsibilities had political but not fiscal responsibilities. Such a scenario precluded politically accountable AC to become "contestable agencies", thus operating on the behalf of their constituents rather than subject to central-state coordination.

In a decentralized model of healthcare provision there is substantial scope for policy and technology innovation. There are remarkable incentives for policy experimentation (e.g. testing the repose to providers' incentives) and coverage extension. On the other hand, the visibility of healthcare coverage provides incentives to innovation as mechanisms to signal government activity. This feature, coupled with a uniform funding, provides incentives for regional incumbents to implement programs already developed in other regions, and which have already shown evidence of appreciable success.

4. Regional inequalities and policy innovation

4.1. Regional inequalities

As discussed earlier, one of the major issues in the discussion on devolution is the extent to which devolution fits within the so-called strategy of equality. Importantly, evidence from Spain from 2001 onwards, when decentralization was completed by extending healthcare responsibilities to all region states, reveals that regional inequalities did not expand. Instead, evidence suggests very much the opposite. Figure 4.1 shows that regional inequalities dropped from a variation coefficient of 0.006 in 2001 to a coefficient of 0.004 in 2009. This indicates a 33% drop in the overall level of inequalities

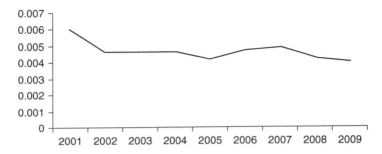

Figure 4.1 Regional inequalities on unadjusted healthcare output (coefficient of variation of regional expenditures per capita, 2001–2009)
Source: Ministerio de Sanidad, Política Social e Igualdad, 2011.

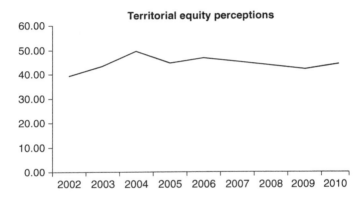

Figure 4.2 Perceptions of territorial equity (% of the population that receive the same health care irrespective of what regional states they live in)
Source: Spanish Health care barometer, several years.

in unadjusted health outputs, consistent with other studies (Costa-Font 2010b).

Such a pattern is not only an empirical regularity, but appears to be a feature that citizens come to perceive as well. Figure 4.2 reveals evidence on perceived territorial equity throughout Spain. Importantly, after devolution there is no evidence of an increase in perceptions of territorial differences throughout the country. Overall the percentage of the population that perceives there is more equity seems to slightly improve since 2002 when healthcare decentralization was completed.

Explanations of such regularity are twofold. First, there is a limited degree of diversity that Spanish decentralization allows. Indeed, the funding of the system is based on soft budget constraints that do not encourage savings, but instead they appear to drive toward expanding activity instead.

Framework laws limit the extent of diversity, and important responsibilities such as pharmaceuticals pricing are still largely centralized. This implies that there is limited leeway to obtain price discounts of pharmaceuticals for patent products, and regional policies primarily refer to generics instead (Costa-Font and Puig-Junoy 2007). Similarly, the extent of tax autonomy is limited, which constrains the degree of diversity and incentives for keeping the budget under control.

Second, policy innovation and experimentation implies that region states that are typically more dynamic and more prone to innovate take the plunge, and once there is evidence of success, such innovations are extended to other region states. Examples are explained in the following section. However, a system based on experimentation and costless diffusion would be expected to lead to policy convergence, which ultimately would result in a reduction of inequalities in activity and output.

4.2. Policy innovation

Given that policy innovations might be disseminated to other regions, I scrutinize whether innovation leads to inter-regional externalities to other regions though a process of policy imitation. Incentives underlying policy innovation for regional incumbents might be improving the re-election chances. Nonetheless, we do not suggest that, ceteris paribus, centralized governments are less successful in promoting policy innovation, but that the financial magnitude of potential risks can be sizeable in centralized government structures. Furthermore, large administrations (e.g. the central state in a 40-million population country like Spain) might need to deal with important heterogeneity in health needs and preferences that might make region-specific policy innovation more suitable.

Policy dissemination takes place through the influence of political interactions. In the absence of complete information, other ACs act as reference groups to collect information on new policies. Thus, once a specific policy has demonstrated success in one region, an incentive exists to free ride on policy experiments of other ACs. As Besley and Case (1995) find, it is efficient for decentralized governments to choose policies of similar (benchmark) jurisdictions as long as voters use relative rather than absolute performance for their inference on the quality of locally provided services.

Evidence from Spain, examined in Costa-Font and Puig-Junoy (2007), suggests that the role of devolved regions was paramount in promoting policy innovation during the 1990s. This was particularly the case within the fields not explicitly contemplated by the 1986 Act, such as the organizational status of healthcare centers, management structures and tools, and payment systems. In the sub-sectors, preventive programmes, mental health care, and long-term care were also subject to considerable regional experimentation, although often restricted to one or a few regions. Although this has often been interpreted as a source of potential territorial inequalities in the accessibility and delivery of care, there is also evidence of cross-regional diffusion processes, which might push toward territorial convergence in the medium to long term. This was possible because – with the exception of Navarra and the Basque Country – regions are constrained with equivalent per capita funds. In addition, Spanish evidence confirms the advantage of being the first, as Catalonia and Andalucía have played the role of leaders in introducing innovations. In the case of Catalonia, this has been, in the setting up of health technology agencies, in the purchaser–provider split, and in several experiences with long-term care. In Andalucía, innovation has been in coverage of dental care, exchange and opposition to negative lists. The Basque Country is another front-runner, among other reasons due to the higher expenditure per capita at its disposal.

5. Conclusions

This chapter has argued that decentralization of Spanish health care is an institutional reform with a twofold purpose, namely a strategy of democratization and modernization, as well as an efficiency-attainment goal of managing heterogeneity in healthcare preferences and needs throughout the territory. The decentralization process has taken a gradual speed so that only when region states were perceived as having the capacity to take over the responsibility to manage a regional health service, transfers too place.

The design of the system appears to provide the political incentives for innovation and diffusion, though limited incentives for patient mobility. The latter appears to demise progressively with the full decentralization of health care that only limits mobility to Madrid and Barcelona to complex and urgent needs. In centralized states, lack of political accountability provides little incentive to regional incumbents to improve the quality and quantity of care. Instead, decentralization opens up some regional diversity, which entails a genuine expression of local values and specific regional, and minority needs (Banting 1987) that puts into question the so-called "strategy for regional equality" (Powell and Boyne, 2001). The latter is especially relevant in Spain where concerns over regional inequalities date back to the concerns over fragmentation from the centralist policies in line with the logic of the Francoist uniform political view of Spain. Evidence from Spain suggests that regional inequalities have declined dramatically by one-third after the completion of the decentralization process.

Perhaps the biggest concern of decentralization in Spain has to do with the existence of soft budget constraints, which explain that public health care has risen, although less than in other European countries. That is, vertical imbalances result from a certain mismatch between political and tax autonomy. That is, moral hazard emerges when regional incumbents do not bear the ultimate consequences of expanding expenditure as the health system is financed centrally with the exception of two region states. The consequence is the emergence of healthcare deficits in those regions where moral hazard incentives exist that is all but the two regions that are fully fiscally accountable (Basque Country and Navarra) where deficits are almost negligible. Importantly, healthcare debts mount especially when regional incumbents are from a different party than national incumbents. This is explained by a softening of the so-called "double agency" problem, as it is not when this is the case that loyalties to regional constituents become far more important than to meeting central-level coordination standards.

Note

1. A constitutional reform in 2011 has been put urgently in place to limit the extent of public debt public administration can accumulate.

References

Banting, K. (1987). *The Welfare State and Canadian Federalism*. McGill-Queen's University Press, Kingston.

Besley, T. and Case, A. (1995). Incumbent behaviour: vote-seeking, tax-Setting, and yardstick competition. *The American Economic Review*, 85 (1), pp. 25–45.

Costa-Font, Joan (2005). Inequalities in self-reported health within Spanish regional health services: devolution re-examined? *International Journal of Health Planning and Management*, 20 (1), pp. 41–52.

Costa-Font, Joan (2010a). Devolution, diversity and welfare reform: long-term care in the "Latin Rim". *Social Policy & Administration*, 44 (4), pp. 481–494.

Costa-Font, Joan (2010b). Does devolution lead to regional inequalities in welfare activity? *Environment and Planning C: Government and Policy*, 28 (3), pp. 435–449.

Costa-Font, Joan and Moscone, Francesco (2008). The impact of decentralization and inter-territorial interactions on Spanish health expenditure. *Empirical Economics*, 34 (1), pp. 167–184.

Costa-Font, Joan and Pons-Novell, J. (2007). Public health expenditure and spatial interactions in a decentralized national health system. *Health Economics*, 16 (3), pp. 291–306.

Costa-Font, Joan and Puig-Junoy, Jaume (2007). Institutional change, innovation and regulation failure: evidence from the Spanish drug market. *Policy and Politics*, 35 (4), pp. 701–718.

Costa-Font, Joan and Rico, A. (2006a) Vertical competition in the Spanish National Health System (NHS). *Public Choice*, 128 (3–4), pp. 477–498.

Costa-Font, Joan and Rico, A. (2006b) Devolution and the interregional inequalities in health and healthcare in Spain. *Regional Studies*, 40 (8), pp. 1–13.

Lopez-Casasnovas, G., Costa-Font, J. and Planas, I. (2005). Diversity and regional inequalities: assessing the outcomes of the Spanish "system of health care services", *Health Economics* 14 (S), pp. S221–S235.

Powell, M. and Boyne, G. (2001). The spatial strategy for equality and the spatial division of welfare. *Social Policy & Administration*, 35, pp. 181–194.

Revelli, F. (2002). Testing the tax mimicking versus expenditure spillover hypothesis using English data. *Applied Economics*, 14, pp. 1723–1731.

Rico, A. and Costa-Font, J. (2005). Power rather than path? The dynamics of institutional change under health care federalism. *Journal of Health Politics, Policy & Law*, 30 (1), pp. 231–252.

Salmon, P. (1987). Decentralisation as an incentive scheme. *Oxford Review of Economic Policy*, 3, pp. 24–43.

Tiebout, C.M. (1956). A pure theory of local expenditures. *Journal of Political Economy*, 64, pp. 416–424.

5
The Rise and Fall of Territory in UK Health Politics

Scott L. Greer

Health policy in the UK is experiencing a curious double movement. On the one hand, in what was long considered a highly centralized unitary state, the central UK government is showing steadily less interest in the health policies and outcomes of devolved Northern Ireland, Scotland, and Wales. And on the other hand, within England and the individual devolved health systems, policymakers have created increasingly centralized systems that aspire to dislodge doctors and local boards from their positions of importance.

How is it that the UK government simultaneously involves itself in ever more intimate decisions in English health policy while disengaging from most aspects of devolved health policy? The answers, in large part, are to be found in the constitutional structure of the UK. In a country dominated by the English and governed by strong parliamentary governments, there is little to interest a UK government in Scotland and much to interest them in the performance of the English NHS. Electoral concerns lead ministers into concern for the English NHS, while the politics of a multinational state discourage UK government interest in Northern Irish, Scottish, or Welsh policy. The result is the paradox of constitutional decentralization and policy centralization that we see today.

1. Allocation of authority

The salient fact about the UK's territorial politics is its asymmetry. The UK has four component polities: England, Northern Ireland, Scotland, and Wales. England makes up about 85% of population, voters, and economy. Northern Ireland, Scotland, and Wales are much smaller.

The devolution settlement is, like the UK, asymmetrical, and lacks an overall legal framework. Devolved government in Northern Ireland, Scotland, and Wales is constituted by a series of specific laws that give them different legal and practical autonomy.[1] This section briefly explains the content and form of the different jurisdictions' health policy powers. In content, they are quite similar; the asymmetrical settlement means that their form is quite different, and the ensemble is like no other country. It also has a level of devolved autonomy over health policy that, combined with the very different devolved politics, produces policy divergence – but atop a fragile institutional base. The result is a "fragile divergence machine" (Greer 2007a).

1.1. England

England has little fixed institutional identity. There is no English government and there are no English regions (the Conservatives in office, many of whom had early political experience opposing Labour's plans for elected regional governments in England, have been dismantling even very pragmatic regional structures). The English show no signs of wanting them and in a referendum the most "regionalist" of England's voters, in the North East, overwhelmingly opposed the creation of an elected region (Sandford 2009). English voters feel much more identified with their local areas (counties, towns), but do not even support any significant measure of local autonomy; localism has at best as much political impact as sporting loyalties (Aughey 2007).

So how is English health policy made? The UK government directly rules England. In fact, the whole UK settlement should be viewed as consisting of an English core to the UK state, with special arrangements for three smaller areas. This means that the departments in charge of health and social care in England are the UK government departments. The UK Department of Health is essentially the department for the English NHS, with a few other functions (such as relations with international organizations) that it provides for the UK as a whole. This asymmetric organization reflects an asymmetric country; on one hand the whole UK votes for the UK government, so the Scots and Welsh can play a major role in decisions for England, but the UK government has no authority over health services in Scotland or Wales. The UK government's investment in dealing with devolved governments, or even thinking about relations with them, is limited and it is accordingly accident-prone in most areas, including health (Greer & Trench 2010).

1.2. Scotland

Scotland has the highest degree of legal autonomy of the three devolved administrations. The Scottish Parliament has "primary legislative power", which means that it can legislate without reference to Westminster, and stature, even down to its symbolically significant name. It also enjoys a "negative list"; the Scotland Act enumerates the areas in which the Westminster Parliament legislates, and leaves all other areas to the Scottish Parliament. Health policy in general, including public health and social care (as against income replacement, such as disability or unemployment insurance) is within the powers of the Scottish Parliament.

There are still areas of overlap with the UK. For example, occupational health and safety is a UK power, so when Scotland banned smoking in public places it had to do it as a public health power (rather than as a measure protecting the health of staff, which was how it was born). Policymakers did not view the identification of a legal base as a serious problem (Cairney 2007), though the Ministry of Defence (MoD) was inconvenienced when it found that Scotland had banned smoking in its Scottish barracks – something neither the Scots nor the MoD were aware of during the legislative process. The interface with benefits, which are a UK power, has produced some difficulty. When the Scottish Executive[2] decided to make long-term personal care for the elderly a universal benefit funded out of its health budget, the UK government promptly quit paying the allowances that had helped the poorer elderly afford long-term personal care services in Scotland (Simeon 2003). Throughout the UK, the Conservative–Liberal Democrat coalition, with its agenda of cutting disability and other welfare payments, is likely to provoke tensions as cuts in benefits transfer needs and the needy to relatively stable health budgets; in the devolved administrations, including Scotland, this will take on a tinge of intergovernmental conflict.

1.3. Wales

The legal situation of Wales is vastly more complex than that of Scotland. The power of the Welsh Assembly Government[3] is substantially less than the power of the Scottish government, but for health policy purposes this is less of an impediment to Welsh policymaking than might be imagined. In terms of content, the National Assembly for Wales has roughly the same health powers as Scotland – power over healthcare services, public health, and social care, but not health and safety, pharmaceuticals and medical device regulation, or benefits. In terms of form, the National Assembly has powers to enact so-called "secondary legislation", which originally meant implementing laws that primary legislation allowed the government to enact. In a rolling process of reform it gained access to a complex legal operation by which legislation could pass the Assembly and Westminster that allowed it to legislate afterward in an area (Trench 2006). In a March 2011 vote, a solid majority voted in a referendum to have primary legislative powers in 20 policy areas including health.

1.4. Northern Ireland

In terms of form and content, Northern Ireland resembles Scotland. It has primary legislative powers and a negative list that gives it access to almost any relevant health and social care power; in addition, it inherits the always theoretically separate social security apparatus for Northern Ireland (which is funded by the UK government and operates in lockstep with UK policy).

There are some major qualifications though (Carmichael et al. 2007; Wilford 2001, 2010). These reflect the unusual circumstances and politics of a place with one of Europe's longest histories of civil conflict. First, the Northern Ireland Executive, formed out of the Assembly, is a weird body with little parallel outside some parts of Austrian local government. The Executive is formed out of the Assembly by proportional representation, so any party of significant size is included in the Executive, and there is little discipline in a government that joins such opposed parties. It is then filled with provisions that ensure that each "community" can veto major decisions (the communities are, realistically, Protestants and Catholics – people who have other approaches to religion, or who try not to base their political identities on sectarianism, are not "communities" and have no veto powers). Second, Northern Ireland's Executive is enmeshed in a web of other bodies born of the peace process; these include all-Isles and North-South bodies (with the Republic of Ireland). Third, the Northern Ireland Assembly repeatedly collapsed due to various crises in the peace process for much of its first ten years; London would during such times suspend devolution and revert to "direct rule" by UK government ministers, which was how Northern Ireland had spent most of its time since the 1970s.

1.5. Finance

Finance of health systems means two different things: the finance of the governments in question, and their decisions about how to allocate finances within their budgets and health systems.

1.5.1. Devolution finance

The key fact about devolution finance until now has been that it was a block budget raised by the UK and allocated by a formula. This meant that the devolved governments did not have or use serious tax-raising or borrowing powers; they were basically in the business of spending and neither bore the blame for taxes nor enjoyed tax policy tools. It also meant that they were autonomous insofar as they could use their budget allocation on anything they were allowed to do, without Westminster interference. The formula is likely to change, but Westminster is, if anything, going to see its minimal ability to influence devolved budgets reduced still more.

For the first ten years of devolution, the financial formula was essentially the same for all three; changes in finance were distributed by the Barnett formula, which gave them a pro-rated per capita share of changes in English spending. This meant that if England got an extra pound per capita of "new" spending in an area that was devolved in the devolved administrations, such as health, the devolved administrations' block budgets would each receive new pence equal to their percentage of the UK population. The devolved per capita budgets were already higher than the English, so ceteris paribus the effect is to very slowly drive the UK toward equal per capita budgets.

As fiscal policy, this left something to be desired. The block formula separated taxing and spending powers. The devolved administrations spend, and the UK taxes, which is not particularly good for democracy or for devolved policy autonomy. The formula itself did not have much to recommend it, since it took one number with no obvious basis in "need", the pre-existing devolved budget allocation, and modified it with another, namely crude per capita equality in any changes. There has never been a needs analysis that suggested either the baseline or simple per capita equality is a good idea for the UK. The logic is, if anything, political – it enshrined past victories of territorial lobbies (such as the Scots) in the baseline and made incremental changes that would very slowly do away with those inherited funding inequalities without making big policy decisions. But put another way, the formula had the disadvantage of potentially offending everybody, by dividing the UK into places with lower per capita spending and places that were having their per capita spending reduced with every budget.

The devolution finance debate had been grinding along since devolution started, with not much payoff for the participants – the Treasury under Gordon Brown simply refused to engage. After the SNP took office in Scotland in 2007, the debate took on more interest. The SNP was calling for "full fiscal autonomy" that amounted, in government finance terms, to independence. Labour's counterattack was to create the Calman Commission, made up of all the unionist parties, with a remit to think of ways to enhance devolution within the UK (Commission on Scottish Devolution 2009; Trench 2009). It marked out the unionist end of the political debate in Scotland, but was taken in London as the devolutionist extreme. The Brown government watered it down substantially but was thrown out of office before it could implement the Calman proposals in any strength (Scotland Office 2009). As ever, the UK governments' need to solve a problem in Scotland gave Welsh devolutionists their opening. There had been a string of Welsh committees that had tried to make the case for greater fiscal autonomy – and greater formula financing, since unlike Scotland, Wales is clearly a poor part of the UK. The Holtham Commission, which put out a good analysis of UK devolution finance, proposed many of the same things for Wales, though with interesting differences (e.g. the power to vary the progressivity of income taxes (Independent Commission on Funding & Finance for Wales (Holtham Commission) 2010)).

At the time of writing, it seems quite likely that the coalition government will pass more or less Calman, and quite possibly Holtham – which would mean both greater financial autonomy for Scotland and Wales and a new formula for allocating funding. Both involve a mixture of transferring some taxes and transferring part of a given tax (e.g. the UK government would cut income tax in a given area by X%, and the devolved government would be able to immediately take over that X% without changing the tax; the devolved tax could also vary in both Calman and Holtham's proposals). Calman essentially proposed giving the Scottish government the ability to vary about 20% of its current spending. The taxes were selected to total up to about 20%, and secondarily to avoid distorting economic activity. It is not clear what would happen to Northern Ireland, which faced a substantial "Barnett squeeze" under Labour (because of its high per capita historic funding) and is now seeing its budget cut under the coalition. Under Barnett, the devolved governments will face absolute (not inflation-adjusted) cuts in their block budgets through to 2014 as consequences of the UK government's 2010 Comprehensive Spending Review.

It is worth noting that none of the proposed changes would create hypothecated (dedicated) revenue streams for health or create UK government earmarked funding for health. They all operate on the revenue side, with no automatic consequences for spending. The fragile divergence machine might become less fragile, but will continue to operate.

1.5.2. Spending within systems

All of the NHS systems, when created in 1948, inherited a highly unequal landscape of services that was deeply marked by the caprice of donors. Rich towns and London had more hospitals and doctors; rural areas and poor areas were underserved. The postwar history has been of policymakers awakening to this reality and trying to change it, replacing local initiative and inequity with national expenditures (Gorsky & Sheard 2006; Mohan 2002). In 1968, a Hospital Plan set out to build new infrastructure that would redress some of the imbalance. The next step was to reallocate spending to underserved areas, through a formula developed by the "Resource Allocation Working Party" (RAWP) (Mays & Bevan 1987; Welshman 2006). Over decades, the RAWP has narrowed the gaps. We can see this in the fact that the substantial differences in health spending between devolved governments and in overall government spending between English regions are not replicated in health; while there are huge variations in the amount of overall government spending between English regions (McLean et al. 2009), the differences between regions in health spending are much smaller, as discussed below. The structure of finance in the post-2011 NHS remains to be seen, but presumably will allocate money to GP consortia on an adjusted per-patient basis that, depending on the calculation, could increase regional inequality within England.

Health was already administratively devolved to Northern Ireland, Scotland, and Wales by the time that the RAWP came around, although there were some Hospital Plan facilities in Wales. The result was that they financed health care out of their block allocations, with specific decisions generally made in an ad hoc manner. After devolution, both Scotland and Wales adopted new financial formulae intended to rebalance spending toward areas of greater need (Greer 2004). The result was that England has and had a relatively egalitarian distribution of health spending within its territory, while Scotland and Wales have their own systematic, needs-based formulae since devolution.

2. Constitutional politics and the allocation of authority

The origins of the UK's allocation of authority lie in the constitutional history of a multinational state. The UK is a "union state", in which a single state united a variety of nations and earlier political formations without imposing a single, unitary state form such as happened in France (Mitchell 2007). Hence its name; it was born as the "United Kingdom" when the Treaty of Union merged the Scottish and English parliaments in 1707. The UK went on with one Parliament, in Westminster, and one government, in Whitehall.

National differences meant "administrative devolution", in which separate government departments, headed by a Secretary of State (high-ranking minister) administered increasingly large parts of domestic policy in the different areas. The effect was that by the 1970s there were large "territorial offices", known as the Scottish Office, and Welsh Office, that ran services including health and social care other than benefits (Mitchell 2003). The rough political calculation was that the territorial offices provided a measure of proximity and accountability, and a shell that allowed regional political and other elites to influence policy and implementation. Northern Ireland, meanwhile, had an autonomous, devolved, and bigoted Protestant government known as Stormont, after its location. It operated health and social services, seeking mostly to keep them at the same overall levels as the UK (part of their Unionist commitment). Administrative devolution provided an institutional infrastructure for the territorial lobbies – the Northern Ireland, Scottish, and Welsh elites and politicians lobbying for their interests in Westminster – while containing their concerns. The result was that even if the headline policies influencing (for example) Scottish health policy were UK-wide, the Scottish implementation might be somewhat different, and implementation took place among Scots. The political and administrative framework sustained the different "feel" of devolved health care, and higher per capita funding, without permitting significant policy divergence.

Administrative devolution was broadly successful at keeping regional mobilization channeled until the 1960s, when nationalist parties (Plaid Cymru in Wales, and then the Scottish National Party) entered Westminster and Northern Ireland's Catholics rose up again against the discriminatory Stormont governments, plunging the region into what can only be called a civil war. The UK government's response to the problems in Northern Ireland was to impose "direct rule", suspending devolution and taking over all significant services in Northern Ireland. UK government responses to the mobilizations in Scotland and Wales were confused, but they concluded in 1979 referenda on the creation of elected assemblies. The Scottish referendum lost narrowly – on an unusual definition of majority – and the Welsh referendum lost heavily. The failure prompted a general election.

The 1979 election brought Margaret Thatcher into power and would, in retrospect, ensure devolution. As a civil servant once noted to me, "Thatcher put the Great back in Britain but took the United out of Kingdom". The combination of deindustrialization, much of it caused by government policy and changes in government spending both hurt the Scottish and Welsh populations and offended many of the elites in areas such as health who had long enjoyed funding, respect, and autonomy in implementation (there was special insult in that the government benefited from revenue from North Sea oil that would have floated an independent Scotland) (Greer 2007b; Holliday 1992). The populations of Scotland and Wales, badly hit by deindustrialization and Conservative policies, also noted that the Conservatives had majorities in England, but not Scotland or Wales. It was hard not to challenge the territorial structure of the UK. The result was that Thatcher and her successor John Major created strong coalitions for devolution in Scotland and Wales – which manifested themselves in the descent into irrelevance of both Labour anti-devolutionists and all Conservatives in Scotland and Wales. By 1997, when Blair was swept to power, devolution was guaranteed and no Conservative MPs were elected in Scotland or Wales. The devolution legislation simply put new elected legislatures atop the existing territorial offices.

The important fact about this story is that while the concerns and powers of health elites mattered, devolution was at no point a health policy decision. In Northern Ireland, devolution was part of a larger peace process intended to lure Northern Ireland politicians out of violent conflict into government. In Scotland and Wales, health (and many other) regional elites had often preferred to be governed through administrative devolution. When the Conservatives overrode their limited but informal autonomy, their influence contributed to the sense that political devolution was necessary, while nationalist parties and an increasingly devolutionist Labour channeled voters. The arguments for devolution in Scotland and Wales were a mixture of nationalism and democratization, including calls for a more open and participatory "new politics", but they amounted to the same proposal: Scottish and Welsh policy should never be determined by governments, such as the Thatcher and Major governments, that did not have majorities in Scotland and Wales. And what was a Northern Ireland, Scottish or Welsh policy? One of the policies already carried out by the territorial offices. Health was long part of those offices, and there was no debate about its transfer to the devolved administrations (Wincott 2006). That is how path dependency works in politics.

3. Equity, quality, and efficiency

There are two ways to approach the devolution settlement's equity, quality, and efficiency. One is to consider the different policies that the four jurisdictions have adopted. The other is to consider the overall settlement and its effects.

3.1. Policy divergence and convergence

Devolution produced first a natural experiment in politics and then a natural experiment in policy.[4] The most pronounced fact about health policy early in devolution was the presence of the past. When the devolved legislatures first met, and in fact when Labour made its pre-devolution reforms in 1997–1998, the priorities and strategies reflected the particular, distinctive, policy communities and party politics inherited from before devolution. History directly influenced policy because it explained who was present and influential in Belfast, Cardiff, and Edinburgh. But over time, the role of history changed. As time wore on, pre-devolution legacies were joined by the legacies of devolved politics and policies, and new actors joined the old.[5]

In other words, devolution means two things. It means democratization, opening up devolved policymaking, and it means autonomy, devolved governments' ability to do different things. In the early years of devolution, autonomy was crucial – many of the same people who had influenced policy at the margins before devolution were in a position to influence policy overall after devolution. But over time, democratization came to matter more; the new actors, and the groups activated by devolved policies, began to play a role and shape the distinctive devolved politics. History no longer means a simple carry over from pre-devolved bureaucratic and professional politics; it also means the accumulated consequences of devolved politics and decisions.

What kinds of policy divergence have we seen, then? There have been a few politically salient cases of policy divergence (Birrell 2009). The most salient and expensive is long-term personal care for the elderly in Scotland. The Scottish government opted to make this benefit, which covers nonmedical aspects of elderly care, universal, despite strenuous objections from their Labour Party colleagues in London (Simeon 2003). Other salient policy divergences include charging for parking in hospital car parks, free prescription medicines for teenagers or everybody, and the constant stream of decisions by one system or another to cover or not cover a given treatment. What is striking is how little these issues illuminate in health policy.

The real differences have been, predictably, in the organization and finance of healthcare services, and in public health policy. They grow from the different politics of the four different systems. Political systems are (more or less) efficient decision-making systems, and four separate systems will only produce similar outcomes insofar as they work in similar ways or face similar problems. The four political systems do not work in the same way, institutionally or politically. Furthermore, they are either not sharing or are not feeling many shared pressures; their similarities are generally due to either path dependency (very similar starting points) or the influence of England on grounds of sheer size (e.g., over the medical workforce) (Greer & Trench 2010).

To summarize Greer (2004), Scotland inherited strong professional elites and a party system that put an emphasis on Scottishness; the result was a perfect environment for a consensus on a set of priorities such as population health and an approach to management built on partnership and professional input. Wales inherited a more fragmented party system, but one that put value on distinctiveness and not the health policy elites of Scotland; its policy accordingly catered to groups that are strong only in Wales, such as unions and local government, and it tried to promote joint working and localism in pursuit of health rather than the narrow management of healthcare delivery. Northern Ireland's party politics are not about health and its structure gave politicians little incentive to seek the portfolio or make changes in it, so it drifted. England, distinctively, had a left-right party structure that meant the NHS was actually challenged by a major sector of the political elite and media. As a result, Labour under Blair and Brown reformed as well as spent in order to entrench the NHS, while Conservatives have had difficulty persuading the public that they are committed to its sustainability. Both parties, therefore, are prone to adopt reforms intended to shake it into greater efficiency through competition. This meant a variety of Labour experiments under Blair, such as more autonomous foundation trusts and expensive contracts with outside firms, justified by the need to impose competitive discipline at the margins.

Later, particularly after 2005, it became possible to speak of devolution as a set of policy-learning exercises (Greer 2009). The first thing that happened after devolution was policy divergence. England, Northern Ireland, Scotland, and Wales all have very different politics, and so the new governments, flush with money, developed different approaches and priorities. By the end of 2003, each had their theories: policy in England focused on increasing efficiency through market and management mechanisms, policy in Scotland focused on running the health service better by aligning it with professions and trying to increase local accountability, and policy in Wales tried to de-emphasize healthcare services in favor of public health. In Northern Ireland, where health policy produced headaches but no votes in a sectarian political system, there was drift.

By the end of 2009, there was learning in each system. England was drawing back from Labour's grand plans for markets, choice, and private sector competition. The party ran into the problem faced by all introductions of market mechanisms in public services: markets require the threat of failure and misdirected investment, and that looks like waste of public funds, while public sector managers and politicians both know that avoiding public failure is more important than success. The last Blair government, let alone the Brown government, lacked the energy, political strength, and money to keep pushing for more market, and Brown returned to trying to improve clinical engagement and management. The legacy of more and more tools for imposing priorities on the NHS – whether by intricately designed market mechanisms such as tariffs, or by direct management – remained, as did the eroded and eroding role of intermediate groups such as organized professions and territorial boards. English health care might not have responded instantly to government priorities, but Labour and its Conservative predecessors had eliminated their rivals for formal power in the NHS.

Wales also reaffirmed a different kind of wisdom about the NHS; its efforts to improve health foundered on the fact that the key determinants of health lay outside the command of the health minister (e.g. education, housing) if not the Welsh Assembly government altogether (e.g. taxes, benefits, and the macro-economy). A workforce of healthcare providers turned out to be useful for, at best, preventive work – and inherited problems that went unaddressed meant they did less of that than might be desired. Scotland, meanwhile, achieved a much higher level of political and administrative stability, but found its health politics constantly turning into local fights about hospital closures, played out against a backdrop of public skepticism about the decisions of health elites. The result was a long series of "partnership" models that strove to produce better service integration and better community relations, up to pilots for expanded public participation and even partially elected health boards.[6] The Scottish focus on a number of seemingly intractable problems, particularly population health and mental health, has also been internationally noteworthy for its consistency over time and professional leadership.

The result is that we can see something like a "devolved model" of NHS organization. It is based on territorial boards that deliver most health care, are small enough in number to have tight relations with the center, and are complemented by special agencies for functions such as ambulances or public health. In Northern Ireland, the UK government designed the structure eventually adopted, so there is an overlay of market (a single "commissioning" body that will plan care), while in Scotland and Wales there are just the large boards and the minister. It stands in increasingly stark contrast to the English combination of plural provision and tight central control.

Moving beyond structure to process and outcome, the data start to fail us. It is hard to characterize the effects of devolved policies overall; the comparative data are often flawed, and often patternless, and the data that are most likely to have interesting patterns are also most likely to be noncomparable or flawed (Connolly et al. 2010; Sutherland & Coyle 2009; Greer 2010b). There is, indeed, scope for significant research and policy intervention on the question of comparable data; it is hard for governments to compete if nobody knows how they are doing, and almost inevitable that comparison will focus on some of the most easily understood and perhaps trivial policy differences such as unlikely experimental drugs or parking charges.

The single most useful conclusion to be drawn from a review of available literature is that most comparisons that seem to suggest the clear superiority of one system or another are untrustworthy. It would be nice to have more, and more credible, comparable data – and a debate that focused on meaningful indicators such as adjusted survival rates for particular cancers, rather than aggregate variables whose value as indicators is unclear. For example, Welsh health care is not usually good, but Welsh cancer care is good by UK standards. Furthermore, Welsh health care was never very good for a variety of reasons (e.g. it is hard to get doctors to live in parts of Wales), and it is not clear what part of the problems lay in the baseline.

It could be that devolution is finally shining a light on longstanding failures of the system. Welsh acute waiting had always been something of a problem; the Welsh Assembly government tried to de-emphasize waiting times to focus on other goals; and it learned that waiting times are what matter to voters. It could be that the Welsh finally had a government that they could blame for waiting lists, and they did. The Welsh Assembly government, unlike Westminster governments, had incentive to pay close attention to the operation of public services in Wales. Decentralization has elsewhere created governments that are electorally accountable for longstanding bad performance, and thereby created governments with reason to fix it. That might be the case with aspects of devolved health policy.

3.2. Devolution as a health policy variable

Drawing back from the policies enacted by the different governments since 1998, what can we say about the overall effects of devolution on healthcare policy in the UK? The first finding has the most evidence: devolution produces autonomy and democratization and therefore produces divergence. Northern Ireland, Scottish, and Welsh politics are not like English politics; both the party systems and the policy elites are different. As a consequence, the policies reflect different political agendas, priorities, problems, and debates. The UK's party systems are particularly strongly differentiated in comparative perspective; Scotland's Labour-SNP cleavage is nothing like England's two-and-a-half-party system organized around the Labour-Conservative cleavage (with the Liberal Democrats presently functioning as the left wing of the Conservative Party) and the two different systems produce different debates.

The second finding proceeds from this democratization: when there has been public interest in a topic, politicians in all four systems (even Northern Ireland!) have been able to move to address the problem. This gives us our few cases of competition (Greer 2010d): when, in 2005, the UK government was boasting about its achievements in reducing waiting times in England, the Scottish and Welsh governments learned that their voters also disliked waiting – and pushed waiting times down sharply. Likewise, once hospital-acquired infections (or their synecdoche, MRSA) became a major public concern, all four governments pushed rates down. And once Scotland had banned smoking in public places and shown major immediate health

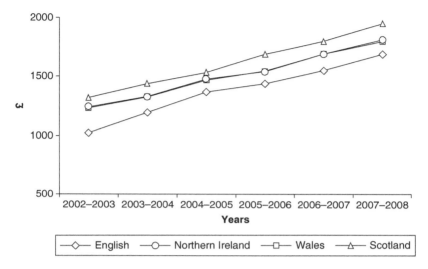

Figure 5.1 Public expenditure on health care, per head (2002/2003–2007/2008)

gains as a result, the rest of the UK adopted such bans (Donnelly & Whittle 2008). Of course, competition (or learning) also routinely fails to happen; the high-profile and popular universal long-term personal care decisions, or free medications, were not picked up across the UK.

Spending data show the interaction of divergent politics and institutions. Figure 5.1 shows the increase in per capita health spending by England, Northern Ireland, Scotland, and Wales under Blair. Notably, the lines are substantially parallel; a 45% increase (from the highest baseline, Scotland) and a 55% increase (from the lowest baseline, in England) are not that different. Both are impressively large amounts of money, but the per capita differential remains quite similar.

Figure 5.2 then shows the variation between the devolved and English regions. They show, first of all, that variation within England is relatively low, and there is lower health spending (by English standards) in the relatively healthy East and South East. That is almost certainly attributable to the RAWP and reflects a successful effort to even out government health spending within England that is not replicated in other policy areas. Second, they show that there is more variation between devolved and English spending, which is not surprising because the Barnett formula operates off baselines with large differentials in per capita spending the North East of England has need as great as any devolved area. Third, they show no evidence of convergence. The large increases in English spending, mostly mediated through the RAWP, have been distributed in a way that does not change inter-regional differentials. Devolved governments could have opted to change the extent

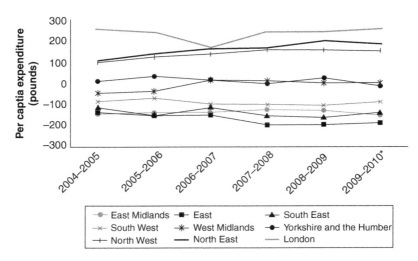

Figure 5.2   Variation in per capita health expenditures by region (2004–2010)
Source: National Statistics.

of per capita health spending, but instead increased it more or less in parallel with English spending, thereby producing no direction in the coefficient of variation.

The UK, in short, is a natural experiment in the relationship between public spending and territorial politics. England is centralized and should show any egalitarian or inegalitarian effects of centralization; the three devolved administrations have the liberty to show divergence (because their overall, not health, budgets are constrained by the financial formula). It is a qualified victory for the thesis that centralization produces equality, since the democratically decentralized devolved governments opted to preserve differential per capita spending while the RAWP formula made and kept it relatively egalitarian within England.

4. Tensions and directions

The UK, with its centralized budgeting, City dominance, strong governments, and consequent tradition of policy innovation and reversals, has long been an exciting case for students of policy. It is really outdoing itself in the early twenty-first century. It has also been increasingly likely to see voters and political elites channel a variety of policy and economic concerns through constitutional politics: a center-left Scot unhappy with coalition policy could support Labour (to put a more left-wing government in Westminster) but could also support the SNP (to free Scotland of

Westminster, and thereby the English, and thereby the policies of English Conservatives).

The Conservative-Liberal Democrat coalition in office since 2010 is promising major changes. These will come through finance, affect health policy less than most other policy areas, and possibly trigger major political changes that will shape at least health care and quite possibly the future of the entire UK. They will come through the confluence of three factors.

First, the coalition is trying to seriously cut the UK budget. This has consequences for devolved budgets: small increases or cuts. This will put devolved governments under considerable threat and make unionist parties work harder to justify the institutional structure of the country. The UK, by centralizing finance, also centralizes political responsibility, credit and blame – so the same tight Treasury control of the fiscal resources also means that the UK government is responsible for the fundamental ability of a devolved government to carry out its chosen policies. That will put pressure on the politics of the UK as the price of managing its economics (Greer 2010b).

It will also raise serious questions about the large allocations devolved governments have made for health. The per capita differentials in spending remained more or less the same during the Blair boom years of health spending. In a time of shrinking resources, will devolved administrations see fit to permit more convergence in per capita spending? Will Scottish policymakers ask more questions of their health managers? Figure 5.3 looks more like convergence than Figure 5.1.

The Cameron government is cutting back in essentially every area, but less in health. On current spending plans, this will leave the English with a

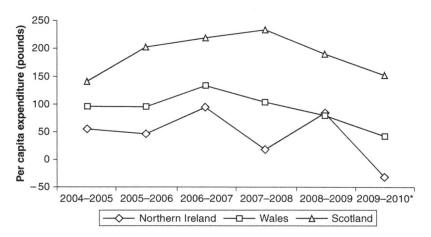

Figure 5.3 Variation in per capita health expenditures (2004–2010)
*2004–2005 to 2008–2009 data are national statistics; 2009–2010 data are not.

welfare state heavily focused on health care at the expense of areas such as social housing or care that most clearly serve the poor. Health is a large part of the basis on which devolved budgets are calculated under Barnett (still the financial formula), which helps to shield them against some of the worst cuts. That still does not mean they will continue to indulge health, though it would not be a bad bet that they will.

Second, the implementation of Calman and perhaps Holtham – and any overall changes that would come from such implementation – will change the budgetary basis of devolution. On the one hand, it might give devolved governments more tools to shape their economies and societies (taxation is a powerful policy tool). On the other hand, it might also make them ask more questions of their health services by creating at least one more trade-off – namely, the trade-off between health spending and lower taxes. As it stands, devolved governments essentially spend a fixed sum on three budget items: health, education, and local government. Adding taxation powers would change their electoral accountability and priorities.

No proposal would transfer significant new benefits or income replacements to devolved governments, so there is no likely change in the allocation of powers. There might be border wars, however, at the intersection of health and benefits. Coalition benefits cuts interact with healthcare services – because it is doctors that make decisions about disability, and because devolved governments deal with any casualties of benefits cuts. Health and benefits budgets have a way of affecting the same people, and turbulence in the benefits system usually affects health needs and spending. In England, for example, coalition plans for substantial cuts to local government (which provides personal social services) will increase pressure on health resources. This will be direct, with policymakers trying to shore up social care budgets by putting them on health budget lines, and indirect, with people who do not receive local government care ending up in healthcare facilities.

Third, the party politics are such that conflict is unsurprising. The coalition has big plans for England. The 2012 Health and Social Care Act marked the furthest point yet of the double movement in UK policy – toward more decentralization to the "Celtic fringe" and more centralization in England. UK governments, fundamentally elected by the English, care deeply about England's health service and try to manage it on a level of detail few other countries would try with a population of 52 million – while trying mostly to avoid distraction from devolved concerns that touch fewer people, combined, than are paid pensions or ride trains in and out of London during a year. In the spirit of this centralization with England and decentralization within the UK, the UK government quite surprisingly decided to forge ahead with Secretary of State Andrew Lansley's comprehensive plans for the reorganization of essentially the whole English NHS. These plans, prefigured in a 2007 Conservative Party paper, received no mention in a coalition agreement that promised not to reorganize the NHS. The detail is still being worked out after the bill's 2012 passage, but the law is the apotheosis of centralization via market mechanisms in the English NHS – attempting to turn primary care doctors into delegates of a powerful Commissioning Board, and eliminating territorial autonomy. The effect of this English development on devolution politics or health is likely to be background instability and conflict.

On the other side, the 2011 devolved elections produced a majority SNP government in Scotland (as well as a Welsh Labour government, no longer in coalition). The SNP government in Scotland is now a strong single-party majority and by far the strongest government in the UK. The remarkable SNP victory, in a system designed to prevent majority government, was probably as much in appreciation of its work in government as a vote for independence. It has elected a government in Scotland committed to a referendum on independence (one eased by years of work blurring the concept of "independence"). The first, minority, SNP government organized its activity around creating a Scotland that would be willing to vote for independence (i.e. create the "winning conditions" for a referendum by increasing both the country's self-confidence and accentuating the limitations imposed by the Union); this is likely to continue. The central UK government has not been notably strategic about intergovernmental relations, and is likely to be wrong-footed on tactical issues by the Scottish government.[7] Given that ill health is a serious problem in Scotland, a government concerned about creating a self-confident country is likely to keep its focus on population health and health statistics.

5. Conclusion

As with most of Europe's constitutionally decentralized countries, health politics explain policy divergence and choices, but broader politics of nationalism and autonomy explain the overall allocation of authority in the society. The devolution of health policy in the UK is determined in content, form, and timing by the politics of devolution rather than some kind of technocratic analysis of health policy efficiency. We see this in the timing of devolution, which came at the end of a long period of mobilization by advocates and regional elites in Scotland and Wales, and as part of the peace process in Northern Ireland. We see it in the content of devolution, which is the activity of the old territorial offices. We see it in the form of devolution, in which the degree of autonomy for the three devolved administrations tracks their historic differentiation and support for self-government. We also see it in England, which has never had much public support, or a significant movement, for its own constitutional dispensation, and which has neither its own political identity nor its own regional institutions.

The UK is thus a standing rebuke to those who might suggest that decentralization is some sort of health policy. The scope and importance of decentralized health politics are, rather, dependent on the power and autonomy of regional governments, and those are products of constitutional contestation. Other advantages – of policy divergence, local coordination, and open politics – were certainly discussed or assumed, but as the English experience shows they have not impressed generations of UK politicians. Nationalist mobilization, however aided by regional elites, impressed them.

The UK is, rather, engaged in a curious double movement born of its combination of decentralization and Westminster government. On the one hand, governments with the high level of accountability of Westminster governments are energetic by any standards in trying to control healthcare systems; hence the ongoing destruction of territorial intermediate governance in the English NHS. On the other hand, the UK government is quite relaxed about reducing its contact with devolved concerns and politics. The result has been more and more centralization in England and more and more decentralization in the UK. This approach is very British in a sense, but in quite a novel way.

Acknowledgment

I would like to thank Denise Lillvis for her research assistance.

Notes

1. Useful works on the institutional structure of devolution include Bogdanor (1999), Hazell and Rawlings (2005), Rhodes et al. (2003), Trench (2007). See also Alan Trench's "Devolution matters" blog at https://devolutionmatters.wordpress.com/ . For overall discussions of social policy, see Birrell (2009), Greer (2004, 2009), Wincott (2006).
2. From 1998 to 2007 the executive was called the Scottish Executive. In 2007 the incoming SNP ministry renamed itself the Scottish government.
3. The National Assembly for Wales was originally an odd committee-based Labour experiment that did not divide between government and backbenchers. The Welsh have gradually converted it into a more conventional body with a Welsh Assembly government, backbenchers supporting the government, and opposition parties. The National Assembly is, like the Scottish Parliament, a mixture of local and regional list-based representatives. As in Scotland, this gives it a tendency to coalition or minority government and more representatives from smaller parties than the UK electoral system produces. For the political evolution of Wales (Rawlings, 2003; Trench, 2010).
4. The very short discussions of policy here are based on Greer (2004, 2009, 2010d); Trench and Jarman (2007).
5. Path dependency does not mean that things just persist. It means that previous steps determine present positions and trajectories.
6. Greer et al., 2012 [cite interim report when it comes out].

7. It might seem that the Conservatives have an electoral incentive to break up the UK since Scotland is much more important for UK Labour. There is no evidence now that they have formulated or acted upon such an incentive. They are just weak at Scottish politics and focused on England. The inevitable future studies in political science that suggest such an explicit partisan incentive was at play in 2010–2011 will misunderstand the situation.

References

Aughey, A. (2007). *The Politics of Englishness*. Manchester: Manchester University Press.
Birrell, D. (2009). *The Impact of Devolution on Social Policy*. Bristol: Policy.
Bogdanor, V. (1999). *Devolution in the United Kingdom*. Oxford: Oxford University Press.
Cairney, P. (2007). Using devolution to set the agenda: The smoking ban in Scotland. *British Journal of Politics and International Relations*, 9(1), 73–89.
Carmichael, P., Knox, C., & Osborne, R. (2007). (Eds.) *Devolution and Constitutional Change in Northern Ireland*. Manchester: Manchester University Press.
Commission on Scottish Devolution (2009). *Serving Scotland Better: Scotland and the United Kingdom in the 21st Century*. Edinburgh: Commission on Scottish Devolution.
Connolly, S., Mays, N., & Bevan, G. (2010). *Funding and Performance of Healthcare Systems in the Four Countries of the UK Before and After Devolution*. London: The Nuffield Trust.
Donnelly, P., & Whittle, P. (2008). After the smoke has cleared – reflections on Scotland's tobacco control legislation. *Public Health*, 122, 762–766.
Gorsky, M., & Sheard, S. (2006). Introduction. In M. Gorsky, & S. Sheard (Eds.), *Financing Medicine: The British Experience Since 1750* (pp. 1–15). Abingdon: Routledge.
Greer, S. L. (2004). *Territorial Politics and Health Policy: UK Health Policy in Comparative Perspective*. Manchester: Manchester University Press.
Greer, S. L. (2007a). The fragile divergence machine: Citizenship, policy divergence, and intergovernmental relations. In A. Trench (Ed.), *Devolution and Power in the United Kingdom* (pp. 136–159). Manchester: Manchester University Press.
Greer, S. L. (2007b). *Nationalism and Self-Government: The Politics of Autonomy in Scotland and Catalonia*. Albany: State University of New York Press.
Greer, S. L. (2009). (Ed.) *Devolution and Social Citizenship in the United Kingdom*. Bristol: Policy.
Greer, S.L. (2010a). Devolution and health: Structure, process and outcome since 1998. In Lodge, & Schmuecker (Eds.), *Devolution in Practice 3* (pp. 141–166). Newcastle-upon-Tyne: ippr north.
Greer, S. L. (2010b). Options and the lack of options: Healthcare politics and policy. In V. Uberoi, A. Coutts, I. McLean, & D. Halpern (Eds.), *Political Quarterly* (79: 117–132.
Greer, S. L., & Trench, A. (2010). Intergovernmental relations and health in Great Britain after devolution. *Policy and Politics*, 38(4), 509–529.
Greer, S. L., I. Wilson, E. Stewart, and P. Donnelly (2012). *Health Boards and Alternative Pilots: Evaluation Report*. Edinburgh: Scottish Government Social Research.
Hazell, R., & Rawlings, R. (2005). (Eds.) *Devolution, Law Making and the Constitution*. Exeter: Imprint Academic.
Holliday, I. (1992). Scottish limits to Thatcherism. *Political Quarterly*, 63(4), 448–459.
Independent Commission on Funding & Finance for Wales (Holtham Commission) (2010). *Fairness and Accountability: A New Funding Settlement for Wales*. Cardiff: Welsh Assembly Government.

Mays, N., & Bevan, G. (1987). *Resource Allocation in the Health Service: A Review of the Methods of the Resource Allocation Working Party.* London: Bedford Square Press.

McLean, I., Lodge, G., & Schmuecker, K. (2009). Social citizenship and intergovernmental finance. In S. L. Greer (Ed.), *Devolution and Social Citizenship in the United Kingdom* (pp. 137–160). Bristol: Policy.

Mitchell, J. (2003). *Governing Scotland: The Invention of Administrative Devolution.* Basingstoke: Palgrave Macmillan.

Mitchell, J. (2007). The united kingdom as a state of unions: Unity of government, equality of political rights and diversity of institutions. In A. Trench (Ed.), *Devolution and Power in the United Kingdom* (pp. 134–145). Manchester: Manchester University Press.

Mohan, J. (2002). *Planning, Markets, and Hospitals.* London: Routledge.

The Northern Veto (2009). *The Northern Veto.* Manchester: Manchester University Press.

Rawlings, R. (2003). *Delineating Wales: Constitutional, Legal and Administrative Aspects of National Devolution.* Cardiff: University of Wales Press.

Rhodes, R. A. W., Carmichael, P., McMillan, J., & Massey, A. (2003). *Decentralizing the Civil Service.* Maidenhead: Open University Press.

Scotland Office (2009). *Scotland's Future in the United Kingdom, cm7738.* London: Stationery Office.

Simeon, R. (2003). The long-term care decision: Social rights and democratic diversity. In R. Hazell (Ed.), *The State and the Nations: The Third Year of Devolution in the United Kingdom* (pp. 215–232). Exeter: Imprint Academic.

Sutherland, K., & Coyle, N. (2009). *Quality in Healthcare in England, Wales, Scotland, Northern Ireland: An Intra-UK Chart Book.* London: The Health Foundation.

Trench, A. (2006). The Government of Wales Act 2006: The next steps in devolution for Wales. *Public Law,*1, 687–696.

Trench, A. (2007). (Ed.) *Devolution and Power in the United Kingdom.* Manchester: Manchester University Press.

Trench, A. (2009). The Calman commission and Scotland's disjointed constitutional debates. *Public Law.* October 2009, 686–96

Trench, A. (2010). Wales and the Westminster model. *Parliamentary Affairs,* 63(1), 117–133.

Trench, A., & Jarman, H. (2007). The practical outcomes of devolution: Policy-Making across the UK. In A. Trench (Ed.), *Devolution and Power in the United Kingdom.* pp 45–56 Manchester: Manchester University Press.

Welshman, J. (2006). Inequalities, regions and hospitals: The resource allocation working party. In M. Gorsky & S. Sheard (Eds.), *Financing Medicine: The British Experience Since 1750* (pp. 221–241), London, UK.

Wilford, R. (2001). *Aspects of the Belfast Agreement.* Oxford: Oxford University Press.

Wilford, R. (2010). Northern Ireland: The politics of constraint. *Parliamentary Affairs,* 63(1), 134–155.

Wincott, D. (2006). Social policy and social citizenship: Britain's welfare states. *Publius,* 36(1), 169–189.

6
From Centralization to Decentralization, and Back: Norwegian Health Care in a Nordic Perspective

Jon Magnussen and Pål E. Martinussen

1. Introduction

In the Nordic countries, health care is an integral part of what is often termed the Scandinavian (or Nordic) model of the welfare state (Esping-Andersen 1990). Thus, health care is generally seen as a public responsibility, with universal access, negligible user fees, and a strong focus on equity (Martinussen & Magnussen 2009). In this chapter we discuss the Nordic model of health care primarily by focusing on one country, Norway. We also highlight similarities and differences between Norway and the other Nordic countries. While Norway is a small country in terms of population, it covers a large area and thus geographical equity is an important issue. This is reflected throughout the system; in structural issues, in choice of (political and administrative) governance models, and in choice of financing system. Although Norway, as are the other Nordic countries, is characterized by a tradition of locally elected governments (municipalities and counties), health policy and healthcare reforms in the past 15 years serve as illustrations of the potential conflicts between public participation, local governance, and a stated goal of national equity.

This chapter describes recent trends in what has been a period of change and reform in the Norwegian healthcare system. The discussion will be made with references in particular to the other Nordic countries, whose healthcare systems bear many similarities, but also some fundamental differences, to the healthcare system in Norway. Section 2 provides some historical background, while Section 3 lays out the basic structure of the healthcare system. This is followed by Section 4, which attempts to illustrate both the effects of the present structure and some current challenges. Section 5 concludes with a discussion of some likely future options and developments.[1]

2. The Nordic healthcare systems

The four Nordic countries share a common history, culture, economy, and social structure, as well as close geographical proximity, and thereby also a number of fundamental health policy ideas. The countries' healthcare systems, like other social sectors, have been built on the principle of universality: all inhabitants have the same access to public health services regardless of social status or geographic location. Thus, the goal of equity has in the Nordic countries been closely related to equal access regardless of gender, age, place of residence, and social status. The two last points have recently been in particular focus: geographical equity is an understandable concern given the number of low-density rural areas in these countries, while social equity reflects a long history of social democratic thinking. This strong emphasis on equity has been combined with a tradition of decentralization to regional democratic control by way of county institutions in Denmark, Norway, and Sweden, and of the municipalities in Finland. Municipalities play an important role in all four countries, as they are responsible for providing all (Finland) or part of primary health services as well as various prevention, rehabilitation and health promotion activities (plus specialized health services in Finland) for their inhabitants.

A second important health policy goal in the Nordic countries is public participation. A key aspect of participation is the institutionalization of arenas for democratic decision-making at local, regional, and national levels. This has been seen as an important way to ensure transparency and public participation in decision-making and as a way to promote efficiency as decisions would fit the local and regional preferences and needs. Taken together, this is believed to improve the legitimacy of the public delivery systems. Another traditional argument has been that local and regional democratic government is an effective way to promote local innovation of organizational and management models. The decentralized structure would thus in essence serve as a series of local laboratories for developing solutions that might subsequently spread throughout the system (Vrangbæk 2007). With this focus on local governance, locally elected politicians have traditionally played an important role in the design, implementation and monitoring of health policy. This has been further accentuated by the role of organized local interest organizations, such as the federation of county councils and/or the federation of municipalities in all four countries.

The governance structure of the Nordic countries has been (and is) decentralized, with the responsibility for service provision resting on a regional, county, or municipal level – although often within a framework of centralized supervision, regulation or coordination. What distinguishes the Nordic countries from other tax-based and/or decentralized systems, however, is its focus on political governance through locally elected political bodies. Thus, the Nordic model has been one of devolution – transfer of power to a local political level – combined with the ability of these local units to raise taxes. This specific form of multilevel public governance varies substantially between the countries, and these differences have increased in the last decade after the recent Norwegian and Danish reforms. However, all four countries still share a tradition of centrally supervised local governance. This combination of elected political bodies and the possibility to raise local taxes is what has traditionally distinguished the Nordic countries from the more centralized tax-based National Health Service (NHS) in the UK, a system that also belongs to the family of public integrated systems.

3. The Norwegian healthcare system

Norway has a population of five million, but among the lowest population densities in Europe.[2] It is a constitutional monarchy, with a parliamentary system of governance. There are three levels of government; the state, the 19 counties, and the 430 municipalities. Parliament, county councils, and municipal councils are elected in four-year cycles, with local elections positioned in-between the national elections. Counties have the responsibility for secondary education, road maintenance and dental care, while municipalities are responsible for primary and long-term health care, elementary education, local load maintenance, local infrastructures, and culture. Specialized health care is the responsibility of the state.

While taxation is the main source of financing for health care, taxes are not earmarked. Thus, healthcare competes with other public tasks for funding. Specialized health care is funded directly from the state, while municipalities fund primary care. Municipalities in turn get their income in part from local taxes and in part via tax equalizing grants from the central government. Relative to other Nordic countries, Norway has a lower share of autonomously raised local taxes and also a lower share of unconditional intergovernmental grants. Norway therefore ranks as one of the most (fiscally) centralized Nordic countries (Sellers & Lidstrøm 2007; Rehnberg et al. 2009).

3.1. How the system has evolved – Phase 1: Decentralization

After the Second World War, health care in Norway evolved as the result of mostly uncoordinated efforts by counties, municipalities, private non-profit organizations, and sometimes the state. In 1969, Parliament passed a Hospital Act, thereby attempting to put the planning and operating of a sector that previously had been subjected to few centralized decisions into a national perspective (Hansen 2001). The Hospital Act placed the responsibility for specialized health care (hospitals) as well as nursing homes with the 19 counties.[3] GPs, on the other hand, were partly state employees and partly private practitioners. Over the next 20 years a three-level system of healthcare governance gradually evolved. Primary health care was made the responsibility of municipalities in 1980, and the responsibility of nursing homes was transferred from the counties to the municipalities in 1988. The financing system gradually changed from a retrospective per diem/fee for service system to a needs-adjusted capitation-based system. Furthermore, transfers from the state to the counties and municipalities went from being conditional (i.e. one transfer for health care, one transfer for education, etc.) to unconditional – that is, the local level was free to determine the allocation of resources between different tasks.

The choice of the counties as the level of government responsible for hospitals was based primarily on the presumption that it would be best to place this responsibility at the same administrative level.[4] With municipals deemed too small to handle the task of coordinating hospital care the choice fell on the counties.

This structure was clearly inspired by the principles of fiscal federalism. Here the basic argument is that public goods that are consumed locally should also be produced locally (Oates 1999). Local authorities will presumably be more responsive to local needs and preferences and are at the same time assumed to be more efficient in their operation (purchasing) of activities. Thus, there is a theoretical welfare gain in decentralization of administrative, financial and political power from the state to local (elected) authorities.

In its pure form, fiscal federalism builds on four assumptions: first, there should be local discretion in the ability to tax ("benefit taxation"); second, there should be mobility of people and firms across locations; third, there should be no spillovers or externalities; and fourth, social costs and benefits should equal the corresponding local costs and benefits (Tiebout 1956; Musgrave 1959).

These assumptions are not fully met in Norway in that local tax levels are fixed,[5] mobility is low compared with other countries, and generally there will always be both spillovers and externalities in health care. Together this can be used to argue in favor of more centralized solutions in health care. The Norwegian solution has been a mixture of decentralized and centralized financing (and governance), implying financial transfers from the central government to local governments. From this arises the *double common pool problem* (Rattsø 2002) where local decision-making in setting service levels combined with central financing easily leads to individuals overusing local government services. The result is a local deficit that has to be financed from central funds from the common pool generated by general taxation.

As discussed in Magnussen et al. (2007), health system design in many cases implies a trade-off between the benefits that come from utilizing local information and the value of internalizing spillovers. Recent trends in decentralization may suggest that the balance has been in favor of local information. On the other hand, this may lead to situations that are efficient in the sense that services are delivered at minimum cost and in accordance with local preferences, but nevertheless deemed undesirable because of the resulting distribution of services. This may be one explanation behind the recent attempts to recentralize as seen in Norway, Denmark, and Finland, and to a lesser extent in Sweden.

3.2. How the system has evolved – Phase 2: Gradual recentralization

Although the period from 1970 to 1990 was characterized by a general belief that decentralization was the preferred model, there was also a search for the "right degree of" decentralization. As noted, Norway is a country with three levels of government: state, counties, and municipalities. Nursing homes, initially a county task, were transferred to municipalities in 1988. In the case of specialized health care, however, the focus of the discussion was whether counties were sufficiently large to provide a full set of services to their population. It soon became clear that cooperation across counties would be necessary, and this was reflected in the principle of *regionalization*. In short, the small size of the population in some counties combined with large geographical distances provided opportunities for economies of scale through centralization. Thus, in 1974, the country was divided into five health regions, each with one large teaching hospital. Notably, the regional level did not have any formal authority, but was merely a way of identifying larger geographical areas that needed to exploit (medical) economies of scale.

It soon became apparent, however, that planning of capacity and the division of tasks both between and within regions was limited. Instead, the hospital sector was in some areas characterized by excess capacity due to duplication of services (Magnussen 1994).[6] Since counties did not seem to cooperate voluntarily, regional cooperation was made mandatory in 1999 (Ministry of Health and Social Services 1998). Under the new regulation, appointed regional health committees were responsible for the development of regional health plans in accordance with national guidelines. These plans also needed to be approved by the Ministry of Health.

Under the period of decentralization, transfers of funds from the state to the counties were sector-specific until 1986 when counties were given a general grant in line with the (central) political goal of local prioritization of different tasks. The rhetoric of the time strongly stressed the importance of the principle that the level responsible for providing services should also be responsible for the financing of services. Since the 1990s however, the state's share of financial involvement increased. Partly this came in the form of Parliament repeatedly providing extra (general) funds, partly in the form of specific funding packages (i.e. heart, orthopedic patients, patients on sick leave, etc.). These packages coincided with an increased frustration with the counties' inability to cope with long waiting lists.

After a relatively short period of piloting and discussions, a system of partly activity-based financing (ABF) was implemented in the Norwegian hospital sector on a full-scale basis from 1997. For counties this meant that a portion of their grants equal to (at first) 30% of expected DRG-costs were withdrawn and made conditional on hospital activity. The share of ABF increased rapidly up to a level of 60% in 2002, before it was reduced to 40% from 2005. We will return to the implications of the change in the level of ABF below; in this context the main point is that the introduction of ABF effectively meant an end to the principle that the level which delivers services also finance them. Thus, in 2001 the counties' share of total hospital expenses was as low as 41% (Samdata sykehus Somatikk 2002). Replacing a system of global budgets with an open-ended system of ABF also took its toll on county finances. The net operating surplus as share of county revenues increased from a 3.1% surplus in 1995 to a 1.8% deficit in 2001 (Ministry of Local Government and Regional Development 2003).[7]

3.3. How the system has evolved – Phase 3: State takeover

By the end of the century, the original decentralized model (of specialized care) was in effect eroded by state interventions in the form of mandatory regional planning and a large share of central funding. The county model was also characterized by fiscal imbalance; while demand (and to some extent) supply decisions were decentralized, financing was increasingly centralized. ABF had led to a substantial growth in activity, and resulting budget deficits. Hagen and Kaarbøe (2006) argue that increased central intervention led to lack of transparency in the financing system and a blame game over the responsibility for increased deficits at the county level. The result was an erosion of trust between central authorities and the county councils.

There is an inherent conflict in Norwegian health policy between a desire to decentralize decision-making and a goal of equity. Thus, one of the premises behind the county model was that it could/should lead to differences in prioritizing between, for example, education and health. Increasingly, however, differences between counties in population use of services and county expenses were regarded as a problem rather than as the result of variations in preferences. When hospitals were recentralized in a state takeover in 2002, one of the main motivations was therefore a goal of reducing geographical variations in utilization of specialized healthcare services (Ministry of Health and Social Affairs 2001).

There were two main elements in the 2002 hospital reform (Ministry of Health and Social Affairs 2001). First, the central government took over responsibility for all somatic and psychiatric hospitals and other parts of specialist care. As a result, about 100,000 employees, or 60,000 person-years, and nearly 60% of county councils' budgets were transferred from the counties to the state (Magnussen et al. 2007). Second, centralization of ownership was followed by a deconcentration (i.e. administrative decentralization) in the form of five regional health authorities (RHA), under the Minister of

Health. The Regional Health Authorities (RHAs) were given the responsibility of providing specialized health care to the population either through local health enterprises (which they owned) or through a contract with private service providers.

4. Delivery of services

4.1. Primary care

4.1.1. Overview

The 430 municipalities are responsible for primary health care and long-term care services. There is a wider variation in the municipality populations in Norway than in for instance Denmark and Sweden; from only 215 in the smallest municipality to 600,000 in the capital of Oslo.[8] The average population size is around 10,000 inhabitants, and as many as 234 municipalities have less than 5000 inhabitants.

Councils govern municipalities and are elected every fourth year. Their main income sources are local taxes and central tax equalizing grants. While municipal revenue can be freely allocated between education, health care, childcare, social services, and other municipal tasks, health and care services consume most of the municipal budget; more than 40% of municipal employees are in the health and care services.

The majority of long-term care services are provided by publicly owned and run institutions, a smaller share by not-for-profit private suppliers, and increasingly by for-profit private suppliers. These services typically represent more than 80% of the budget for health and care services in the municipalities. GPs, on the other hand, are all self-employed,[9] acting since the Regular General Practitioner scheme was introduced in 2001 as family doctors (i.e. serving a specific patient list).

4.1.2. Financing of primary care

The financing scheme for GPs builds on a combination of per capita, per case, and reimbursement from the national sickness fund. Currently, 30% of the income is to be based on capitation (list size) and 70% on a fee for service basis. The fee for service consists of two parts, patient co-payments and refunds from the national sickness fund. Long-term care is financed through global (fixed) budgets, but with substantial co-payment for patients living in institutions.

4.1.3. Reforms

After the Regular General Practitioner reform in 2001, GPs must be contracted with a municipality to receive public payment, and each municipality will have a number of GP contracts based on the size and composition of the population, from which the inhabitants can choose between. Thus, it is mandatory for each inhabitant to be on the list of one GP ("family doctor"). As outlined above, GPs are financed partly based on the size of the list (average list size is around 1500), and partly based on the number of services delivered. The Regular General Practitioner reform replaced a system where inhabitants could choose to see any GP in their area of residence. In practice, however, two-thirds of the population were already in a steady doctor–patient relationship, thus the change was not that fundamental. The motivation behind the reform was a perceived lack of stability in doctor–patient relationship, as well as tendencies of "doctor shopping" (i.e. patients would switch doctor to get better access to prescription drugs). The reform aimed at improving equal access across all parts of the country, as well as increasing effectiveness through better coordination across the primary–secondary interface, and between primary care physicians and emergency care services.

In 2012, the so-called "Coordination reform" will be implemented (Parliamentary proposition no. 47, 2008–2009). The reform is an attempt to tackle the challenges related to patients' needs for coordinated services not being sufficiently met, that there is too little initiative in the health services aimed at limiting and preventing disease, and the ageing population and changing range of illnesses among the population. The reform gives the municipalities more responsibility for health prevention and public health work, with the most important financial instruments being municipal co-financing of the specialist healthcare services and municipal financial responsibility for patients ready for discharge. As the reform documents state, the intent is for the financial schemes to encourage the municipalities to assess whether positive impacts on health can be achieved by using resources differently, for example through more appropriate use of the hospitals.

4.2. Hospital care

4.2.1. Overview

As noted above, in 2002 ownership of hospitals was centralized from the 19 counties to the state, and the responsibility for the provision of specialized health care delegated to five (later four) independent regional health authorities (RHAs). The RHAs coincide with the former regions, thus preserving and formalizing the principle of regionalization.

The state owns the four RHAs, with each authority governed by a board of trustees appointed by the minister of health and care services. The state executes its strategic and operational governance through the Ministry of Health and Care Services; more specifically through the department of hospital ownership within the ministry. This department prepares annual "task documents" to signal that the central authorities primarily are concerned with strategic rather than operational governance. In addition to these task documents there is an annual enterprise meeting, similar to the general assembly in private firms.

At the lower level, the RHAs own the hospitals, which are organized as *independent* health trusts with governing bodies (hospital boards) appointed by the RHAs. These boards have the same mix of politicians and other representatives as the regional boards, with some variation between the RHAs with respect to who fills the roles as the chair of the health trusts' board. While some regional authorities place their own representative as chair of hospitals boards, other RHAs choose an external representative to fill this position. The strategic and operational governance of the health trusts is done – as on the regional level – through "task documents" and annual enterprise meetings.

The responsibilities and tasks are clearly divided between the state, the RHAs, and the local health trusts. The RHAs are regulated by a set of statutes that clearly defines as the responsibility of the RHA to "coordinate the activity and division of tasks between the local health trusts in such a way that it is appropriate and efficient".[10] Furthermore, the local health trusts also operate under a set of statutes regulating among other things tasks and investment decisions.

4.2.2. Hospital financing

There is little tradition for fiscal decentralization in the Norwegian system, which distinguishes it from the other Nordic countries. A main characteristic of the former county model was vertical fiscal imbalance: demand decisions were decentralized, while financing was centralized. Counties were thus unable to fund the provision of health services through taxes, as the main financial sources were a fixed tax base, ABF of hospital services and a block grant from central government (Magnussen et al. 2007). The hospital reform did not change this, with the state still maintaining control over hospital financing.

In the current model, two financing decisions must be made; first, central government needs to finance the RHAs, and second, the RHAs must finance the local health trusts. RHAs are financed by a combination of needs-adjusted capitation and ABF. The capitation model is similar to capitation models found in other tax-based countries, such as the other Nordic countries and the UK. Thus, each RHA receives a share of the total budget for specialist health care that in effect is the size of the population weighted by a needs index. Separate needs indices have been constructed for somatic care, mental health care, substance abuse, and ambulances and patient transport. To account for differences in the costs of providing services there is also a regional cost index.

The present regional model dates back to 2009. Previous models have, however, been built on the same principles (needs-adjusted capitation plus compensation for costs), but there has been a substantial political discussion about the criteria used to adjust for needs, as well as to what extent regional differences in costs are unavoidable, and thus should be compensated through the financing system. Somatic care is also partly financed

Table 6.1   Health expenditure in the Nordic countries

	Denmark	Norway	Sweden	Finland	OECD-average
Share of GDP to Health	11.1	9.4	9.6	8.9	9.5
Public share of total Health care expenditures	85.1	85.5	8.1	74.5	72.2
Average growth rate real terms 2000–09	3.6	3.7	3.9	4.3	4.7

Source: OECD Health data 2012.

based on activity. The unit of payment is hospital discharges, classified by using DRGs. The share of ABF is 40%. This system of partly ABF dates back to 1997, when hospitals were owned and run by counties. The share of ABF has varied between 30% and 60% (see Table 6.1).

The RHAs are, in principle, free to choose their own way of financing the local health authorities (hospitals). In the period from 1980 to 1997, hospitals in Norway were financed via global budgets, in a way that often resembled a form of cost-compensation. Thus, a hospital budget would be set based on historical costs adjusted for inflation. With the introduction of partly case-based financing in 1997, the idea was both to provide incentives for higher levels of activity and higher levels of productivity. Initially, this model was prolonged after the reform, but gradually replaced by a capitation-based model also within the RHAs. Hence, a local health authority now receives its budget partly based on the population in its catchment area and partly based on activity as measured by DRGs. To cope with cross-border movement of patients there is also a system of transferring funds between local health authorities based on cross-border activity levels.

5. Structure, governance, and financing in the Nordic countries

As noted above it is possible to define a "Nordic model of health care" as a system that is tax-based, with universal access, (almost) free at point of use, dominantly public and decentralized (devolved). Within these broad characteristics however, the Nordic countries are remarkably different both with respect to aggregate spending, structural issues, type of governance, and financing mechanisms. Some of these differences are highlighted in this section and further discussed below.

Table 6.1 shows differences between the Nordic countries in spending as share of GDP, share of spending that is public, real annual growth and physician density. Although blurring lines between what is considered social services and what is considered health care services implies some caution when interpreting these numbers, they still provide some useful insight. First, share of GDP that is spent on health is close to OECD average of 9,5 (2010) for Norway and Sweden, but substantially higher in Denmark. Differences in the share of public financing between the four countries are smaller than differences in aggregate spending, reflects the similarities in the health care systems and is well above OECD average. We also note that real annual growth rates are quite similar in the four countries, and below OECD average. As neither of the Nordic countries face the fiscal austerity that is seen in other parts of Europe, the relatively low growth rate may be surprising.

Table 6.2 shows differences in governance structure between the Nordic countries (excluding Iceland). There are some important differences that emerge from this table. All four Nordic countries have a history of decentralized management and political responsibility of health service delivery to either the county or municipality level. This phase of decentralization, however, has been replaced by a phase of recentralization more so in Norway and Denmark than in Sweden and Finland. Hence, there are differences between the four countries both with regard to the degree of devolution of political and fiscal authority.

Table 6.2 Governance structure in the Nordic countries

	Long-term care	Primary care	Specialized care
Norway	Municipal (430) (political)	Municipal (430) (political)	State (political) decentralized to Regional (4) (administrative)
Denmark	Municipal (98) (political)	Regional (5) (political)	Regional (5) (political)
Sweden	Municipal (289) (political – can set tax rate)	County (21) (political – can set tax rate)	County (21) (political – can set tax rate)
Finland	Municipal (336) (political – can set tax rate)	Municipal (336) (political – can set tax rate)	Municipal (336) (political – can set tax rate) centralized to Districts (21) (administrative)

In Sweden both political and fiscal authority lies with the 21 counties. To create a new regional system with clearer roles and clearer division of responsibilities, Sweden did discuss a model where the county councils would be replaced with six to nine directly elected regional authorities with overall responsibility for regional development and health and medical care (SOU 2007), but no changes have so far been implemented.

As in the other Nordic countries, a large part of the funding of the Swedish healthcare system is through taxes. The degree of fiscal decentralization is quite high, with the bulk of the total health sector revenue for the county councils stemming from county-level taxes. The municipalities also generate a high share of their revenues through local taxes, with expenditure on care for the elderly and disabled constituting around a third of their total expenditure (Federation of Swedish County Councils 2004; Glenngård et al. 2005). Note that counties and municipalities are free to set tax rates. The sum of county and municipal income tax varies between 30% and 33% (2011); roughly one-third is county tax and two-thirds is municipal tax.

A similar case of fluctuation between decentralization and centralization in health care can be found in Finland. In 1993, a reform decentralized all hospital financing to the municipalities, and it could be argued that the Finnish healthcare system thereby became more decentralized than any other country (Häkkinen 2005). The municipalities are small; more than 75% have less than 10,000 inhabitants, and 20% have less than 2000. As there is little detailed central regulation of the municipal health service provision, the municipalities enjoy relatively more autonomy in terms of deciding income tax rates (generally between 15% and 20%), healthcare investments and organization of services (Vuorenkoski 2008).

In recent years, however, there have been growing concerns that high waiting lists, diseconomies of scale, and geographical inequalities in access can be attributed to a decentralized model. Thus, Finland is now rebalancing national and local decision-making roles, and is in particular actively promoting mergers of small municipalities to create larger, and more sustainable units (Vuorenkoski 2008).

With regard to fiscal decentralization, the national government played a relatively large fiscal role until the state subsidy reform of 1993, with health sector revenues split 50–50 between national and municipal sources (Saltman & Bankauskaite 2006). The most significant change in the financing of health care has been the shift from state to municipalities, with the municipalities in 2005 financing approximately 40% and the state 21% of total healthcare costs, while the rest was covered by the National Health Insurance (17%) and private sources (22%). The municipal income tax is the major source of tax revenue for the municipalities, constituting 87% in 2005 (Vuorenkoski 2008).

With a major structural reform, implemented in 2007, which eroded the counties' role as healthcare providers, Denmark has also chosen a strategy of recentralization. The reform merged 14 counties into five regions and the number of municipalities was reduced from 275 to 98. Directly elected politicians govern both the regional and local levels. The main responsibility of the regions is to provide health services, while the municipalities are responsible for prevention, health promotion, and rehabilitation outside of hospitals. To ensure coordination between the two administrative levels, health coordination committees are established in which municipalities and regions are to enter into binding partnerships (Strandberg-Larsen et al. 2007).

Since 1970, Denmark has had a shared structure of healthcare funding between state and counties. The main financial sources have been general taxation at county and national levels, with redistributional mechanisms from central to county level and between counties based on demographic and economic criteria. With the structure reform, however, Denmark has reconfigured its health governance arrangements to resemble those of Norway, with fiscal decisions taken centrally and administrative responsibilities located within the five new regional units. The new financing scheme is a combination of central tax-based financing (80%) through ABF payments and block grants, and municipal tax-based financing (20%) through a combination of per capita and ABF. By removing the independent right to raise taxation at regional level, the system breaks with the tradition of having responsibility for management and financing at the same political level. Instead, healthcare activities are to be financed largely through a national earmarked health tax (8% of income), which will be redistributed in terms of block grants to regions and municipalities. Earmarked health taxation is a novelty in Denmark and is thought to improve transparency in the sector and to reduce the potential of redistribution between healthcare and other service sectors. Furthermore, the idea behind the municipal co-financing is to create stronger incentives for municipalities to reduce hospitalization through, for example, investing in preventive activities (Vrangbæk 2005; Strandberg-Larsen et al. 2007).

Compared with the other Nordic countries, Norway is the only country where political governance of the specialist healthcare sector is centralized to the state. Since the administrative responsibility for the hospitals is delegated to the four RHAs, Norway also differs from its Nordic neighbors by being the only country where the hospitals are not run by democratically elected bodies. We would hypothesize that the combination of local political and fiscal authority would lead to more variation in healthcare spending within a country than a system of centralized political and fiscal authority. Unfortunately, we do not have access to local-level data from Finland. For the three other countries we present county (Sweden) and regional (Norway/Denmark) spending measured as deviation from the national average after adjusting for geographical differences in need.[11]

In the 21 Swedish counties county healthcare spending[12] varies between counties, ranging from 7.5 percentage points below expected to 13.5 percentage points above expected levels. Six out of 21 counties have a level of spending that deviates with more than five percentage points from the expected level. In Denmark, on the other hand, regional healthcare spending[13] is close (within a percentage point) to or almost identical with expected (need- and cost-adjusted) levels. In Norway[14] two out of four regions have an actual level of spending that is almost identical to the expected; while the two others are approximately 3.5 percentage points off. To some extent, however, the differences between the countries reflect that variations will be smaller when a country is divided into 4/5 regions than 21 counties. Also, we have no information about variations within Norwegian or Danish regions. Nevertheless the numbers would suggest that the decentralization of fiscal and political authority in Sweden may have as a consequence that geographical variations are larger.

6. Discussion

The hospital reform of 2002 represents one of the most dramatic changes in Norwegian health care to date and is considered quite controversial in several respects. First of all, in contrast with its neighboring Nordic countries, the Norwegian reform was a centrally initiated "big bang" reform that was implemented almost overnight. It took only a year from initial proposal in Parliament to a decision, and an important precondition for why the reform was so rapid is the shift in position within the Labour Party. In a Nordic comparative light it may also have played a role for the willingness to experiment with new organizational forms that the macroeconomic situation was exceptionally good due to oil revenues. In Norway, major policy changes and reforms are generally implemented through central initiatives and cover the whole of the country. In some cases, if there is doubt as to whether changes will work as expected, there may be "local trials". Such pilot projects were implemented before introducing ABF in 1997 and before introducing the family doctor model for primary care in 2001.

A similar, general approach is taken in Denmark. The Danish structure reform was also quite rapid, taking only a little over two years – from 2002 to 2004. Other recent large Danish reforms (the financial reform in 1999 and the structural reform in 2007) were centrally initiated and nationwide, yet many other policy initiatives have been taken at the regional levels or in collaboration between state and regions. In contrast to this, both Sweden and Finland rely more on local initiatives and experiments. The Swedish reform process has been much longer and less streamlined than in Denmark and Norway, which is due to the political/administrative traditions for long and careful deliberation of reforms. This also reflects a situation with a comparatively stronger position of regions and regional interest organizations than in the other Nordic countries. Sweden therefore has a tradition of more consensus-based policies with stronger veto points for regions.

Secondly, with the new organizational reform in Norway the hospitals were turned into separate legal entities. While ownership is still public, the hospitals are no longer an integral part of the central government administration. In the new model the hospitals correspond to the general meeting in ordinary companies, with central regulations primarily taking place through the enterprise meetings. The introduction of this type of enterprise model represents a distinct break with earlier administrative traditions, since it builds on a new management philosophy: the enterprise structure implies an organizational division between the activity and the superior political body. In short, the argument for adopting the enterprise model rather than the common directorate model was to "keep politicians at arm's length". The Hospital Act underlines that hospital leaders must be allowed control and responsibility of all input factors, the authority to choose an organizational structure that advances the purpose of the activity, and to have complete responsibility for the management, without interference from other administrative levels. Thus, the hospital reform can be viewed just as much as a responsibility – and leadership reform as an ownership reform. More important, the essential keywords are precisely the same as those associated with the New Public Management (NPM) doctrine: distinct objectives, output demands, and – not least – professional and genuine leadership.

Another interesting observation is the inherent duality in the reform. On the one hand, the reform signifies a recentralization of the hospital sector: ownership was transferred back to the central state, the Minister of Health took over the overall responsibility, and the five regional health authorities assumed responsibility for coordinating and steering the hospitals. On the other hand, the reorganization of health regions and hospitals into health enterprises represents decentralization, which signifies a change from devolution (to a lower political level) to deconcentration (to an independent lower administrative level) (Magnussen et al. 2007). When the reform was implemented in 2002, there were 82 hospitals and clinics. Following a series of mergers this number is now reduced to approximately 22, and in 2007, the two largest regional health authorities, East and South, were also merged into one region covering 55% of the Norwegian population.

There seems to be weak political support for the current model of specialized health care (Magnussen 2011). The only political party defending the current model is the governing Labor Party. We might therefore see changes after the parliamentary election in 2013. As noted in Magnussen (2011) there are in broad terms five issues that need to be dealt with: (i) How large a share of the public budget should be allocated to health care?[15] (ii) How should these funds be distributed evenly among geographical areas? (iii) How should the delivery of hospital services be structured; that is, what types of services should be offered where?[16] (iv) Is capital special, in the sense that capital financing needs to be more centralized? (v) How should hospitals be paid; capitation, cost-volume contracts, global budgets or activity based financing? In this setting, the choice of governance model implies choosing a degree of political centralization, choosing the types of issues that should be politicized and those that could be handled administratively, and finally choosing the degree of administrative decentralization.

The healthcare services represent a policy sector where one must constantly make difficult decisions. How are priorities to be made in the area of tension between what is medically and economically possible? Which patient groups need special efforts to receive services that are suited to their needs? Should certain types of treatments be given lower priority to give other patients with more critical needs better services? Is it important to keep small local hospitals to secure emergency medicine and maternity wards for the inhabitants in peripheral municipalities, or is it better to build on the larger and more advanced medical professional communities in the central hospitals? With the central takeover of the hospitals in Norway, health policy was essentially removed from the regional political arena. But this did of course not mean that the problems and challenges that defined this policy area disappeared. It does however mean that the decisions are made in other arenas and by other types of decision-makers. By removing politics from the traditional political arena important decision-makers become more discrete and less visible, and are outside the control of citizens.

An increasing market orientation implies that hierarchies of power based on traditional political institutions are replaced with an intricate system where public, private, and voluntary actors participate in local decision-making processes together with the elected local politicians. Important key elements in this development involve delegation of authority, consumer involvement, market- and competition-orientation, privatization, contracting out, the creation of micro delivery agencies, and the introduction of new budgeting systems. The essential point to be made is simply that central public decisions on health care will take place more in long-term relationships between key individuals in a diverse set of organizations located at various territorial levels rather than within hierarchically organized bureaucracies. The emerging healthcare governance thus implies reduced possibilities for democratic elected representatives to control public decisions. Furthermore, this model may diffuse decision-making and weaken its clarity, and it certainly becomes difficult to hold power holders to account when it is hard to locate which body formally makes the decisions. After all, there remains a crucial "dismissability" in elected representatives: the politicians offer the citizen the only obvious focus for discontent or anger, as they are the ones that can be held responsible for the outcomes of the policy decisions (cf Goss 2001; John 2001).

As noted in Section 2, the reliance on decentralized democratic institutions for health service delivery means also accepting that the solutions chosen in different areas can be somewhat different. The increased national steering ambitions in the Nordic health systems are related to a general trend of reduced acceptance of geographical differences in service delivery (Magnussen et al. 2007; Vrangbæk 2009). The decentralized democratic structure has been considered a positive feature in the Nordic context; indeed, it is what has made the Nordic countries different from, for example, the UK. While local decision-making and public participation still are important principles, the Nordic healthcare systems – and in particular the Norwegian – makes for good examples of the oscillation between political/administrative centralization and decentralization. The pendulum is now swinging in favor of more central (state) governance.

Constitutionally, the Norwegian health minister is responsible for everything that happens within the healthcare sector. It is the health minister and the government, which he or she is part of, that must face the political repercussions if citizens want to assign blame for the performance. But needless to say, not all decisions belong at the national level. National health policy also contains numerous local aspects, which gives ground for local expressions. An important question in the wake of the Norwegian reform therefore becomes whether local health policy will disappear when the local health political arena is closed down. The development in Norwegian politics has in general been distinguished by a withdrawal of politics in accordance with the NPM concept, as documented by the government-initiated research project on "Power and democracy 1998–2003".[17] Reflecting this trend, the hospital reform implied delegation of authority, discretion for managers and boards, and limited involvement of politicians, but so far there is little evidence that the reform has served to change the health policy process in the way it was supposed to do.

A study by Opedal and Rommetvedt (2005) of the involvement of Parliament in hospital matters reflects a considerable gap between explicit intentions and practical results. They found that while the formal governance model is influenced by NPM, in practice the model has not influenced the governing style of the Parliament. Their analysis, based on data from the Parliament and the health enterprises, indicates that politicians are still involved in hospital issues. Opedal and Rommetvedt therefore conclude that Parliament is challenging the balance of political control and enterprise autonomy, which formed the basis of the hospital reform. The years following the hospital reform have demonstrated this rather clearly: whenever the health enterprises have attempted to restructure their organization, typically through the closing down of small local hospitals, maternity wards or emergency wards, the health minister has intervened and forced the boards of the RHAs to reverse their decisions. People's movements to keep local hospitals, maternity wards, emergency wards, and so on have a long tradition in Norwegian health policy (e.g. Olsen 1988), and the national politicians have found it hard to withstand the pressure from broad and strongly articulated interests in the local communities, just in the same way as the local politicians did before them.

This then leads us to what seems to be the dilemma of the present Norwegian debate; which decisions should be taken at what political level? Or, put differently, how devolved should the system be? A return to the devolved model of county councils owning and running hospitals seems unlikely; even among the critics of the present model it is hard to find people who express nostalgic feelings about the period of county ownership. Therefore, the most likely solution is to strengthen the central political governance of the sector (i.e. the role of Parliament). The proponents of this solution point in the direction of using a national health plan as a more detailed policy instrument. Under the general (and presumably quite specific) framework laid out by such a health plan the administrative burdens would be reduced, there would be no need for the RHAs, and local health authorities could be governed directly from the Ministry of Health (or a directorate).

Notes

1. Readers interested in a more thorough discussion of the Nordic countries are referred to Magnussen et al. (2009). The present text builds in part on that book, in particular chapters 1 and 2.
2. The area of Norway is three times that of England, with one-tenth of the population.
3. With some exceptions (e.g. a National Hospital, owned and run by the state).
4. Although a few hospitals remained the responsibility of the state (e.g. the National Hospital and the National Cancer Hospital).
5. Meaning that all municipalities and counties have the maximal allowed tax rate (21% for municipalities and 7% for counties).
6. Ironically, limited patient choice led to situations with waiting lists in some counties and excess capacity in others.
7. The net operating profit shows how much the counties have at their disposal after working expenses, interest, and repayments are paid.
8. The second- and third-largest municipalities have 260,000 (Bergen) and 175,000 (Trondheim) inhabitants.
9. And thus represents an element of privately provided care in an otherwise publicly dominated system.
10. Authors' translation.
11. Source Sweden: http://www.skl.se/vi_arbetar_med/statistik/publikationer_ -statistik/landsting_och_regioner_i_diagram_och_siffror_2009, Denmark and Norway, authors' own calculations based on regional formulas for need and cost adjustment and actual costs.
12. Specialized and primary care, excluding dental care.
13. Specialized and primary care, excluding dental care.
14. Specialized care.
15. Private supplementary funding is not an issue in Norway, so we'll leave that be.
16. Remember that Norway is a large, but sparsely populated, country.
17. For publications from the project, see http://www.sv.uio.no/mutr/english/ publications.html.

References

Esping-Andersen, G. (1990). *Three Worlds of Welfare Capitalism*. Princeton: Princeton University Press.

Federation of Swedish County Councils [Landstingsförbundet] (2004). *Sjukvårdsdata in Focus*. [*Health Care Data in Focus*.] Stockholm: Landstingsförbundet.

Glenngård, A. H., F. Hjalte, M. Svensson, A. Anell & V. Bankauskaite (2005). *Health Systems in Transition: Sweden*. Copenhagen: WHO Regional Office for Europe on behalf of the European Observatory on Health Systems and Policies.

Goss, S. (2001). *Making Local Governance Work: Networks, Relationships and the Management of Change*. Houndmills: Palgrave.

Hagen, T. P. & O. Kaarbøe (2006). The Norwegian hospital reform of 2002: Central government takes over ownership of public hospitals, *Health Policy* 76: 320–33.

Hansen, F. H. (2001). "Sykehusstruktur i historisk perspektiv", In F. H. Hansen (ed): *Sykehusstruktur i endring. SINTEF report STF78 A015017*. Trondheim. [Hospital Structure in a historical perspective.]

Häkkinen, U. (2005) The impact of changes in Finland's health care system, *Health Economics* 14: 101–18.

John, P. (2001). *Local Governance in Western Europe*. London: SAGE Publications.

Magnussen, J. (1994). Hospital efficiency in Norway. A non-parametric approach. PhD dissertations in Economics no 6. University of Bergen.

Magnussen, J. (2011). Recentralization 10 years later. Success or failure, *Euro Observer* 14: 10–12.

Magnussen, J., T. P. Hagen & O. Kaarboe (2007). Centralized or decentralized? A case study of the Norwegian hospital reform, *Social Science & Medicine* 64: 2129–37.

Magnussen J., R. Saltman, K. Vrangbæk & P. E. Martinussen (2009). "Introduction: The Nordic model of health care", in J. Magnussen, K. Vrangbæk & R. Saltman (eds): *Nordic Health Care Systems: Recent Reforms and Current Policy Challenges* (pp. 3–20). London: Open University Press.

Martinussen, P. E. & J. Magnussen (2009). "Healthcare reform – the Nordic experience", in J. Magnussen, K. Vrangbæk & R. Saltman (eds): *Nordic Health Care Systems: Recent Reforms and Current Policy Challenges* (pp. 21–53). London: Open University Press.

Ministry of Local Government and Regional Development (2003). Rapport fra Det tekniske beregningsutvalg for kommunal og fylkeskommunal økonomi. Rundskriv H-8/03 April. [Circular letter. The municipalities' and counties' economic situation.]

Ministry of Health and Social Services (1998). Om lov om spesialisthelsetjenesten m m Ot.prp. nr. 10 (1998–99), [The Specialized Health Care Act].

Ministry of Health and Social Affairs (2000–2001). Parliamentary proposition No. 66, 2000–2001: Om lov om helseforetak mv [On the law of health authorities etc]. Oslo: Ministry of Health and Social Affairs.

Musgrave, R. (1959). *The Theory of Public Finance*. New York: McGraw Hill.

Oates, W. E. (1999). An essay on fiscal federalism, *Journal of Economic Literature* XXXVII: 1120–49.

Olsen, J. P. (1988). *Statsstyre og institusjonsutforming*. Oslo: Universitetsforlaget.

Opedal, S. & H. Rommetvedt (2005). Sykehus på Løvebakken. Stortingets engasjement og innflytelse før og etter sykehusreformen, *Journal of Social Research* 46: 99–132.

Parliamentary Proposition No. 47 (2008–2009). *The Coordination Reform: Proper Treatment – at the Right Place and Right Time*. Oslo: Norwegian Ministry of Health and Care Services.

Rattsø J. (2002). "Fiscal controls in Europe: A summary", in B. Dafflon (ed.): *Local Public Finance: Balanced Budget and Debt Control in European Countries*. Cheltenham: Edward Elgar.

Rehnberg, C., J. Magnussen & K. Luoma (2009). "Maintaining fiscal sustainability in the Nordic countries", in J. Magnussen, K. Vrangbæk & R. Saltman (eds): *Nordic Health Care Systems. Recent Reforms and Current Policy Challenges* (pp. 180–198). London: Open University Press.

Saltman, R. B. & V. Bankauskaite (2006) Conceptualizing decentralisation in European health systems: A functional perspective, *Health Economics, Policy and Law* 1: 127–47.

Samdata Sykehus Somatikk (2002). Trondheim: SINTEF Unimed. [Samdata hospital reports].

Strandberg-Larsen, M., M. B. Nielsen, S. Vallgårda, A. Krasnik, K. Vrangbæk & E. Mossialos (2007) *Health Systems in Transition: Denmark*. Copenhagen: WHO Regional Office for Europe on behalf of the European Observatory on Health Systems and Policies.

Sellers, J. M. & A. Lidström (2007). Decentralization, Local Government, and the Welfare State, *Governance* 20: 609–32.

SOU (2007). *SOU 10. Hållbar samhällsorganisation med utvecklingskraft*. Stockholm: Ministry of Financial Affairs.

Tiebout, C. (1956). A pure theory of local government expenditures, *Journal of Political Economy* 64: 416–24.

Vrangbæk, K. (2005) Health policy in Denmark: Leaving the decentralized welfare path? *Journal of Health Politics, Policy and Law*, 30: 29–52.

Vrangbæk, V. (2009). "The political process of restructuring Nordic health systems", in J. Magnussen, K. Vrangbæk & R. Saltman (eds): *Nordic Health Care Systems: Recent Reforms and Current Policy Challenges* (pp 53–78). London: Open University Press.

Vuorenkoski, L. (2008). The new health care act, *Health Policy Monitor*, October 2008; available at www.hpm.org./en/Downloads/Half-Yearly_Reports.html (accessed October 2011).

Part III

Cross-Country Evidence in Social Insurance Systems

7
Decentralization in Health and Social Care in Poland: Does Resource Allocation Matter?

Katarzyna A. Kuć-Czajkowska and Małgorzata Rabczewska

1. Introduction

Countries are increasingly recognizing the benefits of decentralization,[1] mostly because it can be a way of improving access to services, tailoring government actions to private needs, and increasing the opportunities for state–society interactions. However, decentralization traditions in Central and Eastern Europe (CEE) appear to be a phenomenon that has been developed relatively recently. Similar to the Spanish case (see Chapter 4), it follows from a democratization strategy. Indeed, after the fall of the communist system, democracy was planned to emerge out of the blue from a monolithic state. Regulski (2000) back in 1990s pointed out that the main challenge for reformers in CEE countries were the breaking of the five monopolies of the communist state:

- the doctrine of "homogenous state authority", which implied the vertical, hierarchical dependency of lower on upper tiers of government;
- the political monopoly of the communist party – in spite of its democratic facade, candidates in local elections before 1990 had to be nominated or approved by the local committee of the communist party; such a situation left no real choice for voters;
- the monopoly of state property – municipal property could not exist separately from state property before 1990;
- the monopoly of the state budget – local budgets were treated as part of central government finance and the state budget approved by Parliament formed very strict frames for local budgets;
- the monopoly of state administration – local bureaucrats were treated as part of central government administration and were subordinated to branch ministries more strictly than to local councils or local executives.

Evidence from CEE countries exhibits heterogeneous approaches and routes to decentralization, although mostly boil down to three models (Swianiewicz 2002). Namely, the first model, the *"step-by-step"* approach, meant that the fundamental reforms of the 1990s had some background in earlier events. The political disintegration of 1989 and 1990 met with pre-prepared suggestions for legal and economic changes (e.g. Hungary was the closest to this model).

The second strategy, the *"it's all happening too fast"* approach was related to very rapid and unexpected political change. In this model, central government was very hesitant to decentralize the country. The main argument was that the local self-governments were not ready to take on responsibility and real devolution of power because it would bring political and economic chaos; such an approach was typical in Bulgaria and Romania.

The third model was *"jump in at the deep end"*; in this case there was no time to prepare or discuss new laws in advance. Reformers were determined to introduce decentralization very quickly. Polish decentralization was the closest to this strategy. In 1999, Poland experimented simultaneously with four reforms, including the pension system reform, local self-government change, public education reform, and the reform of public healthcare services.

The main goal of this chapter is to assess the effects of Poland's decentralization on health and social care. Before turning to a description of the empirical research, we describe the existing territorial division of Poland, and more generally the institutional underpinnings that preceded decentralization. The second section examines the decentralization of public health care in Poland that has evolved from a centralized health system (before 1990) through to decentralization reforms (1990–2003) to newly introduced re-centralization processes. The final section discusses the delivery of social care from the decentralized perspective. It should be added that the expressions "social care" and "social welfare" are used interchangeably.[2]

2. The territorial division of Poland and health and social care tasks

The Polish Constitution of 2 April 1997 paved the way for the transfer of political, fiscal, and administrative powers to subnational (local) levels of government. The most important form of decentralization has undoubtedly been local self-government reforms. At present, Poland is divided into 16 provinces (regions), 314 districts, 65 urban districts (i.e. cities with district status) and 2478 municipalities. Subsequently, the national government decentralized the responsibility for health and social care services to local self-governments. The basic unit at the local level – the municipality – performs all the tasks of the local administration not allocated to other units (i.e. district and province). The Local Self-Government Act of 8 March 1990 gave responsibilities in about 20 areas to Polish local authorities. The fields of municipal activity involve, among other things:

- healthcare – the municipality is mainly responsible for primary health care in outpatients clinics (municipal health centers);
- social care (welfare) – providing benefits and essential social services, such as organizing care and education, the provision of homecare services, and the allocation and payment of benefits like regular or periodic targeted social security.

The second level of local self-government is the district. The urban district has been commanded to carry out many tasks on behalf of central government. Therefore these duties are financed from the state budget. Among other factors this results in a small share of the district's own revenues in their budgets. This level of local self-government (according to the District Local Self-Government Act of 5 June 1998) performs many tasks relating to everyday local life. The areas of district activity involve, among others:

- health care – the district is responsible for hospitals and a large number of medical centers for outpatients;
- social care (welfare) – the district realizes specialist tasks like diagnosing the social problems as well as finding effective solutions, running a crisis intervention center, organizing and managing care homes, providing training and in-service training of social care workers.

The province/region is a sort of double-nature entity, being the highest level of local self-government on the one hand, and the largest unit in the territorial division of Poland for purpose of public administration on the other. The province as the level of local self-government (according to the Province Local Self-Government Act of 5 June1998), performs tasks not reserved for municipalities and districts. These tasks include:

- health protection – the province is responsible for main and specialized hospitals, clinics, and polyclinics;[3]
- social care (welfare) – province plays the role of coordinator of social policy, so that organizing vocational training and staff welfare; it also inspires and promotes new solutions for social assistance (Staręga-Piasek et al. 2009: 209).

3. The decentralization of the healthcare system

The reform of the healthcare system (according to the Act of Universal Health Insurance of 1 January 1998) has aimed to improve the efficiency and quality of care, especially through the decentralization of ownership, financial and management responsibility to municipalities, districts and regions, the creation of new payment and contracting methods, and the development of the family-doctor model.

3.1. The organization of healthcare system – formerly and nowadays

The healthcare system, which was incepted in 1 January 1999, established that the essential responsibility for healthcare services rested with the Ministry of Health that takes on board a coordination role. These were decisions involving the directions and priorities in healthcare policy, regulatory decisions regarding prevention and treatment measures against the main health hazards, monitoring, assessment and analysis of the health of the population, and the provision of certain specialized care (Girouard and Imai 2000).

The newly established institution was the Health Insurance Fund (HIF). There were 16 Health Insurance Funds (covering at least one million insured each) corresponding to Poland's administration division into 16 regions (provinces) plus one additional branch fund for soldiers and officers in services subordinated to the Ministry of the Interior and Administration and the Ministry of Justice. HIFs were independent and autonomous organizations responsible for financing the majority of healthcare services in Poland. They were designed as non-profit organizations that cannot run, own, or hold shares in healthcare institutions. The task of HIFs was to ensure the availability of health benefits through contracting and financing medical services rendered by medical facilities. The source of financing HIFs was health insurance contributions. The contributions collected from members of each of the HIFs were the incomes of the given fund. The main brief of HIFs was to handle the money; the other was to sign contracts with healthcare providers. The providers of healthcare services were: hospitals, primary care practices (family doctors), specialist care practices, dental clinics, rehabilitation centers, nursing services (run by qualified nurses), obstetric services (run by qualified midwives), emergency services, and others who offered any service for the consumption of care for the health of population.

As of 1 January 1999, residents of each region were automatically members of one HIF. There was on opt-out mechanism, and from 1 January 2000 patients were free to change HIFs. On their part, healthcare funds were allowed to register members living outside the fund's region, so that they were to compete with each other for members (Girouard and Imai 2000).

The introduction of HIFs in each Polish province was consistent with the policy of decentralization. Decentralized institutions had numerous advantages. They could be more skilful in responding to changing needs, more effective in identifying problems, more innovative in the type of solution they adopted and could generate stronger commitment and greater productivity in the workplace (Saltman and Figueras 1997). On the other hand, decentralized arrangements were not without weaknesses. Examples were the risk of high administration costs and regulatory difficulties with multiple funds, the inequities and financial difficulties arising from an inadequate equalization mechanism, and the risk of the weak governance of HIFs (Girouard and Imai 2000). Gilowska (2000: 32) argues that the system actually resembled another tax rather than a real health security organization. The HIFs turned out to be no more than another layer in the bureaucratic institution and hence largely useless. The managers working for the funds earned up to USD 3,750 a month, as compared with Poland's average monthly wage of USD 500 per month.

The explicit aim of healthcare reform was to separate the delivery and the financing of health care. Shortly after the commencement of the operations of the HIFs it turned out that the insured had problems with obtaining a referral to a doctor, waited a long time for basic medical tests and, above all, there was no clearly specified scope for medical services under the insurance (Malinowska-Misiąg et al. 2008: 72–73). Another problem was the serious financial difficulties of HIFs. Unfortunately, nobody involved with reforms predicted the breakdown of a social security service that was responsible for gathering individual premiums and forwarding them to HIFs. It resulted in many patients being refused necessary examinations and treatment because of constant financial problems. There were considerable differences in the standard of medical services provided by different HIFs due to different efficiencies of HIFs.

3.2. Re-centralization of central state coordination

The unsuccessful experience with the decentralization of the public healthcare service made Parliament pass a new healthcare solution – the Act of Common Insurance in the National Health Fund of 23 January 2003. This legislation anticipated returning responsibility for health policy to the state (the government has a strategic role in health politics). Under this reform a National Health Fund (NHF) with 16 regional branches replaced 17 HIFs. Instead of 17 separate HIF budgets we have one central budget directly subordinate to the Minister of Health. The funding for the NHF comes from mandatory social insurance contributions paid by every employee. The percentage of income tax for the NHF is 9%. It is necessary to note that the Minister of Health is responsible for the division of those funds and – which is Poland's problem – should ensure the same standards of healthcare services throughout the whole country. On the one hand, advocates of this solution expect that it will guarantee a uniform standard of healthcare service. It seeks to unify the principles on which contracts are concluded with the reality of medical procedures, and implement a single health system for the whole country. On the other hand, its opponents think that this project is perceived as a step backwards in health reform – it assumes a centralized system of health care, and it transfers all healthcare responsibility from local self-governments to the state.

The organizational structure of primary health care was under the supervision of the NHF. First, a regional NHF would set up a tender for primary healthcare services in a given area. At that time the scope and standards of primary health care would be set. Next, when healthcare centers were commissioned a service, they were expected to provide round-the-clock primary health care for those willing to register. A lump sum was paid by the NHF every month for every registered person. There was no fee-for-service payment that included the operational costs of running healthcare centers.

The choice of beneficiaries is conducted in the form of competitions for tenders. Contracts concluded between the NHF and entities rendering medical services determine the range of services (procedures) and the top quantitative limit of benefits provided in a given financial year. Medical units, doctors and dentists, on the basis of contracts concluded with the NHF, or – in the case of highly specialized procedures – with the Ministry of Health, deliver healthcare services. Medical units are funded, run and supervised by public and private providers. Outpatient healthcare centers are mainly private (Malinowska-Misiąg et al. 2008: 74–75). The number of outpatient healthcare centers is presented in Table 7.1.

Within the framework of public health care, a patient has the right to choose a doctor, nurse, or midwife for primary health care, as well as – on the basis of a referral from a family doctor – to be a beneficiary of outpatient specialized benefits and hospital. A referral is not necessary in the case of benefits in the fields of dermatology, gynecology, ophthalmology, oncology, or stomatology.

3.3. The development of family doctors

One of the important and successful effects of the decentralization of the healthcare system is the strengthening of primary care services, in particular the strengthening of the function of family doctors. Patients use them as gatekeepers to the healthcare system. Outpatient services in specialist healthcare centers and hospitals treatment are provided on the basis of a referral from a family doctor, with the exception of services provided by clinics for those such as gynecology, mental health, drug addict rehabilitation and HIV carriers' care. Each family doctor should not have more than 2500 patients (Girouard and Imai 2000). Patients are entitled to the choice of any service provider. It is worth noting that primary-care-doctor practices function as private institutions but are financed from public funds gained as a result of negotiating a contract with an NHF. Among several advantages of this solution is that it improves the accessibility of primary healthcare services, and also reduces waiting times, improve consumer satisfaction, free

Table 7.1 Outpatient healthcare centers in the country and cities, with division into provinces (2003–2006)

Provinces	In urban areas				In rural areas			
	2003	2004	2005	2006	2003	2004	2005	2006
	per 10,000 inhabitants							
Dolnośląskie	2.7	3.0	2.9	3.7	1.9	2.1	2.1	2.6
Kujawsko-pomorskie	2.9	2.8	3.0	3.2	2.2	2.2	2.3	2.3
Lubelskie	4.0	4.5	4.5	5.0	2.3	2.4	2.5	2.6
Lubuskie	3.4	3.3	3.6	4.6	1.6	1.4	1.7	2.5
Łódzkie	4.3	4.6	4.7	4.8	2.7	2.6	2.7	2.7
Małopolskie	4.6	4.6	4.7	4.7	2.5	2.4	2.5	2.6
Mazowieckie	3.9	3.5	3.4	3.7	2.2	2.1	2.1	2.4
Opolskie	3.4	4.0	4.2	4.1	1.2	2.1	2.1	2.3
Podkarpackie	4.7	4.8	5.0	5.7	2.6	2.3	2.5	2.7
Podlaskie	4.4	4.5	4.9	5.5	1.9	1.8	1.9	2.5
Pomorskie	2.8	2.7	2.5	3.0	1.5	1.6	1.8	2.0
Śląskie	4.3	4.3	4.2	4.4	2.6	2.9	2.7	3.0
Świętokrzyskie	3.5	3.9	4.5	4.5	2.6	2.4	2.7	2.5
Warmińsko-mazurskie	4.0	4.0	4.0	4.3	1.7	1.6	1.5	1.7
Wielkopolskie	3.5	3.6	4.0	4.7	1.2	1.2	1.3	1.6
Zachodniopomorskie	4.0	4.2	4.0	4.3	1.3	1.2	1.3	1.5

Source: Personal study based on the date from the Central Statistical Office.

up private enterprises' time, and substantial savings such as a reduction in administrative staff (Halik 2001: 139–140).

3.4. Health care and the tasks of local self-government

As a result of the territorial division in Poland, three levels of local self-government are responsible for health care. The municipality is responsible for primary health care in outpatient clinics (health municipal centers). The district is responsible for hospitals and outpatient medical centers. Provinces, which perform tasks not allocated to municipalities and districts, are responsible for main and specialized hospitals, clinics, and polyclinics. All levels of local self-government have the legal status of the owner, supervisor, and manager of medical units. In particular their activity involves (Frąckiewicz-Wronka 2002: 173):

– providing conditions for the existence of various types of medical center;
– repairing medical facilities and capital investment in this field;
– ensuring administrative, financial and organizational services for medical units;
– equipping medical units with the necessary medical equipment;

- creating the whole strategy of healthcare policy in one's area;
- initiating actions related to public health;
- initiating the actions connected with protecting and promoting a healthy lifestyle.

This means influencing local self-governments that run medical units in at least two ways. First, local governments own large shares of indebted hospitals. It is very easy to point to many towns in Poland where for 40,000 inhabitants there are 400–500 short-term-care beds. The best solution in that situation might be a "reduction" in the number of short-term-care beds and an increase in the number of long-term-care hospitals. Secondly, a big problem is a lack of liaison (especially at the district and municipality levels) between the particular NHF and local authorities. The key to healthcare reform was the separation of the organizer and payer of healthcare services. NHFs (payer) cover about 60% of the costs involved in treatments. Local self-governments (organizers) have to cover 30–40% of total expenditures, which is too small in relation to the needs of indebted hospitals (Halik 2001: 136–138). Paradoxically, representatives of local self-governments have no opportunity to influence NHF negotiations, decisions, or the level of contracts.

Local self-governments are also responsible for the protection and promotion of healthy lifestyles. In reality these tasks are not realized due to a lack of funds, a lack of professional programs, and a lack of officers employed as medical specialists in local self-government units. Quite often in the development of civil society, non-governmental organizations sector fills that role best.

3.5. Financing of healthcare services

The healthcare reform anticipated that the state would be no longer responsible for the greatest part of health care (and the cost of it). In view of the growing needs and soaring costs of the medical service, it was hoped that linking healthcare funding with the income of individual citizens would provide a solid financial base. Therefore the public sector was financed by the insured as a premium for the coverage of healthcare costs. The insured/employed were obliged to pay 9% of the employee's gross salary after deduction of the employee's portion of social insurance premiums. This amount was withheld from the employee's take-home pay. Moreover, other forms of financial benefits, such as disability benefit, old-age pension, and scholarships were also subject to deduction of the premium. It should be noted that all people were covered, including the homeless, unemployed, soldiers, and others. In these cases, insurance was paid by the state budget. In this system insurance was not related to age, gender, or state of health. It may even be regarded as a health tax. There were also other options for getting medical treatment (e.g. private-sector health care or private health insurance, principally provided by employers as a part of a social-benefit package). Outside health care was not exchangeable with the regular service provided by NHFs (Jasiutowicz 1999).

Since the foundation of the NHF in 2003, incomes from contributions to health insurance are treated as uniform resources, subject to division into expenditure limits awarded to individual departments of the NHF. The expenditure limits of NHF branches for a given financial year are established according to a four-phase procedure. First of all, the total income for a given year is estimated. The assessment of incomes marks a total limit of expenditures for healthcare benefits financed from public sources. In the second stage, expenditure limit is divided into two parts: expenditures of central NHF and total expenditures of 16 NHF branches. In the third phase, the total amount allocated for financing highly specialized procedures is separated from the amount of expenditure by NHF branches. Next, the expenditures of particular NHF branches are specified (Malinowska-Misiąg et al. 2008: 77).

The procedure has a few weak points. First, to estimate expenditures for all provinces, the same nationwide indicators are used. It means that in the division of resources for provinces, not taken into account are the level of urbanization, having an influence on costs of primary health care (in rural areas costs are higher), and the inter-province diversity of inhabitants' state of health. Secondly, taking into consideration migration-factor increases (to the cost of other provinces) transfers to the regions, which have a good medical infrastructure achieve a positive balance of "export" and "import" of medical services. Therefore the rules of dividing resources cause further diversity in the state of the medical infrastructure and the standards of medical services in particular provinces (Malinowska-Misiąg et al. 2008: 78).

In the years 2003–2004, NHF branches set different rates for the same procedures, which influenced the diversity in the financial situation of medical establishments in individual provinces. The division of resources among NHF branches did not take into account additional factors such as the transfer of patients to other provinces (e.g. to use highly specialized medical services).

The replacement of HIFs with one NHF was done to ensure equal and territorially unlimited access to health benefits. In reality, the reform had the opposite effect. For instance, in 2000 the highest income per insured person amounted to 106.3% of the average, and the lowest was 95.3%. In 2006, the highest income per insured person increased to 112.6%, and the lowest decreased to 87.5% of the average. It means that the stratification of resources – per insured person – managed by NHF branches is currently larger than when separate HIFs functioned. The centralization of the healthcare financing system did not solve the problem of big liabilities in some provinces (Malinowska-Misiąg et al. 2008: 87).

The unbalanced division of resources among province NHF branches has an impact on, among other things the value of the liabilities of public

Table 7.2 The total liabilities of public medical establishments (2004–2006)

Provinces and ministries	Total liabilities (million USD)			Including due liabilities (million USD)		
	2004	2005	2006	2004	2005	2006
Dolnośląskie	473.83	496.23	460.47	376.20	343.93	259.27
Kujawsko-pomorskie	142.57	154.67	172.63	86.20	63.80	75.87
Lubelskie	177.37	177.23	187.47	112.37	81.17	41.73
Lubuskie	178.60	199.67	216.63	146.33	141.37	121.93
Łódzkie	292.47	326.26	333.93	204.27	168.03	123.53
Małopolskie	202.20	224.43	223.17	93.07	64.00	46.03
Mazowieckie	345.80	405.67	401.40	208.07	191.90	124.00
Opolskie	56.40	55.27	40.20	29.17	17.53	5.97
Podkarpackie	100.43	113.57	113.40	33.73	22.17	24.57
Podlaskie	89.77	93.17	85.50	52.07	31.80	19.67
Pomorskie	229.40	278.90	318.40	153.67	154.60	112.90
Śląskie	315.67	331.23	352.03	155.47	126.23	109.73
Świętokrzyskie	122.27	124.97	112.47	79.47	69.90	37.27
Warmińsko-mazurskie	75.33	73.53	64.87	38.53	18.77	15.07
Wielkopolskie	111.20	125.47	130.37	45.83	34.20	31.00
Zachodniopomorskie	100.93	106.03	107.87	59.63	53.07	40.50
Ministry of Defence	67.10	60.03	55.67	39.77	22.47	18.30
Ministry of Interior and Administration	68.67	78.17	73.13	43.57	39.57	33.80

Source: Personal study based on the date from the Central Statistical Office.

medical establishments. In some provinces (Table 7.2), despite the low incomes of the NHF department from contributions, the NHF's debt level is relatively low (in the Podkarpackie, Opolskie and Warmińsko-Mazurskie provinces). On the other hand, other regions with NHF incomes above average (Mazowieckie and Śląskie) are distinguished by a low level of liabilities of medical establishments, but at the same time, in provinces with a high level of liabilities of medical establishments, NHF branches' incomes are relatively low. In spite of these regularities, the differences in incomes of individual NHF branches are not the factor deciding the level of liabilities of public medical establishments in particular regions.

The Act of 2005 on restructuring public medical establishments was intended to, among other things, support the restructuring liabilities of public medical establishments from public sources. With the aim of financing the restructuring program, medical establishments received a loan from the state budget or that grant from budget of a founding organ (a local self-government unit). They could also issue bonds or contract bank credits (Malinowska-Misiąg et al. 2008: 81).

The restructuring of medical establishments' debt did not have the expected effects. In spite of the fact that part of the debt was erased, the total amount of liability in two years increased from USD 2.07 billion in 2004 to more than USD 2.23 billion in 2006. In place of the amortized liabilities new and higher ones arose. The improvement in the situation was short-term, since in place of the amortized liabilities medical establishments raised new loans. The negative assessment of the effect of the restructuring is confirmed by analyses of medical establishments' liabilities published by the Ministry of Health. According to those data, the total amount of medical establishments' liabilities increased from USD 3.15 billion in 2004 to USD 3.45 billion at the end of 2006 (Malinowska-Misiąg et al. 2008: 81).

It is necessary to emphasize that Polish health care was (and is) very far from a universal system. One of the most significant problems includes the widespread use of informal payments (*de facto* corruption). While officially medical services were provided free of charge, patients started making informal payments to doctors to obtain faster and more personalized service. According to the results of a public opinion poll published by Transparency International, Poland, 45% of patients in 1997 and 43% in 1999 reported feeling obliged to make some form of payment when visiting a doctor (Borowczyk-Przyborowska 2000: 315). The situation has not changed to date. These findings suggest that the good things in Polish healthcare services are privatized. But then the pecuniary incentives may be working to limit the supply of services at public hospitals available to the low-income earner (Girouard and Imai 2000).

Financing health care in Poland is one of the key economic, social, and political problems. Decisions related to the sources and rules of financing influence the kind of healthcare system that is present and also determine the level and structure of expenditure. Total expenditures on health care in Poland, despite constantly growing, belong to one of the lowest in Europe. The average annual expenditure growth rate during 1998–2008 was at the level of 9% (Table 7.3). Going through the detailed structure of healthcare expenditure is also interesting. The share of private expenditures in the total healthcare expenditure amount oscillated around 30%. The highest level achieved was 31.4% in 2004. During 1998–2004, it displayed a growth trend. During the aforementioned 2004, a considerable growth of private expenditures, and a reduction of public expenditure[4] were observed. Since 2005, the expenditure structure reversed and the share of financial expenditures from public sources began to grow, while private expenditures shrunk.

In Poland, healthcare expenditures in the GDP, similar to total expenditures, are one of the lowest in Europe. Between 1998 and 2008, a slow growth (from 5.9% to 7%) of the share of expenditures in GDP could be observed (Table 7.3). An analysis of total expenditures on health care, on a per capita basis, indicated that during the said period, they grew from USD 264 to 729.

Table 7.3 Expenditure on health care in Poland (1998–2008)

Year	Expenditure on health care			% GDP	Expenditure on health care per capita	
	Total (million USD)	Of which public expenditure (%)	Of which private expenditure (%)		in USD	in USD PPP (purchasing – power parity)
1998	11829.7	65.4	34.6	5.9	264	556
1999	12724.7	71.1	28.9	5.7	249	566
2000	13699.3	70.0	30.0	5.5	247	590
2001	15225.0	71.9	28.1	5.9	292	647
2002	17079.0	71.2	28.8	6.3	328	734
2003	17550.7	69.9	30.1	6.2	354	754
2004	19119.7	68.6	31.4	6.2	411	814
2005	20313.3	69.3	30.7	6.2	494	865
2006	20685.7	69.2	30.8	6.2	543	910
2007	23610.7	70.5	29.5	6.4	619	1049
2008	27798.0	72.2	27.8	7.0	729	1213

Source: Personal study based on the date from the Central Statistical Office.

Similarly, healthcare expenses have doubled according to purchasing power parity (from USD 556 to 1213).

Table 7.4 shows healthcare expenditure per region (province). These amounts comprise the sum of the expenditures of municipalities, districts, urban districts, and provinces segregated by each province. Taking into consideration the general amounts, the largest pool of money for health care was allotted by local self-government units in the provinces of Dolnośląskie, Mazowieckie, Śląskie and Wielkopolskie. Analyzing healthcare expenditures on a per capita basis, we observe a similar situation. The largest pool of funds is allotted for the Mazowieckie province (during 2005–2009, this amount grew from USD 35 to 53 per resident). During 2005–2007, local self-government units located in the Dolnośląskie province spent one of the largest sums. In 2009, aside from the Mazowieckie province, about USD 45 per capita was allotted for health care in the provinces of Lubuskie, Opolskie, and Świętokrzyskie.

Summing up, the experience in the functioning of the healthcare system shows that the issues that require the greatest attention are:

– difficult access to specialized healthcare (especially to hospitals) and patients waiting in long queues;
– the unsatisfactory level of healthcare services provided;
– low salaries in the healthcare sector, which are a direct cause of the emigration of specialized medical staff to other EU countries;
– the indebtedness of hospitals (the due liabilities of public hospitals in the years 1999–2007 is presented in Figure 7.1).

Table 7.4 Expenditure on health care by provinces (regions) (2005–2009)[5]

Provinces	Total (thousand USD)					Expenditure on health care per capita (thousand USD)				
	2005	2006	2007	2008	2009	2005	2006	2007	2008	2009
Dolnośląskie	81,615	112,811	109,125	105,977	90,372	28	39	38	37	31
Kujawsko-pomorskie	46,185	64,702	69,431	75,034	76,422	22	31	34	36	37
Lubelskie	42,991	41,552	49,728	67,067	60,360	20	19	23	31	28
Lubuskie	19,249	21,863	17,199	19,850	45,586	19	22	17	20	45
Łódzkie	48,922	54,861	57,044	77,552	95,277	19	21	22	30	38
Małopolskie	48,947	63,402	56,937	69,332	89,664	15	19	17	21	27
Mazowieckie	180,683	230,423	239,986	245,751	276,388	35	41	46	47	53
Opolskie	22,186	23,207	20,320	20,652	46,911	21	22	20	20	45
Podkarpackie	31,249	40,067	35,881	51,158	53,450	15	19	17	24	25
Podlaskie	15,123	19,189	16,521	29,794	30,912	13	16	14	25	26
Pomorskie	43,052	55,435	55,793	81,940	85,838	19	25	25	37	38
Śląskie	131,173	119,361	109,401	143,447	157,988	28	26	23	31	34
Świętokrzyskie	23,918	29,388	36,321	45,471	60,271	19	23	28	36	47
Warmińsko-mazurskie	24,000	27,286	31,645	29,653	38,337	17	19	22	21	27
Wielkopolskie	57,550	73,664	65,766	87,151	100,998	17	22	19	25	30
Zachodniopomorskie	43,616	44,840	49,293	77,071	59,419	26	26	29	45	35

Source: Personal study based on the date from the Central Statistical Office.

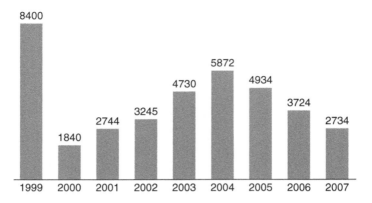

Figure 7.1   The due liabilities of public hospitals (1999–2007, million PLN)
Source: Personal study based on the date from the Central Statistical Office.

The following should be highlighted among the most problematic issues in the functioning of the healthcare system (Kaczmarczyk 2010):

- the system's unsatisfactory level of funding from public funds;
- the monopolistic position of the public payer – the NHF;
- the lack of a defined range of benefits available within the insurance provided by the NHF;
- the unclear policies in the medication reimbursement area;
- the unsatisfactory qualifications of public hospitals' management staff (due to the fact that the main management staff of public hospitals constitute doctors);
- the lack of an integrated IT system in health care (the Medical Services Register has remained unfinished since 1992).

3.6. The decentralization of the social care system

In response to the huge social costs of the transformation,[6] at the beginning of the 1990s the work to reform the social-benefits system began. As a result, a decentralized model was introduced and within this model local self-government not only performed the role of supplier of social benefits but also that of coordinator and organizer of the actions aimed at helping to resolve the problems of the local communities. The reformers gave priority to decentralization and handing social services to local self-governments. Due to this fact, the necessary conditions were created for a greater activity by public institutions and organizations providing assistance in resolving social problems within local communities. In addition to this, it was presupposed that the local self-governments are more conscious of the local situation and because of that, they will be more effective in spending the money on public services (Kulesza 2002: 5–6; Cherka 2004: 15–19). The social services provided on the local level made it possible to shorten the reaction time for the emerging social problems. Also, it was easier to give a closer look into the local needs and the already applied mechanisms of fulfilling them.

The social services system created in the 1990s was frequently modified, mainly to reduce the public social expenditure. According to J. Rybka (2006: 4–6) the plan was unachievable in relation to its implementation possibilities: there were not enough funds and not enough sufficiently qualified staff. The bureaucracy hindered the coordination and cooperation of different services and non-governmental organizations. The basic range of social services was systematically being extended and the new benefits were introduced along with the responsibility for the implementation of the new support programs. It led to a situation where the social services system became a bottomless pit into which the new tasks and new unsolved problems were put. After a few dozen of amendments, the Social Services Act from 1990 was replaced in 2004 with a new one. At present, the Act from 12 March 2004 and the Act from 26 January 2007 define the rules of social-benefits allocation.

4. Definition, objectives, and the basic range of social services

Social Security constitutes an institutional element of the country's social policy aiming at helping individuals and families to overcome difficult times, which they cannot overcome by means of their own powers, resources, and opportunities. Social Security provides support in the endeavors to fulfill the basic needs and makes it possible to live the life in the conditions, which assure human dignity. It is also up to Social Security to prevent difficult life situations by means of actions aimed at helping individuals and families to become independent and to integrate into society.

Social Security benefits are allocated, in particular, to individuals and families who are eligible under the following conditions: poverty, orphanhood, homelessness, unemployment, disabilities, long-term or serious illness, the need to protect victims of human trafficking, pregnancy, a great number of children, difficulties in integrating the refugees, alcoholism and drug abuse, acts of God and crisis situations, and natural or ecological disaster.

4.1. Social care (welfare) and local self-government tasks

Local self-governments (districts and municipalities) are mainly responsible for social welfare. The range of the municipality's task is the following: internal mandatory tasks, internal non-mandatory tasks,[7] and commissioned tasks related to government administration (Table 7.5). Likewise, at the district level, the tasks are divided into internal and commissioned tasks related to government administration (Table 7.6). The district's tasks are a complementary and compensatory character in relation to the municipality's tasks.

The division into internal and commissioned tasks implies diversity in terms of the organizational and financial supervision of government administration over these services. Internal tasks are funded from the municipality's budget (often also co-financed by the government administration agencies) and their supervision is accounted for by the law. As for the commissioned tasks, the necessary funds are transferred from the national budget and they are supervised in terms of the following criteria: legality (lawfulness) purposefulness, reliability, and thrift. The supervision over the implementation of the internal and commissioned tasks in every province exercises the province governor.[8]

The division of tasks in the social welfare area was carried out in proportion to the size of the local self-government unit and, thus, according to the available implementation means. The municipality provides basic services such as running welfare centers, providing a visiting-nurse service, and allocating and paying regular, seasonal, passported and social benefits. The district conducts special tasks (i.e. running crisis-situation centers, establishing and running care homes and providing counseling services for managerial staff and welfare centers employees (Koczur 2002: 165)). The province conducts tasks of a special nature and provide support for municipalities and districts in the implementation of their own tasks. The province's task range includes:

- providing education, running public schools for social welfare employees and providing the professional training of social welfare employees;
- identifying the causes of poverty and developing regional social-aid schemes, which would be help for local self-governments in their actions in curbing the phenomenon;
- inspiring and promoting new solutions in the social welfare area;
- organizing and running regional welfare centers;
- running a database with information on vacancies in 24-hour care homes in the region.

The division of responsibilities in social welfare between the different organizational levels is illustrated by Table 7.7. Units of local self-government fulfill management and executive roles. Municipalities and districts focus on implementing social tasks, while on the provincial level, a needs diagnosis, planning and raising the qualifications of civil servants take place. The Ministry of Labor and Social Policy, together with 16 province governors, are only responsible for oversight.

Table 7.5 The range of the municipality's task in respect to social welfare

Internal mandatory tasks	Internal non-mandatory tasks	Commissioned tasks related to the government administration
– elaboration and implementation of the municipal strategy on resolving social problems – augmentation of the social-needs register – provision of shelter, meals and clothes for the needy – allocation and repayments of seasonal benefits including benefits paid in the event of Acts of God, health benefits, health benefits for the homeless and the unemployed and those unable to obtain benefits accounted for in NHF insurance regulations – allocating and paying benefits through the Funded-Ticket Scheme – paying social security contributions on behalf of a persons who are forced to give up work to take care of family members undergoing long-term treatment and co-residing mothers, fathers or siblings – providing social work – organizing and providing care services including specialized home care services – running and guaranteeing vacancies at welfare centers and welfare youth centers – creating a municipal prevention and childcare system – providing extra food for children – arranging funeral services	– allocation and payments of special passported benefits – providing assistance for those who want to become economically independent in the form of allowances, loans, help in kind – running and assuring vacancies at municipal welfare centers and referring people who need help there – undertaking other actions in the social welfare area resulting from the local needs and implementation of social protection schemes	– organization and providing the specialized care services for the mentally ill – allocation and repayments of the passported benefits allotted to cover expenditures connected with natural or ecological disasters – running and expanding the network of mutual aid centers for mentally-ill people, – implementation of the tasks set out in governmental social welfare schemes aiming to maintain the level of life conditions of individuals, families and other social groups

Source: Personal study based on the Social Welfare Act of 12 March 2004 and the amended Social Welfare Act of 26 January 2007.

Table 7.6 The range of the district's/urban district's task in respect to social welfare

Internal tasks	Commissioned tasks related to the government administration
– elaboration and implementation of the strategy on resolving social problems in district – providing specialized counseling services – providing foster families for children and assistance from the funding of children's stay in foster care centers, and also repaying benefits for willingness to receive a child or the care and adoption of a child not connected with professional foster families – providing care and education for parentless children, especially by organizing and running care and adoption centers and care homes, and also establishing and implementing family and child assistance schemes – covering foster children's and families' living costs – allocating financial support for the continuation of education and becoming financially independent – providing support for people with difficulties in adjusting to normal life after leaving care homes and welfare centers for intellectually disabled children and young people, single-parent centers for pregnant women and women with young children, foster families, and shelters for underage people, reformatories, special care homes and care homes for young people – providing support for refugees and former convicts who find it difficult to integrated or reintegrate into society – running welfare centers in the district – providing free accommodation and district support centers for single mothers and pregnant women – running crisis situation centers – training new people in the social welfare area for district residents – providing counseling services for managerial staff and welfare center employees from the district	– providing help to refugees in the form of an individual integration scheme and paying health insurance contributions on behalf of these persons – running and expanding a network of mutual aid centers for mentally-ill people – implementation of the tasks set out in governmental social welfare schemes aiming at maintaining the level of life conditions of individuals, families, and other social groups

Source: Personal study based on the Social Welfare Act of 12 March 2004 and the amended Social Welfare Act of 26 January 2007.

Table 7.7 Division of responsibilities for social welfare between organizational levels (since 1999)

Tasks	Municipalities	Districts	Provinces	Province governor	Ministry of Labor and Social Policy
Monetary and non-monetary support	x	x			
Services	x				
Social and advisory work	x	x			
Institution creation and oversight	x	x	x		
Needs diagnosis	x	x	x		
Planning	x	x	x		
Employee development		x	x		x
Control and coordination				x	x

Source: Personal study.

It is worth to mention that local self-governments are fully independent in making decisions about the allocation of funds for the implementation of internal welfare tasks. This means that provinces, districts, and municipalities are empowered to shape their own social welfare policy. To conduct these tasks, local self-governments establish special units at different levels (i.e. municipal welfare centers, district family-support centers, which in cities with district rights are known as municipal family support centers, and in provinces are called regional welfare centers).

Social welfare institutions are organized and funded collectively by the state and local self-governments, yet they may still collaborate with non-governmental organizations. They are funded both through local self-government funds and the national budget funds allocated to local self-governments for the implementation of the tasks related to government administration. Local self-government units and government administration institutions are obliged to work together with social welfare and non-governmental organizations, churches, religious groups, legal persons and corporate entities (Koczur 2002: 164). There are approximately 15,000 non-governmental organizations providing welfare services. Altogether, they account for 29.6% of all third-sector organizations in Poland (Krzyszkowski 2004/2005).

4.2. Financing of social welfare

A consequence of the division of responsibilities for activities related to social welfare is a constant trend to increase the share of local self-government budgets in providing social welfare, combined with the reduction of national budget spending for these goals. Since introducing new regulations for the functioning of social welfare in 2004, the share of local self-government started to considerably exceed the expenditures from the national budget. Figure 7.2 is an analysis of municipal budget spending on social welfare in the years 1990–2009, separating between internal tasks and commissioned tasks. As can be seen, from the beginning of the 1990s, a growth of expenditures incurred by local self-government units for social welfare grew. This was paired with broadening of the scope and form of benefits in the range of activities performed by municipalities. In other words, municipalities and districts have to a greater degree, single-handedly financed a growing number of activities, at the same time reducing the

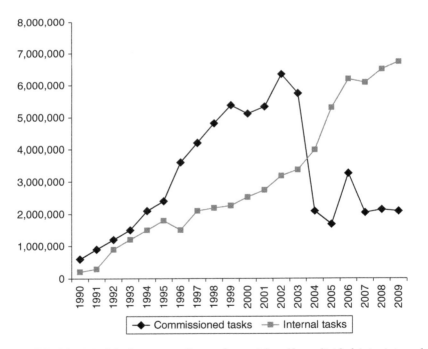

Figure 7.2 Municipal budget expenditures for social welfare, divided into internal tasks and commissioned tasks (1990–2009, thousand USD)

Source: Personal study based on annual reports from the Ministry of Labor and Social Policy on social welfare benefits.

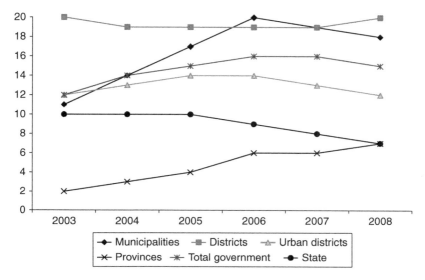

Figure 7.3 Comparison of the share of expenditures from the national budget and the budgets of local self-government units on actions related to social welfare (2003–2008, %)

Source: Personal study based on *Budżety . . . 2009; Sprawozdania . . . 2009*.

share of commissioned tasks (tasks for which funds are transferred from the national budget).

Figure 7.3 confirms that the highest percentage share of expenditures on actions in the field of social welfare belongs to districts (19–20%) and municipalities (11–20%). The national budget (with a share in the area of 7–10%) finances this type of activity to a very small degree. Since 2005 the national government's share in these expenditures has been declining constantly. The last position belongs to provinces, whose social welfare expenditures oscillate around 2–7%.

An analysis of the expenditure amounts of province, districts, urban districts, and municipalities placed in a given region indicates that the groups of the biggest beneficiaries of social welfare are the inhabitants of: Mazowieckie, Śląskie, and Wielkopolskie (Tables 7.8 and 7.9). However, taking into account per capita expenditures, the highest amounts for social welfare and other actions of social policy are received by the inhabitants of the Lubuskie province and one of the poorest regions, located in Eastern Poland – Warmińsko-Mazurskie. These funds are mainly directed to support payments. To a lesser degree, they are used to raise the inhabitants' qualifications or activating individuals who are stricken by poverty and require support.

Table 7.8 Expenditure on social welfare by provinces (regions) (2005–2009)[9]

Provinces	Total (thousand USD)				Expenditure on social assistance per capita (in USD)			
	2005	2006	2007	2008	2005	2006	2007	2008
Dolnośląskie	392,996	447,370	461,549	487,624	137	155	160	169
Kujawsko-pomorskie	324,646	397,185	399,098	412,411	157	192	193	199
Lubelskie	272,850	360,672	366,677	377,743	126	167	170	175
Lubuskie	165,926	194,410	201,941	203,882	164	192	200	202
Łódzkie	331,588	410,536	421,138	454,339	130	161	166	179
Małopolskie	369,995	482,480	507,647	512,694	112	146	154	155
Mazowieckie	566,242	710,866	733,238	782,837	108	136	140	150
Opolskie	127,299	149,401	138,953	164,931	123	145	135	160
Podkarpackie	272,751	350,994	383,684	393,113	130	167	182	187
Podlaskie	144,932	194,783	196,641	200,229	122	164	165	168
Pomorskie	313,594	368,344	386,468	401,251	141	165	173	180
Śląskie	545,781	631,066	657,537	686,545	118	136	142	148
Świętokrzyskie	171,701	232,091	239,652	249,876	135	183	189	197
Warmińsko-mazurskie	252,023	303,141	319,115	334,769	176	212	224	234
Wielkopolskie	425,123	540,281	565,368	585,516	125	158	166	172
Zachodniopomorskie	273,549	308,667	319,946	326,673	161	182	189	193

Source: Personal study based on the date from the Central Statistical Office.

Table 7.9 Expenditure on other actions in the range of social policy by provinces (regions) (2005–2009)[10]

Provinces	Total (thousand USD)				Expenditure on other actions in the range of social policy per capita (in USD)			
	2005	2006	2007	2008	2005	2006	2007	2008
Dolnośląskie	29,208	43,073	53,735	54,840	10	15	19	19
Kujawsko-pomorskie	19,230	27,566	30,033	46,935	9	13	14	23
Lubelskie	18,501	31,026	34,649	38,732	8	14	16	18
Lubuskie	12,104	16,354	16,868	23,549	12	16	17	23
Łódzkie	23,878	33,668	40,220	41,763	9	13	16	16
Małopolskie	23,539	35,281	40,408	54,639	7	11	12	16
Mazowieckie	47,668	65,867	78,533	87,250	9	13	15	17
Opolskie	9943	14,829	16,123	23,856	10	14	16	23
Podkarpackie	16,251	28,427	34,673	35,952	8	13	16	17
Podlaskie	10,362	19,690	21,891	25,942	9	16	18	22
Pomorskie	17,591	27,746	30,829	45,894	8	12	14	20
Śląskie	39,437	50,818	59,678	64,885	8	11	13	14
Świętokrzyskie	10,931	19,807	19,639	29,481	9	15	15	23
Warmińsko-mazurskie	17,086	25,601	22,920	42,150	12	18	16	29
Wielkopolskie	32,242	39,900	43,826	61,529	9	12	13	18
Zachodniopomorskie	18,489	26,973	30,869	55,679	11	16	18	33

Source: Personal study based on the date from the Central Statistical Office.

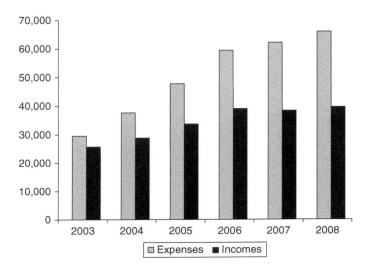

Figure 7.4 Comparison of expenditures and incomes for local self-government units in the field of social welfare and other actions of social policy (2003–2008, million USD)

Źródło: Personal study based on *Budżety … 2009; Finanse … 2009.*

It is worthwhile to note that the comparison of expenditures and incomes of local self-government budgets related to social welfare and the remaining tasks of social policy (Figure 7.4) shows that a great disproportion exists between the growth rate of expenditures and incomes for social welfare. In the case of expenditures, the growth rate amounted to 142%; however, in the revenue part, it was only 53%. This means that local self-government expenditures are growing faster than incomes. This difference grows from year to year. Local self-government units are burdened by new activities and the resulting costs of social welfare. However, revenues for this cause remain at a similar level. The authorities of local self-government units are forced to cover increasing costs with revenues from sources other than social welfare and social policy.

4.3. Strategies for solving social problems

Local self-governments in Poland are obliged to develop strategies for solving social problems. It is the task of municipalities and districts to prepare such documents, whereas provinces develop and update their strategy in respect of social policy. This is not a separate document, but constitutes an integral part of the province development strategy. While preparing the strategy for solving social problems, it is essential to diagnose social problems and to establish related social care programs concerning, in particular, preventing and solving alcohol- and drug-related problems in municipalities, as well as to support the disabled and to activate the unemployed in districts. These programs aim at the integration of people from groups at particular risk. If they are prepared and implemented properly, they contribute to solving key social problems.

Nevertheless, according to the Institute for the Development of Social Services, only 60% of districts and 40% of municipalities had such strategies in 2007. The main drawbacks of documents prepared by local self-governments were too low a level of commitment by communities and representatives of non-governmental organizations to the development of social services and the fact that the knowledge of authors concerning social problems was based on data coming from the offices they represent, and only in some particular cases were residents asked about their problems and needs. Additionally, less than half the strategies included indices through which the accomplishment of intended goals could be verified.

4.4. The system of benefits within the scope of social care

There are two kinds of social care (and two types of benefits): *community care* implemented at the place of residence of beneficiaries, and *institutional care* provided in nursing homes and support centers of various types – community self-help centers, "doss-houses", and care-education centers. Both community and institutional help may be provided in the form of money, goods, and services. Community care may be limited to one of these forms, indispensable in a given situation, whereas the institutional care is a complex character and embraces all the needs of the beneficiary (Koczur 2002: 152).

The decentralization of the social care system is not perfect as it is focused on the implementation of care functions at the expense of activation benefits and support for self-help initiatives. The experiences of the last 20 years have shown that the Polish social care system leads to the dependence of beneficiaries.[11] People entitled to any financial benefits become regular clients of social care centers. Instead of regaining independence, they gradually become dependent on aid funds.[12] Furthermore, social care benefits are often granted on the following basis: if there is money, it is given to the greatest possible number of people entitled to it in accordance with legal rules. That is why an accurate determination of social care recipients constitutes, undoubtedly, a huge challenge for the social care system.

Dependence on social benefits by subsequent generations will be higher without changes to the system. According to the social care system established after 1989, local self-governments were to help families and people encountering difficulties overcome difficult situations and get back onto the labor market. These experiences show that the established mechanisms did not work. Living month to month, from one benefit to another, is a way of life for more than 1.3 million families in Poland. The highest proportion of people using social care services (60% of all people receiving help) live in small towns and villages, mainly in the north and east of Poland. These are mainly poorly educated people. Unemployment is also the highest in these regions. The lack of workplaces, together with poor qualifications, leads to the dangerous phenomenon of long-standing dependence on the help guaranteed by the state. Over 80% of people who receive benefits have been receiving them for over ten years. Because of the guaranteed monthly benefits, beneficiaries often do not look for a job or legal employment. Among the beneficiaries of social care, who are working age, only every fifth person is employed and every third person is registered as unemployed. As many as 44% of them are professionally inactive (Topolewska 2010).

4.5. Social workers

Performing social work should be the fundamental task of social workers. Their aim is to improve the functioning of persons/families in the local community and at the same time improve their activity and independence. Thus, social work should be the fundamental form of help given to families using social care services. Monetary benefits should only complement it. In reality, it is the other way round. Help consists of paying money. The main task of social workers is limited to conducting community interviews which ascertain the income, family, and financial situation of a person applying for support. The decision concerning benefits is issued on the basis of a form consisting of a few pages. Social workers devote most of their time to filling in and updating these forms (Topolewska 2010).

Another problem is that (due to lack of funds) local self-governments do not observe the rule of one social worker per 2000 residents. When local self-governments want to save some money, they reduce expenditures related to the employment sector of social care. This, in turn, leads to the situation where one social worker takes care of too many families. He/she has to visit each family and confirm this fact by an entry in the files and that is why there is not enough time to deal with the problems of these families (Topolewska 2010).

Furthermore, social workers are not financially motivated. They belong to the lowest paid group of people working in local self-governments. Their salaries do not depend on the effects of their work (i.e. how many families they were able to help, to what extent these families are no longer dependent on benefits). This leads to the professional burnout of social workers, who then do not care about the improvement of situation of the families for whom they are responsible. Moreover, social workers are burdened with many additional tasks. Most local self-governments have handed over tasks related to the payment of family benefits and benefits from the Alimony Fund to the social care centers. Thus, instead of helping families, social workers have to collect money from debtors who do not pay alimony (Topolewska 2010).

In conclusion, the decentralization of tasks related to social care is necessary, but it is not enough if we want to improve the quality and effectiveness of public services (Skawińska and Dąbrowska 2009: 23–33). While fulfilling the tasks related to social care, units of local self-governments (especially the smallest of them) have to cope with many problems (e.g. the lack of funds and qualified staff, and having a great number of urgent tasks). The fact, that authorities are elected for definite terms is also a problem hindering strategic planning (Sierpowska 2007: 80–81).

5. Conclusions

Local self-governments will only be effective when they have access to the necessary human and financial resources to undertake the services they have been allocated. Meanwhile, experience with the decentralization of public health and social care services in Poland shows that the perception of those reforms has become worse. Why?

The key question in the debate over the decentralization reforms lies in the finances in line with other European countries. The Polish example illustrates that some duties of central government were transferred to local self-governments with no financial means to exercise them. Leaders of local authorities used to talk about "decentralisation of public duties without decentralization of public finance" or "decentralisation of budgetary problems" (Gilowska 2000: 31). Local governments complained that under-financed services were transferred the most willingly, and that central government was decentralizing problems rather than resources. It is necessary to emphasize that the principal trend of increasing the role of local self-governments in public services cannot be questioned. On the other hand, local authorities – although very unsatisfied with present financial regulations – are not very active in lobbying for more fiscal autonomy and extensive local tax-raising powers. Very often they are more interested in receiving more shares in central taxes that would give them financial security without political risks (Swianiewicz 2002).

As a comment, it is worth evoking the words of J. Regulski, who identifies half-hearted decentralization as one of the main problems of the CEE countries. "After the initial proclamation of decentralisation, it has become apparent that *de facto* deconcentration rather than decentralisation is taking place" (Nyiri 2000: 482–483). The signs that only deconcentration is taking place have included the creation by the central government of new institutions at the regional or local level (in the case of NHF), increased (or maintained) fiscal control of resources at the state level, and the delegation of new responsibilities to local self-governments without the allocation of the appropriate financial resources to fulfill them.

Last but not least, the problem in CEE countries relates to the risk of re-centralization. Young democratic traditions in Poland mean that if something functions badly, Polish's legislators instinctively incline toward centralizing solutions. We can observe the risk of re-centralization, particularly as regards the financial system of public healthcare services. Perhaps the best way for healthcare services will be, paradoxically, next to reform and transfer all responsibility for them to local self-governments.

Notes

1. In the context of considering, it is useful to define the term "decentralization" precisely. This is a term used with different meanings. It can refer to all forms of sharing or transferring authority or responsibility between the national government and any other level of government, including local or regional offices of the national government. An alternative use of the term is narrower, covering only the transfer of authority for certain functions from the national to local self-governments. A further look at decentralization shows that it is not simply one whole concept – rather it has different varieties. It includes political, administrative, fiscal, and market decentralization, although these can appear in different forms and combinations in a country's decentralization program (e.g. if we examine the aspects of decentralization, devolution will result in political decentralization; deconcentration implies a process of administrative decentralization; while privatization focuses on such devolved functions as deregulation or contracting out (CEU 2003; UNDP 2002: 4)).

2. The term social care was formerly official terminology from the time of the first Welfare Act of 1923 to the Welfare Act of 1990. Introduction of the new terminology relating to social welfare in the Welfare Act of 1990 was not only for political reason, to change everything that was in use during communist times (especially since social care had been introduced before the communist system was established), but also to change the whole philosophy of social services. The former domination of social worker and care over client and the consequent creation of the welfare dependency syndrome was to be transformed into a help for self-help approach, where social welfare was to be a system of temporary support, so that clients could regain the coping skills (Krzyszkowski 2004/2005).

3. Among all duties of the province, hospitals are the greatest burden. In some regions there are many of them and they are often much bigger than needed, thus causing huge expenditures. Closing them would worsen health protection and contribute to social worries.

4. Public spending is a sum of expenditures from the national budget, local self-government unit budgets and the National Health Fund.

5. Expenditure on health care by provinces encompass the expenditures of municipalities, urban districts, districts, and province.

6. The extent of poverty in Poland, measured on the basis of the minimum subsistence level, reached 34% in 1991, while the number of the unemployed exceeded 2.5 million.

7. The internal non-mandatory (or facultative) tasks are the tasks performed by the local self-government if such need arises and sufficient funds are available.

8. The tasks of the province governor include the assessment of the status and effectiveness of the social welfare benefits provided, establishing schemes for the implementation of tasks related to government administration and conducted by

local self-governments, supervision of the standards of the services provided by the appropriate organizations, issuing and revoking permits to run welfare centers, holding the register of welfare centers, coordinating actions in the refugee integration area, and coordinating the integration of people who have obtained refugee status in Poland.

9. Expenditure on social assistance by provinces encompass the expenditures of municipalities, urban districts, districts, and province.

10. Expenditure on other actions in the range of social policy by provinces encompass the expenditures of municipalities, urban districts, districts, and province.

11. Beneficiaries may apply for three kinds of benefits: permanent, temporary, and designated benefits. *Permanent benefits* are granted to: (1) a person of age running the household alone, totally unable to work due to age or disability, if his/her monthly income is lower than USD 154; (2) a person of age living with his/her family, totally unable to work due to age or disability, if his/her income (or income per capita in the family) is lower than monthly USD 105. The amount of the permanent benefit cannot be higher than USD 139 per month (in the case of a person running the household alone) and USD 110 (in the case of a person living with the family). The amount of permanent benefit cannot be lower than USD 10 per month. *Temporary benefits* are granted on account of long-term illness, disability or unemployment, to a person running the household alone, whose income is lower than USD 154 per month and to a family, whose monthly income per capita is lower than USD 105. The amount of benefit cannot be higher than USD 139 per month (in the case of a person running the household alone) and USD 105 (in the case of a person living with the family). The amount of the temporary benefit cannot be lower than USD 7 per month. The period for which the benefit is granted, is determined by the social care center. *Designated benefits* are granted to satisfy some particular needs (e.g. the purchase of food, medicines, fuel, clothes, articles of everyday use, financing minor repairs at home, treatment, and reimbursement of funeral costs). Designated benefits may be granted to uninsured persons, for covering the costs of health care (e.g. hospitalization). The amount of the benefit granted depends, on the one hand, on the financial situation of the applicant, and on the other hand, on the financial means of the social care authorities. Designated benefits may also be granted to a person/family, who suffers losses as a consequence of natural or ecological disaster or random incident (e.g. flood or fire).

12. Solutions have been developed in social care to prevent beneficiaries from becoming dependent on benefits for periods of many years. The first of these solutions, used when benefits are wasted, is the possibility of exchanging them for help in the form of goods and services. The social welfare contract is the second solution. It is a type of contract entered into to improve the person's independence in life, professional activity, and to counteract social exclusion. In the contract, the social care worker and the person applying for help undertake in writing to take joint action to overcome difficult life situations in which the beneficiary has found himself or herself. The beneficiary may undertake to find a job or participate in drug rehabilitation. The social care worker may for example assist the beneficiary when visiting the Employment Agency, or help in preparing the documents necessary to look for a job. If the beneficiary does not fulfill the provisions of the contract, or refuses to sign it, the municipality may decide not to grant the benefit, or to revoke it. In practice, social care centers take this mobilization measure

only rarely. In 2009, 71,000 contracts were signed, while more than 3.7 million members of families received benefits in the same period (Topolewska 2010).

References

Borowczyk-Przyborowska, M. (2000). "Problem korupcji w publicznej służbie zdrowia." In J. Pope (Ed.), *Rzetelność życia publicznego – podręcznik procedur antykorupcyjnych* (pp. 132–156). Warsaw: Transparency International – Poland.

Budżety jednostek samorządu terytorialnego w latach 2003–2008. (2009). Warsaw: Central Statistical Office.

CEU (2003). *International Fiscal Relations and Local Financial Management: Distance Learning Modules.* Budapest: CEU Summer University.

Cherka, M. (2004). "Decentralizacja – czy "reaktywacja" pojęcia jest groźna?" Studia Iuridica, No XLIII, Warsaw: Wydawnictwo Uniwersytetu Warszawskiego.

Finanse samorządów. Sprawozdania budżetowe 2003–2008, Ministry of Finance, http://www.mf.gov.pl/index.php?const=5&dzial=229&wysw=4&const=5, 20 November 2009.

Frąckiewicz-Wronka, A. (2002). "Samorządowa polityka ochrony zdrowia." In A. Frąckiewicz-Wronka (Ed.), *Samorządowa polityka społeczna.* Warsaw: Wydawnictwo Wyższej Szkoły Pedagogicznej TWP.

Gilowska, Z. (2000). "Regionalne uwarunkowania reform strukturalnych." *Studia Regionalne i Lokalne,* No. 2, Warsaw: Euroreg.

Girouard, N., Imai, Y. (Eds.) (2000). *The Health Care System in Poland.* Paris: OECD Economics Department Working Papers No. 257.

Halik, J. (2001). "Utworzenie powiatów a funkcjonowanie ochrony zdrowia na szczeblu lokalnym." In G. Gorzelak, B. Jałowiecki, M. Stec (Eds.), *Reforma terytorialnej organizacji kraju: dwa lata doświadczeń.* Warsaw: Scholar.

Jasiutowicz, K.P. (1999). "Health Care Reform in Poland 1999." http://www.republika.pl/kpjas/en/basic_body.html, 14 March 2003.

Kaczmarczyk, A. (2010). "Taniec z pacjentami." *Dziennik Polski.* 25 May 2010.

Koczur, W. (2002). "Zadania samorządu terytorialnego w zakresie pomocy społecznej." In A. Frąckiewicz-Wronka (Ed.), *Samorządowa polityka społeczna.* Warsaw: Wydawnictwo Wyższej Szkoły Pedagogicznej TWP.

Krzyszkowski, J. (2005). "Social services system in Poland." No. 10.

Kulesza, M. (2002). "Polskie doświadczenia w zarządzaniu reformą decentralizacyjną." *Samorząd Terytorialny,* No. 9. Briefing.

Malinowska-Misiąg, E., Misiąg W., Tomalak M., (2008). *Centralne finansowanie ochrony zdrowia i edukacji w Polsce. Analiza regionalna.* Warsaw: Zakład Wydawnictw Statystycznych.

Nyiri, Z. (2000). "Decentralisation and good governance: Hungary's ten-year experience." In J. Jabes (Ed.), *Ten Years of Transition: Prospects and Challenges for the Future of Public Administration.* Budapest: NISPAcee.

Polish Ministry of Finance (2009). *Sprawozdania z wykonania budżetu państwa za lata 2003–2008,* Ministry of Finance, http://www.mf.gov.pl/index.php?const=5&dzial=36&wysw=2, 14 November 2009.

Regulski, J. (2000). *Samorząd III Rzeczypospolitej. Koncepcje i realizacja.* Warsaw: PWN.

Rybka, I. (2006). "Diagnoza pomocy społecznej w Polsce w latach 1991–2006. Możliwości i bariery zastosowania instrumentów ekonomii społecznej w pomocy społecznej." *Ekonomia Społeczna. Teksty.* No. 23. Warsaw: Agencja Rozwoju Spółdzielczości.

Saltman, R.B., Figueras J. (1997). "European Health Care Reform: Analysis of Current Strategies", WHO Regional Publictions, European Series, No. 72.

Sierpowska I. (2007). *Prawo pomocy społecznej*. Warsaw: Wolters Kluwer Polska.

Skawińska, M., Dąbrowska A. (2009). "Pomocniczość wsparcie jako nowe kategorie polityki społecznej współczesnego państwa (na przykładzie Polski)." In M. Miłek, G. Wilk-Jakubowski (Eds.), *Stan realizacji polityki społecznej w XXI wieku*. Kielce: Wydawnictwo Stowarzyszenia Współpracy Polska-Wschód.

Staręga-Piasek, J., Golinowska S., Morecka Z. (2009). "Pomoc społeczna. Ocena działania instytucji." In B. Balcerzak-Paradowska, S. Golinowska (Eds.) *Polityka dochodowa, rodzinna i pomocy społecznej w zwalczaniu ubóstwa i wykluczenia społecznego. Tendencje i ocena skuteczności*. Warsaw: IPiSS.

Swianiewicz, P. (2002). "Reforming Local self-government in Poland: Top-Down and Bottom-Up Processes." Stuttgart: the Conference of IPSA's RC05 and the German Political Science Association *Reforming Local self-government: Closing the Gap Between Democracy and Efficiency*. http://www.uni-stuttgart.de/soz/avps/rlg/papers/Poland_Swianiewicz.pdf. 29 May 2003.

Topolewska, M. (2010). "Polski system pomocy społecznej prowadzi do uzależnienia od zasiłków." Dziennik Gazeta Prawna. 31 May 2010.

UNDP (2002). *Rebuilding Effective Government: Local-Level Initiatives in Transition*. Bratislava: UNDP.

8
Federalism in Health and Social Care in Austria

Birgit Trukeschitz, Ulrike Schneider, and Thomas Czypionka

1. Introduction

In Austria, health and social care are organized in separate systems, which themselves are fragmented and display substantial degrees of fiscal as well as parafiscal federalism. While a major part of healthcare funding is based on contributions to mandatory social health insurance, social care is not part of the country's Bismarckian tradition and remains essentially tax-funded. As a consequence, health care, on the one hand, and social care, on the other hand, are characterized by different degrees and flavors of federalism. The federal government as well as the country's provinces take responsibilities in health and social care. Self-governed social health insurance is a more visible player in health care, where its regional bodies determine financing and delivery in outpatient and rehabilitative care.

This plurality in systems and political responsibilities is striking given that Austria is a comparatively small country (8.4 million inhabitants) in Central Europe. Whereas one in five Austrians lives in the capital city of Vienna (1.7 million people), more than every second Austrian lives in smaller towns and villages with less than 10,000 residents. Notwithstanding its smallness, the country comprises nine provinces (*Länder*) as compared with 16 in Germany or 17 in Spain, which are ten and six times as large. Similarly remarkable, Austrian provinces differ greatly in population size (284,000–1.7 million) and population density. Overall, the size of the Austrian provinces only warrants a classification as NUTS 2 regions.

The political system of Austria's Second Republic (after World War II) is based on the constitution of 1945, which essentially reintroduces the constitution from 1920 to 1929. The Austrian federal constitution assigns legislative authority to both the Federal State and to each of the nine provinces. The provinces are further divided into districts (*Bezirke*) and statutory cities (*Statutarstädte*). Districts are subdivided into municipalities (*Gemeinden*). In a meta-analysis of various studies on the degree of autonomy, federalism and decentralization, Austria is unanimously classified as federal as well as decentralized (Keman 2000). Vetter and Soós (2008) assign Austria to the countries with the highest regional political power.

A high degree of federalism and decentralization appears counterintuitive in the case of a small country such as Austria. However, the ideal allocation of responsibilities between different levels of a federal system is not just a matter of overall population size but depends on a variety of factors such as the homogeneity of society, the characteristics of the issues, and the goods to be regulated and provided (Apolte 2008; Bussjäger 2008). Thus, the degree of federalism usually varies between different policy matters. This chapter will highlight Austria's institutional response to those specifics of health and social care services that need to be addressed by public policy.

In Austria, the degree of federalism is comparatively high in the field of health and social care. Competencies in this area are not only spread across provinces but are also divided up between regional entities of the parafiscal social health insurance. It is important to note that health and social care systems are organized in different ways. Even though there is overlap in some areas, integrating health and social care remains a challenge for policy design in Austria. Given the current divisions between both policy areas, we will discuss the federalist structures for health care and social care in separate sections.

In what follows, we will first introduce the legal and political foundations of Austrian federalism (Section 2). We will then move on to a more in-depth discussion of federalism in health care (Section 3) and social care (Section 4), where both sections will offer some historical background on how the current institutional setting has evolved over time and an overview of how competencies are allocated in health and social care. In Section 5, we discuss the performance of Austria's multilevel policy in health and social care in terms of quality, efficiency and equity. Section 6 offers a brief account of current policy initiatives that are likely to affect the institutional design of health and social care in this country. The chapter on the Austrian health and social care system concludes with a summary of findings and conclusions (Section 7).

2. Legal and political foundations of federalism in Austrian health and social care

The allocation of authority is a crucial point in understanding the problems that health and social care face today. The central passage of the Austrian constitution[1] governing the relationship between the governmental units comprises arts. 10–15, also stating that all matters not otherwise specified fall into the competency of the nine provinces (art. 15). Art. 10 defines all matters exclusively regulated by the federal level, and this is where most of the health-related matters are found. Art. 11 defines all areas where the federal level has legislative power, but the provinces rule implementation.

Art. 12 delineates all matters where the federal level is restricted to framework legislation, with the provinces enacting specific laws. Under this article, hospitals (with the exception of sanitary supervision) and social care facilities are the most notable areas in our context, resulting in nine different legal frameworks for institutional health and social care.

Art. 15a designates that for all cross-sectional matters (i.e. where competencies are split between levels) the federal state and the provinces can negotiate agreements to improve coordination. This instrument is well institutionalized. Approximately every five years, an agreement according to art. 15a is concluded and enacted by Parliament, the latest being the agreement for the period 2008–2013.[2] Moreover, 15a agreements may form the basis of discretionary policy design as in the case of long-term care. These 15a agreements also imply changes in many other laws, including the laws concerning fiscal relations.

A different constitutional law is called the *Finanz-Verfassungsgesetz* (F-VG) (constitutional law governing fiscal matters). It lays out the basic principles of taxation and fiscal relations between governmental units. The current and actual fiscal relations are enacted as the *Finanzausgleichsgesetz* (FAG) (law governing fiscal equalization). Remarkably, this is a simple federal law, seemingly assigning great power to the federal level. However, in political reality, it is enacted by the federal level only after meticulous negotiations between all levels of government for two reasons: first, to avoid legal action by other governmental units and second due to the strong political influence of governors (Matzinger and Pröll 2010).

Along with this system of fiscal federalism, there is also a system of parafiscal federalism. Governed by federal laws, social insurance is organized in self-governed bodies and has three branches: pension insurance, health insurance, and accident insurance. Social care is not part of the social insurance system. However, by various modes (see Section 4.3), interactions with the social insurance system can also be found for social care. Therefore, parafiscal federalism also affects the field of social care. The Federation of Austrian Social Insurance Institutions (*Hauptverband* (HVB)) has the role of coordinating the activities of all social insurance institutions.

3. The Austrian federal system in health care

3.1. Historical background[3]

In the pre-industrial era, the family or immediate community mainly provided social security in Austria. In the developing medieval towns, the emerging guilds as well as the miners' associations provided the first form of institutionalized social insurance. With respect to public health, the Court Sanitary Delegation (*Sanitäts-Hofdeputation*) was established under

Empress Maria Theresia (1717–1780) with sanitary commissions in all parts of the Empire. In 1852, district offices were opened. These institutions were later integrated in the federal and provincial administrations when Austria became a constitutional monarchy. The Imperial Sanitary Act of 1870, which is basically still in effect, established today's institutions of the Supreme and Provincial Health Boards (Richter 1970). The public health service is currently being reformed (Sax et al. 2009).

With industrialization, social insurance increasingly became the task of the factories and some of these established welfare funds. To overcome problems when switching jobs, in 1868 the first general fund for sickness and invalidity insurance for Viennese workers was established. In the following years, associations of regional funds were formed in Austria (1873) and for the whole Austrian–Hungarian Empire (1876). Following the example of the Bismarckian Reforms in Germany, a mandatory health and work accident insurance was finally introduced after much political debate in 1888, with contributions paid by employees (two-thirds) and employers (one-third). By the end of the First World War in 1918, there were already 600 sickness funds, with various umbrella organizations. In the following years, a strong tendency of concentration can be observed, and by 1925, there were 186 funds left. During the German reign in Austria, self-government of social insurance was abolished. It was reintroduced in 1947 (Social Insurance Transition Act, *Sozialversicherungsüberleitungsgesetz*). This law, together with the new General Social Security Act of 1956 (*Allgemeines Sozialversicherungsgesetz* (ASVG)), laid out the basic principles underlying today's social insurance. Accordingly, in 1948, the Federal Association of Austrian Social Security Institutions (*Hauptverband der Österreichischen Sozialversicherungsträger* (HVB)) was founded, establishing a single umbrella organization for the three branches of social security in Austria: pension, work accident and health insurance (see Section 3.3). The ASVG unified all three branches for all blue- and white-collar workers, but not for the self-employed, farmers and civil servants. For these groups, proprietary laws were enacted during the 1960s, all with the ASVG as a kind of guideline.

The most important event for today's division of power concerning health care is the constitutional debate after World War II. Whereas some politicians advocated a unitary state, others favored a federal state, resulting in a kind of compromise in 1945, which recreated the constitution of 1929, with health care being a cross-sectional matter between the governmental units, thus separating responsibility for hospitals and their financing from social health insurance (SHI). In the following years, hospital financing had to be borne by and pooled together from SHI and all governmental units. In 1997, the largest hospital financing reform came into effect. The federal hospital fund was split into nine provincial hospital funds in political exchange for the introduction of a diagnostic related group (DRG)-system, replacing the previous payment system according to length of stay only. This step also meant that SHI would henceforth contribute only a lump-sum payment valorized according to revenue growth, but effectively losing all say in hospital matters.

The healthcare reform of 2005 implemented an attempt for more coordination of care through the provincial health platforms, a body with representatives from SHI and all relevant governmental units (see Section 3.4). The possibility to found health funds by more than one province has never been used. A common quality initiative on the federal level (*Gesundheitsqualitätsgesetz*), is effectively mostly dead law due to resistance from various groups. The reform also revived the framework planning of healthcare provision (*Österreichischer Strukturplan Gesundheit* (ÖSG)), but only its latest revision in November 2010 managed to include the outpatient sector as well.

3.2. Fiscal federalism in health care

3.2.1. Federal level

At the federal level, the main players are Parliament and the Ministry of Health (MoH). In changing the regulatory framework of health care, it is usually the MoH that, after negotiations with all stakeholders, submits bills for new legislation to Parliament. However, the MoH lacks direct control over health care. Whereas in inpatient care, the provinces have considerable discretionary power, the self-governed social health insurance determines financing and healthcare delivery in outpatient and rehabilitative care. Nevertheless, legislation in this latter area is very detailed, extending also to the contribution rates and obligations on how to contract with healthcare providers, effectively limiting the discretionary power of SHI.

In its tasks, the MoH is supported by several other bodies. The Supreme Health Board[4] (*Oberster Sanitätsrat*) consisting of 39 members appointed by the minister of health for three years mostly from all medical professions advises the minister in matters of state-of-the-art medicine and public health. The Health Austria Company (*Gesundheit Österreich GmbH* (GÖG)) has three business units. One of these business units, the Austrian Federal Institute for Health (*Österreichisches Bundesinstitut für das Gesundheitswesen* (ÖBIG)), is the MoH's applied research and planning institute. It also prepares the Austrian Structural Plan for Health (*Österreichischer Strukturplan Gesundheit* (ÖSG)), which is an instrument for capacity planning in health care. Through the second business unit, the Fund for a Healthy Austria (*Fonds Gesundes Österreich* (FGÖ)), projects in public health are sponsored. The youngest business unit, the Austrian Federal Institute for Quality in Healthcare (*Bundesinstitut für Qualität im Gesundheitswesen* (BIGQ)) was founded in 2007 and is tasked with improving quality assurance and reporting in Austrian health care.

The Federal Health Agency (*Bundesgesundheitsagentur* (BGA)) holds the federal level's funds for hospital financing and some minor tasks (e.g. coordination of transplantation). Its executive body is the Federal Health Commission (*Bundesgesundheitskommission* (BGK)), which at the same time is the supreme board for coordination and decision-making in health care in Austria. It consists of seven representatives from the MoH, one from each of the nine provinces, one each from the associations of municipalities and the cities, six from SHI, and one from the Chamber of Physicians (*Ärztekammer*), the patient ombudsmen and the order hospitals, and some non-voting members. Its chair is the minister of health.

Most activities concerning strategy and operative business in health care, however, are not administered by the MoH or one of its agencies, but by the self-governed SHI, which is explained in Section 3.3. The MoH acts only as a supervisory body for SHI and sets the regulatory framework by changing SHI-legislation through Parliament.

3.2.2. Provinces

As previously mentioned, the provinces have considerable political power in Austria. Each provincial government has a health department, through which it exerts its power as supreme health authority in the province, which is also responsible for public health activities. Another responsibility is the regulation of the medical professions' job market and training facilities (both with the exception of physicians). The department is supported by the provincial health board (*Landessanitätsrat*).

The most relevant political field is hospital care. In every province, the provincial parliament passes legislation on hospital organization and financing, following the framework legislation by the federal level. The provinces hold the right to regulate access to the hospital market (extending due to the legal definition of "hospital" to outpatient clinics as well, although they are mostly paid by SHI) and also run most of Austrian acute-care hospitals, either directly or through publicly owned companies.

With the hospital financing reform of 1997, hospital financing was brought to the provincial level in "exchange" for provinces' approval of the introduction of a DRG-like reimbursement system. With the healthcare reform of 2005, the provincial funds for hospital financing were enhanced and renamed to provincial health funds (*Landesgesundheitsfonds*). Their administrative body is the health platform (*Gesundheitsplattform*), which consists of representatives from the province, the federal level, SHI, the association of Austrian cities and the association of Austrian municipalities and the Austrian Chamber of Physicians. As the composition of the health platform is subject to provincial law, there can be additional stakeholders involved as well. Most notably, the Viennese health platform also comprises representatives of the political parties, whereas only Burgenland and Upper Austria also include representatives from the association of registered nurses.

The health platform in each province is supposed to discuss all matters related to the health system in the province. In sharp contrast to this intention, the province alone automatically has the majority of votes concerning hospital matters, whereas SHI automatically has the majority on matters of outpatient care. Some matters concerning both, inpatient and outpatient care, have to be decided upon unanimously by both SHI and the province, the most important of which is the Reform Pool. The Reform Pool is an attempt to improve integration of care at the interface of inpatient and outpatient care by granting funds to related projects. Due to flaws in its incentive mechanism, however, it has not achieved this goal (Czypionka and Röhrling 2009).

3.2.3. Districts and municipalities

The district level in Austria (99 including independent cities) has no elected but only a professional administration. Notwithstanding, it plays an important role in the public health service. In the district health office, the district medical officer is responsible for sanitary matters and sanitary supervision of the hospitals[5] located in the district.

The municipalities have an elected administration with an appointed municipal health officer. A few sanitary matters are located on this level (mainly sanitary inspections). Because municipalities are rather small in Austria (there are 2357 of them), they tend to cooperate in this matter, forming joint health districts. The municipalities and very few districts act as owners of hospitals as well. At the same time, the municipalities are involved in hospital financing.

3.3. Parafiscal federalism in health care

Health insurance is mandatory in one of the 19 sickness funds on the grounds of occupation (and in some cases also region). Therefore, different social insurance bodies are responsible for different parts of the population (with a coverage of nearly 99%), and the three branches of social security (pension, health and work accident insurance) are integrated to varying degrees. Table 8.1 provides an overview of the institutions as well as the relevant laws.

Sickness funds have discretionary power over the use of their respective contributions, subject to legal requirements, and their bodies are elected by employers and employees. The nine most important sickness funds (76.5% of all directly insured, HVB, 2010) are the regional sickness funds, which operate on the level of the nine provinces. Hence, parafiscal federalism clearly reinforces regional variation in health care that is already implied by fiscal federalism.

For most employees, health insurance is provided by these regional sickness funds (*Gebietskrankenkassen* (GKKs)). Six very large companies provide health insurance through company health insurance funds

Table 8.1 Matrix of social security branches, institutions, and laws

Federation of Austrian social insurance institutions (HVB)			
Accident insurance	Health insurance	Pension insurance	Law
General work accident insurance institution (AUVA)	9 Regional health insurance funds (GKKs) 6 Company health insurance funds (BKKs)	Pension insurance institution (PVA) for wage and salary earners	ASVG
		Insurance institution for the self-employed (SVA)	GSVG
	Insurance institution for railways and mining (VAEB)		ASVG
	Insurance institution for farmers (SVB)		BSVG
Insurance institution for public sector employees (BVA)			B-KUVG
		Pension insurance institution for notaries	NVG

Source: IHS HealthEcon (2011).

(*Betriebskrankenkassen* (BKKs)). The railway and mining workers have their own insurance institution (*Versicherungsanstalt für Eisenbahnen und Bergbau* (VAEB)). All these institutions are based on the General Social Security Act (*Allgemeines Sozialversicherungsgesetz* (ASVG)), which therefore is relevant for approximately 77% of the population.

Farmers have their own social insurance institution under the Farmers' Social Security Act (*Bauern-Sozialversicherungsgesetz* (BSVG)) covering approximately 4.5% of the population (and declining). All other self-employed[6] must be insured with their insurance institution (*Sozialversicherungsanstalt der Gewerblichen Wirtschaft* (SVA)) on the basis of the Social Security Act for the Self-Employed (*Gewerbliches Sozialversicherungsgesetz* (GSVG)), thus covering 7% of the population.

Civil servants are in general insured by the *Versicherungsanstalt der Beamten* (BVA) (8.5% of the population). However, the respective law, the Act on Civil Servants' Health and Accident Insurance (*Beamten-Kranken- und Unfallversicherungsgesetz* (B-KUVG)), allows for public bodies to have their own health insurance institutions, called health welfare institutions (*Krankenfürsorgeanstalten* (KFAs)), currently 17 of them being in existence covering roughly 200,000 people.

The Federation of Austrian Social Insurance Institutions (*Hauptverband der Österreichischen Sozialversicherungsträger* (HVB)) is the umbrella organization of social security in Austria. For historical reasons, however, the KFAs are not part of the HVB.

The relation between the social insurance institutions and the HVB is complicated with the chairpersons and vice-chairpersons of the aforementioned social security institutions[7] and three representatives of retirees form the Conference of Social Security Institutions (*Trägerkonferenz*), the supreme body in the HVB. It sets the framework for the HVB, monitors its financial performance, issues or approves guidelines, and has to approve any agreements of the HVB. The Conference also appoints the board of the HVB, with 15 members (3 without voting rights). Of the 12 members with voting rights, 10 have to be from social security institutions. Of these, 5 are from the Austrian Chamber of Labour (*Bundesarbeitskammer* (AK)) and 5 from the Austrian Chamber of Commerce (*Wirtschaftskammer Österreich* (WKO)). One member is appointed by the Federation of Trade Unions (*Österreichischer Gewerkschaftsbund* (ÖGB)) and 1 from the Presidents' Conference of the Austrian Chamber of Agriculture[8] (*Präsidentenkonferenz der Landwirtschaftskammern*).

The chairman of the Board of the HVB is sometimes called its president. The Board of the HVB is responsible for the management of the HVB. However, consisting mainly of political functionaries, it appoints a chief executive director and three deputies as the management team of the HVB. We shall discuss the implications of this rather complex system in Section 5.2.

SHI is responsible for all outpatient care (by physicians, dentists, and other medical personnel), all rehabilitative care, the provision of pharmaceuticals, and therapeutic aids (through contracts with pharmacies and other providers). Inpatient acute care and outpatient wards of hospitals, however, are funded by SHI and all other governmental units together, constituting one of the major problems in Austrian health care.

3.4. Hospital organization and financing as a cross-sectional matter

As previously mentioned, responsibilities for hospitals are regulated in art. 12 of the constitution; therefore, the provinces pass hospital legislation according to the federal framework legislation, and they are responsible for administrative matters with the exception of sanitary supervision. According to the definition of the federal act on hospitals and health facilities (*Kranken- und Kuranstaltengesetz* (KaKuG)), there are some 1000 hospitals (BMG 2008). However, only 269 have beds with the rest actually being outpatient clinics. Of these, 132 are called fund-hospitals[9] (*Fondskrankenanstalten*), which are publicly funded acute-care hospitals (BMG 2008) and represent 75.9% of all hospital beds. Today, most provinces[10] have founded hospital operating companies as legal entities of private law, but maintain the shares directly or indirectly. Some hospitals remain in the ownership of municipalities or districts. However, their number is declining due to increased financial pressure with the provinces taking over ownership.

Hospital financing is a very complicated matter in Austria and a concise discussion would exceed the scope of this chapter.[11] Basically, the federal government, the provinces, the municipalities, and SHI dedicate shares of their VAT revenue and certain lump-sum payments to being distributed among the provincial health funds according to a number of (mostly negotiated, some population based) allocation tables (currently five). Some health funds receive advance payments previous to this distribution, to reflect certain differences like guest patients from other provinces. This system leads to an initial share of about three-quarters of SHI in the financing of provincial health funds. However, on the provincial level, some provinces contribute additional funds to their health fund according to provincial legislation. Most of the health funds money is then spent on inpatient and outpatient hospital care. Whereas the funds for inpatient care are divided up by the number of DRG-points provided by the hospitals each year, the outpatient departments in most provinces receive only a global payment. However, the Austrian DRG variant LKF was never designed to reflect all current costs incurred. So each hospital is left with costs initially uncovered, called *"Betriebsabgang"* (BAG). This BAG is partly or fully covered by the province and the municipalities according to (greatly varying) provincial legislation (*Betriebsabgangsdeckung*). The rest has to be borne by the respective hospital company, which in most cases is owned by the province anyway, but sometimes by NPOs like the religious orders, requiring them to negotiate for additional funds with the governor of the province.

4. The Austrian federal system in social care

4.1. Historical background

From a historic point of view, the year 1993 marked an important change in Austria's benefit system for people in need of care. Prior to 1993, various types of legislation mainly at the provincial level regulated benefits and services targeted to people in need of care or support. In addition, cash benefits were granted from social insurance bodies, namely the social pension insurance and the social accident insurance systems. The social insurance provided a cash benefit for pensioners in need of care (*Hilflosenzuschuss*). Although the social insurance body administered this benefit, it was covered by the federal budget. Thus, with regard to this benefit, the insurance principle had receded in importance over the years (Gruber and Pallinger 1994). Not only the refunding mode between the social insurance body and the federal budget, but also huge differences in both eligibility criteria and level of provincial cash benefits resulted in policy action to consolidate responsibilities in terms of legislation and funding in the 1980s.

The 1993 legislation on social care is regarded as a major step toward reducing the fragmentation and differentiation in benefits and support across Austria. The "15a agreement" between the federal state and its provinces on common measures for people in need of care can be regarded as the first framework regulation for a comprehensive social care system. It clarifies the responsibilities of the federal state and the provinces for social care and at least acknowledges the need for support of informal caregivers, the main actors in care for dependent (elderly) people. Interestingly, up to date[12] both regulatory and financial responsibilities for the care allowance are split between the federal state and its provinces. By contrast, social care service provision remained a sole responsibility of provinces and is mainly regulated by provincial social assistance laws and equivalent legislation (for details see Section 4.2).

In Austria, social care has been widely separated from health care, with some exceptions discussed in Section 4.3. Medical home care (*Medizinische Hauskrankenpflege*) was introduced as a social health insurance benefit on a voluntary basis in 1977. Since 1992 people have been entitled to medical home care services paid for by social health insurance. This improvement was motivated by the need to reduce hospital beds. Taken together, the ways of organizing and funding the post 1993 social care policy in Austria appear to be path-dependent.

Austria's system supporting people in need of social care has always stressed subsidiarity and hence the role of families, nonprofits, and the immediate community in providing help.[13] Even after the 1993 reforms, families still play an important role, as almost 70–80% of dependent older persons rely on help provided by spouses and children. The public social care system was designed to complement these efforts. In recent years, especially since the early 2000s benefits for informal caregivers have been successively introduced on both the federal and the provincial level (Schneider and Trukeschitz 2008; Trukeschitz and Schneider 2011). Major aims and elements of today's public social care system will now be presented in more detail in the following two sections.

4.2. Fiscal federalism in social care

The Austrian federal constitution (see Section 2) assigns public responsibilities in social care to both the federal state and to each of the nine provinces. It states that framework legislation pertaining to social welfare and nursing homes is a responsibility of the federal state, whereas defining measures within the broader framework, implementing and executing laws is the business of the provinces (art. 12 B-VG). The constitution's art. 15a allows both government levels to negotiate agreements in areas where their competences overlap. Two such "15a agreements" exist, which clarify the division of tasks, financing responsibilities and the inter-governmental clearing of payments in the area of social care (Trukeschitz 2010: 18; Trukeschitz and Schneider 2011).

Both governmental levels, the federal state and the nine provinces, are responsible for regulation and public funding of social care for dependent people. Beyond the level of the provinces (*Länder*), districts (*Bezirkshauptmannschaften*), communities (*Gemeinden*), and other public bodies such as public associations of welfare agencies (*Sozialhilfeverbände*) are relevant public social care actors but do not have any legislative power in Austria. Communities contribute financially to social care service provision.

The aim of the public social care system is to assure an adequate supply of social care services in terms of quantity, quality, choice, and geographical coverage. Second, it should secure access to social care services, which at present time is attempted by granting universal and selective financial support to people in need of social care. Third, and contrary to health care, public support not only for people in need but also for their caring relatives is perceived as an important element of the social care system.

The Austrian social care system comprises financial benefits (care allowances, cash benefits supporting 24-hour care, tax exceptions) and social care services. Responsibilities for regulating, providing and funding vary across these different types of benefits. Responsibilities for benefits under the social care allowance and 24-hour standby care program and are divided between the federal state and its provinces, whereas provinces have the full responsibility for social care services.

Figure 8.1 summarizes major institutional actors and respective funding flows in the Austrian federalist social care system[14]; explanations in Sections 4.2 and 4.3 are linked to the respective parts of this figure. As was the case in health care, two types of federalism also shape the picture of social care: funding flows from different government levels system and entities (fiscal federalism) characterize the federalist structure of the Austrian social care. In Section 4.2, we explain structure and functioning of the federalist system in social care by discussing fiscal federalism. Parafiscal federalism will be addressed in Section 4.3.

Given the shared legislative responsibilities for social care allowances, eligibility criteria and benefit levels are laid down in ten legal acts (namely one federal act and one for each of the nine provinces). People in approved need of at least 60 hours of care[15] per month for an expected period of at least six months are eligible for the social care allowance, irrespective of their income or assets. The lump-sum cash benefit is graded into seven levels of care dependency ranging from EUR 154.20 to EUR 1.655,80 per month. Although both levels of government agreed on harmonizing their respective entitlement laws, eligibility criteria, need assessment and levels of care allowances have all differed slightly between the federal and the provincial benefit programs as well as across provinces over the past two decades (for further details, see Rechnungshof 2010a; Trukeschitz and Schneider 2011).

Whether federal or provincial regulation applies relates partly to pension eligibility and (for a minority of beneficiaries) on the causality behind care

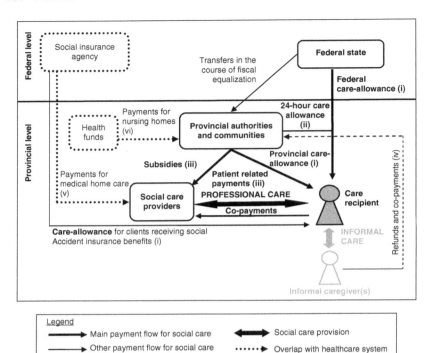

Figure 8.1 Institutional design and funding flows in Austrian social care
Source: Own display based on BMASK (2010).

dependency. The federal state covers social care allowance expenditures for care dependent pensioners (and for people receiving related benefits that are based on federal statutory provisions), the social accident insurance bears the costs for federal care allowance for people who are in need of care due to an accident at work or due to an occupational disease, and the provinces agreed to cover cash benefits for the remaining groups of people in need of long-term care.

As a consequence, there is no need for a separate financial clearing mechanism. Each governmental level bears the cost of their cash benefit and the social accident insurance pays for their clients' care allowances as regulated by the federal act. The majority of care allowance recipients are covered by the federal act. In 2008 the federal state faced expenditures of approximately 85% of all social care allowance recipients; the aggregated cost of federal care allowance for the social accident insurance is of minor importance. The expenditures for the remaining 15% of care allowance recipients are paid for by the provinces (see Figure 8.1 – (i) and Table 8.2). As noted in Section 4.1, in 2012 a single care-allowance scheme will be implemented that is regulated

Table 8.2 Overview of the division of legislative and financial responsibilities in social care between the federal state and its provinces in Austria (2011)

Type of benefit	Benefit	Regulation	Public financial responsibilities	
Cash benefit	Social care allowance	1993–2011: F; P; 2012–2014: F	F: 85%	P: 15%
	Subsidy for 24-hour care	F, P	F: 60%	P: 40%
Tax expenditures		F	Forgone revenues, F: 100%	
Care services	Social care services	(F), P	P: 100%	

Note: F: federal state, P: provinces
Source: Own illustration.

and administered by the federal state only. Provinces will still contribute to funding the care allowance system.

Twenty-four hour care is a care arrangement where the caregiver (either employed by the dependent person or self-employed) resides in the dependent person's private household. The level of public financial support for this type of care (*Förderung der "24-Stunden-Betreuung"*) depends on the level of care allowance, the net income of the care client, and the type of engagement (for details, see Trukeschitz and Schneider 2011).

From the legislative point of view, federal laws needed to be amended to enable this specific form of live-in caregiving.[16] Eligibility criteria for the financial support of 24-hour care are laid down at both the federal level (Federal Act governing social care benefits) and currently in four of the nine provincial laws on social care allowance (namely Vorarlberg, Tyrol, Lower Austria, and Carinthia). Provincial laws may stipulate that eligibility criteria are to be specified by provincial guidelines (e.g. in Vorarlberg and Lower Austria).

Contrary to the universal social care allowance where responsibilities between the federal state and its provinces are divided by characteristics of the target group of the benefit, the federal state and the provinces agreed on a 60:40 division of total expenditures for the financial support of 24-hour care (see Figure 8.1 – (ii) and Table 8.2).

These main social care-related cash benefits of the Austrian social care system are anchored at both the federal and provincial governmental levels. In addition to direct spending, the federal state offers tax deductions for care-dependent people. Care related expenditures, such as costs of professional care services or housekeeping is acknowledged as a kind of "extraordinary financial burden" (*außergewöhnliche Belastungen*) and reduce taxes to be paid (see Table 8.2).

When it comes to social care service provision, legislative responsibilities exclusively lie with the provinces. Again, the agreement based on art. 15a of the Austrian constitution binds the provinces to assess an area-wide social care service provision, to set minimum standards for social care services, and to issue regulations for the supervision of care service provision (for further details, see Trukeschitz 2010: 18). The provinces are particularly responsible for ensuring that all offers for home care, semi-institutional, and institutional services are coordinated, and that information and counseling for the same is guaranteed.

Social care services are regulated by the provincial laws on social assistance and respective laws in provinces where social assistance has been replaced by new forms of basic social security (e.g. the Carinthian Law on Guaranteed Minimum Standards and the Tyrolean Law on Basic Benefit Provision). Some provinces have issued additional laws regulating specific types of long-term care services, especially institutional care. Ordinances (*Verordnungen*) and guidelines (*Richtlinien*) for home care and residential services substantiate and interpret these laws on the provincial level.

With regard to quality criteria of social care services, the federal state interfered. The "15a-agreement" between the federal state and its provinces introduced in 1993 defines some basic characteristics of domiciliary and residential social care services labeled as "minimum standards" and "quality criteria". These characteristics are specified by provincial laws and/or derived regulation, like ordinances and guidelines (for further information on quality regulation as part of the legal framework for social care, see Trukeschitz 2010).

Provinces are not required to provide social care services themselves. Social care services can also be offered by other organizations suitable to the needs of dependent people, according to the principles of convenience as well as cost-effectiveness. From an institutional point of view, social care services are provided by public and private (for-profit and nonprofit) organizations in Austria. For example, in 2008 about 48% of all residential care and nursing homes were run by public bodies and 52% by private (for-profit and nonprofit) organizations. Taking into account the number of beds available in these homes, 49% of beds are offered by public and 51% by private providers.[17]

Provinces subsidize social care service costs of care-dependent people and contribute to covering the building costs of care homes (for details, see Trukeschitz and Schneider 2011) (see Figure 8.1 – (iii)). For domiciliary care, the substitute payment per hour of care worker activity can be regarded as the dominant public funding arrangement in Austria. The level of public funding usually depends on the care client's income; some provinces also take the level of care allowance into account. For institutional care, provincial authorities provide subsidies for authorized providers to cover parts of the building costs of private care homes. Residents living in an authorized care home can get public financial support if their income/asset is not sufficient to pay the monthly fees. The financial means come from the social assistance system of the provinces as lender of last resort. Provincial authorities have the right to reclaim refunds from the residents as soon as their financial situation improves or – which occurs more frequently – from their relatives, heirs, and donees (Trukeschitz and Schneider 2011) (see Figure 8.1 – (iv)).

4.3. Parafiscal federalism in social care

Although the federal state and the nine provinces are the major players with legislative power in social care, parafiscal authorities, mainly the social insurance agency, represent a supporting pillar of the social care system in Austria. To begin with, a significant share of care allowances on the federal level as well as on the level of provinces is being administered and disbursed by social insurance bodies, notably by the pension insurance. Second, parafiscal entities finance federal care allowance for care-dependent people who had a work accident or suffer from an occupational disease.[18] Third, contrary to the main social care services, medical home care (MHC) (*Medizinische Hauskrankenpflege*) is not part of the social care service system organized by the provinces. It is rooted in the General Social Security Act (§ 151) (*Allgemeines Sozialversicherungsgesetz* (ASVG)).

Medical home care (treatments like giving injections, artificial feeding, decubitus care) is paid by the health branch of the social insurance agency and therefore represents the link to the health insurance system (see Figure 8.1 – (v)). It covers time-limited nursing by educated health and nursing staff at home, if the hospitalization period can thereby be shortened or avoided altogether. MHC may be carried out only under medical supervision, in principle for a maximum period of four weeks. For care beyond this period of time, medical approval by the chief physician and controlling medical authority of the insurance body is required.

Other examples for the overlap of health and social care are payments by the provincial health funds to nursing homes. Health funds, founded to plan, govern, and finance health care at the local level, contribute to the building of nursing homes or support operating nursing homes (see Figure 8.1 – (vi)).

5. Critical appraisal of federalism in health and social care in Austria

In this section we will explore the impact of federalism on the performance of Austria's health and social care systems in terms of quality, efficiency, and equity. This endeavor presents a challenging task, given the lack of empirical studies investigating this issue. Thus, our analysis will be broadbrush. Our approach is twofold. We will start with a brief reflection of the theory and concepts discussed in Section 5.1. More specifically, we will evaluate the degree of federalism against two normative theories in public finance and assess the preconditions and degree of interjurisdictional competition. In addition, we will define our assessment tools for quality, efficiency, and equity and reflect on the causal relationships between these dimensions of performance, on the one hand, and federalism, on the other hand. In sections 5.2 and 5.3 we will examine the impact of federalism on the three dimensions quality, efficiency, and equity, offering empirical illustrations for the Austrian healthcare and social care settings.

5.1. Criteria for assessing the impact of federalism on system performance

5.1.1. Economics of federalism: Two approaches

To assess the impact of the federal structure in health and social care, we can make use of Oates' theory of fiscal federalism (Oates and Schwab 1991), Wicksell's theory of institutional congruency (Wicksell 2010 [1896]), and theories of interjurisdictional competition, particularly, Tiebout's theory (1956) and the theory on yardstick competition (Salmon 1987; Besley and Case 1995).

Oates' theory basically states that governmental units for a certain public task should be of a size that makes them homogenous within and heterogeneous compared to other units with respect to preferences. Public services provided within such a unit must have non-increasing returns to scale, and external effects should be minimal. Wicksell's institutional congruency comprises three different aspects originating from the field of political economy. Its first aspect is the democratic principle. It states that the collective users of public services should be the electorate for the relevant decision-makers. The connexity principle states that the political body responsible for a task should also be responsible for financing it. Finally, the principle of fiscal equivalence states that the population benefiting from public services should be the one paying for it. Last but not least, economic theories also address modes and effects of interjurisdictional competition. According to Tiebout (1956), interjurisdictional competition is mobility driven. People move to a province when the public service/tax package seems attractive to them. By contrast, yardstick competition is driven by voice. Residents (re-)elect a party if they are happy with both the service/tax packages provided and the tasks fulfilled.

5.1.2. Federalism and quality in the provision of health and social care

The most well-known definition of quality is being "the degree to which a set of inherent characteristics fulfills requirements" (ISO-9000). However, this basic definition is of little use in the assessment of quality on the macro level. For this end, the OECD has compared system-wide approaches and identified the most common dimensions used in assessing healthcare quality: effectiveness, patient-centeredness, accessibility, equity, efficiency, and safety (Kelley and Hurst 2006). As we will discuss efficiency and safety separately, we can therefore reduce our definition of quality to a narrower sense. Patient-centeredness is similar to responsiveness, meaning that the system adapts to the preferences and (subjective) needs of its patients or clients. By contrast, effectiveness is more technical, meaning how well and fast the objective or physical needs of a patient/client are addressed. This, however, requires defined standards. Accessibility is the most commonly used dimension of system-wide quality, with waiting times as a proxy.

Federalism can affect these three aspects of quality in various ways, and for good or bad. Responsiveness is said to improve due to the subsidiarity principle. However, this is only required if there is no market, where responsiveness is expected anyway. Accessibility can sometimes vary between provinces, thus raising concerns about equal access. Effectiveness can either be strengthened by closer proximity to patient/client, or weakened because the decentralized actors cannot create an evidence base of good care themselves (which probably has to be provided centrally).

5.1.3. Federalism and efficiency in the provision of health and social care

Turning to efficiency as a second dimension of performance, we look at whether a better level of service provision could be reached with the same amount of funding or whether a given standard or level of service provision is achieved at minimal cost. Our focus is hence on productive or cost efficiency, and of course on scale efficiency. First and foremost, Oates and Schwab (1991) derive that public services must be provided at a level of government or by a political district such that production displays non-increasing returns to scale. As long as there are increasing returns to scale, it makes sense to reallocate the powers to govern and the provision to the next level of government (or to enlarge political districts). In health care and social care, the optimal catchment areas of hospitals, or efficient operating distances in mobile services depend on population size and density. Yet, the size of provinces also has been mentioned above, with regard to homogeneity or heterogeneity of preferences. It is conceivable that serving a population with homogeneous preferences and needs is less costly from a production point of view than providing services to a more diverse population.

From a dynamic perspective, another question to be addressed is whether the Austrian flavor of federalism in health and social care displays adaptive capacities and is conducive to innovation. This question brings us back to the concept of interjurisdictional competition. The general expectation in the theoretical literature is that competition sets incentives for an improvement of services (and hence quality) and processes (reducing the cost per service unit). Whether or not this is the case in the Austrian system hinges upon the degree of competition, which again is related to the number and size of competitors (provinces and/or providers of health and social care services), transparency, and mobility.

5.1.4. Federalism and equity in the provision of health and social care

Our third dimension of performance is equity, which can be defined as a service provision, and/or funding that is considered socially just. This dimension is particularly hard to grasp theoretically, let alone empirically. There are different concepts of justice or equity reaching from egalitarianism (from which one could derive a claim for uniform access to services or uniform standards in all parts of Austria) to needs-based or desert-based concepts. The WHO framework (WHO 2008) for healthcare system performance distinguishes between equity in financing and equity in utilization. The WHO uses the common measures of income distribution and distribution of cares expenditures or tax/SHI contributions relative to income. Similar correlations can be calculated for the income-dependence of the use of care services. The WHO also provides a normative framework, being of the (egalitarian) opinion that care should be provided independently of income and only based on need. Therefore, equity in financing is best represented by the ability-to-pay principle, whereas utilization should be strictly needs based. In other words, pooling is required across income groups and risk groups.

The impact of federalism on equity in financing is related to fiscal equivalence. If, for example, health care is mainly the task of a small government unit, the pool of income and risks might be too small, requiring some form of financial equalization. However, in such a case the principle of fiscal equivalence will be violated. Also, there is an intrinsic conflict between the democratic principle and equity, because the normative approach of equal access and financing is typically one decided upon behind the "veil of ignorance". It is quite reasonable to assume that "having stepped out from behind", people will not vote for policies of equity.

5.2. Federalism and the performance of the Austrian healthcare system

When applying our public finance approaches to the Austrian healthcare system, we would expect rather large governmental units, as the Austrian population is quite homogenous, with only one language and only minor differences in cultural respects. Yet, Austrian provinces are quite numerous and vary considerably in size. Still, each of these provinces has legislative power in health care.

As regards Oates' second aspect, returns to scale, it can be questioned whether the critical size for efficient provision of a variety of hospital services can be met. In fact, the resulting large number of small hospitals is seen as one of the major fields of potential efficiency gains (Czypionka et al.

2008; Rechnungshof 2010b). Provinces like Vorarlberg (370,000 citizens) or the Burgenland (285,000 citizens) are simply too small to provide higher-tier health care. As a consequence, the third Oatesian aspect, minimal external effects, can also be seen as violated. Health care is not a strictly local public service when coming to more complex interventions. The share of guest patients from other provinces is considerable in some provinces as shown in Figure 8.2. In contrast to this, the provinces have not used the possibility provided by the 2005 healthcare reform to form overarching health funds.

Furthermore, a certain degree of competition between providers seems reasonable to improve quality and efficiency in elective interventions. It is in fact the case that choice in Austrian health care is not very limited. Several aspects, however, do sharply impede free and informed choice. First, there is little information on quality and efficiency made available in Austria, in outpatient as well as in inpatient care. Second, most hospitals are run (directly or indirectly) by the provinces. Substantial (non-price) competition is limited to some regions like Vienna or Upper Austria.

Therefore, medical services for a "guest patient" in another province are not reimbursed, at least not at the time of service consumption. Guest patients are only taken into account when negotiating the distribution of tax and SHI contributions between the provincial health funds for the *next* five years.

Against the background of patient migration between provinces, all aspects of institutional congruency (see Wicksell's theorem) are violated: a patient from the province of Lower Austria who received treatment in another province, say Vienna, does not vote for the governor of Vienna (democratic principle), s/he does not pay taxes there (principle of fiscal

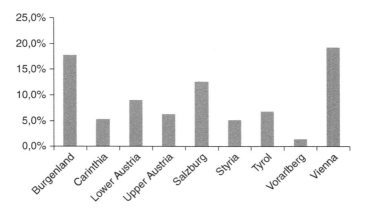

Figure 8.2 Share of hospital patients from other provinces
Source: Own display, according to BMG (2010).

equivalence; in fact, nearly all taxes are collected by the federal level), and the Viennese government does not bear all the costs of the Viennese hospitals (connexity principle). In fact, the latter two aspects are the most criticized problems in Austrian health care.[19] For the connexity principle to be positively fulfilled, the decision-makers and the cost-bearers must be the same. However, SHI pays for about 44.9%[20] and the provinces for about 30% of acute hospital care (Czypionka et al. 2011), while SHI has *no* say in any aspect of hospital care, as in the provincial health platform (see above), the province has the automatic majority of votes concerning hospital matters.

The fragmentation of healthcare financing is in fact at the core of the problems for the Austrian system as a whole, because the other side of the coin is that SHI pays only a lump sum and no marginal contribution to hospital care. In outpatient care, however, SHI bears the full costs of any volume increase.[21] Hence, for SHI there is a strong incentive to make people use the hospital, whereas for hospitals it is profitable to push people to care outside the hospital, especially if they only need services from the (globally paid) outpatient departments.[22]

Finally, with regard to fiscal equivalence, the Austrian system of financial equalization is mainly based on common federal taxes. There are next to no provincial taxes. Therefore, the political benefit from opening a new hospital falls to the governor, whereas the tax burden is attributed to the minister of finance. Experts see this as one of the main reasons why the number of acute-care hospitals in Austria is one of the highest in Europe (6.1 acute-care beds per 1000 inhabitants). This financing mechanism also contributes to the ongoing current debate about healthcare financing reform and continuous tensions between the federal level and the provinces, as the costs have been rising for a long time now at unsustainable rates.

As discussed in Section 3, the influence of the social partners is very strong within SHI. There are however two different lines of conflict within this construction. To begin with, it is employers' vs. employees' representatives, for the largest part congruent with the two largest political parties (the Social Democratic Party (SPÖ) and the Conservative People's Party (ÖVP)) that elect the health insurance bodies. Secondly, the HVB's power is almost entirely dependent on the will of its member institutions. The members of the HVB board (and thus the entire management) are appointed with the votes of chairpersons and vice-chairpersons of member institutions. Even the Data Protection Act mirrors this dependency relation between HVB and the social security institutions. Thus the HVB can coordinate the activities within social security, provide common services, and formulate and implement strategies only "on a short leash" of its members, effectively ruling out a stronger leadership role or yardstick competition. This is a problem because the sickness funds are not subject to competition, have only a very indirect democratic legitimization (as a side-effect of social partner elections), but nevertheless enjoy a high degree of autonomy, whereas the HVB is the main interlocutor of the political level. This problem is currently mitigated by the fact that the HVB's president is also vice-president of the Chamber of Commerce, as was the case when the vice-president of the Federation of Trade Unions was president of the HVB in the period 1997–2001. Nevertheless, as is very common in Austria, the formal institutions often do not wield the real political power. A suggestion for reform in this area would be a more clear-cut distribution of competencies alongside actual social elections for the bodies of sickness funds and HVB.

The contractual relationships are also subject to parafiscal federalism. Whereas the HVB negotiates contracts with pharmaceutical companies and "small" providers (e.g. optometricians), the individual health insurance funds in coalition with the regional chambers of physicians insist on retaining negotiations on the regional level. This has led to differing reimbursement schemes for physicians, which decreases transparency and comparability. The HVB is part of the negotiations and signs the contracts alongside the insurance funds to enforce some degree of uniformity, despite the fact that according to law, the HVB is the main negotiator and the respective sickness fund is only required to approve. It has also set up the "meta-reimbursement scheme" in a (hitherto) futile attempt to improve comparability.

Applying the Oatesian principles to SHI is obviously a bit tricky. The sickness funds could form more suitable (i.e. homogenous) populations of insurees, and of an "optimal" size, at least in theory. In reality, however, the size of sickness funds varies considerably and is determined by profession and region, which are probably not the best criteria. There are only very few studies on the scale efficiency of sickness funds, and the evidence is mixed. The Wicksellian criteria can be used more easily. In theory, in SHI, the users of services automatically are the payers (fiscal equivalence), the electorate (democratic principle) and the decision-makers are accountable for financing (connexity principle). In reality, however, this opportunity is missed, because as we have seen, with the fragmentation of hospital financing, fiscal equivalence and connexity are not positively fulfilled, and the democratic principle is weakened by the very indirect way of social elections in Austria.

When coming to quality, the satisfaction of Austrians is quite high (ISA 2010) albeit hard data on quality are widely missing. The provinces seem to be rather opposed to collect standardized data on quality, let alone publish it, so assessing effectiveness is difficult. Responsiveness should in theory be high due to the rather large number of provinces and sickness funds. However, as of yet, there is no institutionalized patient survey, neither in the provinces nor in SHI. Due to widely free choice, access is not very limited, albeit of course the density of providers varies considerably between regions, and information is lacking. Underserved areas are mapped in the ÖSG, and thus improvement is likely.

As previously mentioned, the fragmentation between SHI and the provinces as well as the size of hospitals all affect efficiency to a rather large extent. The lack of information on quality also impedes actual or yardstick competition in "both worlds". For 2006, we measured the efficiency in the hospital sector (Czypionka et al. 2008) by means of Data Envelopment Analysis and subsequent econometric regression. We found considerable room for improvement in terms of technical and scale efficiency. Due to political reasons, province-based data are not free for publication. However, from administrative data, sound comparative measures can be calculated as well. In Figure 8.3, three of these measures are shown for the provinces head-to-head, standardized to the overall Austrian values. The term "actual bed" refers to an adjustment that has to be made to account for holidays and changes during the year. The costs per acute-care bed are especially high in Vienna. The university hospital there cannot account for all of the difference as Graz (in Styria) and Innsbruck (in Tyrol) also run university hospitals, albeit the Viennese is the largest.

Unlike other provinces, Vienna also has to serve an urban area only with respect to emergencies, but admittedly receives more severe cases from other parts of Austria. To adjust for this, a cost/DRG measure can be used. However, as the LKF-system, the Austrian variant of DRG, applies only to the inpatient sector, only inpatient costs must be used. Despite the fact that an

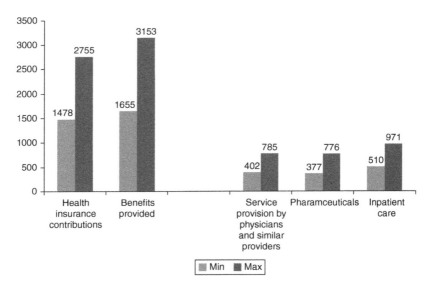

Figure 8.3 Range of contributions received and benefits provided, in euros per capita (2008)
Source: IHS HealthEcon (2010), data provided by HVB.

LKF-point is supposed to represent an equal unit of effort and expenditure, the ratio is also considerably higher in Vienna. This might also be the reason why, given the already high level, Vienna at the same time has the lowest expenditure growth rate. Especially troubling in this regard are the provinces of Lower Austria,[23] Upper-Austria, Salzburg, and Styria. The policies of these provinces concerning their hospitals have led to growing tensions between them and the federal level, because despite the over-capacity of acute-care beds in Austria, beds have not been reduced quickly enough and even some new hospitals have been constructed. This has led to proposals by the minister of health to pool more funds centrally and thus exert more pressure. However, a sanctioning mechanism, on the one hand, already exists but has so far never been used, and on the other hand, changes in these matters require the provinces themselves to approve. In the meantime, and under the impression of the recent decision by Eurostat to attribute the debts of public hospital companies to the government sector when calculating the figures for the Maastricht criteria, Vienna, Upper Austria, and Styria have enhanced plans for hospital reform.

With respect to SHI, sickness funds are opposed to the idea of yardstick competition. However, measures to reduce administrative costs have been employed and have led to a decreasing share of revenues spent on administration. In a recent study (Czypionka et al. 2010), we found a drop from 4% in 1994 to 2.8% in 2008, with some sickness funds "gaming" these comparisons by shifting personnel, but a generally favorable trend, in contrast to hospital administrative costs, which show efficiency gains. Again, sickness funds were opposed to having the data published on an individual level. Following an agreement between the HVB and the government in February 2009 (agreement of Sillian), social health insurance also engaged in an effort of "dampening" the growth rate of expenditures by negotiating four agreements with their major contractual partners. The effort seems to have been at least partly successful, and also marks an important step by the sickness funds for more concerted action.

When coming to equity, the rather cooperative federalism in Austria leads to considerable subsidies from richer to poorer areas. However, in contrast to for example Denmark or the Netherlands, fiscal equalization between provinces is based on negotiations and not mainly on actual population characteristics. A problematic point in SHI is the lack of an equalization scheme between funds. Income and expenditures vary greatly among funds (see Figure 8.3). However, only 2% of contributions are redistributed among the regional health insurance funds, and this is mainly due to the fact that the Viennese sickness fund runs a hospital on behalf of SHI. When applying the equity goal of WHO for healthcare systems, the recommendation would rather be the pooling of incomes and risks and setting up a yardstick competition between sickness funds (Czypionka and Röhrling, 2009).

In Austria, there is a strong tradition of cooperative federalism in health care, as equal access is highly valued (ISA 2010). Paradoxically, among governmental units as well as sickness funds, autonomy is quite strong. What is more, this autonomy also creates a large number of veto-players, considerably slowing down reform efforts. The fragmentation in health care and variability between provinces and among sickness funds, which can be attributed to this complex network of fiscal and parafiscal competencies and financial flows, is not outweighed by dynamic efficiency gains, because provinces and sickness funds, in concordance with the provincial chambers of physicians, are largely opposed to the idea of actual or yardstick competition.

5.3. Federalism and the performance of the social care system

This section aims to assess whether federalism in the Austrian social care system comes with advantages or disadvantages in terms of quality, efficiency, and equity. In doing so, we follow the assessment criteria laid out in Section 5.1.

Similar to the allocation of authority in health care, it seems surprising that social care regulation competences are to be found with nine provinces in such a small country. As explained in Section 2, this phenomenon has historic roots that go back to the design of the constitution of the state in 1920. Path-dependent decisions led to the federal system of social care rather than care-related rationales. Despite split competences for social care, the federal state and its provinces principally agreed on nationwide benefit levels and eligibility criteria. Both levels of government also agreed on coordinating type, amount, and quality of social care services across the provinces but implementation has not been as successful as intended.

The continuing differences across provinces in levels and patterns of service delivery could reflect differences in social care needs between regions. The claim to better respond to such diverse needs in a decentralized and federalized system might then explain why the reforms in the early 1990s have brought little change in terms of governance structures.

Data from the social care allowance database in fact display considerable variation across the nine provinces in social care needs measured as the share of care allowance recipients on all residents. In comparison, the two most westerly provinces, Tyrol and Vorarlberg, face the lowest share of dependent people (3.9% each) and the most southern province, Carinthia, records the highest share (6.1%) of dependent people (Austrian average: 5%). As a measure for distribution of severe dependencies across provinces we apply the share of people receiving care allowance of level five to seven on all care allowance recipients. The share of highly dependent people on all dependent people ranges from 10.1% in Carinthia to 20.2% in Vorarlberg (Austrian average: 13.1%).

Also Austrian data from the Special Eurobarometer that addressed health and long-term care issues in 2007[24] in fact point to interregional differences in attitudes with regard to respondents' own preferred forms of long-term care should they come to depend on help.[25] When it comes to preferences with regard to specific types of care arrangements, differences between provinces are quite pronounced. In particular, preferences differ for home care by family members (29–77% approval), the use of domiciliary care services or personal carers (22–55% approval), and the move into a care home (0–21% approval). Thus there might be a case to be made for a federalized rather than a centralized long-term care system in terms of responsiveness.

It seems fair to say, however, that compared to health care there is less reason to expect externalities and increasing-returns to scale in the provision of social services, which would add to the cost of a federal system (see for further analysis of efficiency).

As regards Wicksell's democratic principle – the collective users of public services should be the electorate for the relevant decision-makers – we first note that in contrast to health care, fiscal federalism rather than parafiscal federalism prevails in social care. Thus, decision-makers in this field can claim direct democratic legitimacy. However, the lack of accessible information and poor transparency on the different provincial social care service systems hinders political accountability as well as policy learning through comparative reflective analysis of strategies and measures taken elsewhere.

The connexity principle – stating that the political body deciding a benefit should also bear its costs – is fulfilled in the area of social care in Austria. The provinces pay for subsidized service provision consumed by their residents. With regard to fiscal equivalence – the population benefiting from public services should be the one paying for it – it has to be remembered that provincial financial means are generated via fiscal equalization rather than via provincial taxes. On the other hand, a province's budget is allocated to different tasks so that high priorities in one area imply lower financial means in other areas. The respective residents do not directly pay for social care but indirectly by other collective goods forgone.

Assessing the type and degree of interjurisdictional competition in social care we look at three main preconditions of competition in Austria's federal social care system: (a) transparency and information about social care service/tax packages; (b) mobility of dependent people, caring relatives, and professional care service providers; and (c) elective power.

To ensure transparency of provincial social care service provision, two measures have been taken. First, provinces are obliged to set up requirement and development plans for future social care provision (*Bedarfs- und Entwicklungspläne*). Second, a working group[26] at the federal level (*Arbeitskreis für Pflegevorsorge*) has been established to recommend aims and principles of social care and to develop minimum standards. Although this working group publishes a report every year, information on social care service provision in the provinces particularly on a comparative basis remains sketchy. Even some basic information on social care provision is missing in a provincial comparative perspective (e.g. there are no official data on the number of social care users or social care providers (private, nonprofit, public)).

As regards mobility, the number of persons in need of social care who relocate can be assumed to be negligible. First, frail and dependent people are very much limited in their mobility. Secondly, professional care services are typically delivered to private households. A smaller percentage (15–17%) of those in need of social care receive institutional care. Hence, there is little service travel involved in daily life on the side of care clients, let alone travel across the boundaries of a province: under current regulation publicly subsidized domiciliary care services can only be accessed when the care-dependent person has lived in the province for a certain amount of time (e.g. a couple of months). Thirdly, family and neighbors in Austria mainly provide care. About 70–80% of frail dependent people in private households rely on this source of care. Given that family networks are not ubiquitous or easily replaceable, household relocation appears to be less likely for households with social care needs.

The analysis above suggests that concepts of direct interjurisdictional competition by mobility might not apply to the Austrian social care system but there might be still room for yardstick competition. Theorists of yardstick competition hold that citizens compare (social) care benefits or costs across provinces. If they perceive (social care) benefits in their own province are not as good as in any other province they will no longer give their vote to the party in power. Contrary to theoretical considerations horizontal competition in social care in Austria regards benefits only. This is due to the fact that most of the provincial revenues[27] are transferred by the federal state to the provinces in the course of fiscal equalization. With regard to benefits, it is in fact well documented in a variety of analyses by the Austrian Court of Auditors (see Rechnungshof 2010a) that provinces use their rights to adapt their care allowance laws to allow for more generous cash benefits. It looks as if some selective changes in social care benefits and accessibilities are used for gaining political advantage in election campaigns.

Despite the general regulation of the nature of social care services (like provision in an area-wide manner, definition of basic "quality" criteria) (Trukeschitz 2010) accessibility, type of social care services available, level of public support and share of private co-payments vary significantly between the nine provinces (Trukeschitz and Schneider 2011). However, there is little effort to engage in systematic benchmarking and policy learning.

Concluding with regard to public finance approaches, provinces are differently affected by care needs of their residents and residents seem to differ in their preferences for care arrangements. Theory suggests that local authorities rather than a central authority might be more appropriate to solve social care issues as they should be more informed about both care needs and preferences of their residents. At the same time, the preconditions for interjurisdictional competition in the area of social care are not fulfilled in

Austria. This is mainly due to the characteristics of vulnerable immobile people but also due to lack of transparencies in comparative social care provision. We will now turn to the effects of the federal social care system on quality, efficiency, and equity.

Quality of social care service provision is roughly regulated by the art. 15a agreement between the federal state and the provinces. This agreement mainly addresses criteria of quality of structure, like capacities of care homes, fixtures, and fittings (for details, see Trukeschitz 2010). It is up to the provinces to regulate and supervise quality of social care provision. Different quality-assessment systems have been developed by the regulators at the provincial level and inter-regional exchange about quality measurement and quality management is limited. One exemption to this phenomenon is the National Quality Certificate (NQZ) for care homes. This certificate can be regarded as the attempt to promote nationwide standards and quality management processes for Austrian care homes (for details on the NQZ, see Trukeschitz 2010).

Quality of social care services in a dynamic perspective requires both substantial potential of innovation and adaptive capacities. Poor transparency does not only affect accountability. It also implicates on innovation and adaptive capacities. In theory innovation is usually thought to be driven by competitive pressure – be it competition in political terms or competition on markets for the goods and services in question. Yet, as has already been elaborated, major preconditions for interjurisdictional competition are not met in Austria's federal system.

Turning to efficiency issues caused by the federal system in the area of social care funding and provision, one has to account for information and transaction costs. Austria is characterized by social care service regulation that varies from province to province (see Section 4.2 and Trukeschitz and Schneider 2011). The variety of different funding systems and differences in regulation on the provincial level increase the transaction cost of service providers who intend to serve clients in more than one of the nine Austrian provinces.

It is difficult to assess productive efficiency in addition to transaction costs, given that data on this issue are not easily accessible for social care and, consequently, the lack of empirical studies on the economics of social care in Austria. Projections of the Court of Auditors, though, reveal that differences in total costs for care home services between provinces are not always due to differences in quality of care. This raises issues of inefficient social care service provision.[28]

The last performance dimension to discuss in conjunction with federalism is equity in terms of funding and service use. We will assess this aspect from the financial side and from the perspective of benefit design.

From the perspective of funding, similar to health care, negotiations rather than formulae-based transfers determine the flow of funds to provinces.

Negotiations underlie the FAG, which is (re-)enacted only every four years. There are no specific taxes or grants to finance social care and no transfers from the federal budget to the provinces that are earmarked for social care (see Trukeschitz/Schneider 2011). Hence, there is some fiscal equalization but is unlikely that full fiscal equivalence can be achieved.

From the perspective of benefit design, the introduction of the universal care allowance together with the intended coordination of social care service provision in the early 1990s has been perceived as a step toward reducing regional inequalities.

The federal structure of social care regulation, though, raises some equity issues: (i) substantial variation in the duration of proceedings for care allowances (40–137 days) between the administrative entities, (ii) differences in time of transmission of care allowances (some administrative entities paid them at the beginning of the month, the majority at the end of the month), and (iii) substantial differences in fees of care homes across provinces that could not be explained by differences in service provision.

With regard to the administration of care allowances, substantial changes are under way. Instead of approximately 300 administrative units just eight administrative bodies will deal with care allowance issues. This change in the federal system of social care will not only affect efficiency but also increase equality. By contrast, the design of the social care service systems has not been touched. Access to social care services still varies between provinces due to differences in both availability and in eligibility criteria.

Overall, Austria's social care system comprises care allowance, social care services, 24-hour care for dependent people, and support for informal care-givers. Depending on the type of benefit, different levels of the federal system regulate benefit design. The fragmented administration of the universal care allowance – introduced in 1993 – led to inefficiencies and inequalities in benefit provision. It will be replaced by a single cash benefit regulated by the federal state and administered by a couple of entities in 2012. With regard to social care service provision, nine provinces are still responsible for service regulation. Therefore, type, volume, and funding modes of social care services vary considerably in Austria. On the one hand, this offers an excellent opportunity for policy learning. Systematic evaluation of the existing models of service provision and funding within one country could put forward the chance to learn more about good and best practices in this field of social policy. Unfortunately, in Austria this has not been taken up so far. Intransparencies and lack of comparative data on both service provision and needs/preferences of dependent people and their relatives hinder policy learning. On the other hand, the different modes of social service regulation and provision across provinces led to different levels of quality and to inefficiencies and inequalities in social care service provision as has been repeatedly reported by the Court of Auditors.

6. Austrian health and social care: the future

6.1. Health care

Austria has one of the most expensive healthcare systems in Europe (USD 3763 PPP per capita in 2007) and its strong reliance on inpatient care is not in accordance with recommendations from health sciences. Apart from the most expensive hospital sector in Europe (USD 1025 PPP per capita in 2008, prices 2000), the fragmentation between inpatient and outpatient care and a lack of competition despite high autonomy of provinces and sickness funds are the main problems in Austria. While most stakeholders accept these basic facts, and even the main direction of reform is clear, the large number of veto-players is mainly responsible for the slow pace of reform.

The most recent reform propositions are a good example of this. In spring 2010, the HVB announced it would issue a "Masterplan for Health" in autumn of the same year because it deemed the pace of reform too slow, and fought hard to bring all sickness funds together on this. Only two weeks before the presentation, the minister of health announced his own reform concept for hospital financing. This has led to a struggle about the hege-mony in healthcare reform on various fronts, with the provinces opposing the minister and favoring the HVB's plan in some cases.

The disheartening aspect is that the two reform proposals have very differ-ent scopes and could be easily brought together: whereas the "Masterplan" covers all of health care and is meant as a reform process spanning decades, the minister's proposal is a concrete model of increased centralization of funds for hospital financing. Early in 2011, the provinces themselves issued a crude plan for reform, effectively demanding healthcare financing to be con-centrated on the provincial level. Some sickness funds indeed sympathized with the plans, seemingly oblivious of the serious shift in power and severe difficulties when unifying insurance/employment-based and residence based principles of funding and care delivery, for which there is no specification in the reform concept. In the meantime, all parties have agreed to start reform negotiations within the Federal Health Agency, but basically limited in scope to the upcoming 15a-agreement negotiations (to be finished in 2013), in contrast to the more visionary process-based "Masterplan".

Under the impression of the inclusion of the debts of hospital companies in the public debt as of 2011 by Eurostat (Austria is subject to the Maastricht criteria), Vienna, Styria, and Upper Austria announced increased efforts and plans to curb hospital costs, but political viability and actual success remain uncertain.

This slow pace of reform poses a threat for the sustainability of the healthcare system, as the growing share of the elderly, alongside with a decrease in the employable population to be expected within the next 20 years will put considerable pressure on costs and revenues alike. A solution would have to include more streamlined structures and competencies within the fiscal as well as parafiscal federal system.

6.2. Social care

It has not been long since long-term care dependencies as social risk appeared on policy agendas. Compared to social security systems against sickness, unemployment or old age poverty, policy approaches for covering the risk of long-term care dependency are comparatively new. This is striking, given that a risk that almost everyone will be confronted with care dependency in his/her life, be it directly (as potential recipient of care) or indirectly (family caregiver) (Schneider and Trukeschitz 2008).

As will other European countries, Austria will face significant demographic changes, predominately a marked increase in the share of old people on the whole population. Even with optimistic predictions on the expected number of healthy life years at age 50 or 60, it is common knowledge that the number of people in need for long-term care will increase in the future. However, half of the remaining life years (men: 14.6 years, women: 18 years) could be troubled by health problems and functional limitations (Jagger et al. 2008).

Even today, care dependency in old age presents a financial challenge to private households as well as public budgets. The most recent measures to consolidate public budgets also affected social care. For the first time since 1993, the year universal care allowances were introduced, the eligibility thresholds relating to care needs were actually raised and hence access to cash benefits tightened starting in 2011. Also, as public spending on long-term care continues to grow, provinces start realizing that they will not be able to assume sole responsibility in securing adequate infrastructures for long-term care. Therefore, rethinking the current allocation of the powers to govern in this policy area is of eminent importance for people in need of care as well as from a taxpayer's perspective.

Recently, the federal government (the Federal Ministry of Social and Consumer Affairs) and the provinces agreed on a new funding model in social care for 2012–2014. The basics were laid down in the federal government's program for the years 2008–2013. The plan is to set up a tax-funded "social care fund" (*Pflegefond*) to cover the additional estimated cost of long-term care that will accrue in the period 2012–2014 and to develop a longer-term funding model for the decades to come by 2014. In the interim period 2012–2014 funding responsibilities for the social care funds will be shared between the federal government and the nine provinces. The provinces agreed to contribute about one third of the funding.

7. Summary and conclusions

The Austrian health and social care systems show substantial degrees of federalism though the country is one of the smallest in Europe. The Austrian healthcare sector is marked by the strong tradition of (fiscal and parafiscal) federalism and thus characterized by a fragmentation of competencies. Executive legislation, administration, regulation, and ownership (of the majority) of hospitals lie with the provinces, with the federal level only providing framework legislation. Profession-dependent mandatory social health insurance consists of 19 sickness funds of greatly varying size, with next to no equalization scheme, but covering nearly the entire population. Financing of the hospital sector is split between all governmental units and SHI, the latter paying only a lump sum. Despite its dominating role in hospital financing, SHI has no say in these matters. All in all, the principles of institutional congruency are all violated. What is more, this financing mechanism leads to incentives to shift patients between payers, as in the non-hospital sector, SHI pays for nearly all costs incurred.

The small size of many hospitals has been sharply criticized, but provinces are reluctant to lose these due to their importance for the local labor market. Fiscal illusion helps to keep these capacities as the federal level levies most taxes, with shares belonging to the other governmental units. In addition to this, the tradition of cooperative federalism in Austria "socializes" the costs to some extent. Therefore, hospital costs are among the highest in Europe, and ever increasing, threatening the sustainability of healthcare financing. Attempts for more central planning, common quality monitoring, and financing are met with resistance by the provinces. What is more, the large number of players keeps the pace of reform very slow, despite the fact that Austria is entering an era of double ageing.

In social care, the financial responsibility for the care allowance is currently split between the federal state and the provinces, whereas the responsibility for securing an adequate supply of care services rests entirely on the provincial level.

At first sight, the Austrian universal care allowance seems to be a nationwide-consistent benefit system. However, a closer look at the federal and provincial social care allowance laws and derived legislation as well as at administrative procedures still reveals significant variety of differences in benefit levels, eligibility criteria and need-assessment procedures (Rechnungshof 2010a). A major change will take place in 2012. Legislative and administrative responsibilities for the care allowance will be shifted to the federal state. As a result, only eight authorities will be tasked with administration of the care allowance starting 2012.

Due to the fact that the responsibility for provision of social care services is allocated exclusively to the provincial level, additional differences emerge in the design of service benefits. At the same time, transparency about comparative issues of health social care service regulation is very low in Austria which makes comparisons between provinces very challenging. In the late 1980s and early 1990s, policymakers recognized that exchange about aims and developments of social care services and policies is an important issue and started to take action. Yet, the window of opportunities that different solutions of social care service regulation offer is still quite far from being used for policy learning.

In assessing the impact of federalism on the Austrian health and social care system we found basic principles from the public economic literature to be violated. Federalism could be beneficial to some extent if there was effective competition, if scale efficiencies were fully exploited, and if the allocation of responsibilities and funds would imply fiscal equivalence and connexity. However, in the current state of affairs there is little mobility-driven competition, transparency (as a precondition for yardstick competition), and little willingness to adjust the allocation of powers in a way to better meet fiscal equivalence.

Cooperation of multiple actors and/or government levels or centralization both offer a chance to reduce or overcome such difficulties. Particularly in a time where an increase in the demand for health and social care service is predicted for the near future, information exchange and the development of common strategies will be necessary to avoid unnecessary information and administration costs. Incentives are needed to increase transparency, encourage communication on different levels of government and administration, and arouse interest in comparative analysis to learn and to take advantage of the different systems of social care service provision in Austria.

Notes

1. All legal documents can be accessed through a website of the federal chancellery, albeit only in German: http://ris.bka.gv.at.
2. As this term will be frequently used, we refer to it simply as the "15a-agreement" from this point on.
3. This section is based on information provided by the HVB on its website: http://www.hauptverband.at/portal27/portal/hvbportal/channel_content/cmsWindow?action=2&p_menuid=58408&p_tabid=6 (retrieved on 27 December 2010).
4. The law governing the Supreme Health Board is currently being reformed.
5. Note that this is the only aspect in hospital legislation that is sole responsibility of the federal level, executed by the district level.
6. With some exceptions like medical doctors, who can opt out in favor of full private health insurance.
7. Of the BKKs, only the largest sends a representative.
8. The Regional Chambers of Agriculture have no federal institution other than their presidents' conference.
9. This term is a common abbreviation of the technical term "hospitals financed by the regional health funds" (*landesgesundheitsfondsfinanzierte Krankenanstalten*).
10. With the exception of Lower Austria and Vienna.
11. For a more detailed analysis, see Czypionka et al. (2008) and Czypionka and Röhrling (2009).
12. In spring 2011, the federal state and the nine provinces decided to concentrate the legal and administrative responsibilities for the care allowance at the federal level. The provinces will still contribute to funding the care allowance system.

This regulation will be in force from 2012–2014. In this book section we report on the current system (2011).

13. This is why the theoretical literature on social care regimes assigns the Austrian system to the "Continental European Subsidiarity Model" (see Trukeschitz and Schneider 2011).
14. Private long-term care insurance is not popular in Austria, therefore not displayed.
15. The entry threshold of more than 60 hours of care per month applies to new applications from 1 January 2011 on; from 1993 to 2010 more than 50 hours of care per month were required.
16. Among them the Act of Home Care (*Hausbetreuungsgesetz*) and the Industrial Code Act (*Gewerbeordnung*): the former forms the legal basis for this specific type of care. It specifies scope and care service activities. The latter states criteria for running a commercial enterprise that offers person-related care service provisions.
17. Based on BMASK (2008a), BMASK (2008c), BMASK (2008b), own calculation.
18. In March 2011, it was not only decided that both legislative and financial responsibilities will be with the federal state, but also that only one authority will be involved in administrating the care allowance.
19. See numerous publications of the Austrian Court of Auditors and IHS, like the problem-analysis paper for the administrative reform group (Rechnungshof 2010b).
20. Calculations are for 2006; recent legislation is supposed to have reduced the share of SHI a bit.
21. An important piece of background information is that in contrast to many other countries, but similar to Germany, secondary care is also provided by independent contract specialists in the outpatient sector.
22. The target functions of (and within) an Austrian hospital are far more complicated, though. For a more detailed analysis, see Czypionka et al. (2008).
23. In the case of Lower Austria, it is often argued that cost increases are due to the absorption of community hospitals into the provincial hospital holding. Notwithstanding, these figures comprise all hospitals within a province, no matter the owner, therefore rendering this argument invalid.
24. Special Eurobarometer 283/ Wave 67.3 (2008): Health and long-term care in the European Union. See http://ec.europa.eu/public_opinion/archives/ebs/ebs_283_en.pdf; respondents age 15 and over.
25. However, the small case numbers ($n = 1009$ for the entire country) only allow to give a first impression based on descriptive statistics. Whether emerging differences are statistically significant remains an open question.
26. The working group consists of the members of the federal state, the provincial authorities, the social insurance body, the Austrian Working Group for Rehabilitation.
27. Only of minor importance are taxes that can be influenced by the provinces themselves.
28. http://www.rechnungshof.gv.at/berichte/ansicht/detail/altenbetreuung-in-kaernten-und-tirol.html (retrieved on 25 April 2011).

References

Apolte, Thomas (2008): Zentralisierung, Dezentralisierung und institutioneller Wettbewerb, in: Bauer, Helfried; Pitlik, Hans; Schratzenstaller, Margit

(Eds.): *Reformen der vertikalen Aufgabenverteilung und Verwaltungsmodernisierung im Bundesstaat*. Wien: NWV Neuer Wissenschaftlicher Verlag, pp. 23–25.

Besley, Timothy; Case, Anne (1995): "Incumbent behavior: vote seeking, tax setting, and yardstick competition", in: *American Economic Review*, 85 (1), pp. 25–45.

BMASK, Bundesministerium für Arbeit, Soziales und Konsumentenschutz (Hg.) (2008a): Altenheime und Pflegeheime in Österreich, Ost [Care homes in Austria, East].

BMASK, Bundesministerium für Arbeit, Soziales und Konsumentenschutz (Hg.) (2008b): Altenheime und Pflegeheime in Österreich, Süd/West [Care Homes in Austria, South/West].

BMASK, Bundesministerium für Arbeit, Soziales und Konsumentenschutz (Hg.) (2008c): Altenheime und Pflegeheime in Österreich, Mitte [Care Homes in Austria, Central].

BMASK, Bundesministerium für Arbeit, Soziales und Konsumentenschutz (Hg.) (2010): Österreichischer Pflegevorsorgebericht 2008 [Annual Report on Long-term Care in Austria]. Vienna: Bundesministerium für Arbeit, Soziales und Konsumentenschutz.

BMG, Bundesministerium für Gesundheit (2008): Krankenanstalten in Zahlen [Hospitals in Austria]. Vienna.

BMG, Bundesministerium für Gesundheit (2010): Krankenanstalten in Zahlen: Überregionale Auswertung 2009 [Hospitals in figures: Supraregional analysis 2009]. Vienna.

Bussjäger, Peter (2008): Does federalism matter?, in: Bauer, Helfried; Pitlik, Hans; Schratzenstaller, Margit (Eds.): *Reformen der vertikalen Aufgabenverteilung und Verwaltungsmodernisierung im Bundesstaat*. Vienna: NVW Neuer wissenschaftlicher Verlag, pp. 60–62.

Czypionka, Thomas; Riedel, Monika; Röhrling, Gerald (2010): Verwaltung im Gesundheitssystem: Bestandsaufnahme und Einsparungspotenziale in Österreich, Reformen im Vereinigten Königreich [Administrative costs in the Austrian healthcare sector and examples of administrative reforms from the UK]. Health System Watch, II/Sommer 2010.

Czypionka, Thomas; Röhrling, Gerald (2009): "Analyse der Reformpool-Aktivitäten in Österreich: Wie viel Reform ist im Reformpool? [Analysis of 'Reformpool' activity in Austria: How much reform can be found in the 'Reformpool'?]", in: Health System Watch, II/Summer 2009.

Czypionka, Thomas; Röhrling, Gerald; Kraus, Markus; Alexander, Schnabl; Eichwalder, Stefan (2008): Fondsspitäler in Österreich: ein Leistungs- und Finanzierungsvergleich [Publicly financed hospitals in Austria: A comparison of their performance and financing structure]. IHS final report.

Czypionka, Thomas; Röhrling, Gerald; Sigl, Clemens (2011): Vertrauliches Projekt [confidential project]. IHS final report.

Gruber, Gerd; Pallinger, Manfred (1994): *BPGG, Bundespflegegeldgesetz: Kommentar*. Vienna: Springer.

HVB, Hauptverband der österreichischen Sozialversicherungsträger (2010): Statistisches Handbuch der Österreichischen Sozialversicherung [Statistical Manual of Austrian Social Security]. Vienna.

ISA, Institut für Strategieanalysen (2010): Gesundheitsbarometer 2010. Study commissioned by the Austrian Ministry of Health. Vienna.

Jagger, Carol; Gillies, Clare; Moscone, Francesco; Cambois, Emmanuelle; Oyen, Herman Van; Nusselder, Wilma; Robine, Jean-Marie (2008): "Inequalities in healthy life years in the 25 countries of the European Union in 2005: a cross-national meta-regression analysis", in: *The Lancet*, in press, corrected proof, available online 17 November 2008.

Kelley, Edward; Hurst, Jeremy (2006): Health Care Quality Indicators Project, Conceptual Framework Paper, OECD Health Working Paper No. 23, DELSA/HEA/WD/HWP(2006)3.

Keman, Hans (2000): "Federalism and policy performance: a conceptual and empirical inquiry", in: Wachendorfer-Schmidt, Ute (Eds.): *Federalism and Political Performance*. London and New York: Routledge, pp. 196–227.

Matzinger, Anton; Pröll, Gerlinde (2010): Finanzausgleich, in: Steger, Gerhard (Eds.): *Öffentliche Haushalte in Österreich*. 3rd Edition. Vienna: Verlag Österreich, pp. 63–109.

Oates, Wallace E.; Schwab, Robert M. (1991): "The allocative and distributive implications of local fiscal competititon", in: Kenyon, Daphne A.; Kincaid, John (Eds.): *Competition among States and Local Governments: Efficiency and Equity in American Federalism*. Washington: Urban Institute Press, pp. 127–145.

Rechnungshof (2010a): Vollzug des Pflegegeldes. Rechnungshof.

Rechnungshof (2010b): Gesundheit und Pflege. Problemanalyse zum Arbeitspaket 10 der Verwaltungsreform. Rechnungshof.

Richter, H (1970): "Das Reichssanitätsgesetz und seine Bedeutung für die öffentliche Gesundheitsverwaltung. Mitteilung der österreichischen Sanitätsverwaltung", pp. 71 (6–7).

Salmon, Pierre (1987): "Decentralization as an incentive scheme", in: *Oxford Review of Economic Policy*, 3, pp. 97–117.

Sax, Gabriele; Patzer, Gerhard; Rottenhofer, Ingrid (2009): ÖGD-Reformprozess. Bericht zum Stand der Arbeit.

Schneider, Ulrike; Trukeschitz, Birgit (2008): Changing long-term care needs in ageing societies: Austria's policy responses. Vienna. WU Vienna University of Economics and Business, Research Institute for Economics of Ageing.

Tiebout, Charles (1956): "A pure theory of local expenditures", in: *Journal of Political Economy*, 64 (October), pp. 416–424.

Trukeschitz, Birgit (2010): "Safeguarding good quality in long-term care: The Austrian approach", in: *Eurohealth*, 16 (2), pp. 17–20.

Trukeschitz, Birgit; Schneider, Ulrike (2011): "Long-term care financing in Austria", in: Costa-Font, Joan; Courbage, Christophe (Eds.): *Financing Long Term Care in Europe: Institutions, Markets and Models*. Basingstoke: Palgrave Macmillan, pp. 187–214.

Vetter, Angelika; Soós, Gábor (2008): "Kommunen in der EU", in: Gabriel, Oscar W.; Kropp, Sabine (Eds.): Die EU-Staaten im Vergleich: Struktur, Prozesse, Inhalte. 3. Auflage 2008. Wiesbaden: VS Verlag, pp. 579–604.

WHO (2008): *Health Financing Policy: A Guide for Decision-Makers*. World Health Organization – Regional Office for Europe. Copenhagen.

Wicksell, Knut (2010 [1896]): *Finanztheoretische Untersuchungen: nebst Darstellung und Kritik des Steuerwesens Schwedens*. Fischer, Jena: Nabu Press.

9
Federalism and Decentralization in German Health and Social Care Policy

Margitta Mätzke

In Germany, regional and local jurisdictions are the place where in many policy fields administrative resources are located, and where the relevant organizational actors – both public and private – implement social policies (Banting and Corbett 2002). Decision-making about benefits and beneficiaries as well as social policy financing, however, tend to be highly centralized. Subnational (*Länder-*) governments have strong participation rights in such decisions, yet there are few areas in which individual *Bundesländer* can shape institutions or policies unilaterally or autonomously (Ziblatt 2002: 628ff.). There is, therefore, no clear allocation of authority over the making and implementation of (health) policy across territorial levels (Jordan 2008: 168). Decision-making, control over finances, implementation, and supervision of performance are in different hands.

Historically the structure of cooperative federalism has promoted uniform living conditions across the country (Manow 2005: 236), a widely accepted social policy goal in Germany (Jeffery 2006). At the same time it is one of the institutional safeguards against excessive concentrations of executive power in the central government (Katzenstein 1987). In terms of administrative norms we find not only federalist political structures as means of dispersing executive power, but also subsidiarity, a preference for the smaller social unit as primary locus of social service provision (Wassener 2002: 73), shaping implementation in many service-intensive social policy fields and providing potent normative support for decentralized administrative capacity. Part of that positive assessment of social service delivery controlled at the subnational level and even by non-governmental organizations is also the notion that small and local organizations are more efficient in delivering services and more responsive to community needs.

In view of these varied political rationales underlying decentralized organization it does not come as a surprise that decentralization has different forms in different policy fields (Webber 1988: 160), depending on how urgently and in what form the conflicting motives of policy harmonization, reservations against concentrations of executive power, and responsiveness to local needs present themselves in different substantive policy areas. Furthermore, even within the health policy field we find not only various degrees of decentralization, but also varied forms of decentralized governance, depending on what subfield of health policy is at issue. Decision-making about the benefits paid by the public health insurance system is fairly centralized, as is healthcare financing. In hospital investment and public health, by contrast, the *Bundesländer* play an important role. Many aspects of outpatient care, such as surveillance quality and professional conduct and negotiations over doctors' compensation are decentralized but without giving much power to subnational governments, and in social service delivery[1] the local level of government is crucial, although decisions about financing are often made by the *Bundesländer* or the central government.

The following section of the paper therefore presents the structures and the role of subnational politics in a range of subfields of the health system where the subnational level is significant. It gives an overview over the varied forms of territorial organization that can be found in the German health system. The second section briefly analyzes the common long-term trend that has led to the combination of centralized decision-making with decentralized implementation. It also indicates the logic behind this historical development. The third main section of the paper then turns to the tensions and controversies that this gradual unification has engendered, especially with regard to the distributional question of inter-regional transfers of resources. In conclusion the paper examines the solutions that policymakers have devised in their attempts to resolve these tensions.

1. Subnational health politics in Germany

There are several areas of the German health system in which subnational levels of government play a significant role, but as we will see, the institutions of decentralized governance and the central government's roles and policy measures are different in each field. Thus, one could not generally call the German health system "centralized" or "federalist". Significant parts of the German health system, such as the quality standards and financing of medical service delivery (both inpatient and outpatient care) through social insurance, the main structures of professional governance and (partially) supervision of health insurance organizations, are determined at the national level. Primary care is organized in a large sector of private practitioners, who work on their own account, but under tight supervision and according to detailed standards of quality and professional conduct. Still, privatized outpatient care is a form of decentralization in that sector. Another form of partial decentralization and autonomous practice of medicine is in the hospital sector, where municipalities, large welfare associations, universities, and (increasingly) private companies are owners of hospitals, and doctors have varied degrees of autonomy in practicing medicine.[2]

Health services in the large field of activities adjoining clinical medicine have developed still other models of decentralized governance: public health services are the responsibility of municipal (or district-level) and *Bundesländer*-level public health authorities. Social service delivery – organizing retirement homes, nursing homes, daycare centers for children or the elderly, or all kinds of initiatives trying to reach out to vulnerable groups and ease access to the health systems for them – tends to follow a governance model that grants even more autonomy to the local level and accords a large role to voluntary welfare associations. Although many of the organizations in that voluntary sector are large and centralized, the motive of autonomy from direct *state* intervention is very strong here.

In different parts of Germany's health system, therefore, different models of decentralized governance are employed. In general administrative decentralization tends to play a more important role than decentralized *decision-making* authority in the hands of subnational governments with independent democratic legitimation and financing bases. *Bundesländer* governments have strong parliamentary veto powers, but they cannot unilaterally shape the design, financing, or implementation of health benefits. Different models of administrative decentralization each find answers to the problems of efficiency and responsiveness, and they each prevent excessive concentrations of executive power in the central government, but they do so in different ways. The following passages will therefore briefly describe the most important forms of decentralized governance in the different areas of the health system where subnational politics matters most. They will point out the rationales of policy decentralization and say a few words about important aspects of their historical development as well as current debates on the benefits and drawbacks of decentralized governance.

2. Social services

Social services for families, the elderly, the unemployed, and all kinds of vulnerable groups are areas of the German welfare state where decentralization is most firmly entrenched. In part simply an outgrowth of the historical roots of municipal social service delivery (Evers and Sachße 2003), this also has a purposeful aspect to it, as it is one of the power-dispersing organizational forms typical of large areas of domestic policymaking in Germany. One of the administrative norms constraining the policymaking autonomy is the principle of subsidiarity, which guides much of social service provision in the German welfare state. Rooted in Social Catholic thought (Sachße 2000), subsidiarity defines a cascade of responsibility for social services that places priority on the lowest possible level of aggregation. The family takes precedence over service provision in the public realm (Schulz 1998), non-profit welfare associations take precedence over public providers (Sachße 2000), and local service provision takes precedence over all kinds of centralized social assistance (Nell-Breuning 1957).

There is one less prominent dimension to subsidiarity, however, which is very important for the funding and implementation structure of many social services: the principle is itself ambiguous, oscillating between a liberal variant that emphasizes individual responsibility and private provision wherever possible, and a variant in which Social Catholic thought is stronger (Sachße 2000), and which emphasizes the responsibility of public authorities to enable individuals, families, and voluntary sector associations to provide social protection for themselves and those close to them (Nell-Breuning 1957). This second, *enabling* dimension of subsidiarity forms the basis of large-scale public (municipal and regional) subsidies granted to the welfare associations' welfare service facilities. It also forms a gateway for stronger central government intervention, in defining nationwide standards and requiring increasingly strict adherence to procedural rules.

This can be observed in unemployment assistance benefits[3] or in the area of long-term care for the elderly. The introduction of long-term care insurance as fifth branch of social insurance in 1994 introduced rules and practices, and with them standards for care and documentation, engendering "processes of de-municipalization and de-localization of care" (Evers and Sachße 2003), yet at the same time allowing for "the establishment of a competitive social care market, which treats the established voluntary sector and the newer for-profit providers equally" (Evers and Sachße 2003) On one level, therefore, subsidiarity is about principled beliefs on how and where to provide social services. At the same time it is also – and one might say, increasingly (Bode 2006) – about struggles among different kinds of providers of social services, quarrels between welfare associations and public authorities, and among different territorial jurisdictions over local autonomy versus binding, uniform standards of social care.

3. Public health

Public health is another area of health policy with policymaking capacity primarily at the subnational level. Concerned with tasks such as food inspection businesses and professions handling food and serving people's health, school health services, surveillance and controlling communicable diseases, public health services also have their historical origins on the local and regional levels. The common roots in municipal social relief account for the fact that the local and regional levels long seemed the most natural and undisputed place for service delivery for both social services and public health services. At the same time, with public health tasks being among the oldest responsibilities of public bureaucracies in the in the health policy field, central government capacities in that area were quick to develop as well.[4] An *imperial health office* was founded as early as 1876 (Lee and Vögele 2001); reconstructed in 1952, the Federal Republic's central government public health agency existed until 1992, albeit both organizations focusing their activities on coordinating the activities of lower-level agencies and public health surveillance, with only limited resources and authority to actually intervene on public health grounds. The federal health office was dismantled in 1993 and shortly after, all health policy functions (including healthcare finances) were consolidated in a health ministry at the federal level. Public health institutes and agencies in charge of disease surveillance, medicinal products, and health education now directly report to the federal health minister, and public health activities are not joined in one organizational unit at the federal level.

While federal resources mostly concentrate on data collection, research, documentation, and licensing of medicinal products, resources and organizational capacities to actually implement public health campaigns – such as vaccination campaigns or installing safeguards against contaminated food – are located in the *Bundesländer* and in local health offices. *Bundesländer* are in charge of buying vaccines for their populations; in the recent outbreak of Escherichia coli (EHEC) bacteria, local health authorities were responsible for collecting food-samples and transferring them to the federal research facilities only indirectly, via the regional agencies. *Länder*-level authorities were authorized to issue warnings and bans against foodstuffs suspected of carrying the bacterium, a situation in which the German public health infrastructure generally created the impression of being disorganized, difficult to control, and duplicating functions across the different territorial jurisdictions.

An additional problem is that on all territorial levels, public health agencies in many areas share responsibility with neighboring agencies in the public bureaucracies. In the case of food-borne health risks, the ministries of agriculture and consumer protection are also involved; acquiring and stockpiling vaccines also concerns pharmaceuticals regulation. The allocation of public health authority across territorial jurisdictions, therefore, is fraught with disputes over competencies among functional units in the public bureaucracies, so that overall the public health segment of Germany's health system presents an image of not very strong, and rather disorganized administrative capacities.

4. Hospital planning and hospital financing

Public health and social service delivery grew out of municipal bureaucracies and the local poor relief system. While many hospitals are in municipal ownership too, the functions of hospital investment and hospital planning have completely different historical roots. Planning competencies for the

Bundesländer were established here much later, after medical progress and rising demands on the standards of care overcharged the financial resources of the public health insurance system and led to a crisis of underinvestment in the hospital sector in the mid-1960s. Lacking hospital capacities and substandard conditions in existing hospitals put hospital financing on the agenda (Kahlenberg and Hoffmann 2001). Never firmly entrenched as a task of local government, hospital investment was defined as a public task, to be managed on the *Länder*-level of government.

The Hospital Financing Act of 1972 established a statutory responsibility of the *Bundesländer* for ensuring sufficient hospital capacity in their territory (the service guarantee, *Sicherstellungsauftrag*), and as tools that enable them to reach these goals it put them in charge of hospital planning and hospital investment (Böhm 2009). Since then hospital investment has been the responsibility of the *Bundesländer*, and covering hospitals' operating costs is the public health insurance system's task. With this division of labor a central role for the *Bundesländer* was established not only in planning capacity in the hospital sector and supplying funds for hospital investment (Sell 2001), but also in health policy decision-making at large. Public health insurance funds have to cover the cost of treatment in these hospitals, and since the range of benefits covered by the public health insurance system has become increasingly standardized and subject to negotiations at the national level, "dual hospital financing" soon turned out to be prone to imbalances and overcapacities. For regional governments extending hospital capacity was attractive investment, especially as until the beginning of the 1990s the public health insurance system had to reimburse the costs of treatment in the new hospitals (Sell 2001).

New prospective payment systems for hospital services developed out of dissatisfaction with this situation and moved hospital budget negotiations gradually away from the regional level and toward the national level, until, after the turn of the century, hospital operating costs were fully calculated on the basis of DRGs that are determined on the national level and uniform across the country (Böhm 2009). In recent years the budgetary pressures in the *Bundesländer* dictated that their financial contributions for hospital investment have declined, so that hospital investment is already partially funded from social insurance revenues. Nevertheless, regional governments seek to hold on to their role in hospital financing and investment, because ensuring hospital capacity and the service guarantee had become one of the central pillars of hospital planners' and hospital administrators' professional commitments (Bode 2010). Moreover, the service guarantee also secures the *Bundesländer*'s role in federal health legislation. As long as regional governments are involved in hospital investment, most health reforms are subject to *Länder* chamber's approval, so that even if they cannot impose particularistic interests on national legislation, the *Bundesländer* have veto powers over legislative decisions.

In public health and social services the *Bundesländer* appeared primarily as administrative agents and organizational arenas for negotiations. Hospital financing, by contrast, is an area which introduces them as *political actors*, involved in not only shaping healthcare provision within their territories, but also accelerating or containing the development of healthcare costs and having a say in legislation about benefits. Even if these political actors cannot unilaterally determine decisions about benefits and payments, collectively they wield considerable influence over health policymaking.

5. Outpatient care and its financing through social insurance

Outpatient care is the sector in which governance structures are probably most complex and most politicized. Several different forms of devolving authority to decentralized or para-public institutions co-exist, but while the regional level often defines the administrative arena – doctors' associations and the public health insurance system operate on the level of regional associations – none really amounts to federalist government; as none of them really empowers the *Bundesländer*. Provision of outpatient care is organized in a sector of physicians in private practice. Economically independent, and in their professional conduct under the supervision of medical chambers, these private practitioners and the (regional-level) associations in which they are all members (*Kassenärztliche Vereinigungen*) are the decisive actors and organizations on the provider-side of the outpatient care sector (Simon 2010). On its revenue side, the bulk of financing is organized through social insurance (Gerlinger 2008), which raises its funds by levying income-based contributions from the members of public health insurance.[5] Doctors' compensation, and thus distribution of health insurance monies among the private physicians, is determined in corporatist negotiations among the associations of statutory health insurance doctors (the *Kassenärztliche Vereinigungen*) and the associations of statutory health insurance funds. Corporatist institutions exist on both regional and national levels.

At the national level corporatist consultation is primarily concerned with the fundamental parameters of (outpatient) health care: the range of benefits covered by public health insurance plans, issues of quality control (Gerlinger 2008; Urban 2001), and establishing guidelines for the compensation of medical services. Actual reimbursement for doctors' services is negotiated at the regional level, and regional associations of statutory health insurance doctors are then in charge of administering the distribution of funds among the physicians practicing in their jurisdictions (Wassener 2002; Simon 2010).

Thus, when considered from an organizational perspective, not only service provision, but also the statutory health insurance system is highly decentralized. There are currently about 150 public statutory health insurance funds (the result of continuous decline from more than 1800 in the

1970s[6]). Some of these organizations are strictly regional (the former blue-collar workers' health insurance funds), others operate on the national level (the so-called subsidiary funds, formerly the public health insurance system for white-collar employees. Since 1992 this distinction is no longer relevant, but the differences in the types of health insurance funds' scope of activity remained). Even where the regional and the local level plays a role as administrative unit, regional and local governments have no say in health governance. This holds for both health insurance organizations and for provider associations: They are (roughly) organized at the regional level,[7] but unlike in hospital planning there are no procedures or institutions empowering the regional level of government.

There are, thus, alternative routes to power dispersion (Katzenstein 1987), which in public health insurance takes the form of delegation to corporatist decision-centers, not to decentralized levels of government. Within those corporatist institutions the regional level has been losing ground over the course of the 1990s and 2000s (Gerlinger 2008, 2009). Corporatist consultation on the federal level has become increasingly important (Bandelow 2009; Urban 2001; Burau 2007) but at the same time federal government regulation and intervention in these macro-corporatist bodies has become more dense (Mätzke 2010; Gerlinger 2008).[8] By 2009 public health insurance organizations had almost completely lost control over their finances, and their funding consisted of grants allocated to them on the basis of a fixed set of criteria reflecting the risk-structure of these organizations' membership base. At the same time strengthening the micro-level – individual doctors' and patients' decisions and market competition among health insurance funds and (recently) healthcare providers – has been the declared goal of government policy since 1992. As of 1997 patients have been allowed to choose their health insurance fund and encouraged to choose those that manage their resources most efficiently. While competition on the financing side had been promoted by public policy since the beginning of the 1990s, by the turn of the century policymakers began to implement it in the area of healthcare provision as well. Individual health insurance funds and individual doctors or groups of doctors were allowed to contract outside the collective bargaining agreements, putting pressure on corporatist bargaining at the regional level (Gerlinger 2008). Micro-level behaviors – of patients, when choosing efficient health insurance plans, and of doctors when choosing economical treatment methods or innovative models of integrated care – supplemented and partially replaced governance structures in which associations had negotiated on the regional level.

Movement of governance processes to the micro-level is the more recent development in the German health system. It started 20 years ago as part of explicit government attempts at using managed competition as a tool for cost control. The older is a tug of war between centralizing tendencies, advancing federal government policymaking capacities and decentralized forms of health policy administration. The former grew out of efforts to contain health expenditures (Banting and Corbett 2002); the latter were historically the principal organizational location of public healthcare provision, valued not only for this long tradition, but for their quality and responsiveness advantages as well. This controversy has long lineages in the policy history of German health care. As we will see below, it has an important redistributive dimension to it. Before turning to that, the following section briefly reviews some of the main themes and important events in the historical struggles over the right mix of centralized or decentralized elements in healthcare governance.

6. Consolidation of central government health policy capacity

The previous sections suggest that one would have to tell separate histories for each of the health subfields that have been discussed. Indeed in social service delivery the public policy norm of subsidiarity is well and alive, and there are few political initiatives aimed at replacing decentralized administrative capacity. As we have seen, however, social service decentralization pertained primarily to implementation, not to decision-making. The public health field, too, is relatively stable with regard to its *Länder*-level organizational position. Part of the reason is that some of the tasks in that area (ranging from prohibiting certain foodstuffs all the way to quarantine and restrictions on the freedom of movement) are very close to the state's police functions, and those are often located at the regional level in Germany. The motive of seeking to avoid power concentration and therefore limiting the amount of executive capacity at the disposal of central governments plays a role in this firm commitment to the regional level as the proper place for police functions (Sell 2001). Decentralized public health authority is part of that commitment (Lee and Vögele 2001). The most interesting developments with regard to the question of centralization or decentralization are in those health system subfields in which social insurance financing plays a major role (i.e. inpatient and outpatient medical care).

As historical scholarship convincingly argues, social insurance has been a tool of centralization from the beginning (Manow 2005). Bismarck's main intention with his (1883) social health insurance legislation was an agenda of nation-building, of trying to undermine internationalist ideologies of Socialism and political Catholicism alike by creating connections between workers and the new central German state (Tennstedt 1997), thereby weakening alternative arenas for political identification, such as the *Länder* or various kinds of voluntary associations (Bauer 1976; Tennstedt 1976) or party- or church-affiliated welfare organizations.

If social insurance was a tool for achieving policy centralization, so was federalism. "The federalist structure of the 'belated German nation' was simply an acknowledgement of the fact that the German states were already autonomous, sovereign entities. Therefore, the constitution was clearly meant to be an institutional structure that would allow and foster national integration and help overcome federalist fragmentation" (Manow 2005). The tendency to leave administrative capacity on the regional and local levels therefore does not mirror the intention to create constitutional safeguards for regional particularism; instead, prior to the Federal Republic, it reflected the fact that German unification could realistically only happen through the delegation of power from the states to the Reich (Manow 2005). It was only later, during the early years of the Federal Republic that the rationale of keeping the German central state "semi-sovereign" as a safeguard against dictatorial ambitions became part of the logic of executive decentralization.

Therefore, during the Weimar years (and of course under National Socialism as well), policy innovation further centralized. It was most likely where it involved social insurance funding, the new financing mode for public policy that did not interfere with established *Länder* and municipal finances. Attempts at unifying local public health services (1934) or youth welfare services (1922) tended to assert the crucial administrative role of regional and local authorities. In the public health subfield an Imperial Health Office (1876) and a Federal Health Office (1952) both served advisory and coordinating, rather than actual policy implementation functions (Lee and Vögele 2001; Kahlenberg and Hoffmann 2001). In outpatient care the system of corporatist negotiations between health insurance associations and doctors' associations was codified in a series of laws that turned doctors' associations (1937) and health insurance associations (1955) into public law institutions (Tennstedt 1976), increasing state oversight over these organizations, but delegating the tasks of fee negotiations, quality control, and service guarantees (in the outpatient care sector) to them.

Regulation of hospital planning (1971) and a series of cost-containment laws (1977–1983) introduced elements of state participation in these corporatist structures. In the hospital sector the *Bundesländer* became a central player in planning and investment, and in outpatient care 1977 legislation created a macro-corporatist arena that involved representatives of public health insurance, doctors, and various government agencies (Wiesenthal 1981). Tripartite consultation was supposed to help contain health costs, but its solutions tended to be short-lived, so that while corporatism as a governance tool in the health sector enjoyed high esteem among policymakers and observers (Döhler 1991), central government capacity turned out to be increasingly important. With the growth and consolidation of the central government, its intervention also rose (Döhler 1995). The federal health ministry (founded in 1961) remained a rather weak actor in federal health policymaking because for a long time, until 1991, responsibility for health finances – public health insurance – was not part of its responsibility; public health insurance was perceived as a general social policy institution, organizationally located with the other social insurance systems in the labor ministry, and social insurance institutions for a long time were not part of specific health policy debates (Bauer 1976). This changed after 1991 when responsibility for health insurance moved into the remit of the federal health ministry (Mätzke 2010). Centralizing tendencies drastically increased almost immediately after this step of consolidating policymaking capacity on the level of the central government.

The trend toward increasing amounts of central government regulation and intervention greatly accelerated in the 1990s with government-mandated risk-sharing and financial transfers among the health insurance funds and it culminated in two recent reforms. The first was in 2007 and amounted to pooling all health insurance revenues on the federal level, making decisions about the contribution rate a central government prerogative and eliminating financial autonomy of the health insurance funds. The second centralizing step was a reform of fee schedules for outpatient health services, which came into effect in 2009. The reform sought to rationalize negotiations over doctors' compensation, make the basis for doctors' income more transparent and understandable, move away from budgeting as a means of cost control, and, last but not least, remove some distributional inequities between different groups of doctors and between regions that the previous system had generated (Nolting and Schwinger 2009). While the details of the reform had been negotiated among doctors, health insurance and state representatives, the reform still implied a major centralizing move, extending central government rule-setting from area of financing organization into the realm of medical service provision. Especially the aspect of interregional transfers became highly controversial issues in the 2007 and 2008 reforms of financing organization and compensation for outpatient medical services. To these aspects the next section will turn.

7. Distributional repercussions of health policy centralization

Centralization has been an underlying trend of health policy development over much of its history. This trend sharply accelerated in the 1990s and 2000s when, as part of attempts at achieving cost control through (quasi) market mechanisms, traditional institutions of professional governance and self-government got under pressure, and public health insurance finances, quality standards, nationwide service guarantees, and doctors' compensation became subject to federal interference and regulation. Managed competition[9] as a tool for cost control brought to the fore all kinds of distributional questions. Increasing central government intervention aimed at resolving these distributional tensions worked to increase the political salience of redistributional issues.

Health inequality existed, and redistribution became necessary as an outgrowth of the funding mode of public health insurance. As health insurance revenues are raised due to contributions levied on a health insurance fund's members, there will be stark differences in the contribution bases of different funds, depending on the kind of people they insure. To maintain organizational diversity in the statutory health insurance system and prevent competition in the public health insurance system from driving the poorer funds out of the market (Wassener 2002), the 1992 legislation had installed a risk-sharing scheme designed to equalize risk structures among the public health insurance funds with regard to the most important factors of income, age, gender – distributions among the members of different health insurance funds, and numbers of dependents per contribution-paying member. The risk-sharing scheme channeled resources to health insurance funds that have older and poorer members and cover many people (children or nonworking spouses) who do not pay contributions, that way leveling the playing field of competing health insurance organizations and removing incentives to compete for "good risks" (i.e. young, healthy, wealthy members) rather than on the basis of service quality and efficiency (Bohm 1997).

The salient distributional issue in the debates about risk equalization, therefore, was membership structure: redistribution in the risk-equalization scheme was framed as an issue of class-inequality. As managed competition spread across the nation, however, questions of uneven healthcare coverage across regions and interregional transfers of resources also came to the fore. Such disparities had always existed in the German health system, because contribution-based financing of public health insurance makes the system extremely responsive to differences in economic conditions. As regional economic conditions are highly unequal across Germany, but the commitment to uniform standards of health care is fairly strong, regional transfers of resources is an almost inevitable result. Regional health insurance funds have more resources in the richer southern *Bundesländer*, doctors' compensation is more generous there, and without risk sharing health insurance organizations in the poorer *Länder* tended to need higher contribution rates to cover their costs.

As long as the primary decision-making arena in the corporatist governance structure of health care had been the regional level, such disparities were not so strongly politicized. Corporatist negotiations took place in specific regional contexts, and one could perceive the system of health finances as being in equilibrium at regionally diverse levels of cost and service quality. Interregional transfers had always happened within the insurance funds that were active nationwide (Oldiges 1994), where cross-subsidization from richer to poorer regions was implicit and was rarely even observed or documented (Leber 1992; IGES et al. 2001; Rürup and Wille 2007). Interregional redistribution became a political issue to the extent that a nationwide public health insurance market was evolving, and to the extent that the risk equalization scheme was steadily growing. Decision-makers from different regions now came together in increasingly important bodies of macro-corporatist consultation, debating intensifying attempts at equalizing risk structures versus returning to regionalized structures in the public health insurance system (Leber 1992; Jacobs and Reschke 1994).

A 2005 constitutional court ruling confirmed the legitimacy of nationwide risk-sharing. Stark differences, in terms of economic bases and health service quality, existed between East and West Germany, and the risk equalization scheme was initially implemented separately for East and West Germany and was only gradually consolidated (IGES et al. 2001). In this situation the wealthy southern German *Bundeländer* Bavaria and Baden Württemberg had filed a complaint against the risk-sharing scheme, challenging in general the federal government's right to intervene in the *Bundesländer's* finances to such an extent (BVerfG 2005) and arguing, more specifically, that the risk-sharing scheme would put West German health insurance funds at a disadvantage by imposing financial burdens only upon them (BVerfG 2005). This kind of unequal treatment could not be justified with reference to a dictate of solidarity, because in social insurance systems solidarity is defined only with reference to circumscribed groups, in the case of health insurance the members of individual health insurance funds (BVerfG 2005). The court dismissed these charges, arguing that because of the federal government's mandate to attain uniform living conditions, solidarity requirements extend beyond the risk communities of social insurance funds (BVerfG 2005). Such solidarity requirements are typical of all social insurance schemes, in which financial transfers from stronger to weaker members are very common (BVerfG 2005). In principle social insurance finances are outside federal or *Bundesländer* budgets, as social insurance is a form of administrative organization fundamentally different from the *Länder's* public finances, so that *Länder* autonomy in managing their finances is no basis on which the risk-sharing scheme could be unconstitutional (BVerfG 2005).

With this decision, the court not only confirmed that risk-sharing among public health insurance organizations is constitutional. It also asserted that fiscal federalism, as one form of decentralization, is fundamentally different from social insurance as another form of devolving financial capacity from the federal government to other organizational units. As Rürup and Wille (2007: 4) put it, "the regional organizational principle is alien to social insurance", and the finances of health insurance funds operating in Bavaria and Baden Württemberg are not Bavarian or Baden Württemberg resources at all (Wasem et al. 2008). They are part of social insurance. And social insurance has been a "centrist" organizational form from the beginning.

8. Conclusion

Distributional tensions arise from centralizing policy commitments that were formulated in a polity in which economic bases are unevenly distributed and public health insurance revenues are a direct function of these economic bases. These tensions, and especially the constitutional court's judgment regarding these tensions, underline that by now the German health system has become an essentially unitary one, and decentralized organization – all public declarations about the advantages of decentralized governance notwithstanding – is not much more than an administrative convenience. There are few areas of health policy left in which regional governments are indeed still powerful and significant political actors.

In a sense, therefore, the historical rationale of federalist institutions – federalism as a tool for achieving national unification in the face of entrenched regional power centers – has served its time; federalist institutions are no more needed to tame the regions. Whether federalist institutions are still necessary for taming the political center (Peter Katzenstein's rationale for decentralized organization) is another question, but health policy developments clearly indicate that potent constraints on central executive intervention are unlikely to be found in the health policy field. Responsiveness to local demands and efficient organization remain a hope and a promise, with all the limitations that arise when decentralization is so strongly intertwined with market-coordinated allocation: uneven responsiveness to local needs and economical use of resources only in select settings plague decentralized policy implementation in the health policy field, requiring ongoing and heavy doses of micro-level central government intervention.

Governance of the outpatient care sector is a case in point. Risk-sharing among public health insurance funds has been steadily growing in volume, sophistication,[10] and political salience until, as of 2009, the public health insurance have funds lost control over most of their contribution revenues and now receive grants out of a centralized pool of health insurance revenues. Ongoing political tensions over risk equalization reveals the extent to which managed competition is an artificially staged enterprise, with participants as far removed from market agents as cats are from lions. Risk-sharing did, however, continue to produce severe financial imbalances, so that further intervention became necessary. This time, centralization addressed the other side of health finances, medical services, and their compensation (Wasem and Walendzik 2008).

A reform coming into effect in 2009 imposed tight rules on the kind of contracts that health insurance funds could negotiate with the statutory system's doctors practicing in their jurisdictions, issuing a full schedule of prices for most of the important diseases and mandating that these fees be uniform across Germany, with only limited possibilities to diverge from the nationwide standards (Knieps and Leber 2008). With central government control reaching the area of service provision and compensation for services, not only did corporatist negotiations lose a large part of their role, but also competitive processes that those regional negotiations had still allowed were undermined (Wasem and Walendzik 2008). Centralization, it seems, has developed its own dynamic, in which ever increasing amounts of central government intervention become necessary, destabilizing not only traditional governance forms of the policy field, but undermining declared commitments to the advantages of decentralized forms of health governance as well. A "rationale" for the resulting mix of centralized and decentralized elements in the health sector is becoming increasingly hard to identify.

Notes

1. The relevant policy area in the context of health policy here is elder-care.
2. But see the analysis of changes in the structures of hospital administration by Ingo Bode (2010), which shows that this autonomy is coming under increasing pressure (p. 201).
3. Centralized standard-setting in social assistance greatly tightened with the 2004 reform of unemployment assistance (the Hartz IV reform).
4. See Baldwin (2005), pp. 557ff. for an argument about the close (two-way) connection between administrative capacity and public health intervention.
5. Roughly 90% of the population are covered by the public health insurance system; financing burdens are borne by the system's "active members" (i.e. those who have a labor market (or pension) income).
6. See *Anzahl der Krankenkassen im Zeitablauf – Konzentrationsprozess durch Fusionen.* In http://www.gkv-spitzenverband.de/ITSGKrankenkassenListe.gkvnet (accessed 13 October 2011).
7. But health insurance jurisdictions never exactly mirrored the federalist structure of the German state: Manow (2005): 227.
8. This is partially also a side effect of federal, paid out of the general budget, that had been introduced in 2004 and gradually increased since then Simon (2010): 150.
9. Among different health insurance organizations as well as – increasingly – healthcare providers.
10. The set of criteria underlying the calculation of financial need has been improved and meanwhile includes a comprehensive set of morbidity criteria.

References

Baldwin, Peter (2005): *Contagion and the State in Europe, 1830–1930.* Cambridge, NY: Cambridge University Press.

Bandelow, Nils C. (2009): "Health governance in the aftermath of traditional corporatism: One small step for the legislator, one giant leap for the subsystem?" *German Policy Studies* 5 (1), pp. 45–63.

Banting, Keith G., and Stan M. Corbett (2002): "Health policy and federalism: An introduction." In *Health Policy and Federalism: A Comparative Perspective on Multi-Level Governance,* edited by Keith G. Banting and Stan. M. Corbett. Montreal: McGill-Queens University Press, pp. 1–38.

Bauer, Guntram (1976): "Die Finanzwirtschaft in der Krankenversicherung." In *Handbuch der Sozialmedizin,* edited by Maria Blohmke, Christian v Ferber, Karl Peter Kisker and Hans Schaefer. Stuttgart: Ferdinand Enke Verlag, pp. 492–515.

Bode, Ingo (2006): "Disorganized welfare mixes: Voluntary agencies and new governance regimes in Western Europe." *Journal of European Social Policy* 16 (4), pp. 346–359.

Bode, Ingo (2010): "Die Malaise der Krankenhäuser." *Leviathan* 38 (1), pp. 189–211.

Böhm, Katharina (2009): "Federalism and the 'New Politics' of hospital financing." *German Policy Studies* 5 (1), pp. 99–118.

Bohm, Steffen (1997): "Risikostrukturausgleich: Abschaffung bzw. Rückführung sachlich geboten?" *Sozialer Fortschritt* (12), pp. 293–299.

Burau, Viola (2007): "The complexity of governance change: Reforming the governance of medical performance in Germany." *Health Economics, Policy, and Law* 2007 (2), pp. 391–407.

BVerfG (2005): Entscheidung zum Risikostrukturausgleich. In *2 BvF vom 18.07.2005, Absatz 1–287*. Karlsruhe.

Döhler, Marian (1991): "Policy networks, opportunity structures and neo-conservative reform strategies in health policy." In *Policy-Networks: Empirical Evidence and Theoretical Considerations*, edited by Bernd Marin and Renate Mayntz. Boulder, CO: Westview Press, pp. 235–296.

Döhler, Marian (1995): "The state as architect of political order: Policy dynamics in German health care." *Governance* 8 (3), pp. 380–404.

Evers, Adalbert, and Christoph Sachße (2003): "Social care services for children and older people in Germany: Distinct and separate histories." In *The Young, the Old, and the State*, edited by Anneli Anttonen, John Baldock and Jorma Sipilä. Cheltenham and Northampton, MA: Edward Elgar, pp. 55–79.

Gerlinger, Thomas (2008): "Wettbewerbsinduzierte Unitarisierung – Der Wandel der Bund-Länder Beziehungen in der Gesundheitspolitik." In *Föderale Politikgestaltung im deutschen Bundesstaat. Variable Verflechtungsmuster in Politikfeldern*, edited by Henrik Scheller and Josef Schmid. Baden Baden: Nomos, pp. 123–134.

Gerlinger, Thomas (2009): Der Wandel der Interessenvermittlung in der Gesundheitspolitik. In *Interessenvermittlung in Politikfeldern*, edited by Britta Rehder, Thomas Von Winter and Ulrich Willems. Wiesbaden: VS Verlag, pp. 33–51.

IGES, Dieter Cassel, and Jürgen Wasem (2001): *Zur Wirkung des Risikostrukturausgleichs in der gesetzlichen Krankenversicherung: Eine Untersuchung im Auftrag des Bundesministeriums für Gesundheit*. 2001.

Jacobs, Klaus, and Peter Reschke (1994): *Freie Wahl der Krankenkasse: Konzeption und Konsequenzen eines geordneten Kassenwettbewerbs*. Baden Baden: Nomos.

Jeffery, Charlie (2006): "Devolution and social citizenship: Which society, whose citizenship?" In *Territory, Democracy and Justice: Regionalism and Federalism in Western Democracies*, edited by Scott L. Greer. Houndmills and New York: Palgrave, pp. 67–91.

Jordan, Jason (2008): "Federalism and health care cost containment in comparative perspective." *Publius: The Journal of Federalism* 39 (1), pp. 164–186.

Kahlenberg, Friedrich P., and Dirk Hoffmann (2001): "Sozialpolitik als Aufgabe zentraler Verwaltungen in Deutschland – Ein verwaltungsgeschichtlicher Überblick." In *Geschichte der Sozialpolitik in Deutschland seit 1945. Band 1: Grundlagen der Sozialpolitik*, edited by Bundesministerium für Arbeit und Sozialordnung und Bundesarchiv. Baden Baden: Nomos, pp. 103–182.

Katzenstein, Peter (1987): *Policy and Politics in West Germany: The Growth of a Semisovereign State*. Philadelphia: Temple University Press.

Knieps, Franz, and Christian Leber (2008): "Die Neuordnung der vertragsärztlichen Vergütung – Darstellung und Zielsetzung der gesetzlichen Regelungen." In *Vortrag*

auf dem Symposium der Deutschen Gesellschaft für Kassenarztrecht am 6. März.
Berlin.

Leber, Wulf-Dietrich (1992): *Risikostrukturausgleich in der gesetzlichen Krankenverischerung: Ein Konzept zur Neuordnung des Kassenwettbewerbs.* Baden Baden: Nomos Verlagsgesellschaft.

Lee, W. Robert, and Jörg P. Vögele (2001): "The benefits of federalism? The development of public health policy and health care systems in nineteenth-century Germany and their impact on mortality reduction." *Annales de Demographie Historique* 2001 (1), pp. 65–96.

Manow, Philip (2005): "Germany: Co-operative federalism and the overgrazing of the fiscal commons." In *Federalism and the Welfare State: Nowe World and European Experiences*, edited by Herbert Obinger, Stephan Leibfried and Francis G. Castles. Cambridge: Cambridge University Press, pp. 222–262.

Mätzke, Margitta (2010): "The organization of health policy functions in the German federal government." *Social Policy & Administration* 44 (2), pp. 120–141.

Nell-Breuning, Oswald von (1957): "Solidarität und Subsidiarität im Raume von Sozialpolitik und Sozialreform." In *Sozialpolitik und Sozialreform*, edited by Erik Boettcher. Tübingen: Mohr, pp. 313–326.

Nolting, Hans-Dieter, and Antje Schwinger (2009): "Reform des vertragsärztlichen Vergütungssystems." *Gesundheits- und Sozialpolitik* 2009 (1), pp. 12–22.

Oldiges, Franz Josef (1994): "Landes- oder bundesweite Zentralisierung in der Krankenversicherung." *Sozialer Fortschritt* (7–8), pp. 163–167.

Rürup, Bert, and Eberhard Wille (2007): *Finanzielle Effekte des vorgesehenen Gesundheitsfonds auf die Bundesländer: Gutachten im Auftrag des Bundeministeriums für Gesundheit.* Darmstadt und Mannheim 2007.

Sachße, Christoph (2000): "Subsidiarität: Leitmaxime deutscher Wohlfahrtsstaatlichkeit." In *Wohlfahrtsstaatliche Grundbegriffe: Historische und aktuelle Diskurse*, edited by Stephan Lessenich. Fankfurt/M, New York: Campus Verlag, pp. 191–212.

Schulz, Günther (1998): "Soziale Sicherung von Frauen und Familien." In *Drei Wege Deutscher Sozialstaatlichkeit: NS-Diktatur, Bundesrepublik und DDR im Vergleich*, edited by Hans Günter Hockerts. München: Oldenbourg Verlag, pp. 117–149.

Sell, Stefan (2001): "Gesundheitspolitik im Spannungsfeld von Bundesländern und Krankenkassen." In *Föderalismus in Deutschland*, edited by Karl Eckart and Helmut Jenkis. Berlin: Duncker & Humblot, pp. 255–277.

Simon, Michael (2010): *Das Gesundheitssystem in Deutschland: Eine Einführung in Struktur und Funktionsweise.* Bern: Verlag Hans Huber.

Tennstedt, Florian (1976): "Sozialgeschichte der Sozialversicherung." In *Handbuch der Sozialmedizin*, edited by Maria Blohmke, Christian v. Ferber, Karl Peter Kisker and Hans Schaefer. Stuttgart: Ferdinand Enke Verlag, pp. 385–493.

Tennstedt, Florian (1997): "Peitsche und Zuckerbrot oder ein Reich mit Zuckerbrot?: der Deutsche Weg zum Wohlfahrtsstaat 1871–1881." *Zeitschrift für Sozialreform* 43 (2), pp. 88–101.

Urban, Hans-Jürgen (2001): "Wettbewerbskorporatistische Regulierung im Politikfeld Gesundheit: Der Bundesausschuss der Ärzte und Krankenkassen und die gesundheitspolitische Wende." In *Veröffentlichungsreihe der Arbeitsgruppe Public Health: Wissenschaftszentrum Berlin für Sozialforschung*, Berlin.

Wasem, Jürgen, Florian Buchner, and Eberhard Wille (2008): *Umsetzung und empirische Abschätzung der Übergangsregelungen zur Einführung des Gesundheitsfonds: Gutachten im Auftrag der Bundesregierung sowie Sonderauswertung.* Diskussionsbeitrag aus dem Fachbereich Wirtschaftswissenschaften, Universität Duisburg-Essen 2008.

Wasem, Jürgen, and Anke Walendzik (2008): "Reform der ambulanten ärztlichen Vergütung: Mehr Rationalität durch stärkere Zentralisierung?" *Wirtschaftsdienst* 2008 (10), pp. 640–647.

Wassener, Dietmar. (2002): "Federalism and the German health care system." In *Health Policy and Federalism: A Comparative Perspective on Multi-Level Governance,* edited by Keith G. Banting and Stan. M. Corbett. Montreal: McGill-Queens University Press, pp. 69–105.

Webber, Douglas (1988): "Krankheit, Geld und Politik: Zur Geschichte der Gesundheitsreformen in Deutschland." *Leviathan* 16 (2), pp. 156–201.

Wiesenthal, Helmut (1981): "Die Konzertierte Aktion im Gesundheitswesen: Ein korporatistisches Verhandlungssystem der Sozialpolitik." In *Neokorporatismus,* edited by Ulrich von Alemann. Fankfurt/M, New York: Campus Verlag, pp. 180–206.

Ziblatt, Daniel F. (2002): "Recasting German federalism? The politics of fiscal decentralization in post-unification Germany." *Politische Vierteljahresschrift* 43 (4), pp. 624–652.

10
Politiques de Santé: The Territorial Politics of French Health Policy

David K. Jones

1. Introduction

French health policy is in the midst of dramatic changes. Although reform has been ongoing for many years, the pace of change intensified with the passage of legislation known as *Hôpital, Patients, Santé, et Territoires* (HPST) in the summer of 2009. One of the most significant aspects of the bill is the degree to which it alters the political dynamics of health policymaking at the subnational level. As of 1 April 2010, new regional-level bodies known as the *Agences Régionales de Santé* (ARS) were created, with each being assigned the powers and functions previously performed by more than a half dozen organizations in each of France's 26 regions. Unlike many French reforms that have tended to create new bureaucracies and further clutter the administrative landscape (Loughlin 2007), the new law actually eliminates many existing organizations, folding them into the ARS (see Figure 10.1).

The new agencies are particularly interesting to study given that they were created based on the rhetoric of decentralization and the logic of centralization. Ironically, by promoting the development of subnational agencies, the state is able to play a larger role than ever before. The hope is that regionalized control of the implementation of centralized policymaking will reduce disparities better than completely devolving or completely centralizing authority.

That the nation ranked by the World Health Organization (WHO) as having the best healthcare system (WHO 2000) would make such dramatic changes might come as a surprise to some. However, why President Nicholas Sarkozy and the French government pushed for major reform is not necessarily the most interesting question. France is facing the same problems of national deficits, rising healthcare costs, and ageing populations experienced by most industrialized nations. In her speech before the Senate, then Minister of Health and Sports Rosalyne Bachelot-Narquin, described the purpose of the bill as "Réformer pour moderniser, réformer

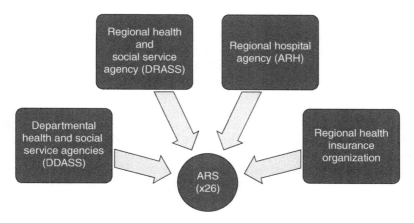

Figure 10.1 Creation of the Agences Régionale de Santé from previous organizations
Source: Own graphic.

pour renforcer" (reforming in order to modernize, reforming in order to strengthen), with the ARS serving to unify efforts instead of dispersing them (Bachelot-Narquin 2009). This reform is also consistent with President Sarkozy's broader efforts to overhaul subnational governance in general (République Francaise 2008).

The questions this chapter will attempt to address are fourfold: first, how does this reform affect the allocation of authority over health policy? Second, how do these reforms fit within the larger context of decentralization in France? Third, what do these reforms mean in terms of actual policy? In other words, how do they speak to issues of equity, quality, and efficiency? Finally, what obstacles stand in the way of implementation and how likely are the reforms to succeed?

The order of these questions is significant, emphasizing the importance of first understanding the political context in which decisions are made before attempting to assess policy outcomes. Fittingly, there are not separate words in many European languages for *politics* and *policies*. In French, the word *politiques* is used for both, suggesting an inherent connection between the two. Although it is too early to know exactly how the regional politics of the ARS will affect the achievement of their policy goals, this chapter provides one of the first in-depth looks at these issues since their creation.

Much of the analysis presented here is based on nearly three-dozen interviews with officials at multiple levels within the regional health agencies of Bretagne (Rennes), Ile-de-France (Paris), and Midi-Pyrénées (Toulouse), officials at the Ministry of Health, leaders of stakeholder groups such as health insurance, hospitals, health policy experts, and scholars of French public administration. With the exception of Ile-de-France, which is unique and important in its own right, the geographic, demographic, and political diversity of these regions make them as representative of the nation as any set of regions could be. Bretagne and Midi-Pyrénées both have urban centers with surrounding suburbs, as well as large areas of sparsely populated farmland. Approximately two-thirds of the interviews took place in person during the summer of 2010, with the rest occurring over the phone during the summer of 2011. In addition to reading official publications, organization websites, and media coverage, I was given access to materials not available to the public, including the opportunity to sit in on private meetings and observe first-hand the interactions between leaders of various organizations and levels of government. In exchange for access to meetings and documents, and for candor during interviews, identity-revealing information is generally not included in this analysis.

2. Allocation of authority

The best way to understand the allocation of authority under the *Agences Régionales de Santé* is to describe how their creation has affected the institutional landscape at the national, regional, and departmental levels. It will first be useful to provide a brief summary of the broader context of both subnational governance and health care in France.

2.1. Overview

France is divided into 26 *régions*, four of which are overseas. Each of the 22 mainland regions is further divided into between two and eight *départements*, for a total of 101 throughout France. Departments as a level of government date back to Napoleon and are historically more significant and powerful than regions that were only given constitutional status in the 1980s. Within each department is a *Préfet*, a person appointed by the national *Conseil de Ministres* to serve as the official representative of the government in that department. The *Préfets* are regarded as the eyes, ears, and arms of the state throughout the country, they are generally not from the area in which they are serving, and rarely stay longer than a few years in each department. One *Préfet* per region is given broader responsibility over the other departmental *Préfets* as the *Préfet de Région*, with recent reforms strengthening the hierarchal nature of this relationship. The elected legislative body of the department is the *Conseil General*, and the elected legislative body at the regional level is the *Conseil Régional*.

The French healthcare system has been described as somewhere between the British and American systems. According to Rodwin, the French dislike the rationing of Britain's National Health Service (NHS) but consider the American approach socially irresponsible (Rodwin and Le Pen 2004). Steffen describes the system as "liberal universalism", in that it is a state-run social health insurance system that "lacks the legitimacy of Bismarckian systems and the leverages of a state-run system" (Steffen 2010).

The vast majority of residents have two types of health insurance. First, all have one of the public, universal insurance schemes financed by the government, with separate plans for different categories of workers. Second, nearly all residents also have private supplemental insurance paid for by employers and employees, with the government paying for those unable to afford it. Reimbursement for services is negotiated between the health insurance funds and unions representing the various categories of workers. Healthcare spending is guided by an annual prospective budget passed by Parliament, though there are few restraints on spending to ensure targets are met. Partly for this reason, health expenditures are among the highest in Europe, estimated at 11% in 2005. Care is generally delivered in three types of institutions: (1) public hospitals (housing 65% of hospital beds), (2) private, not-for-profit hospitals (15% of beds), and (3) private, for-profit hospitals/clinics (20%) (Kaiser Family Foundation 2008).

At the subnational level, health policy and social services have largely been carried out by two sets of organizations: the *Directions Régionales des Affaires Sanitaires et Sociales* (DRASS) at the regional level, and the *Directions Départementales des Affaires Sanitaires et Sociales* (DDASS) at the departmental level. Summarizing the nature and functions of these organizations is no easy task, nor is it entirely necessary for present purposes. However, it is important to understand three elements about the DRASS and DDASS prior to the creation of the ARS: first, there was no direct chain of command between the two sets of organizations. In other words, this was not a hierarchal relationship in which the leaders of each DDASS reported directly to the leaders of their respective DRASS; each had their own unique line to the state. Second, the *Préfets* were responsible for overseeing their DDASS, with the *Préfet de Région* also responsible for the DRASS. Third, the division of competencies between the two organizations created a disjointed policy climate, with each responsible for separate aspects of the same issue. For example, there are a number of areas in which the DDASS were responsible for inspecting and regulating medical establishments within their respective departments, but resources were actually allocated by the DRASS.

At its best, the relationship between the DDASS and DRASS could be described as a partnership; at its worse they were rivals, either duplicating efforts or letting things slip through the cracks. It is interesting to note that for a brief period in the early 1990s, policy management was re-organized on a trial basis in three regions as something similar to what is now the ARS. The DDASS and DRASS of these regions were grouped together in a new experimental organization called the *Direction Régional et Interdépartemental de la Santé et de la Solidarité* (DRISS). Although this arrangement supposedly resulted in better coordination and more efficient use of resources, a handful of well-positioned political opponents remained unconvinced (du Mesnil du Buisson and Jeandet-Mengual 2004).

2.2. ARS: National oversight

At the time of their creation, the ARS fell under the responsibility of two parallel ministries: *Le Ministère de la Santé et des Sports*, and *Le Ministère du Travail, de la Solidarité, et de la Fonction Publique* (see Figure 10.2 for a schematic of the major actors at the national, regional, and departmental levels). Their efforts are coordinated by the *Secrétariat Général des Ministères Chargés des Affaires Sociales* (SG) who is the highest-level person in Paris directly responsible for overseeing the ARS. The cabinet shuffle of November 2010 reorganized these ministries, bringing a new Minister of Health under a new Minister of Labor. The new ministers are described as less invested in the ARS, attending meetings less frequently than their predecessors. It remains to be seen what impact these changes will have, if any, on the oversight of the *Agences Régionales de Santé*. The answer to this question largely depends on the continuously changing nature of the high-level civil service in France (Bezes and Le Ledic 2007).

Beginning 1 April 2010, A *Conseil National de Pilotage* (CNP) was established to provide direction for the 26 ARS and to involve national stakeholders. The Secretary General and her team play a key role in the work of the CNP. The council meets monthly and is responsible for giving directives on how to implement various policies, as well as ensuring consistency between regions. Although the use of contracts in French public administration is becoming increasingly common (Gaudin 1999; Palier 2000; Bezes 2009), the CPOM signed by the ARS directors are somewhat unique given the level of specificity of the requirements over things that will be nearly impossible to

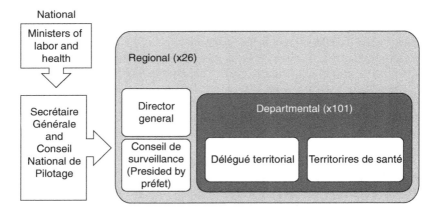

Figure 10.2   Governance of the Agences Régionale de Santé
Source: Own graphic.

control, particularly within a two- or three-year period. For example, the contract signed by Alain Gautron, Director of the ARS in Bretagne, requires that the suicide rate in that region decrease from 37.8 men per 100,000 in 2011 to 35 men per 100,000 in 2013 (Agence Régionale de Santé 2011).

The contracts do not specify the consequences if objectives are not, nor do they specify rewards if objectives are met. High-ranking officials at the Ministry of Health say that in the extreme a director could be removed if his or her region does not sufficiently improve, but that the purpose of the contracts is to help ARS leaders track progress, rather than to catch and punish laggards. In other words, the contracts are less about carrots and sticks than they are about coordination. Even still, ARS officials are motivated to do what they can to achieve the objectives more likely to be within their control, particularly process-oriented goals.

During the initial stages of the development of the ARS, much of the state's guidance came in the form of regular training meetings. Every three weeks between October 2009 and September 2010, the 26 directors were brought to Paris for sessions organized by the Secretary General. Run with the assistance of experts at *l'Ecole des Hautes Etudes en Santé Publique* (l'EHESP), each meeting contained presentations and modules centered on a theme or policy issue. For example, one meeting had experts presenting on disease prevention while another was devoted to overcoming workforce shortages. Interestingly, the dynamic at these meetings seemed to be more of the state providing assistance and resources than the state providing heavy-handed direction. One of the most beneficial aspects of these sessions for the directors was the opportunity to network with each other and learn how other directors were overcoming the challenges of creating a new regional agency.

2.3. ARS: Regional governance

Although each ARS director has some discretion in setting up their organizational chart, the basic structure is the same in each region. At the top, each is led by a director named by the national *Conseil de Ministres*. This fact is significant in and of itself, suggesting the same level of prestige and legitimacy as attributed to the *Préfets*, the representative of the state in each of the 100 departments. As a result, the ARS directors are often described as *"Préfets-Sanitaires"*. The level of sarcasm meant by this term varies by context, with critics implying that the directors will act as detached agents of the state with minimal connection to their region. The term *"Préfet-Sanitaire"* is doubly ironic given that many people predict inevitable clashes between the new ARS directors and the actual *Préfets*.

Within the ARS, the *Préfet de Région* presides over a *Conseil de Surveillance* consisting of a wide variety of stakeholders. This council oversees ARS activities and has the responsibility of approving the agency's budget. Although it is not yet clear how these tensions will play out, there are early indications that a number of *Préfets*, particularly at the departmental level, are still proceeding as if nothing has changed. They believe they have a natural right to be involved in every policy domain, as they are the official representatives of the government in each *Département,* including the Minister of Health. For example, leaders at the *Préfecture* are quick to point out the circumstances under which the ARS are *"sous"* (under) the *Préfet.* Similarly, ARS leaders at the departmental level describe somewhat tense negotiations with their *Préfecture* about how to visually represent their relationship on an organizational chart.

Despite the vertical oversight in the form of contractual obligations to the *Conseil National de Pilotage,* and the horizontal oversight in the form of the *Préfet* and the *Conseil de Surveillance,* ARS directors are given discretion over how to implement programs and reach their targets. In fact, nobody is more important to the future of the ARS than the 26 directors. The first cohort will play a particularly large role in shaping the organizational culture in each region. Chosen from a field of more than 900 candidates most new directors had recently worked within the Ministry of Health bureaucracy at either the regional or departmental level, though some came directly from the health insurance industry, hospitals, and other parts of public administration.

In selecting leaders, the state had to balance two competing incentives. On the one hand, they wanted to select leaders strong enough to implement national policies in resistant regions. On the other hand, the danger of elevating strong leaders is that they would successfully push for higher levels of autonomy and discretion. Interestingly, the way it seems to be playing out is that strong directors such as former Minister of Health Claude Evin in Ile-de-France (Paris) have been able to successfully work with state officials while maintaining cohesion in his agency; whereas other leaders such as Xavier Chastel of Midi-Pyrénées (Toulouse) initially struggled to develop unity. He is seen by many within his agency as a businessman and an outsider with very little experience in health.

Each director had six months before the agencies became operational to begin developing a team to lead divisions responsible for issues ranging from human resources to public health. A large portion of the ARS infrastructure was inherited from the DDASS and the DRASS. The DDASS was split in two, with the ARS responsible for health policy and another organization now responsible for the other welfare policy previously addressed by the DDASS. Whereas the DRASS and the DDASS used to operate sometimes as partners and sometimes as rivals, all activity is now funneled through the ARS director. This creates a hierarchal relationship between the regional and departmental leaders where one did not previously exist, a development not entirely welcomed at the departmental level. This change is additionally significant in that the split of the DDASS significantly alters the *Préfet's* official role over health policy.

At the departmental level, policies are implemented by a *Délégué Territorial* (Territorial Representative) appointed to act as the lead ARS agent within each department. In many cases, the person acting as director of the DDASS on 30 March became the *Délégué Territorial* on 1 April, though to some degree they have experienced a reduction in both competencies and organizational clout. The exact nature of the relationship between the *Délégués Territoriales* and the ARS directors largely depends on the characteristics of the regions, including their geographic size, population, and the number of *départements* they contain, as well as the personalities of the leaders at both levels. Some ARS directors were able to take advantage of the natural course of retirements and transfers to start fresh with a team largely of their making. In Midi-Pyrénées for example, a region that is particularly large both in terms of geography and number of *départements*, six of the eight *Délégués Territoriales* were named to their posts during the six-month transition period after Xavier Chastel was named the incoming director. This gives his team greater opportunities to shape the culture within the agency.

One of the more contentious issues of the reform debate is the inclusion of *L'Assurance Maladie*, or much of the health insurance industry, within the ARS. In particular, this refers to the *Union Régionales des Caisses d'Assurance Maladie* (URCAM) and the portion of the *Caisses Régionales d'Assurance Maladie* (CRAM) that deal with health. This creates an uncomfortable arrangement for the health insurance industry in which they are under the direction of ARS directors within the public administration bureaucracy rather than acting as an independent partner as they had proposed.

The extent to which this potential source of conflict is managed depends largely on the personalities and backgrounds of those involved. Insurance leaders express concern about existing as an outsider in the new organizations and being shut out of the decision-making process. This balance seems a little smoother in regions in which the director had come directly from health insurance. At the same time, they have the challenge of learning how to operate in the public sector, particularly with *Préfets* not necessarily interested in stepping aside. As one departmental leader described, "c'est très spécial de travailler avec les Préfets et les gens de l'assurance maladie n'ont pas habitude de ça" [it is very special (i.e. particular) to work with the Préfets, and people from health insurance are not used to that]. As a result, they rely heavily on the networks and relationships of former DDASS leaders.

Another significant set of bodies folded into the ARS were the *Agences Régionales de l'Hospitalisation* (ARH). Created in 1996 as part of the "Juppé reforms," the ARH were responsible for implementing hospital policies within their region, as well as allocating resources according to a regional budget set by the Ministry of Health (Steffen 2010). The ARH tended to be quite small, run by only a dozen or so civil servants. Even still, for reasons described in the next section, their creation was a significant development in the center–periphery balance of health policymaking.

2.4. Summary

As I discuss in more depth later, the key point about these reforms is that this regionalization is actually a centralization. By consolidating power to regional health agencies, the state has diminished the role of departmental leaders. An important side effect of the allocation of authority described in this section is that with the exception of a small handful of people serving on the *Conseil de Surveillance*, the ARS infrastructure exists almost entirely independent of elected officials. Whereas reforms in other policy domains empowered the elected officials from the *Conseils Régionaux* (elected bodies at the regional level) and the *Conseils Généraux* (elected bodies at the departmental level), the ARS operate largely outside the realm of electoral and legislative politics.

Both Dupuy and Thoenig's *régulation croisée* (cross-regulation) (Dupuy and Thoenig 1983) and Loughlin's mutual interdependence models (Loughlin 2007) are useful frameworks to describe that instead of operating through a single hierarchy, French governance often takes place through parallel hierarchies that at times intersect, are unequal, and are mutually dependent. One implication of this is that ARS agents at the departmental and regional level have no base of authority independent of the Parisian officials who appointed them; in other words, leaders in the ARS have very little leverage with which to challenge potential encroachments. Of course, this also means that the only constituency ARS leaders truly have to please in order to keep their job is the state.

This section has mostly focused on the formal allocation of authority since the creation of the ARS. However, it is important to note that there are many ways in which the actual functioning of the ARS will differ from the relationships designed on paper. For example, there are already examples of *Préfets* reluctant to change making it more difficult for ARS directors to operate autonomously. Similarly, the average citizen is not necessarily aware of the reform and thus continues to go to the *Préfets* with their issues. It is still much too early to be able to predict how these balances will play out; however, the massive changes to the institutional landscape described here foreshadow a number of the obstacles discussed in the final section of this chapter.

3. The ARS in context

What do these reforms indicate about the current state of health management in particular and of French governance in general? Do these reforms represent decentralization, centralization, or some combination of the two? What do the answers to these questions mean for center–periphery relations in the context of health policymaking? To answer these questions it will be useful to place these reforms in a larger context by discussing the two major trends in French governance during the last 50 years: the building up of the welfare state through centralization, and its subsequent decentralization. Some theorists and politicians have wondered aloud whether the institutions have changed so much that it makes sense to start thinking of

France as having entered the Sixth Republic.[1] Le Galès and Pinson provide a more reasonable assessment, predicting the possibility that "the golden age of decentralization may be over" and that the Fifth Republic might have entered a new phase that is "more plural but re-centralizing" (Le Galès and Pinson 2009). I argue in this section that their description of the new phase seems appropriate in the context of health policy, even if the route taken in health policy is different than in other areas. In other words, regionalization is being used as a centralizing tool to enhance coordination rather than to promote local experimentation.

3.1. Centralization (1958–1981)

The high levels of centralization used to build up the welfare state did not begin with the creation of the Fifth Republic in 1958. As the prototypical textbook example of a unitary state, the roots of central control run deep in France, dating to at least the creation of the *départements* in 1790 and the assignment of *Préfets* to each *département* in 1800. This model is viewed as biased against policy diversity, instead prioritizing standardization (Loughlin 2007; Ridley 1973; Schmidt 1990). As was the case in many other nations, the building up of the French welfare state began in earnest during the postwar years. *Sécurité Sociale* was passed in 1945 and became ubiquitous by the early part of the Fifth Republic. Although originally designed only for certain groups of employed citizens, by 1970 *Sécurité Sociale* covered 96% of the French population and was accepted by 89% of French doctors. These percentages have since increased to near universality (Dutton 2007).

3.2. Decentralization: Act I (1982–1986)

Decentralization took place during two major periods, 1982–1986 and 2003–2004, with its roots in the cultural and administrative changes of the 1970s. Although health policy was not the major focus of these reforms, it was obviously impacted. It is important to note that decentralization did not result from one single piece of legislation (Bezes 2009) but was the cumulative effect of more than 40 laws and more than 300 decrees passed between 1982 and 1986. Although the implications of these reforms are too numerous to discuss in detail, it is important to highlight three. First, regions were recognized as a subnational units of government for the first time. Rather than strengthening the hierarchal model, this change greatly confused it. Instead of being legally situated between the departments and the state, regions were given equivalent legal status to the departments. To confuse matters further, the more than 36,000 municipalities throughout France were elevated to the same legal status as departments and regions.

Second, the spreading of power in this way had the effect of significantly reducing the role of the *Préfet*. In fact, many powers traditionally exercised by the Préfets were specifically transferred to the *Conseils Généraux* and the

Conseils Régionales, the legislative bodies of the departments and regions. With regards to health, this meant transferring some competencies from the DDASS to the *Conseil Général*, the departmental-level legislative body (du Mesnil du Buisson and Jeandet-Mengual 2004). Third, the regional councils created in 1982 became fully elected bodies in 1986. Although this was an important development, the historically low turnout of the March 2010 regional elections indicates confusion and apathy among the French over the role of this level of government.

3.3. Decentralization Act II: 2002–2004

After a period in which the *Préfets* were given greater authority relative to the regions, and it seemed that the pendulum might be shifting back toward centralization, Prime Minister Jean-Pierre Raffarin introduced a series of three bills and a constitutional amendment that he described as the second act of decentralization. His proposed change to the constitution was to say that "France is an undivided, lay, democratic, social *and decentralized* Republic". Chirac insisted it instead read "France is an undivided, lay, democratic and social Republic. *Its organization is decentralized*" (emphasis added). It has been suggested that phrasing it this way did not challenge the hierarchal control of the state, ensuring that France would remain a unitary state and not drift toward federalism (Loughlin 2007). In other words, it is important to maintain the perspective that France at its peak of decentralization is (was?) still a relatively centralized system.

3.4. Decentralization and health policy

Understanding this history is important to emphasize how different the trajectory within health care has been from other policy domains. In most areas, the state has been the dominant actor for centuries and has used decentralization to localize decision-making. Although the management of health care was never decentralized *per se* and therefore is not being "re-centralized," the state has not traditionally been the major player as it has been in other policy areas. In the words of one expert, the increased role of the state over health "est très récent, par rapport aux deux siècles qui ont précédé. Donc on a un Etat qui n'a pas de légitimité au niveau de la santé" [the increased role of the state over health is very recent compared to the previous two centuries. Therefore, the state has no legitimacy with regards to health]. Unlike other policy domains in which the trend has been toward greater local control, the state has been pushing for a stronger role within health care. Of course, this is not to say that the France welfare state has not been large – it has, or that the state has not played a role in health policy – it has (Levy 2005).[2] It does however seem fair to say that the state has not had as much of an influence over health policy as one might expect given its role in other policy domains, and that the trend is toward greater state involvement.

Paradoxically, the state has been able to exert more influence by developing stronger territorial organizations (Steffen 2010; Rochaix and Wilsford 2005). As one leader put it, by the 1990s the choice was made for the region to be the level of management in health care, and that despite periodic pressures, this decision has been re-iterated a number of times since. Although the creation of the *Agences Régionales de l'Hospitalisation* in 1996 was seen by some at the time as a move toward regionalization, in practice it tended to strengthen the central government's role in hospital policy setting (Steffen 2010). According to another expert, the ARH were regional agencies operating "au nom de l'Etat" and the state has continued to exercise greater control ever since. In his own words, the ARS represent "l'aboutissement de ces vingt ans d'affirmation du pouvoir de l'Etat ... où l'Etat affirme qu'il est le patron de la santé" (the ARS represent the culmination of these 20 years of the affirmation of the state's power, where the state affirms that it is in charge of health care).

The major distinctions between the ARS and truly decentralized bodies (such as the departmental and regional legislative councils) are the lack of a base of authority separate from the state, and the inability to innovate outside relatively narrow parameters (Richard 2003). The oft-repeated quote in the American federalism literature is that subnational units act as policy laboratories in which the best ideas can rise to the top while the rest are discarded.[3] However, many interviewees described the ARS as being permitted so little experimentation that they essentially have none. From this perspective, the ARS were created to adapt national policies to local circumstances, not to use local differences to shape national policies. We should not expect to observe the type of policy divergence that we see in more decentralized systems, such as the UK since devolution (Greer 2004).

To a large extent the degree of autonomy experienced by the ARS will depend on their budgetary freedom. The ARS do not have a source of income independent of the state and will not be able to set their budgets without approval from the *Conseil de Surveillance* presided over by the *Préfet de region*. Even if a particular region wanted to innovate, its capacity to do so would be severely limited without the state's support.

Some make the mistake of describing the ARS as another example of decentralization. For example, the Health Systems Profile published by the European Observatory on Health Systems and Policies is a bit sloppy with the word "decentralization" when describing the ARS. Using the term too broadly blurs the purpose of each level and the desired effect of the new balance. As Didier Tabuteau described it, "ce n'est pas une décentralisation du tout, pas du tout. Décentralisation – ca veut dire qu'on donne le pouvoir aux collectivités locales. Là, il n'y a pas du tout" [This is not at all a decentralization – not at all. Decentralization means power is given to the local governments. In this case, there is none at all] (interview 2010).

If the ARS do not represent decentralization, how should the agencies be conceptualized? *Déconcentration* is the word that came up most often when speaking with leaders and scholars. Defined as a "système dans lequel l'Etat délègue certains pouvoirs de décision á des agents où organismes locaux qui sont soumis á l'autorité centrale" [a system in which the state delegates certain powers of decision to local agents or bodies who are under a central authority], the term seems appropriate. Rather than giving decision-making power to local bodies subject to constituent pressures, the ARS act as arms of the public administration. Although there is room for a handful of legislators to be involved, the ARS operate without the participation of regional and departmental elected bodies.

Such *déconcentration* can be described as the decentralization of public administration, though doing so greatly overstates the autonomy of local actors. ARS officials have very little room for innovation, no ability to raise money, and a limited ability to spend money without approval from above. The concept brings to mind what Alistair Cole calls "steering at a distance". This framework nicely captures the "top-down impulse of delegating difficult decisions to lower echelons of public administration" (Cole 2008) and suggests that, although regional agencies are making decisions, their policies are largely being "steered" by Paris. As described by Georges Depuis, "La déconcentration n'est que le masque de la centralisation" [*déconcentration* is nothing but a mask for centralization] (Depuis 2000).

3.5. Summary

All of these factors – contractual obligations with the state, direct appointment by the *Conseil de Ministres*, vertical oversight from two ministries, horizontal oversight from the *Préfet de Région*, lack of budgetary autonomy, and so on – support Le Galès and Pinson's prediction about a new centralizing phase of the Fifth Republic, at least with regards to this particular policy domain. What I have argued is unique about health care is that there never was a "golden age of decentralization" (Le Galès and Pinson, 2009) to transition away from. Instead, regionalization ironically seems to serve as the mechanism toward greater centralization.

4. Equity, quality, and efficiency

According to the website of the Ile-de-France ARS, the new agencies were created with four broad objectives (with my translation): (1) to contribute to a reduction of health inequalities, (2) to assure better access to care, (3) to improve the organization and coordination of care, and (4) to assure increased efficiency, meaning both improved quality of care and quality of management. In short, "c'est plus de proximité, plus de simplicité, et plus d'efficacité pour les citoyens, les professionnels de santé, et les collectivités locales" [it's closer, simpler, and more effective for citizens, health professions, and communities] (Agence Régionale de Santé: Ile-de-France 2010). The principle guiding their creation is that each of these goals will be better achieved if stakeholders are brought together rather than acting in isolation. However, few details are provided about how much money this restructuring will save, the mechanisms by which it will improve the quality of care, or how it will address the social determinants of health affecting issues such as obesity.

A common explanation for how the ARS will increase efficiency is through the reduction of redundancy within the bureaucracy. For health care to become more efficient, the incentives of health professionals need to be aligned with all other actors. Bellanger and Mossé argue that all previous attempts to reduce costs and waste have failed due to the path-dependent nature of stakeholder incentives (Bellanger and Mossé 2005). It is unclear exactly how this reform would be different. Although nobody lost their job due to the creation of the ARS, there is an expectation that administrative streamlining should occur over time by leaving vacancies unfilled. It appears that the ARS directors will have a significant amount of discretion over how to achieve this goal. If done well, it could lead to increased efficiency within the ARS. If not, it could lead to increased inequality among the regions. As with most aspects of the newly created ARS, it is too early to know their net impact.

One of the hopes guiding the creation of the ARS is that they will enable the state to target interventions in the areas where they are needed most. Some health issues are ubiquitous enough to deserve national programs; however, each region has its own set of acute problems. For example, leaders in Bretagne are concerned about the high rates of alcoholism reported in the region. Many regions, including Bretagne and Midi-Pyrénées, struggle to attract enough health professionals to work in the vast rural areas relatively far from cities. Although health insurance is near-universal, access to healthcare services is still a major concern in many places. It remains to be seen exactly how much ability ARS leaders will have to craft local solutions to their unique challenges. ARS leaders in Bretagne have taken a particularly interesting approach, defining the borders of their *Territoires de Santé* (planning organizations at the subregional level) according to population and hospital locations instead of according to the departmental borders as was done in most other ARS. The hope is that resources at the most local level can be targeted to where they are needed most.

In many ways these reforms represent a typically French solution to the issues of equality, quality, and efficiency. Dutton suggests that a central question of every French and US health-reform debate is how to balance the principles of *liberté* and *égalité*.[4] Unlike in the USA where liberty tends to be emphasized at the expense of equality, the French are willing to sacrifice some liberty – and accept the centralization it requires – in pursuit of equality (Dutton 2007). Equality in this context generally refers to equal application of the law with the ultimate goal of equal outcomes due to equal provisions of services. The underlying principle is that if regions are allowed to experiment and adapt policies to too large a degree, citizens in some areas will inevitably receive worse services than citizens in others. In other words, the best way to strive for equality is through local adaptation of a clear national strategy rather than by developing myriads of local strategies, and that the potential benefits of local experimentation do not outweigh the importance of consistency between regions. A statement by Jean-Marie Bertrand, of *Secrétariat Général des Ministères Chargés des Affaires Sociales* at the time of the transition, epitomizes this point of view: "Comment les projets régionales de santé peuvent-ils atteindre leurs objectifs si le pilotage national ne donne pas d'orientations cohérentes? Pire, si elles sont inexistantes?" [How can the regional health projects achieve their objectives if the *pilotage national* does not provide coherent orientation? Worse, if they are non-existent?] (Bertrand 2010).

Although this logic of regional agencies requiring strong national oversight to achieve their goals is perfectly consistent with French governing, it would be startling in other contexts, including the American tea party. However, this perspective might have some theoretical support. For example, Cai et al. (2009) argue that centralization might actually lead to more policy experimentation and innovation than decentralization. Similarly, a model developed by Kollman et al. (2000) indicates that once a threshold level of complexity is reached for a given policy domain, centralization is more beneficial than decentralization. In other words, although decentralization is perhaps ideal for problems of medium difficulty, the most challenging issues might best be addressed with higher levels of centralization. One possible explanation is that centralized governing reduces the number of veto-players, thereby reducing the number of compromises needed and the number of potential deal-breaking hang-ups.

4.1. Convergence?

On the other hand, one of the hypotheses explored throughout this book is that democratic decentralization puts pressure on local leaders to ensure that their regions remain competitive. By this logic, we would expect to see convergence over time in decentralized nations in terms of public spending for health as leaders are constantly looking over their shoulders to other regions. Residents would punish leaders who let their region fall behind. Conversely, in centralized nations we would expect a lack of convergence due to a lack of competitive pressure and policy levers by local leaders.

The French case offers an interesting and potentially supportive, though ultimately unsatisfying, exploration of this hypothesis. Although I have argued throughout this chapter that French health care has been relatively "uncentralized," it is important to once again stress that this is not the same as being legislatively or democratically decentralized. In other words, although the center has historically lacked strong control over health, we would still expect to see a lack of convergence on healthcare spending over time.

This exploration is ultimately unsatisfying because of the difficulty of obtaining data on regional health spending that are clear and comparable over time. Perhaps it is an interesting finding in and of itself that such data apparently do not exist. An additional challenge in making such comparisons is accounting for all the factors that affect health spending, including demographic characteristics, actual disease burden, demand for medical services, and supply of accessible medical infrastructure. Although not to be relied on as representative of actual need, the total amount reimbursed by the three major health insurance schemes is a useful indicator of general spending trends in the regions.

From the available evidence there does not seem to be a clear trend toward convergence throughout the 22 regions of mainland France. Although some have argued that disparities in health spending are diminishing, there are still clear disparities. In 2010 (through 31 October) there was an approximate mean of 1735 euros reimbursed per person per region. Spending was as high as 2095 in Provences-Alpes-Cote-d'Azur and as low as 1490 in Pays de la Loire. One example of the change over time is the difference between the regions of Poitou-Charentes and Ile-de-France. This disparity is not new. In 1997, the total reimbursement per person in Poitou-Charentes was 8509 French francs, compared with 10,091 in Ile-de-France. Converted to 2010 euros for the sake of comparison, this is a difference of 1678 and 1990. Rather than diminishing, this difference has actually increased somewhat, with spending in Poitou-Charentes at 1497 euros per person compared with 1875 in Ile-de-France.[5] Although hardly conclusive, there does not seem to be a convergence in terms of health spending throughout the regions. Following the success or failure of the ARS's efforts to reduce disparities over time will be an interesting test of this hypothesis.

5. *La mise en place des ARS*: Obstacles and tensions

Although the success of the *Agences Régionales de Santé* largely depends on the balance of power between the ARS and the *pilotage national*, there are a number of other important obstacles that will need to be overcome. Although it seems too obvious to state, one of the most significant short-term challenges facing the ARS will be their actual creation. Although they have existed at the time of writing for a year and a half, much work still remains. In many ways, creating an agency by combining previously existing organizations might be more difficult than creating one from the ground up. Many people are now working in the ARS at the same desk, in the same building, and with the same team as before. It is only natural, especially for mid-level workers who probably have less at stake in the agency's success, to rely on their previous reflexes and networks. One of the major issues will be how the relationship between health insurance and the ARS evolves over time. It is perhaps an ominous sign that I received somewhat different assessments of the first few months of this relationship depending on who I talked with.

Creating an organizational culture requires developing goals and plans at the macro-level, but it also requires taking into consideration the micro-level adaptations such a reform requires. For example, mid-level workers describe ambivalence bordering on frustration in response to the changes they are facing. To some people, not much more has changed than the sign on the door. For others, particularly those in health insurance, the change brings them into an entirely new type of organization. The process of reform was made somewhat easier in that each person retained their previous employment status, and the associated benefits packages, they had before the creation of the ARS. The unintended consequence of this is the institutional confusion some feel about working side by side with someone they used to consider an outsider. Simple issues like the different number of vacation days and different types of meal tickets for the office restaurant reinforce these differences.

Creating an agency culture is far more than merely a symbolic issue, as streamlining management by bringing stakeholders together is advertised as one of the major mechanisms through which increased efficiency, quality, and equity will occur. Most expect this process to take many years.

Another important obstacle challenging the establishment of the ARS is the fact that they were created during a severe economic crisis. A number of leaders expressed concern that the reforms call for more change and development than could be afforded. This is true both for the policy initiatives the agencies would be undertaking, but also for the physical and symbolic creation of the agencies as a single organization. It is harder to justify the expense of constructing new buildings in this economic climate.

A final potential challenge is the fact that all of these changes are happening after the 2012 presidential and legislative elections, which produced a major Socialist victory. Unlike the American health reform, which delays the initiation of many changes until 2014, the French reform happened quickly enough, and was sufficiently implemented before the elections, to make it relatively safe from electoral politics. A number of interviewees also pointed out that the creation of the ARS themselves is actually a fairly non-partisan issue, that the platforms for both candidates in the 2007 presidential election contained similar proposals. That is not to say that health care will not be a major issue in the next presidential campaign, but that the debate will largely revolve around major financing questions somewhat removed from issues of ARS governance.

6. Conclusion

Analyzing the creation of new regional health agencies in France provides an opportunity to assess common assumptions about decentralization and its effects. On the one hand, the reform is consistent with most definitions of decentralization. Regional-level agencies are responsible for meeting the health needs of their populations. Although the agencies are not overseen directly by locally elected legislative bodies, there are enough connections to elected officials to give the impression of democratic involvement. However, the room for autonomy and innovation is so minimal, and the vertical and horizontal oversight is so strong, that this reform greatly strengthens central control over health policymaking.

As a result of this mix of rhetoric, it is difficult to make predictions about the effects of this reform on disparities. Even if the definitions and assumptions about decentralization were clearer, it would be difficult to know what evidence to apply. In a sense, the French reform attempts to have the best of both approaches, building local input into a system of central coordination. Although the agencies do not have the downward accountability consistent with the democratic assumption of decentralization, there are enough opportunities for stakeholder contributions that an ARS director would ignore grassroots voices at his or her own risk. In the case of an attentive director, perhaps we can expect many of the supposed benefits of decentralization such as high levels of enthusiasm and investment among local actors. At the same time, because the agencies are so tightly monitored from Paris, we might expect many of the supposed benefits of centralization, including information sharing, coordination, cohesion, and actors with an incentive to maintain a perspective broader than their own regions.

Although there are high expectations for this hybrid approach, it may not be exportable to other places or other moments in time. Unfortunately, it will likely be many years before we know the effect of this approach on disparities. When pressed for a prediction about the success of the ARS, the most common reaction among ARS leaders was cautious optimism.

Acknowledgments

This research was made possible in part by a grant from the Center for European Studies – European Union Center at the University of Michigan. Sarah Sacuto deserves particular recognition for her assistance, as do Olivia and Anne Jones.

Notes

1. Loughlin (2007) describes these well. Some are more aggressive than others, calling for a reassessment of French institutions and even a new constitution. For example,

consider Arnaud Montebourg's Convention pour la 6ème République http://www. c6r.org.
2. Many people have done a better job than I could of summarizing the role of the state in the political history of French health care; Dutton (2007) is a particularly good place to start. Palier (2002) provides a comprehensive analysis of the history of *La Sécurité Sociale* in France.
3. Judge Louis Brandeis, dissent in *New State Ice Co.* v. *Liebmann*, 285 U.S. 262, 52 S.Ct. 371, 76 L.Ed. 747 (1932).
4. Although his book was published before the 2009 French health reform and the 2010 US health reform laws were passed, his observation is still valid and important.
5. Data come from DREES, Eco-santé, and INSEE.

References

Acteurspublics. (2009). www.acteurspublics.com. *Les futures ARS ont leurs patrons.* 1 October 2009. http://www.acteurspublics.com/article/01-10-09/les-futures-ars-ont-leurs-patrons. Retrieved on 8 August 2010.

Agence Régionale de Santé (2011) Contrat pluriannuels d'objectifs et de moyens (CPOM) de Bretagne. Agence Régionale de Santé. Paris.

Agence Régionale de Santé: Ile-de-France (2010) *Qu'est-ce qu'une ARS?* http://www.sante-iledefrance.fr/a-propos-2/. Retrieved on 15 July 2010.

Bachelot-Narquin, Rosalyne (2009) *Discussion au Sénat du Projet de Loi 'HPST.'* 12 May 2009. http://www.sante-jeunesse-sports.gouv.fr/discussion-au-senat-du-projet-de-loi-hpst-discours-de-madame-roselyne-bachelot-narquin.html. Ministère de la Santé et des Sports. Retrieved on 10 November 2010.

Bellanger, M.M. and Mossé, P.R. (2005) "The Search for the Holy Grail: Combining Decentralised Planning and Contracting Mechanisms in the French Health Care System." *Health Economics.* 14(S1): S119–S132.

Bertrand, J. (2010) *Le résumé de l'intervention de Jean-Marie BERTRAND, au salon Hôpital Expo.* 30 May 2010. http://www.ars.sante.fr/fileadmin/PORTAIL/Discours/Resume_intervention_JMB_30mai2010.doc. Agence Regionale de Sante. Retrieved on 6 August 2010.

Bezes, P. (2009) *Réinventer l'état: les réformes de l'administration française, 1962–2008.* Presses universitaires de France. Paris.

Bezes, P. and Le Ledic, P. (2007) "French Top Civil Servants Within Changing Configurations: From Monopolization to Contested Places and Roles?" in *From the Active to the Enabling State: The Changing Role of Top Officials in European Nations.* Edward Page and Vincent Wright. eds. Palgrave Macmillan. Basingstoke; New York.

Cai, H. and Treisman, D. (2009) "Political Decentralization and Policy Experimentation." *Quarterly Journal of Political Science.* 4(1): pp. 35–58.

Cole, A. (2008) *Governing and Governance in France.* Cambridge University Press. Cambridge.

Depuis, G. (2000) *Le centre et la périphérie en France: essai historique et juridique.* L.G.D.J. Paris.

Du Mesnil du Buisson, Marie-Ange and Emmanuèle Jeandet-Mengual (2004) "L'Organisation des Services Territoriaus de l'Etat dans le Domaine Sanitaire et Social: Une Evolution Nécessaire." *Revue Francaise des Affaires Sociale.* 4(4): pp. 61–83.

Dupuy, F. and Thoenig, J. (1983) *Sociologie de l'Administration Francaise.* A. Colin. Paris.

Dutton, P.V. (2007) *Differential diagnoses: a comparative history of health care problems and solutions in the United States and France*. ILR Press/Cornell University Press. Ithaca.

Gaudin, Jean-Pierre (1999) *Gouverner Par Contrat*. Les Presses de Sciences Po. Paris.

Greer, Scott L. (2004) *Territorial Politics and Health Policy: The United Kingdom in Comparative Perspective*. Manchester University Press. Manchester.

Kaiser Family Foundation (2008). *International Health Systems: France*. http://www.kaiseredu.org/Issue-Modules/International-Health-Systems/France.aspx#Background Brief. KaiserEDU: Health Policy Explained. Retrieved on November 2010.

Kollman, K., Miller, J.H. and Page, S.E. (2000) "Decentralization and the Search for Policy Solutions." *Journal of Law Economic Organizational*. APR. 16(1): pp. 102–128.

Le Galès, P. and Pinson, G. (2009) "Local/Regional Governments and Centre-Periphery Relations in the Fifth Republic," in *The French Fifth Republic at Fifty: Beyond Stereotypes*. Sylvain Brouard, Andrew M. Appleton and Amy Mazur. eds. Palgrave Macmillan. Basingstoke.

Levy, J.D. (2005) "Redeploying the State: Liberalization and Social Policy in France," in *Beyond Continuity*. Wolfgang Streeck and Kathleen Thelen. eds. Oxford University Press. Oxford.

Loughlin, J. (2007) *Subnational Government: The French Experience*. Palgrave MacMillan. Basingstoke.

Palier, B. (2002) *Gouverner la sécurité sociale: les réformes du système français de protection sociale depuis 1945*. Presses universitaires de France. Paris.

République Francaise (2008) *Nicolas Sarkozy Annonce la Réforme des Service Déconcentrés de l'Etat*. 9 April 2008. http://www.gouvernement.fr/gouvernement/nicolas-sarkozy-annonce-la-reforme-des-services-deconcentres-de-l-etat. Portail du Gouvernement. Retrieved on 10 November 2010.

Richard, P. (2003) *Les citoyens au coeur de la décentralisation*. Editions de l'Aube. La Tour d'Aigues.

Ridley, F.F. (1973) *The French Prefectoral System: An Example of Integrated Administrative Decentralisation*. H.M. Stationery Off. London.

Rochaix, L. and Wilsford, D. (2005) "State Autonomy, Policy Paralysis: Paradoxes of Institutions and Culture in the French Health Care System." *Journal of Health Politics, Policy Law*. FEB-APR. 30(1–2): pp. 97–119.

Rodwin, V.G. and Le Pen, C. (2004) "Health Care Reform in France – The Birth of State-Led Managed Care." *New England Journal of Medicine*. 351: pp. 2259–2262.

Schmidt, V.A. (1990) *Democratizing France: The Political and Administrative History of Decentralization*. Cambridge University Press. Cambridge.

Steffen, M. (2010) "The French Health Care System: Liberal Universalism." *Journal of Health Politics, Policy Law*. 35(3): pp. 353–387.

Tabuteau, D. (2010) Loi: "Hopital, patients, santé, et territoire": des interrogations pour demain! *Santé Publique*. 22(1): pp. 79–90.

World Health Organization (2000) *The World Health Report 2000 Health Systems: Improving Performance*. World Health Organization. Geneva.

11
Devolution, Nationalism, and the Limits of Social Solidarity: The Federalization of Health Policy in Belgium

Janet Laible

1. Introduction

Observers who attempt to situate Belgium in typologies of European healthcare systems inevitably conclude that Belgium is a hybrid, possessing characteristics of different types in a unique "ecosystem" of health care. The Belgian system in part resembles NHS-style systems with their reliance on tax revenues to finance health care; but Belgium also relies, perhaps to a surprising extent in Western Europe, on private expenditure. Belgium has strong elements of so-called mutual aid systems in which government's role largely entails subsidizing and regulating the private organizations that serve as insurers (Immergut 1992). However, the Belgian system goes beyond the limited intervention understood by this model: government spending in Belgium is considerable and insurance coverage is extensive and compulsory. As in the Dutch and German systems, insurers in Belgium act as intermediaries between patients and providers, with extensive market freedom for doctors, hospitals, and patients. Yet compared with its neighbors, Belgium exhibits distinctive traits, for example, being less enthusiastic than the Netherlands about embracing market-based reforms to achieve efficiencies (Schokkaert and Van de Voorde 2010; van Doorslaer and Schut 2000). Overall, Belgium belongs on the spectrum of national insurance healthcare systems, in which the state plays the role of the administrator or "steward" of the health system, not the owner, with a focus on enabling the system to achieve social goals such as redistributive or equity-promoting outcomes (Saltman 2004: 5–6).

The federalization of the Belgian state over the past three decades has imposed a new and intricate institutional infrastructure on top of a complex healthcare system.[1] This chapter demonstrates how the institutions created by federalization catalyzed nationalist political actors to redefine health policy, turning it from a relatively depoliticized area of social policy into a contentious domain encompassing issues of identity, values, and culture. Until recently, the territorial politics of health care in Belgium were largely concerned with managing the process of devolution of authority over health care and financing. Instead, regionalists and nationalists have turned health care – and social security more broadly construed – into issues that threaten to undermine federal authority and the remaining shared institutions of the Belgian state. Belgium, like other advanced industrialized states, must develop mechanisms to cope with increasing expenditures in health care predicted for the coming century. Legislating healthcare reforms that respect the political ideals embedded in the Belgian system and that garner consensus among key policy actors would be difficult under ordinary circumstances, but health care has emerged as a battleground in the highly contentious politics of constitutional reform, in which some nationalists are arguing for the breakup of the Belgian state.

2. Allocation of authority

2.1. Overview of Belgian political institutions

Belgian federal institutions at the beginning of the twenty-first century attempt to address several interrelated social, economic, and political concerns that the unitary Belgian state established in 1830 failed to manage. Current federal arrangements coexist within a political architecture of proportional representation and consociational bargaining to guarantee the protection of language rights and a high degree of territorial self-determination.[2] Policy authority in Belgium has been granted both to territorial authorities (the Flemish, Walloon, and Brussels-Capital regions) and to linguistic groups (the Dutch-speaking or Flemish, French, and German-speaking communities), with the federal government retaining an ever-shrinking policy mandate for Belgium as a whole. Brussels is the only bilingual region in Belgium. Each region and community was initially empowered with its own legislative body, although the Flemish Region and the Flemish Community authorities later fused because these populations are largely coterminous.[3] The federal chambers and regional parliaments have had separate elections since constitutional reforms of 1993, providing for distinct electoral mandates for representatives in these institutions; the French Community Parliament is composed of the members of the Walloon Regional Parliament and the francophone members of the Brussels Regional Parliament.

After four decades of constitutional reform, the Belgian regions have jurisdiction in policy domains that are generally understood to have a territorial component, including economic affairs (excluding monetary and fiscal policy), land use, housing and urban planning, environmental issues, transportation, public works, industrial policy and industrial subsidies, rural development, agriculture, some aspects of energy policy, and employment policy (Laible 2008; Portail Belgium.be). The language communities of Belgium were granted authority over cultural and other "personalizable" matters. These include most aspects of education, culture, media, use of languages, and aspects of health policy, as well as aid to people (youth, families, immigrant accommodation, and social aid). The French community exercises authority in the Walloon provinces, with the exception of the German-speaking communes in the east of Wallonia, and in French-language institutions in Brussels; the Flemish community exercises authority in Flemish provinces and in Dutch-language institutions in Brussels (Portail Belgium.be). Reforms in 2001 extended some powers to Francophones in the Flemish region.

The residual powers of the federal government include aspects of "high politics" such as defense and foreign affairs, citizenship, federal finance, justice, internal security, social security and aspects of health care, to which I return below. Furthermore, the regions and communities have made incursions into policy areas traditionally reserved for central governments: the constitution grants them the capacity to engage in international cooperation (i.e. to make treaties), provided the substance of the treaties concerns one of their policy jurisdictions.

2.2. Allocation of authority in health policy

The challenges of identifying healthcare jurisdictions in Belgium derive from the fact that federalization occurred after the core principles and structures of the healthcare system had been established in the previously centralized Belgian state. Thus decision-making and the implementation of healthcare policy are highly fragmented across the federal and substate levels.

Somewhat remarkably, given the devolutionary pressures on the central state in recent decades, health policy and health insurance remain largely under the authority of the federal government as an element of its social security remit. The federal government has exclusive authority over health insurance, sets the overall budget for health care, and creates framework legislation for healthcare institutions, including hospitals (Banting and Corbett 2002: 10). The central state is responsible for ambulatory care and physician services, legislation on the practice of medicine including professional qualifications, and the regulation and prices of pharmaceuticals.[4] In ambulatory care, the communities' role is limited to organizing and managing home care and to mental health services. With respect to hospital care, the communities' main role is in capital investment: they are responsible for hospital construction, renovations and internal organization, and for managing nursing home care, although they must adhere to the constraints of federal financing and norms established by federal authorities. By law, communities must communicate their decisions to the federal government so that federal authorities can ensure compliance with federal guidelines (de Cock 2002: 53).

The Institutional Reform Act of 1980 federalized personalizable matters to the communities and defined these matters in health care as curative health care (with important exceptions that have left responsibility for much of this care at the level of the federal government) and policy related to health education, health promotion and preventive health care. The communities are responsible for investigating and controlling infectious and non-infectious diseases; managing childhood vaccination programs; managing public health, including informational campaigns; maternity and child health care; occupational and school health care; and data collection (Gerkens and Merkur 2010: 89). Communities are also responsible for implementing accreditation standards. The division of authority in health policy leads to some "mixed competences" for particular diseases. Johan de Cock notes the example of polio: vaccination is a community responsibility unless there is a legal responsibility to vaccinate (as there is with polio), in which case it is a federal responsibility. He also describes hepatitis B as a "mixed" disease, for which the federal government pays for vaccine but the communities must organize the vaccination campaign (the different levels of government signed an agreement for cooperation in this case) (de Cock 2002).

Federalization has produced multiple institutional asymmetries in health policy at the substate level. The fusion of the Flemish Region and Flemish Community authorities represents the clearest example of institutional asymmetry, with implications for health policy in Flanders and in Brussels. The Flemish Agency for Care and Health, which is responsible for developing and implementing health policy for the Flemish community, is located within the Flemish (regional) Ministry for Welfare, Public Health and Family. However, within the French Community, the General Administration of Youth Support, Health and Sport exercises its authority separately from the Walloon region, the health responsibilities of which are largely related to the construction and management of facilities, mental health services, environmental health, and some aspects of home health care (Portal Wallonia). Even this latter set of responsibilities represents an institutional asymmetry, given the constitutional delegation of personalizable matters to *communities*. In 1993, a reform to the Belgian constitution enabled the French Community to transfer some health policy authority to the Walloon Region and to the French-speaking community in Brussels.

Asymmetries in authority over health policy are also produced by the unique status of Brussels as a bilingual region. The Joint Community Commission in Brussels includes members of both language groups from the Brussels Parliament and is responsible for bilingual facilities that belong to neither community (such as some social services and city hospitals). The Commission also has authority over personalizable matters such as the regulation of local nursing, care for the disabled, and preventive care.

To protect the rights of both language groups, the decisions of the Joint Community Commission require a double majority (i.e. a majority from each language group) (Parlament der Deutschsprachigen Gemeinschaft.be). However, when an issue pertains only to institutions working in French, that issue is subject to the authority of the French Community Commission (COCOF), composed of the French-speaking members of the Brussels Parliament. There is no parallel institutional authority for Dutch-speakers in Brussels. Given the fusion of the Flemish Region and Community parliaments, the Flemish Community Commission (VGC) in Brussels is only empowered to implement the decisions of the Flemish Parliament: unlike the COCOF, the VGC is not a legislative body (de Cock 2002: 42–3). Currently, six authorities have a role in health policy in the Brussels region: the federal state, the French- and Dutch-speaking communities, the Joint Community Commission, the COCOF and the VGC (European Observatory on Health Care Systems 2000: 17).

2.3. Financing health care in Belgium

The structure and mechanisms of healthcare financing in Belgium contribute to the dominance of the Belgian federal state in the system. Health insurance in Belgium is compulsory, and health care is largely publicly funded and provided by independent private providers operating on a fee-for-service basis. Patients may choose their providers (including specialists), their hospitals, and the sickness funds that operate as insurers, although the latter all provide the same coverage under compulsory insurance and are subject to the same reimbursement rules. Five private, nonprofit associations of sickness funds and one public national association sickness fund reimburse health benefits and represent their members in the National Institute for Health and Disability Insurance (RIZIV/INAMI).[5] The market for compulsory insurance is closed to new entrants, although supplemental insurance may be offered by private for-profit insurers, as well as by the existing sickness funds (Schokkaert and Van de Voorde 2005; Schokkaert et al. 2010). However, sickness funds do seek to compete for members, in part with supplemental insurance policies but also based on the quality of their customer service and their efficiency in settling claims (Schokkaert and Van de Voorde 2003). More than 99% of the population is covered by a broad package of benefits, with some modifications for the self-employed: benefits include more than 8000 services set out in a nationally established fee schedule (Gerkens and Merkur 2010: 15).

Patients receiving ambulatory medical care pay the full amount to the provider and submit a receipt to their sickness fund for reimbursement. Reimbursements depend on the type of treatment, the insurance status of the patient and the type of provider from which treatment was received. Generally, full costs are not reimbursed: the patient is responsible for a co-payment unless he or she has preferential reimbursement status due to disability, age, income, or other specified types of qualification for social aid. For hospital care and pharmaceuticals, sickness funds are billed directly and patients pay only the co-payment, and for inpatient hospital visits, some additional costs. Again, reimbursement rates vary, for example depending on the classification of a pharmaceutical product as well as the reimbursement status of the patient (Federal Public Service Social Security 2008). Co-payments are about 25% for general practitioner appointments, 35% for home visits by GPs, and 40% for specialist appointments and a variety of other services, with markedly lower rates (approximately half) for patients with preferential status (Gerkens and Merkur 2010).

Major reforms in the healthcare system have occurred in response to concerns about rising costs and expenditures, coupled with a political commitment by the federal state to ensure equitable access to the system (discussed in a later section). Since the constitutional reforms of 1980, reforms of the healthcare system have focused on managing costs by increasing the financial accountability of the major players in the system and by managing the supply side of health provision. The federal government has used its legislative, budgetary, and regulatory capabilities in efforts to achieve these goals. Early reforms in the 1980s sought to reduce hospital costs by restricting the increase in the supply of hospital beds and encouraging economies of scale in facilities; new legislation began to move hospitals in the direction of prospective financing; and a fixed national budget was introduced for laboratory testing.[6] In addition, efforts to manage the supply of providers took the form of quotas for authorized practicing physicians in 1997.

The manner in which RIZIV/INAMI reimburses sickness funds was significantly altered by the Law Moureaux of 1993, to "increase the cost consciousness and cost participation of all the partners in the health care sector". Before this time, the funds were fully reimbursed and had no incentives to control costs. Since the entry into force of the law in 1995, the distribution of resources among the funds has been based on a formula by which the finances of each fund are a weighted combination of its share in a risk-adjusted prospective budget and its share in actual expenditures. A "growth norm" initially sought to restrict the annual maximum increase in health expenditures to 1.5%, although this ceiling was later raised. The sickness funds are also financially accountable for a portion (currently 25%) of the discrepancy between their actual spending and their budget (Schokkaert and Van de Voorde 2005, 2010).

Compulsory health insurance is mainly financed through social security contributions and general taxation, with the Belgian financing mix described as "among the most progressive in Europe" (Schokkaert and Van de Voorde 2005: S27). In 2009, social security contributions accounted for 66% of this financing; state subsidies (revenue from general taxation, which is used by the federal government to subsidize the difference between the a priori health budget and social security contributions) for 10%; alternative financing (mainly value-added tax) for 14%; and "allocated and diverse receipts" (special contributions such as those by employers for early retirement) for 10% (Gerkens and Merkur 2010). Although social security contributions are no longer "earmarked" but are centrally collected and distributed to programs based on projected need, social contributions for particular programs are fixed. Employed workers pay social security contributions for medical care and disability benefits at 4.7% of gross salary; employers' contributions cover medical care, disability benefits, family benefits, occupational illnesses and workplace accidents, and constitute 14.45% of gross salary (Federal Public Service Social Security 2008).

Central government finances cover most medical costs, although sickness funds also receive a small flat-rate premium of about 10 euros per year directly from each member (Schokkaert and Van de Voorde 2005). The Belgian communities have limited fiscal roles in general and have chosen not exercise the constitutional authority granted to them to raise taxes (largely for political reasons related to the linguistic status of Brussels residents). The regions, communities, and local authorities of Belgium combined have increased their spending significantly in the decades since the devolution of health policy but still constitute only about 3.5% of health expenditure (Gerkens and Merkur 2010). Some preventive care is co-financed by the federal government and the communities (Table 11.1).

The federal government also sets the annual a priori total budget for healthcare expenditure, which along with health insurance includes expenditures on RIZIV/INAMI, social and fiscal maximum billing,[7] the hospital budget, various administrative and other costs, and the Federal Public Service of Health, Food Chain Safety and Environment. Yet although the federal government plays the primary role in regulating and financing the healthcare system, this role often involves the consensus-building among social groups that characterizes many aspects of Belgian politics. The governance of the insurance system is negotiated within RIZIV/INAMI under the management of two bodies: the General Council is composed of representatives of employers, employees, the sickness funds and the federal government and deals with financial issues (including the budget). The Insurance Committee manages the organization of the health insurance system and includes representatives of the sickness funds and healthcare providers (de Cock 2002: 47). The latter negotiate annually to establish the *nomenclature*, the fee schedules that cover each type of service, the rules for applying these services, and required qualifications for care providers, although this schedule must conform to federal budgetary targets. Sickness funds also negotiate with pharmaceutical companies on reimbursement rates for their products. The process has been described as a "bilateral monopoly supervised by the central government", with the sickness funds acting like a cartel in negotiations, and with government ultimately having

Table 11.1 Healthcare expenditures: benefits in cash (million euro)

Year	Payments for sickness and invalidity			Industrial accidents			Occupational diseases			Social benefits in cash, other		
	Ins funds	Fed	R&C	Ins funds	Fed	R&C	Ins funds	Fed	R&C	Ins funds	Fed	R&C
12/31/09	4943.4	0	0	190.3	0	0	332.2	0	0	348	242	689.6
12/31/08	4553.5	0	0	189.7	0	0	340.8	0	0	416.8	174.6	649.8
12/31/07	4143.8	0	0	182.7	0	0	325.5	0	0	404.2	171.2	628.9
12/31/06	3838.5	0	0	178.4	0	0	325	0	0	283.8	169.7	577.3
12/31/05	3636.4	0	0	176.1	0	0	327.1	0	0	211.9	190.9	558.6
12/31/04	3485.4	0	0	169.2	0	0	325.5	0	0	257.6	180.6	525.9
12/31/03	3366.1	0	0	164.1	0	0	329.9	0	0	237.2	198.2	484.7
12/31/02	3207.7	0	0	169.1	0	0	326	0	0	203.1	178	448.7
12/31/01	3023.3	0	0	164.2	0	0	325	0	0	136.3	210.7	447.2
12/31/00	2839.6	0	0	161.5	0	0	324.3	0	0	148.7	237.8	447.6
12/31/99	2721.8	0	0	168.4	0	0	316.3	0	0	117	238.4	387.3
12/31/98	2634.8	0	0	158.5	0	0	335.9	0	0	89.6	272.4	394.5
12/31/97	2546.7	0	0	152.8	0	0	336.4	0	0	100.8	269.5	381.5
12/31/96	2543.3	0	0	152.7	0	0	349	0	0	95.9	262.8	368.6
12/31/95	2482	0	0	154.5	0	0	358.9	0	0	129.5	262.4	362
12/31/94	2430.5	0	0	152.6	0	0	365.7	0	0	53.2	239.7	393.2
12/31/93	2415.6	0	0	153.4	0	0	367.5	0	0	41.7	221.8	358.8
12/31/92	2393.3	0	0	153.3	0	0	381.5	0	0	58.4	197.5	341.8
12/31/91	2356.1	0	0	156.2	0	0	372.3	0	0	24	190.6	295.6
12/31/90	2216.6	0	0	149.2	0	0	363	0	0	36.8	152.9	314.4
12/31/89	2078.9	0	0	155.8	0	0	359.8	0	0	36.7	217.7	309.9

Table 11.1 (Continued)

Year	Payments for sickness and invalidity			Industrial accidents			Occupational diseases			Social benefits in cash, other		
	Ins funds	Fed	R&C	Ins funds	Fed	R&C	Ins funds	Fed	R&C	Ins funds	Fed	R&C
12/31/88	1990	0	0	151.9	0	0	354.5	0	0	27.2	408.2	0
12/31/87	1989.7	0	0	155.8	0	0	354.9	0	0	26.8	278.8	0
12/31/86	2092.1	0	0	158.2	0	0	367.4	0	0	27.7	306.9	0
12/31/85	2101.5	0	0	159.4	0	0	376.1	0	0	25.1	324.2	0
12/31/84	2015	0	0	160	0	0	391.1	0	0	19.5	277.1	0
12/31/83	1907.2	0	0	147.5	0	0	391.6	0	0	44.8	206.3	0
12/31/82	1796.6	0	0	129.5	0	0	388.2	0	0	37.2	44	0
12/31/81	1685.3	0	0	118.3	0	0	360.6	0	0	31.9	93.4	0
12/31/80	1560.4	0	0	109.1	0	0	344.2	0	0	7.9	107.7	0
12/31/79	1435.1	0	0	101.9	0	0	321.4	0	0	0.9	199.4	0
12/31/78	1321.3	0	0	97.6	0	0	310.4	0	0	1	227.1	0
12/31/77	1193	0	0	89.3	0	0	285.8	0	0	0	197.2	0
12/31/76	1099.7	0	0	81.9	0	0	259.9	0	0	0	94.8	0
12/31/75	937.9	0	0	69.5	0	0	221.1	0	0	0	178.4	0
12/31/74	726.5	0	0	43.2	0	0	179.2	0	0	0	98.3	0
12/31/73	595.4	0	0	33.2	0	0	147.6	0	0	0	160.7	0
12/31/72	509.7	0	0	30	0	0	141.7	0	0	0	90.2	0
12/31/71	430.5	0	0	24	0	0	121.3	0	0	0	92.8	0
12/31/70	370.1	0	0	22.4	0	0	77.3	0	0	0	96.4	0

Source: National Bank of Belgium, Belgostat Online, http://www.nbb.be/pub/stats, accessed between 1 December 2010 and 12 July 2011. The NBB reports data for all spending on social benefits; the categories presented here are the only ones related to health care.
Ins funds = Expenditure by the social insurance funds.
Fed = Expenditure by the federal government.
R&C = Expenditure by the regions and communities.

veto power over fee levels and the ability to impose unilateral changes if the prospective budget faces difficulties during a given year (Schokkaert and Van de Voorde 2005).

However, private outlays for healthcare costs are considerable in Belgium and are relatively high compared with those of Belgium's neighbors. Out-of-pocket payments after reinsurance, including co-payments, healthcare goods and services not included in the nomenclature, and extra-billing for hospital services, constitute about 20% of total health expenditures in Belgium. According to OECD data from 2007, the figure was 5.5% in the Netherlands, 6.5% in Luxembourg (2006 data), 6.8% in France, and 13.1% in Germany (Gerkens and Merkur 2010). Both sickness funds and private for-profit insurers offer supplemental insurance that covers many costs linked to hospital stays; supplemental insurance is also available to cover "non-nomenclature" treatments and co-payments (Schokkaert et al. 2010). While voluntary and supplemental insurance represents only a small share of healthcare expenditure, this share is growing (Gerkens and Merkur 2010).

3. Nationalism, regionalism, and the allocation of authority

Social security and healthcare policy specifically have emerged as contentious issues in current debates about further policy devolution in Belgium and the potential breakup of the Belgian state. However, their relevance in shaping the allocation of policy authority to date has been negligible. Instead, the transformation of the Belgian state in the postwar period has been driven by linguistic politics and by the efforts of Belgian political leaders to keep the state intact while responding to language-based nationalist mobilization.

When an independent Belgium emerged in 1830, it was a centralized state dominated by French-speaking political and social elites. The Flemish Movement emerged to press for Dutch-language rights, and although the equality of languages was codified in Belgian law in 1898, the political and social status of Dutch remained problematic and Dutch did not become the exclusive language of public administration and education in Flanders until the 1930s (Deschouwer 1991). The census of 1960 indicated that the linguistic border established in 1932 needed reconsideration in light of population shifts. The Belgian government revised the border in response to Flemish concerns about growing French-speaking populations in Flemish villages around Brussels, but this created questions about the status of Brussels itself and about the ability of French-speakers to be accommodated with public services in their language. The census also indicated that the Flemish were underrepresented in the Chamber of Deputies, and the reallocation of seats led to Walloon demands for safeguards against becoming a permanent minority in the legislature and executive. At the same time, Flemish nationalism was finding a political voice in the Volksunie (People's Union), founded in 1954 to promote Dutch language rights and ultimately working to create a federal Belgium with autonomy for Flanders. As popular mobilization in linguistic and regional politics intensified at the end of the 1960s, Belgian political and social institutions, including political parties, began to fragment along linguistic lines (Laible 2008: 58–9).

Reforms in 1970 resulted in the establishment of three cultural communities with limited powers and two cultural commissions in Brussels, initiating the process of state reform that would transform Belgium into a fully federal state by the mid-1990s. The process of reform continued with more radical changes enacted in 1980, including the formal creation of the three Belgian regions possessing more autonomy in economic affairs, and with the communities further empowered to have jurisdiction over personalizable matters.[8] With the 1993 constitutional reforms, the federalization of the state was complete: these reforms provided for the separate and direct elections of the Flemish and Walloon regional parliaments (these had previously been populated by members drawn from the Belgian Chamber of Deputies), the reform of the federal Senate and additional devolution of policy jurisdictions (Hooghe 1991; Falter 1998).

The federalization of Belgium coincided with the rising political fortunes of Flemish nationalism, and in particular with the electoral breakthrough of the extreme right-wing nationalist party Vlaams Blok (later renamed Vlaams Belang, or Flemish Interest). The Volksunie had long contained a far-right element, but when the party joined the Belgian government in the late 1970s, some members argued that it failed to defend Dutch-language rights and defected to create two offshoot parties that together contested the 1978 elections as the Vlaams Blok. Initially the Vlaams Blok focused on independence for Flanders but within a decade it began to emphasize immigration issues along with a commitment to defining the Flemish nation along blood and linguistic lines: party manifestos in the 1980s and 1990s detailed Vlaams Blok concerns about the incompatibility of Flemish culture with particular immigrant communities and proposed the repatriation of non-European immigrants (Gijsels and Velpen 1992; Mudde 2000). By the late 1990s, Volksunie and the Vlaams Blok together captured a quarter of the Flemish vote in Belgian federal elections for the Chamber of Deputies and elections for the Flemish Parliament. In 2004, by which point Volksunie had disbanded, the Vlaams Blok alone won 24% of the vote for the Flemish Parliament (Laible 2008).

The Vlaams Blok represented the most extreme challenge to the Belgian state, but other major Flemish parties also began to apply pressure for further decentralization of power to the regions and communities. The Christian Democrats (CD&V, formerly CVP) adopted an increasingly Flemish regionalist profile with Flemish minister president Luc Van den Brande calling for jurisdiction over social security and for some federal powers in foreign trade and fiscal policy to be transferred to the regions. The Flemish Liberals and

Democrats (VLD) had been long-term critics of Belgian regionalization, arguing that it was economically inefficient. However, in the 1990s the VLD leader in the Flemish Parliament also began to call for greater autonomy and the VLD ultimately succeeded in drawing some moderate nationalists away from Volksunie (Ishiyama and Breuning 1998: 127). The relatively new party N-VA (New Flemish Alliance), which emerged from the remnants of Volksunie, has most markedly embraced an extreme "devolutionist" position. N-VA seeks the independence of Flanders within the European Union but emphasizes a gradualist approach by which the remaining jurisdictions of the Belgian state are devolved to the regions. Following the June 2010 elections, N-VA emerged with a plurality of seats in Chamber of Deputies although its leader, Bart de Wever, was unable to form a government and negotiations continued into 2011.

Although a small Walloon nationalist movement has waxed and waned in recent decades, Flemish nationalism and regionalism have driven the agenda for further federalization and even the breakup of Belgium. A dominant theme in Flemish nationalism and regionalism and a primary justification for further decentralization has been the argument that Wallonia depends on excessive transfers of wealth from Flanders and that Flanders thus legitimately needs greater control over taxation and spending (a point that I develop in a later section). Daniel Béland and André Lécours argue that social policy can fulfill numerous functions in nationalist politics, noting that social policy "represents a tangible manifestation of the existence of a political community". In particular, services that involve person-to-person communication or that are part of everyday life, such as health care, can be important forces for developing a sense of political identity. Yet for this same reason, social protection can become the focus of political competition. Given the redistributive impact of much social policy, nationalist leaders may "argue that social programs are threatened by the selfish and irresponsible actions of . . . [other citizens or] government[s] and that increased political autonomy, or even independence, represents the only way to preserve the quality of social protection for the community", or that one community needs independence because it has different social or economic priorities than the other (Béland and Lecours 2005b: 678–9). Hence, social security has become the target of Flemish demands, with efforts to decentralize revenue collection and policy authority to the regions situated in broader arguments about the justice of Flemish control over "Flemish" resources, and health asymmetries in general have become contentious political issues in ongoing debates about further constitutional reform.

4. Equality and diversity in a federalized healthcare system

Efforts to curb healthcare expenditures have simultaneously confronted the broad commitment to equity that is universally embraced in the Belgian political system, in particular equality of access in a system with relatively high out-of-pocket fees. A consensus exists among major political parties and the public on prioritizing equality in access to health care, which some observers claim was basically achieved in the mid-1990s. However this period also represented a particular challenge to the ideal of equal access in the wake of federal budget tightening and rising co-payments. Policies such as maximum allowable billing and special status for reimbursements had the effect of protecting equality but potentially undermining cost-saving measures and incentives. And, as late as 2004, 10% of the population was postponing medical care for financial reasons, suggesting that the ideal of equal access remained elusive. Nonetheless, both reducing the scope of the compulsory coverage to cut costs and the vision of a "two-track society" where the rich have access to better-quality care and generally unacceptable alternatives, and it is largely the federal government that must continue to manage the challenges of equality under a burden of rising expenditures (Schokkaert and Van de Voorde 2005; Gerkens and Merkur 2010).

A general commitment to equity has not prevented the emergence of distinct approaches to implementing policy in the regions and communities and divergent clinical practices. Stefaan de Rynck and Karolien Deleuze identify five major areas of policy divergence at the community level. First, the communities have different priorities for training doctors in medical schools under their jurisdictions and appear to produce doctors who communicate and "label" health issues differently, potentially leading to differences in how health policy is implemented. Second, the communities have adopted different approaches to federal restrictions (quotas) on the number of accredited doctors, which has created some political tensions. Historically, Belgium has produced a large number of doctors per capita, with a higher density in French-speaking areas resulting in – among other issues – pressure on physicians' incomes. Thus a 1997 federal decree stipulated the numbers of accredited doctors that each community could produce, leaving it to community authorities to determine how this would occur. The Flemish Community opted for an entrance exam to limit numbers; the French-language Community introduced selection mechanisms during the course of medical training. However, the quota is designed to equalize the physician/patient ratio between the two communities over time (i.e. reducing the number of doctors in Wallonia relatively more sharply) and it has therefore remained controversial in the Walloon region and in the French-speaking Community (Schokkaert and Van de Voorde 2005).

Third, each community (including the German community) has established multi-year objectives for disease prevention and health promotion, but these objectives differ, as do the networks of institutions and organizations that have been created or that are coordinated to achieve them.[9] De Rynck and Deleuze indicate that the Flemish Community places a greater emphasis on preventive care than does the French-speaking Community. The activism of the Flemish Community in some of its priority areas for improving quality of care has been particularly influential: its initiatives in palliative care and breast cancer screening have compelled the federal government to take more action in these areas. Higher breast-cancer screening rates in the Flemish Community may ultimately produce a divergence in curative medicine among the communities. As another example, the Flemish Community established a set of quality-control measures in hospitals to parallel federal guidelines, gaining access to data on hospital operations that enabled it better to target capital investment; while this activity does not infringe on the jurisdictions of federal authority, it has been described as "expanding the reality of Community power in health matters" (de Cock 2002).

Fourth, the communities have adopted different attitudes toward the "gatekeeper" function of primary care providers. Patients may choose any provider, including a specialist; however the Flemish Community has been more successful in promoting general practitioners as gatekeepers to specialist care, and patients in the French-speaking Community spend more on specialist visits. Finally, each community exhibits differing emphases in curative care and even in pharmaceutical expenditures: as an example of the latter, the French-speaking Community uses 30% more antibiotics than does the Flemish Community (although overall Belgian usage of antibiotics is higher than the European average).

Thus communities have limited jurisdictions but in some cases have pushed the boundaries of their authority in creative ways to meet their healthcare objectives. The devolution of some authority over health care has clearly resulted in policy divergence with respect to the implementation of federal policy and to prioritizing healthcare objectives. However, other areas of healthcare divergence can less clearly be attributed to policy devolution. Some aspects of clinical practice may be shaped by the allocation of authority to communities while others may result from existing social differences. Some divergences in health demographics in Belgium may be indicative of deep-rooted socioeconomic patterns that neither have been produced by devolution nor are likely to be remedied by additional changes in constitutional authority.

On some basic indicators, there have been evident differences between Flanders and Wallonia since the nineteenth century, although where Flanders lagged in health in previous centuries it now outperforms Wallonia in critical areas. For both men and women, life expectancy is lower in Wallonia and in almost every age cohort, residents of Wallonia were more likely to report being in ill health than were their Flemish counterparts: one study concludes that "people in the Flemish region live longer and feel healthier while doing so", a finding consistent with numerous other studies that identify a greater amount of ill health in Wallonia (Van Oyen et al. 1996). Lifestyle differences that may contribute to these outcomes include higher rates of smoking, lower levels of physical activity and poorer nutritional habits in Wallonia (Corens 2007). Socioeconomic differences between the regions explain part of the difference in health and life expectancy, leading some to argue that public health measures, education and preventive medicine are crucial strategies for addressing health inequalities and focusing attention directly on the ability of the communities to deploy their authority in health policy to produce substantive improvements in basic health indicators (Schokkaert and Van de Voorde 2005; Corens 2007).

Socioeconomic variables may also explain some of the regional disparities in the provision of care. The use of child and family care facilities that provide a variety of preventive, educational and other medical services to expectant parents and families with young children is greater in Flanders, as is use of the Global Medical File (GMD) by which patients establish their files with a primary care provider, aiming to improve the quality of primary care and to reduce the duplication of services (Gerkens and Merkur 2010). Medical expenditures are higher in Wallonia, but this may reflect some of the lifestyle differences and ill health propensities noted above. Patients in Wallonia visit specialist providers more frequently, and French-speaking doctors order more medical tests than do Flemish doctors (de Cock 2002). Nor are the regional variations between Flanders and Wallonia the only ones: some procedures are more prevalent in the east of Belgium than the west (Schokkaert and Van de Voorde 2010).

However, some regional practice variations indicate inefficiencies that cannot be explained solely by need or by patient preferences. Instead, they may derive from informational issues, including doctors' coordinating their behavior with that of their peers (Schokkaert and Van de Voorde 2010). Specifically in the case of Belgium, informational issues about medical norms and practices may rely on language and media, or on shared educational backgrounds, highlighting how policy implementation by the communities will partly be a function of other community jurisdictions that may reinforce certain regional preferences to produce clusters.

Furthermore, Erik Schokkaert and Carine Van de Voorde emphasize that a focus on interregional (or inter-community) transfers largely misses the point that these transfers lack transparency. Noting that all health insurance systems produce transfers, they describe the Belgian system as a collective one that is underpinned by income solidarity and transfers from the healthy to the sick, from the wealthier to the poorer, and from the lower risk to the higher risk. They indicate that while these financial transfers are transparent, this transparency disappears in efforts to compare regions: "those transfers depend on the relative incomes and on the health risks in the different regions... Interregional transfers have to be 'estimated' ". Efforts to produce solidarity between regions would undermine the transparency of transfers among other groups and could damage interpersonal solidarity (Schokkaert and Van de Voorde 2010).

Federalization has enabled the communities to develop divergent strategies in areas of health care under their jurisdiction, but federal-level institutions and political bargaining may prevent or manage divergence in many areas of care. The federal system contains multiple formal veto points to protect minority interests. Constitutional changes, including changes that could devolve further authority over social policy, are subject to veto by the communities and regions, and the so-called "alarm bell" procedure enables members of the federal Chamber of Deputies from one language community to block ordinary legislation if they claim it threatens the vital interests of their community. The French-speaking Community thus far has blocked Flemish efforts to decentralize health policy further and to devolve the financing of social security.

Federal policymaking also contains numerous mechanisms for intergovernmental consultation that promote communication and sometimes mandate cooperation among the different levels of government. These include mutual representation allowing for the representation of a government on an institution that is formally under the jurisdiction of another level of government (e.g., some planning commissions and scientific councils) and formal cooperation agreements on the joint creation and management of common services when the actions of one government may impose a "financial burden" on another. Non-legally binding protocols may be concluded when cooperation is necessary for the implementation of legislation, and a recently created Concertation Committee seeks to prevent "conflicts of interests" between different governments. Finally, communities have a legislative obligation to provide information to the federal government regarding some of their health policy decisions (de Cock 2002).

Perhaps surprisingly in such a fragmented political system, federal-level organizations of the social partners also play a role in restraining further federalization and, possibly, further divergence in healthcare provision and outcomes. Neither Belgian labor unions nor the federal business associations have formally split along linguistic lines. The largest unions in Belgium oppose further decentralization of social security, arguing that economic solidarity should trump linguistic divisions. The main business peak association, the Federation of Belgian Enterprises (VBO/FEB), also rejects further federalization of social policy, which would likely result in a reduction of its staff and resources, and which would possibly produce a regional increase in payroll taxes for Walloon employers. More importantly, additional social policy devolution could undermine the role that employer and employee associations currently play in managing healthcare financing by participating in the General Council of RIZIV/INAMI, challenging their legitimacy as organizations and their relevance in the policy process (Béland and Lecours 2005a).

Constitutional change is responsible both for the creation of communities as institutions and for producing autonomous healthcare jurisdictions in which the communities can set their own priorities. However, in other respects it is difficult to assess the consequences of federalization. Some regional differences (e.g. in life expectancy) predate federalization and appear to be the product of a complex interaction between socioeconomic and cultural variables. Other differences may only now be apparent because data are collected at the community level. What is clear is that regional differences, both perceived and real, have now become part of the high-stakes battle over further decentralization of the Belgian state.

5. Standing still, moving forward, or falling apart? The uncertain direction of health care in Belgium

The ongoing predominance of the federal government in health policy and social security has combined with the politicization of regional differences to make these the most highly charged issues in current Belgian constitutional politics. Health and social security are now regularly invoked in debates among those seeking to dismantle the Belgian state and those seeking to protect it. Despite the constitutional and political counterweights to further devolution noted above, political demands from Flemish politicians for greater authority over health care and social security have intensified. The Belgian state must thus manage political challenges to its authority and to the social solidarity that underpins health care at the same time that it faces continuing pressures to rein in expenditures and protect equal access to the healthcare system.

Like other EU states, Belgium faces rising healthcare expenditures in the coming decades, largely the product of the costs of technological innovation and healthcare resources. The European population has aged rapidly since the 1990s, and increased life expectancy and new treatment possibilities will also transform healthcare utilization and costs in the future (Busse 2001). While the Belgian state began to enact reforms to control expenditures in the 1980s, health economists argue that the political importance of equality, the systemic emphasis on freedom of choice for patients and providers, and reluctance of the public to embrace stronger market mechanisms have limited the ability of the state to rein in expenditures through microeconomic incentives. Restricting coverage and expanding the role of the private sector are also politically unpalatable (Schokkaert and Van de Voorde 2005).

However, these same economists note that the real challenges to the system come not from the unwillingness or inability of politicians to make painful choices but from the politicization of perceived inefficiencies and regional differences. In the 1980s and 1990s, Flemish nationalists began to take note of academic studies and government data demonstrating that the social security system – including health care – increasingly appeared to be shifting funds away from Flanders toward Wallonia. Studies published in the 1980s concluded that per capita social security expenditures were higher in Wallonia than in Flanders, and that Wallonia's share of social security deficits was higher than that of Flanders. An influential study in 1990 claimed that, after adjusting for tax payments and benefits, Walloons had more disposable income than did the Flemish, despite also having lower wages and higher unemployment, a situation that Flemish nationalists claimed illustrated the extent to which Walloons were benefiting excessively from federal programs. Overall, studies (often conducted on behalf of Flemish organizations) confirmed that centralized social security mechanisms resulted in financial transfers from Flanders to Wallonia in almost all program areas: health care, unemployment, pensions, family allowances, and some other benefits. As an illustration of the amount of financial transfer occurring under the federal social security system, some Flemish nationalists noted that every Flemish family paid for a car for every Walloon family every year (Béland and Lecours 2005b).

The rhetoric of Flemish nationalism has subsumed questions about expenditures, financial transfers, and health outcomes into a broad narrative about differences between the linguistic communities and regions, in which cultural attributes and lifestyle choices among Walloons, mediated by a federal social insurance system, place an undesirable burden on the Flemish people. In Flemish nationalist discourse, Walloons are "state dependent," whereas the Flemish are "entrepreneurial"; with regard to health care, Walloons "cost more" to the social security system because of poor lifestyle choices and "excessive" use of healthcare providers, in particular specialists; and Walloons "willingly overuse" social benefits (Béland and Lecours 2005a,b). For Flemish nationalists and regionalists, these differences legitimize arguments that communities should be granted additional authority over social policy, including health care, and that federal jurisdiction over social security should be challenged. In contrast, the majority of French-speakers want to keep health insurance at the federal level (De Rynck and Dezeure 2006).

The language of this debate often invokes the problematic theme of whether regional differences in expenditures and use of services are "justified" (related, e.g., to differences in mortality) or "unjustified" (related to differences in practices and in the supply of health services). Students of nationalism have observed that this debate signals a transformation in understandings of social solidarity in Belgium, from the interpersonal solidarity on which the social security system was founded to a regional or community-based solidarity that now motivates nationalist politics (largely in Flanders) (Béland and Lecours 2005a,b). But this shift complicates efforts by the Belgian federal state to undertake necessary reforms to manage expenditures and to secure the long-term future of the healthcare system. Health economists who have identified regional inefficiencies in health care urge policymakers to respond to these inefficiencies, in order to address public concerns that some groups are "wasting" funds or services and to protect against public unwillingness to pay for those who are seen to abuse the system. However, any federal government efforts to improve efficiency through microeconomic incentives will face obstacles if these incentives are perceived to have a differential impact on the communities (Schokkaert and Van de Voorde 2005, 2010). Nationalism and regionalism have successfully cast health policy debates in terms of (regional) justice and fairness; the ability of the federal government to undertake even minor reforms to health care will depend on its ability to manage the countervailing pressures for greater decentralization and for upholding the status quo emerging from the communities.

6. Conclusions: A constitutional stalemate

Ellen Immergut once described national health insurance as the most controversial of all social programs, noting that it symbolized "the great divide between liberalism and socialism, between the free market and the planned economy" (Immergut 1992). In the case of Belgium, the political charge conducted by health insurance and health policy also involves tensions between a federal government and substate political authorities, between language communities and regions, and between a universal vision of social solidarity and a community-based one. Constitutional reform initially remade the healthcare system by institutionalizing linguistic communities as healthcare actors complementing the federal state. However, neither health care nor health insurance were the political drivers of constitutional reform; instead, the federalization of the Belgian state was superimposed on an existing centralized healthcare system, producing new patterns of authority in health policy as a consequence of broader constitutional debates.

Only in the mid-1990s did nationalist and regionalist politicians seek to justify further constitutional reform with reference to healthcare and social security financing. Nationalist politicians recast health policy debates as issues of social justice. In particular, Flemish nationalists and regionalists deployed health policy as an illustration of how the Belgian state had entrenched a form of redistributive injustice and argued that only further federalization – or even independence for Flanders – would resolve the problem.

The recent politicization of health care ironically may have undermined the likelihood that any major reforms will soon occur. The formal requirements of the Belgian constitution and the political requirements of consensus building already create multiple veto points that challenge the ability of the federal state to act in any way that might have a differential impact across the communities and regions. Furthermore, to the extent that health care and social policy are increasingly framed as part of a high-stakes constitutional game, it is difficult to see how Flemish nationalists will surrender their claims that further reforms are necessary for their constituents' well-being, or how French-speakers will compromise on issues that many of them perceive to be crucial to their understanding of (Belgian) social citizenship. Lowering the volume on the healthcare debate could potentially open a space to allow bargaining over more mundane (i.e. non-constitutional) aspects of healthcare policy. Some observers have expressed concern that the politicization of health policy, in narrow debates about interregional solidarity and in systemic debates about constitutional reform, has drawn attention away from very real, but less politically attractive, discussions about equal access to health care, the role of the market in care provision and in insurance, and the long-term financing of the healthcare system (Schokkaert and Van de Voorde 2010).

But as of this writing, the pressures on the Belgian political system seem to be intensifying. More than seven months after federal elections, Belgium has failed to produce a governing coalition. The strong showing of the secessionist N-VA in the June 2010 elections has precipitated a crisis in which many of the key players have refused to engage with the N-VA leadership due to its proclaimed goal of pursuing Flemish independence. While health care may not figure specifically into any agreement produced among potential coalition partners, it is likely to remain on the agenda as Flemish nationalists test the boundaries of their political power.

Notes

1. In this chapter, I use the terms *federalization, devolution* or *decentralization* to refer to the shift of policy authority away from the central (federal) government to substate authorities, including territorial and linguistic institutions.
2. Johan de Cock offers an overview of the complicated political mechanisms designed to ensure parity between the language communities in some institutions (such as the federal cabinet) and to recognize proportionality in others (including the federal Parliament). Parity in federal institutions represents a guarantee to French-speakers that they will not be marginalized by Dutch-speakers (who are the majority in Belgium). The Brussels Parliament also employs a similar combination of parity and proportional representation, with parity intended to protect the Dutch-speaking minority in the Brussels region. In some cases, institutions require double majorities (of both language communities). See de Cock (2002: 41–2).
3. The Brussels region initially possessed an executive within the Belgian national government but acquired its own elected parliament and government in 1988. Discussion of the federalization of the Belgian state can be found in Deschouwer (1991), Hooghe (1991), De Rynck and Maes (1995/1996), Velaers (1996), and Falter (1998).
4. A description of the main federal health-related departments, agencies and advisory bodies and their respective portfolios can be found in Gerkens and Merkur (2010: 24–35).
5. The funds, or mutualities, originated along ideological, confessional and professional lines in the nineteenth century, although their philosophical roots do not determine their membership and have weakened over time (citizens may select any sickness fund, with the exception of railway workers, who belong to a separate [sixth] mutuality). The nonprofit funds were grouped into national associations according to their background at the beginning of the twentieth century. The Auxiliary Fund, a public body, was founded for patients who cannot or will not affiliate with the other groups (European Observatory on Health Care Systems 2000: 12–13; Gerkens and Merkur 2010: 20). Remarkably, given the split of many

Belgian political and social institutions along language lines, the sickness funds continue to function on a Belgium-wide basis.

6. A detailed discussion of policy efforts to control expenditures is found in (Schokkaert and Van de Voorde 2005), and a list of major healthcare reforms from 1944 to 2006 is presented in (Gerkens and Merkur 2010).

7. Increased copayments in the 1990s created challenges for certain vulnerable social groups: maximum allowable billing (MAB) was introduced to set a maximum annual out-of-pocket ceiling for all health costs for those with low incomes, children, and those with preferential reimbursement rates (e.g. due to disability or chronic illness). After the ceiling is reached, health costs are fully reimbursed by the sickness funds.

8. In 1983, a special law gave the German community of about 65,000 people (around the city of Liège) equal status with the two other communities and its own parliament.

9. See Gerkens and Merkur (2010: Section 5.1) for extensive details of the most recent community objectives and the organizational networks that cooperate to implement them.

References

Banting, Keith G. and Stan Corbett. 2002. "Health Policy and Federalism: An Introduction." In *Health Policy and Federalism: A Comparative Perspective on Multi-Level Governance*. Ed. Keith G. Banting and Stan Corbett. Kingston, ON: Queen's University Institute of Intergovernmental Relations. 1–38.

Béland, Daniel and André Lecours. 2005a. "Nationalism, Public Policy, and Institutional Development: Social Security in Belgium." *Journal of Public Policy* 25 (2): 265–85.

Béland, Daniel and André Lecours. 2005b. "The Politics of Territorial Solidarity: Nationalism and Social Policy Reform in Canada, the United Kingdom, and Belgium." *Comparative Political Studies* 38 (6): 676–703.

Busse, Reinhard. 2001. "Expenditure on Health Care in the EU: Making Projections for the Future Based on the Past." *Health Economics in Prevention and Care* 2 (4): 158–61.

Corens, Dick. 2007. "Belgium: Health System Review." *Health Systems in Transition* 9 (2): 1–172.

de Cock, Johan. 2002. "Federalism and the Belgian Health Care System." In *Health Policy and Federalism: A Comparative Perspective on Multi-Level Governance*. Ed. Keith G. Banting and Stan Corbett. Kingston, ON: Queen's University Institute of Intergovernmental Relations. 39–68.

De Rynck, Stefan and Rudolf Maes. 1995/1996. "Belgium: Regions, Communities and Subregional Authorities in the European Integration Process." In *Regions in Europe, I.* Ed. Joachim Jens Hesse. Baden-Baden: Nomos Verlaggesselschaft. 101–127.

Deschouwer, Kris. 1991. "Small Parties in a Small Country: The Belgian Case." In *Small Parties in Western Europe: Comparative and National Perspectives*. Ed. Ferdinand Müller-Rommel and Geoffrey Pridham. London: Sage, 135–51.

European Observatory on Health Care Systems. 2000. "Belgium." *Health Care Systems in Transition* Report 1–93.

Falter, Rolf. 1998. "Belgium's Peculiar Way to Federalism." In *Nationalism and Belgium: Shifting Identities 1780–1995*. Ed. Kas Deprez and Louis Vos. New York: St. Martin's Press, 177–97.

Federal Public Service Social Security. 2008. *Everything You Have Always Wanted to Know about Social Security*. Brussels: SPF Sécurité sociale.

Gerkens, Sophie and Sherry Merkur. 2010. "Belgium: Health System Review." *Health Systems in Transition* 12 (5): 1–266.

Gijsels, Hugo and Jos Vander Velpen. 1992. *Le Chagrin des Flamands: Le Vlaams Blok de 1938 à nos jours*. Brussels: Editions EPO.

Hooghe, Liesbet. 1991. "A Leap in the Dark: Nationalist Conflict and Federal Reform in Belgium." Occasional Paper 27, Ithaca: Cornell University Western Societies Program.

Immergut, Ellen M. 1992. *Health Politics: Interests and Institutions in Western Europe*. Cambridge: Cambridge University Press.

Ishiyama, John T. and Marijke Breuning. 1998. *Ethnopolitics in the New Europe*. Boulder, CO: Lynne Rienner.

Laible, Janet. 2008. *Separatism and Sovereignty in the New Europe: Party Politics and the Meanings of Statehood in a Supranational Context*. New York: Palgrave Macmillan.

Mudde, Cas. 2000. *The Ideology of the Extreme Right*. Manchester: Manchester University Press.

Parlament der Deutschsprachigen Gemeinschaft, DG in Belgium, Brussels. http://www.dg.be/en/desktopdefault.aspx/tabid-2837/5390_read-35163/ Accessed on 22 December 2010.

Portail Belgium.be, Informations et services officiels. http://www.belgium.be/fr/la_belgique/pouvoirs_publics/regions/competences/ and http://www.belgium.be/fr/la_belgique/pouvoirs_publics/communautes/competences/ Accessed on 22 December 2010.

Portal Wallonia, Action social et santé, Santé http://www.wallonie.be/en/themes/action-sociale-et-sante/sante/index.html Accessed on 24 December 2010.

Saltman, Richard. 2004. "Social health insurance in perspective: the challenge of sustaining stability." In *Social health insurance systems in Western Europe*. Ed. Richard B. Saltman, Reinhard Busse and Josep Figueras. Berkshire, UK: Open University Press, 3–20.

Schokkaert, Erik and Carine Van de Voorde. 2003. "Belgium: Risk Adjustment and Financial Responsibility in a Decentralized System." *Health Policy* 65: 5–19.

Schokkaert, Erik and Carine Van de Voorde. 2005. "Health Care Reform in Belgium." *Health Economics* 14: S25–S39.

Schokkaert, Erik and Carine Van de Voorde. 2010. "Belgium's Health Care System: Should the Communities/Regions take it Over? Or the Sickness Funds?" Paper presented at the Fourth Public Event of the Re-Bel Initiative. 16 December, Brussels.

Schokkaert, Erik, Tom Van Ourti, Diana De Graeve, Ann Lecluyse and Carine Van de Voorde. 2010. "Supplemental Health Insurance and Equality of Access in Belgium." *Health Economics* 19: 377–95.

van Doorslaer, Eddy K.A. and Frederik T. Schut. 2000. "Belgium and the Netherlands Revisited." *Journal of Health Politics, Policy and Law* 25 (5): 875–87.

Van Oyen, Herman, Jean Tafforeau and Marc Roelands. 1996. "Regional Inequities in Health Expectancy in Belgium." *Social Science & Medicine* 43 (11): 1673–78.

Velaers, Jan. 1996. "La Réforme de l'Etat." In *Un parti dans l'histoire 1945–1995: 50 ans d'action du Parti Social Chrétien*. Ed. Charles-Ferdinand Northomb and Frank Swaelen. Louvain-la-Neuve: Duculot. 107–54.

12
Federalism in Health and Social Care in Switzerland

Berit C. Gerritzen and Gebhard Kirchgässner

1. Introduction

Besides its high quality and high costs, the Swiss health system is mainly characterized by its federal structure. The cantons bear not only the strongest responsibilities, but also pay more than 80% of the public money going into the system. Thus, despite some more recent attempts to improve coordination, the system is rather fragmented. This fragmentation has so far prevented the formulation of a consistent national health policy. In the following chapter, first the formal allocation of responsibilities and the financing system are described (Section 1). Section 2 discusses the underlying reasons for the distribution of tasks among the different governmental levels, its legal foundations as well as recent policy developments. In Section 3, the effects on equity, quality, and efficiency of the health system are investigated. We conclude with some remarks on the tensions and likely future development of the Swiss health system (Section 4).

2. Distribution of tasks and financing

2.1. Formal allocation of responsibilities

Due to the federal structure of the Swiss political system, the development and implementation of health policy is mainly the responsibility of the cantons. The confederation only plays an active role in those areas where these competences have explicitly been assigned by the constitution.[1] Cantons are central actors with respect to provision and financing of health services, whereas policymaking, regulation, and monitoring are shared tasks of both the confederation and the cantons. The key institutions on the federal level are the Swiss Federal Office of Public Health (*Bundesamt für Gesundheit* (BAG)), the Federal Office of Statistics (*Bundesamt für Statistik* (BFS)), and the Federal Office for Social Insurance (*Bundesamt für Sozialversicherungen* (BSV)). All three institutions belong to the Federal

Department of Home Affairs (*Eidgenössisches Departement des Innern* (EDI)). The public health departments of the 26 cantons work together in the Swiss Conference of the Cantonal Ministers of Public Health (*Schweizerische Konferenz der kantonalen Gesundheitsdirektorinnen und direktoren* (GDK)). The GDK is meant to strengthen the coordination among cantons as well as between cantons and the confederation. Since GDK decisions only become legally binding if all parties involved sign a formal agreement, the GDK is more a platform for consensus building than an actual decision-maker (OECD 2006).

The responsibilities of the federal health institutions are mainly related to legislative and supervisory tasks, such as quality control of medicines and medical devices, social insurance,[2] promotion of science and research, and so on.[3] Federal competences generally reflect the need for central coordination and the capacity to act fast. This is particularly important in areas that require international coordination, such as the control and eradication of communicable diseases (European Observatory on Health Care Systems 2000; Kocher 2010; Leu 2008; OECD 2006).

Authorities at the cantonal level are responsible for both the provision of health care as well as the (partial) financing of hospital costs. Furthermore, cantonal authorities organize disease prevention and health education, and provide authorization for medical practices and pharmacies. If delegated by the federal government, cantons also overview and ensure the implementation of federal laws. Last but not least, the municipalities take care of implementation tasks that have been delegated by the cantons, for example nursing and home care (European Observatory on Health Care Systems 2000; Kocher 2010; Leu 2008; OECD 2006).

Besides state actors, interest groups play a very important role in shaping health policy outcomes. Because the Swiss constitution grants interest groups access to the design stage as well as to the implementation phase of new laws, this impact is in Switzerland at least more obvious and might actually be stronger than in other countries. The four most important lobbies with respect to health policy are the association of physicians, the association of health insurers, the association of hospitals, and the pharmaceutical industry (Leu 2008).

The large degree of decentralization has led to some differences in the health systems of the 26 cantons. Despite recent efforts to strengthen central governance in the health sector (described in more detail in Chapter 2), up to now there exists no national, overall framework defining the objectives and standards of the Swiss health system (Leu 2008; OECD 2006; Kocher 2010).

2.2. The financing system

The Swiss health system is financed by (1) mandatory health insurance, (2) private out-of-pocket payments, and (3) government payments, other social insurance schemes, and voluntary health insurance. As Figure 12.1

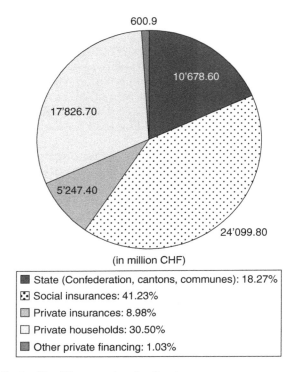

600.9

10'678.60

17'826.70

5'247.40

24'099.80

(in million CHF)

■ State (Confederation, cantons, communes): 18.27%
⊡ Social insurances: 41.23%
▢ Private insurances: 8.98%
□ Private households: 30.50%
■ Other private financing: 1.03%

Figure 12.1   Costs of healthcare system by direct payer

shows, the first two categories together account for about 70% of the total costs.[4] Consequently, the degree of private copayments is very high in Switzerland: out of the OECD countries, only Mexico and South Korea have a higher share of private out-of-pocket payments.[5]

The federal law on health insurance (*Krankenversicherungsgesetz* (KVG)) of 18 March 1994 requires each resident of Switzerland to "purchase basic health insurance from one of a number of competing health funds" (OECD 2006). The basic benefit package is defined by the federal government and is the same for all cantons. The insurance premiums, however, differ between cantons and across health funds.[6] It is further possible for individuals to choose a higher deductible (franchise) in combination with lower monthly premiums. Supplementary private health insurance can be opted for to reduce direct financing of treatments that are not covered by the basic package (Colombo 2001; Leu 2008; Indra et al. 2010).

The per capita premiums implied by the KVG do not differ across income groups and might put disproportionate pressure on people with lower income. To remedy inequities caused by the health insurance premiums, premium subsidies were introduced in 1996 (Bolgiani et al. 2006). In 2008, 2.249 million people (29.6% of the Swiss population) benefitted from premium subsidies. The cantons spent 1,727.4 million CHF on premium subsidies in 2009, whereas the federal payments toward premium subsidies amounted to 1,815.0 million CHF in 2009. Due to the extensive autonomy of the cantons, the premium subsidies differ across cantons.[7]

Eighteen percent of the total costs of the health system are covered by the government, equaling 10,678.6 million CHF in 2008. As Figure 12.2 shows, payments by the cantons account for roughly 86% of this amount, whereas federal payments only cover 2% of it. Thirteen percent of the expenses are paid for by the communes. This breakdown clearly reflects the key role the cantons play within Swiss health politics. It also explains why there is so much reluctance toward greater centralization on behalf of the cantons. After all, he who pays the piper calls the tune.[8]

Figure 12.3 shows the distribution of costs according to the different service types (BFS 2011).[9] Compared with other countries, the share of inpatient treatment is rather high because it covers nearly half of the total costs (Kirchgässner & Gerritzen 2011).

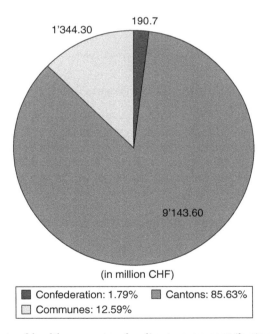

(in million CHF)

Confederation: 1.79% Cantons: 85.63%
Communes: 12.59%

Figure 12.2 Costs of healthcare system by direct payer, contributions of confederation, cantons, and communes

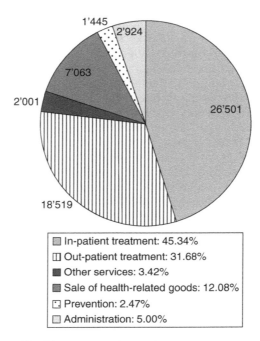

Figure 12.3   Costs of healthcare system by service type

3. Explanations and underlying reasons for the allocation of tasks

The principles of subsidiarity, liberalism, federalism, pragmatism, and direct democracy are considered to be important foundations of the political culture in Switzerland. They are reflected in the constitution as well as in federal and cantonal laws, and therefore also in the legal and institutional framework governing public health (Linder 2004; Vatter 2004; Dafflon 2007).

According to the principle of subsidiarity, responsibility for public provision should be assigned to the lowest possible level. This explains why health policy is first and foremost a cantonal competence and why only those tasks that cannot be taken care of by the cantonal authorities, for example due to insufficient capacity, are delegated to the federal level. Another aspect of the Swiss health system that is clearly influenced by the principle of subsidiarity are the large private copayments (Dafflon 1999). The importance of private actors in the health system (e.g. the privately organized, though publicly regulated, health funds) can also be explained with the liberal orientation of the Swiss state (as expressed by articles 27 and 94 of the Swiss Federal Constitution) (European Observatory on Health Care Systems 2000; Okma et al.

2010; Kocher 2010). According to the European Observatory on Health Systems (2000, p. 9), in Switzerland "the state basically only intervenes when private initiative fails to produce satisfactory results, i.e. it acts only as a safety net or provider of last resort". The principle of federalism is reflected by the large degree of shared responsibilities across different levels of the federal state as well as by the differences between cantons with respect to health policy (Kocher 2010; Okma et al. 2010).

The notion of "Swiss pragmatism" implies that the canton tends to be seen as a testing ground for new ideas and concepts. If a new approach works on the local level it might subsequently be implemented nationwide (Dafflon 2007). For example, in 1995 the canton of Zurich introduced a new hospital funding system called LORAS ("performance oriented resource allocation in hospital care"). Contrary to the traditional approach of covering hospital deficits, LORAS is a New Public Management program focusing on hospital output and performance rather than on the input factors used. Within the framework of LORAS, diagnosis-related treatment groups (DRGs) were adopted. The experiences from the LORAS project have (together with the German experience) influenced the design of the DRGs, which will be implemented on the national level in early 2012 (Schwappach et al. 2003; Lenz & Hochreutener 2001).[10]

The influence of direct-democratic institutions is considerably high in Switzerland: a referendum can be conducted on every federal law – or change of law – if 50,000 signatures are collected (which corresponds to about 1% of the electorate). On the one hand, the threat of a referendum provides interest groups with an additional channel of influence in Swiss politics. On the other hand, referenda make collusion between public bureaucracy and interest groups more difficult. Thus, the range of possibilities to influence government policy might be wider for lobbying groups in Switzerland, but it is unclear whether their impact is really stronger than in a purely representative system (Kirchgässner 2008). Nevertheless, it is obvious that interest groups have important leverage in health policy (Leu 2008). Moreover, given that Swiss citizens can reject nearly every major change in the Swiss health system, (central) governance can be difficult at times (Colombo 2001; Okma et al. 2010). In addition, subject to the fact that basic insurance is mandatory and that the government controls what is included in this, Swiss citizens can choose their own health insurance provider as well as their own insurance policy package from (a restricted set of) different combinations of franchise, premium, coverage, and copayments schedules.

3.1. Legal foundations of health policy

As previously mentioned, the cantons are responsible for all areas of health policy unless responsibility has explicitly been attributed to the confederation.[11] Articles 117–120 of the Federal Constitution (*Bundesverfassung*) can be considered to lie at the heart of the health constitution. These four articles grant the federal authorities encompassing responsibility for the health and accident insurance, health protection, regulation of alternative methods of treatment, gene technology, and transplantation medicine. In addition, all norms and regulations that touch the health status of citizens in a relevant way belong to the health constitution. Among these are the social aims (art. 41 BV), the regulation of medical professions (art. 95 BV), consumption taxes on tobacco and alcohol (art. 131 BV) as well as the utilization of these taxes (art. 112 und 131 BV) (BAG 2011a). Furthermore, regulations concerned with research (art. 64 BV), sports and physical activities (art. 68 BV), protection of the environment (art. 74 BV), consumer protection (art. 97 BV), alcohol consumption (art. 105 BV) and work environment (art. 110 BV) are federal responsibilities (BAG 2011b).

The most important federal laws with respect to health policy are the following laws related to social insurance provision: the federal law on health insurance (18 March 1994, SR 832.10), the federal law on accident insurance (20 March 1981, SR 832.20), the federal law on disability insurance (29 June 1959), and the federal law on military insurance (19 June 1992, SR 833.1). The Federal Office of Public Health is responsible to monitor the health funds and related institutions to make sure that the social insurances respect the law and are conducted in an efficient and effective manner (BAG 2011a; European Observatory on Health Care Systems 2000).

Besides the federal regulations on health policy, there exist 26 cantonal health policies and laws that are all slightly different from each other. Whenever considered necessary, the cantons can also delegate responsibilities to the municipalities. Again, the extent to which this takes place differs from one canton to another. A detailed overview on the different cantonal and communal regulations, however, would be beyond the scope of this paper.

3.2. Policy developments

During the past decade, the federal authorities have been assigned new competences with respect to health policy (Kocher 2010; SGGP 2011). This has happened in three different ways. Either former cantonal responsibilities were taken over by federal institutions, or new federal laws were introduced that were then implemented by federal institutions. The latter was the case with Swiss medic, a newly founded federal institution responsible for registration and market-entry authorization of pharmaceutical products. Thirdly, existing federal laws were revised in a manner that granted more competence to the federal authorities (e.g., the law on the health insurance KVG) (OECD 2006).

As mentioned in Section 1, Switzerland does not have a consistent national health policy so far. However, there have been different policy initiatives to change this. Since 1998, the national health policy project (*Projekt "Nationale Gesundheitspolitik Schweiz"*) is designated to formulate a concise, national health policy. This project is borne jointly by federal and cantonal authorities (GDK and BAG in particular) (GDK 2003). In late 2004, a coordinating institution called *"Dialog Nationale Gesundheitspolitik"* (Dialogue on National Health Policy) was founded. The aim of this forum is to discuss questions related to the development of a national health policy and coordination with respect to issues affecting both cantons and the confederation.[12] Furthermore, the Federal Office of Public Health (BAG) now has a department called "Health Policy" (*Gesundheitspolitik*) (BAG 2005).

4. Effects on equity, quality, and efficiency of health care

4.1. Equity

Except for undocumented immigrants (the so-called *sans-papiers*), all Swiss residents are covered by the mandatory basic health insurance. Besides high coverage, the Swiss health system also offers equal access to health care: important treatments are generally included in the basic package of the statutory health insurance,[13] whereas the supplementary insurance schemes tend to cover additional services assumed not to be necessarily crucial (e.g. alternative treatments, pharmaceutical products that are exempted from the positive list, or non-medical long-term care) (Leu 2008; Kirchgässner & Gerritzen 2011).

Leu and Schellhorn (2004, 2006) analyze equity with respect to health status and healthcare utilization in Switzerland. The authors find that higher income is associated with better health status. However, this holds in practically every society, and given that the distribution of health in Switzerland is among the least unequal in Europe, this is not a major reason for concern. Further, Leu and Schellhorn (2004, 2006) find little or no inequity with respect to healthcare utilization: only specialist visits are "pro-rich" distributed, which is the case in most other OECD countries as well (Doorslaer & Masseria 2004).

Consequently, both health and healthcare utilization appear to be fair and more or less equally distributed across income groups. There are, however, income-related inequalities with respect to the financing of the Swiss health system. Bilger (2008) shows in a decomposition analysis that despite the reform in 1996, Swiss health system financing is still rather regressive. The financing of the health system leads to an increase in income inequality, which is largely caused by a "pro-rich" vertical effect: earners of lower incomes have to contribute disproportionately more to the financing of the health system than those with higher incomes (Bilger 2008).[14] This holds for the direct payments, but even more for the mandatory insurance which is – in principle – financed by per capita premiums and therefore rather regressive. However, people with lower income obtain subsidies, and those with the lowest incomes, for example welfare recipients, get their premiums paid by the government. Today, about 30% of the population get their premium subsidized or even fully paid by the government. Thus, the regressive effect is mainly due to the fact that above a certain income level all insured have to pay the same premiums.[15]

The observed inequity in the financing of the healthcare system is linked to the federal structure of Swiss health politics, mainly via cross-cantonal differences in insurance premiums and premium subsidies. The differences in premiums can, to a large extent, be attributed to different reserve policies of the health insurances. Further, as private health insurance providers determine the insurance premiums, state actors can only indirectly influence this inequality via regulation.[16] The system of premium subsidies, however, is the direct responsibility of the confederation and the cantons. Yet, there exist very large cross-cantonal differences, both with respect to eligibility conditions as well as in the actual level of premium subsidies (OECD 2006; Leu et al. 2008).

The differences in premium subsidies are partly due to underlying differences in the calculation method. In ten Swiss cantons, citizens are eligible for premium subsidies as soon as healthcare expenditure exceeds a certain percentage of the taxable income (so-called percentage models). In eight other cantons, depending on household composition and income, eligibility groups are defined in a way that results in different fixed amounts of subsidies (so-called step models). The remaining eight cantons have hybrid forms that are combinations of the percentage and step models. Furthermore, differences between cantons exist not only with respect to eligibility and the amount of subsidy received, but also regarding to procedural modalities: to receive the premium subsidy, citizens in some cantons will have to apply for it, whereas in other cantons, they will automatically be informed about their eligibility by the cantonal authorities (based on their taxable income) (Balthasar et al. 2008).

In the discussions preceding the introduction of the statutory health insurance, the Federal Council wanted to fix the maximum burden implied by the health insurance premiums at 6% of disposable income. The Swiss Parliament, however, decided to grant more freedom to the cantons to adequately take into account cantonal differences in the tax and social security systems. Consequently there exists no national target parameter with respect to the maximum premium load (Balthasar et al. 2008). As can be seen in Figure 12.4, only in four cantons is the average remaining premium load *after* premium subsidies below 6% of the disposable income.[17] Further, the average premium load differs widely across cantons.[18]

It is often argued that the differences in the premium subsidies are partly legitimate since per capita income, the income tax, and social security system vary across cantons, as does the cost of living. To adequately distinguish between legitimate and illegitimate sources of variation, one would have to control for all inter-cantonal differences. Figure 12.4 accounts for

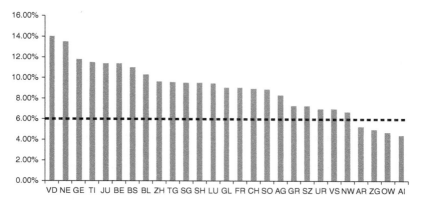

Figure 12.4 Average remaining premium load (after premium subsidy) in percent of the disposable income (2007)

the variation in cantonal taxes (by reporting the average premium load in percent of the disposable income after taxes) (Balthasar et al. 2008). The large remaining variation in premium subsidies, however, indicates that not all of the differences might be legitimate. The inconsistency with respect to the premium subsidies has also been criticized by the OECD (2006) as a major source of inequity in the Swiss health system. Furthermore, over the course of the past years, the funds available for premium subsidies have increased at a lower rate than health insurance premiums, thereby increasing inequality (Bolgiani et al. 2006).

4.2. Quality

In general, the Swiss health system offers a very high quality to its users. Switzerland ranks very well on objective health-quality indicators, such as life expectancy and infant mortality, but also performs very well on subjective health indicators measured by, for example, the SHARE data or the World Value Survey.[19]

Despite its high quality, the Swiss health system suffers from considerable deficits with respect to transparency, particularly when it comes to stationary care (Kommission für Konjunkturfragen 2006). So far, there are no systematic, nationwide performance indicators for quality and efficacy available (Hess & Strauhbaar 2010; Okma et al. 2010). The lack of such indicators has adversely affected the assessment of Switzerland by both the OECD (2006) in its review of health systems as well as its ranking in the Euro Health Consumer Index (Health Consumer Powerhouse 2005–2009). There are quite a few areas where the federal structure of the Swiss political system leads to competition between public providers and thereby triggers innovation, but with respect to public health, the considerable influence of federalism mainly causes the healthcare system to be fragmented and non-transparent (Kocher 2010; OECD 2006).

The federal structure of Switzerland further leads to cross-cantonal differences with respect to the availability of healthcare resources and infrastructure. To assess the impact of these regional differences, Crivelli and Domenighetti (2003) analyze the influence of variation in physician/population ratio on patient satisfaction based on an opinion survey conducted in 1997 and come to the following result: an increase in the physician/population ratio is not associated with an increase in the satisfaction of the population with the provision of ambulatory care. It is not clear, however, whether a "decrease of oversupply" would result in dissatisfaction, at least in the short term. The objective quality of the cantonal health systems, though, does not appear to be affected by the variation in the physician/population ratio: grouping the cantons according to their physician/population ratio does not result in significantly different rates of avoidable mortality.

It is questionable, though, whether the variation in the physician/population ratio really reflects the influence of federalism or whether these differences can be attributed to urban–rural divergence. Stationary care can be expected to reflect the impact of the federal structure more adequately, also because the cantons play a very important role in hospital provision and finance. Unfortunately, so far, there are no studies available on the impact of cross-cantonal differences in the number of hospital beds on patient satisfaction.

4.3. Efficiency

As aforementioned, the Swiss health system is characterized by a very high quality. However, with respect to efficiency, there is still room for improvement – particularly when it comes to in-house treatment. As Figure 12.5 shows, there are very large differences between cantons in the number of hospital beds per 1000 inhabitants: in 2009, this ratio ranged from 11.54 in Basel-City (BS) to 2.13 in Schwyz (SZ); the average over all cantons was 5.02 beds per 1000 inhabitants.[20] Interestingly, the hospitalization rates also vary from one canton to another as is shown in Figure 12.6.[21] Moreover, many of those cantons that ranked high with respect to the number of hospital beds also have a high hospitalization ratio. To analyze this relationship more systematically, Spycher, Bayer-Oglesby and Cerboni (2007) performed a regression analysis using data from the Swiss hospital statistics. According to the authors, 18% of the cross-cantonal variation in hospitalization rates can be explained with differences in the number of hospital beds per inhabitant. All other regressors used in the analysis (e.g., the number of accidents, prevalence of cardiovascular diseases, number of private hospitals and university hospitals, socioeconomic variables, etc.) had lower or even insignificant coefficients. Consequently, the availability of

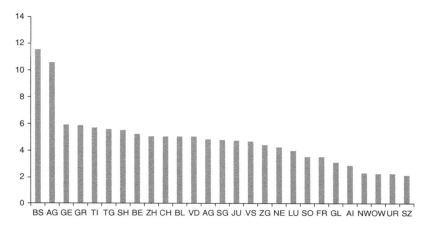

Figure 12.5   Hospital beds per thousand inhabitants

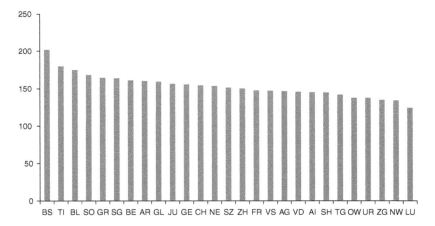

Figure 12.6   Hospitalization rate per thousand inhabitants

stationary care clearly appears to increase usage. However, both the duration in hospitals as well as the number of hospital beds per 1000 inhabitants have decreased in Switzerland over the past decade. Partly, this was due to mergers and increased cooperation between hospitals (Kommission für Konjunkturfragen 2006). One would therefore expect this development to mitigate supply-induced demand in the future (Berger et al. 2010).

In the study mentioned above, Crivelli and Domenighetti (2003) also find evidence for supply-induced demand with respect to the number of physicians per inhabitant: the number of consultations per capita is significantly higher in cantons that have high physician/population ratios.

According to Crivelli et al. (2006), a higher physician/population ratio also corresponds to higher per capita health expenditures. Supply-induced demand is a problem that is often encountered in health economics. However, in the Swiss health system, inefficiencies do not only stem from supply-induced demand, but also from the failure to benefit from economies of scale. This is particularly true for stationary care. Many of the Swiss cantons are rather small and only nine cantons have a population that is above 300,000. Nevertheless, even the smallest cantons are responsible for hospital provision – which then results in a large number of small hospitals. Crivelli et al. (2001) and Farsi and Filippini (2006) have estimated the cost functions of Swiss hospitals. Both studies show that the optimal size of a hospital would be approximately 300 beds. However, most economies of scale can already be benefitted from if a hospital has at least 135 beds. Given that 70% of the public hospitals in Switzerland have less than 135 beds, this clearly points at inefficiencies in stationary care.

Crivelli et al. (2002) as well as Lunati (2009) have further estimated cost functions of Swiss nursing homes and other long-term care institutions. Investigating 850 institutions in 1998 and 356 institutions from 1998 until 2002, the authors derive that the optimal size of a nursing home lies between 70 and 80 beds. However, 50% of the Swiss nursing homes have less than 55 beds. Consequently, institutions of both stationary as well as nursing care in Switzerland do not sufficiently use economies of scale. Furthermore, given the small size and the proximity of many cantons, spillovers across cantons might lead to freeriding effects. To avoid these effects, complex regulation, for example with respect to hospital treatment in another canton, is necessary. Again, this increase in bureaucracy is not likely to make procedures more efficient.

Furthermore, there is an incentive on behalf of health insurance to send patients to the hospital (rather than to ambulatory care sites) as the hospitals are co-financed by the cantons. This is increasing total healthcare costs for two reasons: not only would ambulatory care be less costly in most cases, but also does the co-financing by the cantons make Health Maintenance Organizations less attractive, which achieve a lot of their savings through a larger share of ambulatory treatment and shorter hospital durations.

From an economic point of view, a single-payer system for stationary care would probably be the most efficient option (Kommission für Konjunkturfragen 2006). However, on 1 June 2008, the Swiss people rejected a referendum for the introduction of a single-payer system (*monistische Spitalfinanzierung*) that would have transferred responsibility for hospital finance from the cantons to the health insurances. Consequently, a single-payer system is not going to be an option in Switzerland anytime soon (Kirchgässner & Gerritzen 2011). It is further questionable whether the implementation of DRGs in 2012 is going to improve efficiency in stationary health care (see also Section 4).

Issues with respect to efficiency in a federal health system are not restricted to stationary care, though: with 26 different health policies and a substantial overlap of cantonal and federal competences, governance will always be challenging (Kocher 2010). In its 2006 review of the Swiss health system, the OECD noted that one way to improve efficiency would be to change governance. The report further noted that with respect to prevention, a national (umbrella) law would be needed (OECD 2006; SGGP 2010). According to the OECD (2006), "there is no overarching legislative framework for disease-prevention and health-promotion activities and a lack of clear delegation of responsibilities to the various levels of government". Given that some cost-effective prevention measures (as, e.g., tobacco and alcohol taxation, promotion of physical activities, etc.) appear to be currently underutilized, a national prevention strategy seems to be even more necessary (OECD 2006; Leu et al. 2008; Paccaud & Chiolero 2010). The advice of the OECD has been taken seriously, as the Federal Council passed a national law on prevention on 30 September 2009. It was subsequently accepted by the National Council (12 April 2011) and the Council of States (01 June 2012).[22] In the end, however, the prevention law has not been passed for budgetary reasons. Namely, it failed to meet a qualified majority in the Council of States (27 September 2012) which would have been needed in order to release the debt brake and ensure funding for the implementation of the new law. Despite the failure of the proposal, the discussions related to the prevention law have increased awareness regarding the need of a legal basis in this realm.[23]

Some cantonal representatives argue (in line with a strand of the literature on fiscal federalism)[24] that cost control tends to be easier in a federal system since local authorities understand local needs and capacities better than any centralized authority. This statement might hold for other policy areas, but with respect to health care, the data (not only for Switzerland, but also for other federal states) appear to prove them wrong.[25] Nevertheless, given that the cantons provide a large chunk of the funds available for public health care, it is also understandable that they are rather reluctant toward assigning new competences to the federal level (Frey 2008).

5. Tensions and likely future developments

In 2012, a new financing system for hospital treatment has been implemented in Switzerland. The most important innovation is the replacement of the "payment per day" regulations with the introduction of DRGs. Now, hospital cases are classified into groups (DRGs) and reimbursement is according to the group that the patient has been assigned to (Frey 2008). Under the new regime, the cantons continue to play a key role with respect to hospital provision and financing with a defined cost share of 55%. The remainder of the stationary costs are borne by the health insurers. Some cantons that have previously paid more than 55% of the hospital costs now intend to cut their cost share. According to the association of the Swiss health insurances Santésuisse, this is very likely to lead to health insurance premium increases of at least 1.2%. In its spring 2011 session, the Swiss Parliament has discussed different measures to prevent such a premium increase. The Council of States approved interim regulations that would forbid a rise in premiums due to the new financing system. The National Assembly subsequently rejected the proposal, though. Despite the failure of the proposal, the Council of States remarked that the discussions in Parliament have managed to expose the transfer of payments from (progressive) income taxation to per capita premiums undertaken by some cantons.[26]

Aside from the cost shifting from cantons to insurance providers, it is further of central interest whether total stationary costs are going to decrease due to the introduction of DRGs. The duration in hospitals used to be very long in Switzerland, which was partly attributed to payment-per-day regulations that created an incentive for hospitals to keep patients longer than necessary (Widmer et al. 2007; Kommission für Konjunkturfragen 2006). However, hospital duration in Switzerland has been decreasing over the past years: average duration in stationary care in Switzerland went from 14.7 days in 1995 to 12.8 days in 2000 and 10.7 days in 2008. In Germany, where DRGs have been implemented nationwide in 2004 after pilot projects in several states, average duration in stationary care was 13.5 days in 1995, 11.4 days in 2000, and 9.9 days in 2008.[27] Consequently, both countries have experienced a comparable reduction in duration, even though Switzerland has not yet introduced DRGs. Substantial cost savings due to the introduction of DRGs are therefore questionable. However, DRGs are likely to improve transparency regarding differences between the services of different hospitals. As aforementioned, the federal structure of the Swiss health system often results in a lack of transparency. DRGs, and the quality controls that are implied by it, are therefore likely to improve quality. This comes, however, at the cost of increased bureaucracy (Kirchgässner & Gerritzen 2011).

Like most other industrial nations, Switzerland is more than likely to experience health expenditure increases due to its ageing society (BFS 2007; Imhof et al. 2011; Mösle 2007; Oggier 2010). Up to now, the main responsibility for long-term care lies within the cantons, although medically indicated services are generally covered by the health insurance KVG (Mösle 2007). The degree to which the organization and provision of, for example, nursing homes is delegated to the municipalities, differs from one canton to another. This leads to considerable regional differences, not only in terms of structure, but also with respect to services offered. The pronounced regional variation in long-term care calls for a concise national strategy. It is further questionable, whether the cantonal and communal funds will be sufficient to provide care that matches future increases in demand. Raising the direct copayments of the elderly is not necessarily an option, given that the privately financed contributions to long-term care financing in Switzerland are already very high in international comparison (Leu 2008; Kirchgässner & Gerritzen 2011).

Another issue related to an ageing society is the increased prevalence of chronic diseases. Given that most chronic diseases are not curable, prevention is the key. One of the goals of the new national law on prevention is to coordinate and strengthen preventive efforts with respect to chronic diseases and age-related health issues. As aforementioned, the prevention law has not been passed. Although there is growing awareness regarding the need of a legal basis in this realm, members of parliament could not reach an agreement. In particular, the opponents are worried that a law would result in over-regulation, thereby placing excessive restrictions on personal freedom.[28] Even if eventually a consensus might be found, a prevention law will in many areas increase the number of shared competences of the cantons and the confederation rather than strengthen central governance (Paccaud & Chiolero, 2010).[29] This is, for example, going to be the case with the eight-year national health and prevention aims, one of the central features of the new prevention law: not only will the aims be formulated jointly by the cantons and the confederation, but also, they will only be legally binding for the federal offices and not for the cantons. However, compared with the current, very fragmented system, the increase in coordination under the new prevention regulation would already represent an improvement (Achtermann & von Greyerz 2010; Conti 2010).

Two other proposals that aim to strengthen central governance have received increasing attention over the past few years: first, the creation of a Swiss Health Council, consisting of about 11 experts handling strategic and long-term health policy issues not sufficiently covered by day-to-day politics. Second, the formation of three to five health provision regions (covering at least one million inhabitants each) that would be large enough to benefit from economies of scale (Kocher 2010).

In summary, it can be said that the federal, together with the fragmented insurance structure of the Swiss health system results in a considerable lack of transparency and some pockets of inefficiency, particularly with respect to stationary care. Nevertheless, there exist several areas in health care where federalism leads to competition between providers and thereby to innovation as, for example, the introduction of new methods of outcome measurement shows. Furthermore, knowledge of local needs and capacities might be crucial in some situations and can often more adequately be dealt with on the local level (Kocher 2010; OECD 2006). Actors on all levels of the state are therefore called upon to carefully balance out the positive and negative effects of federalism on the Swiss healthcare system. Authorities on both cantonal and federal levels have repeatedly shown determination to establish a national health policy. There exist quite a few examples where responsibility has been shifted from the cantonal to the federal level. This holds, for example, for the introduction of the statutory health insurance KVG, or the creation of institutions such as Swiss medic. Despite the recent developments, as long as the cantonal payments account for over 80% of the resources available for public health, it is rather unlikely to observe a true competence shift toward the central authorities (SGGP 2011).

Notes

1. See Article 42 of the Federal Constitution of the Swiss Confederation (Bundesverfassung BV) (http://www.admin.ch/ch/e/rs/1/101.en.pdf (8 July 2011)).
2. The Federal Office for Social Insurance (BSV) is responsible for social insurance policies of health insurance, accident insurance as well as disability insurance. The military insurance represents an exception since it is organized and provided by the Federal Office for Military Insurance. For this see European Observatory on Health Care Systems (2000, p. 12).
3. This list is not exhaustive. For a more detailed overview of the organizational structure of the Swiss health system, refer to the European Observatory on Health Care Systems (2000, pp. 10ff.) and Kocher (2010, pp. 133ff.).
4. *Source of the data: Statistisches Jahrbuch der Schweiz* 2011, Table 14.5.3.4, p. 335, or OECD StatExtracts, http://stats.oecd.org/index.aspx (8 July 2011). (All data refer to the year 2008.)
5. See OECD Health Data (2010), as well as OECD StatExtracts, http://stats.oecd.org/index.aspx (8 July 2011).
6. In general, health insurance covers treatment in the home canton only. However, reimbursement is possible for treatments received outside the canton if either treatment was not available in the home canton or if it was an emergency. See also BAG (2010, p. 7).
7. See Bundesamt für Sozialversicherungen, *Schweizerische Sozialversicherungsstatistik 2011*, Gesamtrechnung, Hauptergebnisse und Zeitreihen der AHV, IV, EL, BV, KV, UV, EO, ALV, FZ, Bern 2011, p. 153. http://www.bsv.admin.ch/dokumentation/zahlen/00095/00420/index.html?lang=de (2 August 2012). See for this also Section 3.1.
8. It has to be taken into account, though, that the breakdown of publicly financed healthcare costs does not include payments toward premium subsidies. *Source of the data*: BFS (2011, pp. 27–28).
9. *Source of the data*: BFS (2011, pp. 24–25).
10. See also: C. Schoch, Kantone gegen Einmischung des Parlaments: Zur Umsetzung der neuen Spitalfinanzierung ist kein Notrecht erforderlich, *Neue Zürcher Zeitung* No. 114 of 17 May 2011, p. 13.
11. This is in line with art. 42 of the Federal Constitution of the Swiss Confederation according to which federal institutions are only responsible for those areas where competence has explicitly been assigned to it by the constitution. See http://www.admin.ch/ch/e/rs/1/101.en.pdf (8 July 2011).
12. See also *Dialog Nationale Gesundheitspolitik*, http://www.nationalegesundheit.ch (8 July 2011).
13. An important exception is dental care, which is not included in the basic package. See for this BAG (2011b).

14. Bilger (2008) decomposes the change in income inequality (expressed by the pre- and post-financing Gini indexes) that is caused by healthcare financing into a vertical, a horizontal and a re-ranking effect. The vertical effect shows how households with different pre-financing income are affected by the financing system. In other words, it measures the progressivity or regressivity of the financing (provided that there are no horizontal or re-ranking effects). The horizontal effect measures inequities that stem from unequal treatment of equals.

15. See Bundesamt für Sozialversicherungen, *Schweizerische Sozialversicherungsstatistik 2011*, Gesamtrechnung, Hauptergebnisse und Zeitreihen der AHV, IV, EL, BV, KV, UV, EO, ALV, FZ, Bern 2011, p. 152. http://www.bsv.admin.ch/dokumentation/zahlen/00095/00420/index.html?lang=de (2 August 2012).

16. The Swiss Parliament – together with the interest groups involved – is currently discussing a proposal by the federal council that wants the health insurance providers to refund insured persons in cantons where too many reserves have been accumulated. Before taking a final stance on the issue, though, the Commission for Social Security and Health of the Council of States wants to consult the cantons as well. See also: N. Nuspliger, Rückerstattung von zu hohen Prämien, *Neue Zürcher Zeitung* No. 144 of 23 June 2011, p. 11; AWP/SDA, SGK sistiert Entscheid zur Prämienrückerstattung, *Handelszeitung* 17.04.2012. http://www.handelszeitung.ch/politik/sgk-sistiert-entscheid-zur-praemienrueckerstattung (13 August 2012).

17. Source of the data: own calculations based on Balthasar et al. (2008). (All data refer to the year 2007). The average remaining premium burden is defined as follows: middle remaining premium load = (average health insurance premium – premium subsidy)/(net income – taxes).

18. See also Balthasar et al. (2008). The authors consider five sample cases: (1) a single pensioner with a modest pension income of 45,000 CHF, (2) a middle-class family of four with a gross income of 70,000 CHF, (3) a single parent with two children and a gross income of 60,000 CHF, (4) a large family with two adults and four children and 85,000 CHF, and (5) a family with one child and one young adult in vocational training having a gross family income of 70,000 CHF. The graph shows the average premium load (*after* receiving the premium subsidy) among these five groups. The dotted 6% line in Figure 12.4 shows the remaining premium load proposed by the Federal Council in 1991.

19. For an overview of the performance of the Swiss health system with respect to quality according to the OECD health data, the SHARE data and the World Value Survey WVS, see Kirchgässner and Gerritzen (2011).

20. Source of the data: Bundesamt für Statistik, *Krankenhausstatistik* 2009, Neuchâtel 2011, p. 15, Table D1. http://www.bfs.admin.ch/bfs/portal/de/index/news/publikationen.html?publicationID=4311 (13 August 2012); Bundesamt für Statistik, *Bevölkerungsstand und -struktur: Indikatoren*, Ständige Wohnbevölkerung nach Kanton 2010, Neuchâtel 2011. http://www.bfs.admin.ch/bfs/portal/de/index/themen/01/02/blank/key/raeumliche_verteilung/kantone_gemeinden.html (13 August 2012).

21. Ibid., p. 21, Table F2.

22. See for this also: Bundesamt für Gesundheit, *Entwurf für ein Bundesgesetz über Prävention und Gesundheitsförderung*, Bern, 30 September 2009, http://www.bag.admin.ch/themen/gesundheitspolitik/07492/index.html?lang=de (11 July 2011); Secretariat of the Committees for Welfare and Health, Knapper Entscheid zum Präventionsgesetz, Press Release CSSH-S, Bern, 6 May

2011, http://www.parlament.ch/d/ mm/2011/Seiten/mm-sgk-s-2011-05-06.aspx (11 July 2011); Nationalrat stimmt Präventionsgesetz zu, SR DRS, Zürich, 12 April, 2011, http://www.drs.ch/www/de/drs/nachrichten/schweiz/259482.nationalrat-stimmt-praeventionsgesetz-zu.html (11 July 2011); Ständerat reanimiert Präventionsgesetz: Kleine Kammer tritt nur knapp auf umstrittene Vorlage zur Gesundheitsvorsorge ein, *Neue Zürcher Zeitung* No. 126 of 4 June 2012.

23. In Switzerland, expenditures above a certain amount need to be accepted by a qualified majority in both chambers. In the case of the prevention law, 22 members of the council of States voted in favor and 19 against (27 September 2012). As the Council of States has 46 members in total, this was not sufficient for a qualified majority. See also K. Fontana, Signal gegen behördlichen Aktivismus, Der Ständerat lehnt das Präventionsgesetz aus Sorge vor weiteren Vorschriften ab, *Neue Zürcher Zeitung* No. 227 of 29 September 2012, p. 29.

24. The literature on fiscal federalism goes back to Tiebout (1956) and Oates (1972). For more recent surveys see, for example, Oates (1999, 2005).

25. According to Banting and Corbett (2002, pp. 25ff.), federal states "seem to have greater difficulties in containing cost pressures" with respect to health expenditures as they consistently spend a larger fraction of their GDP on health care than non-federal states. (This result also holds when the USA is being excluded from the analysis).

26. See also: Kommission will Prämienschub verhindern, *Neue Zürcher Zeitung* No. 106 of 7 May 2011, p. 14; N. Nuspliger, Spielregeln nicht in letzter Minute ändern, *Neue Zürcher Zeitung* No. 137 of 15 June 2011, p. 14; Korrektur der Spitalreform beerdigt, *Neue Zürcher Zeitung* No. 138 of 16 June 2011, p. 12.

27. See OECD Health Data (2010), but also http://www.oecd.org/health/healthdata (11/07/11). On the implementation of the DRG system in Germany, see e.g. R. Busse & A. Riesberg, *Health Care Systems in Transition: Germany*, Copenhagen: World Health Organization, Regional Office for Europe, European Observatory on Health Care Systems, 2004, p. 69 & 107.

28. See also Ständerat reanimiert Präventionsgesetz: Kleine Kammer tritt nur knapp auf umstrittene Vorlage zur Gesundheitsvorsorge ein, *Neue Zürcher Zeitung* No. 126 of 4 June 2012.

29. The federal council already tried to implement a prevention act in 1984 that failed due to the resistance of the cantons. See for this also: Bund will aktivere Rolle bei der Prävention, *Neue Zürcher Zeitung* No. 147 of 26 June 2008.

References

Achtermann, W., and S. Von Greyerz (2010), Nationale Ziele für Prävention und Gesundheitsförderung, in: S. Hill (ed.), *Gesundheits- und Präventionsziele für die Schweiz: Ergebnisse der SGGP-Stakeholder-Plattform 2009*, Schweizerische Gesellschaft für Gesundheitspolitik, Bern, pp. 25–54.

Balthasar, A., O. Bieri and B. Gysin (2008), *Monitoring 2007: Die sozialpolitische Wirksamkeit der Prämienverbilligung in den Kantonen*, Experten-/Forschungsberichte zur Kranken- und Unfallversicherung, Bundesamt für Gesundheit, Bern, February 2008.

Banting, G., and S.M. Corbett (2002), *Health Policy and Federalism: A Comparative Perspective on Multi-Level Governance*, Queen's University, Kingston, ON.

Berger, S., M. Bienlein and B. Wegmüller (2010), Spitäler, in: G. Kocher and W. Oggier (eds.), *Gesundheitswesen Schweiz 2010–2012: Eine aktuelle Übersicht*, 4th edition, Hans Huber, Bern, pp. 373–389.

Bilger, M. (2008), Progressivity, Horizontal Inequality and Reranking Caused by Health System Financing: A Decomposition Analysis for Switzerland, *Journal of Health Economics* 27, pp. 1582–1593.

Bolgiani, I., L. Crivelli and G. Domenighetti (2006), The Role of Health Insurance in Regulating the Swiss Health Care System, *Revue Française des Affaires sociales* 6/6, pp. 227–249.

Bundesamt für Gesundheit [BAG] (2005), *Das schweizerische Gesundheitswesen:* Aufbau, Leistungserbringer, Krankenversicherungsgesetz, 2nd edition. Bern.

Bundesamt für Gesundheit [BAG] (2010), *Die obligatorische Krankenversicherung kurz erklärt: Sie fragen, wir antworten*, Bern. (http://www.bag.admin.ch/themen/krankenversicherung/00263/00264/index.html (8 July 2011).)

Bundesamt für Gesundheit [BAG] (2011a), *BAG in Kürze.* Bern.

Bundesamt für Gesundheit [BAG] (2011b), *Rechtliche Grundlagen*, Bern. (http://www.bag.admin.ch/org/grundlagen/index.html?lang=de (8 July 2011)).

Bundesamt für Statistik [BFS] (2007), *Déterminants et évolution des coûts du système de santé en Suisse:* revue de la littérature et projections à l'horizon 2030, Neuchâtel.

Bundesamt für Statistik [BFS] (2011), *Kosten und Finanzierung des Gesundheitswesens*, Detaillierte Ergebnisse 2008 und jüngste Entwicklung, Neuchâtel.

Colombo, F. (2001), Towards More Choice in Social Protection?: Individual Choice of Insurer in Basic Mandatory Health Insurance in Switzerland, *OECD Labour Market and Social Policy Occasional Papers* No. 53, OECD, Paris, September 2001. (http://dx.doi.org/10.1787/664178220717 (8 July 2011).)

Conti, C. (2010), Steuerungsinstrumente im Präventionsbereich: Der Standpunkt der Kantone, in: S. Hill (ed.), *Gesundheits- und Präventionsziele für die Schweiz: Ergebnisse der SGGP-Stakeholder-Plattform 2009*, Schweizerische Gesellschaft für Gesundheitspolitik, Bern, pp. 55–65.

Crivelli, L., and G. Domenighetti (2003), Influence de la variation des densités médicales régionales en Suisse sur la mortalité, les dépenses de sante et la satisfaction des usagers, *Cahiers de Sociologie et de Démographie Médicales* 43, pp. 397–425.

Crivelli, L., M. Filippini and D. Lunati (2001), Dimensione ottima degli ospedali in uno Stato federale, *Economia Pubblica* 31, pp. 97–119.

Crivelli, L., M. Filippini and D. Lunati (2002), Regulation, Ownership and Efficiency in the Swiss Nursing Home Industry, *International Journal of Health Care Finance and Economics* 2, pp. 79–97.

Crivelli, L., M. Filippini and I. Mosca (2006), Federalism and Regional Health Care Expenditures: An Empirical Analysis for the Swiss Cantons, *Health Economics* 15, pp. 535–541. (http://onlinelibrary.wiley.com/doi/10.1002/hec.1072/pdf (8 July 2011).)

Dafflon, B. (1999), Fiscal Federalism in Switzerland: A Survey of Constitutional Issues, Budget Responsibility and Equalization, in: A. Fossati and G. Panella (eds.), *Fiscal Federalism in the European Union*, Routledge Studies in the European Economy, New York, pp. 255–294.

Dafflon, B. (2007), Accommodating Asymmetry through Pragmatism: An Overview of Swiss Fiscal Federalism, in: R.M. Bird and R.D. Ebel (eds.), *Fiscal Fragmentation In Decentralized Countries: Subsidiarity, Solidarity And Asymmetry*, Edward Elgar, Cheltenham and Northampton, pp. 114–166.

Doorslaer, E. van, and C. Masseria (2004), Income-Related Inequality in the Use of Medical Care in 21 OECD Countries, *OECD Health Working Papers* No. 15, Paris, May 2004.

European Observatory on Health Care Systems (2000), *Health Care Systems in Transition: Switzerland*, Copenhagen.

Farsi, M., and M. Filippini (2006), An Analysis of Efficiency and Productivity in Swiss Hospitals, *Swiss Journal of Economics and Statistics* 142, pp. 1–37.

Frey, N. (2008), *Ergebnisbericht 2. Nationale Föderalismuskonferenz*, Sektion Strategie und Controlling, Staatskanzlei Kanton Aargau, Aarau.

Health Consumer Powerhouse (ed.) (2005–2009), *Euro Health Consumer Index*, 2005–2009, http://www.healthpowerhouse.com/media/EHCI2005_EN.pdf (2005). (http://www.healthpowerhouse.com/index.php?option=com_content&view=category&layout=blog&id=36&Itemid=55 (2006–2009) (12 November 2010)).

Hess, K., and P. Straubhaar (2010), Qualität und Qualitätsförderung, in: G. Kocher and W. Oggier (eds.), *Gesundheitswesen Schweiz 2010–2012: Eine aktuelle Übersicht*, 4th edition, Hans Huber, Bern, pp. 335–345.

Imhof, L., I. P. Rüesch, R. Schaffert, R. Mahrer-Imhof, A. Fringer and C. Kerker-Specker (2011), *Perspektiven der professionellen Pflege in der Schweiz:* Literaturgestützte Analyse zukünftiger Entwicklungstendenzen, Schweizerische Gesellschaft für Gesundheitspolitik, Bern.

Indra, P., R. Januth and S. Cueni (2010), Krankenversicherung, in: G. Kocher and W. Oggier (eds.), *Gesundheitswesen Schweiz 2010–2012: Eine aktuelle Übersicht*, 4th edition, Hans Huber, Bern, pp. 177–196.

Kirchgässner, G. (2008), Direct Democracy: Obstacle to Reform? *Constitutional Political Economy* 19, pp. 81–93.

Kirchgässner, G., and B. C. Gerritzen (2011), *Leistungsfähigkeit und Effizienz von Gesundheitssystemen: Die Schweiz im internationalen Vergleich*, Gutachten zuhanden des Staatssekretariats für Wirtschaft (SECO), Bern, April. (http://www.seco.admin.ch/themen/00374/00459/00462/index.html (8 July 2011).)

Kocher, G. (2010), Kompetenz- und Aufgabenteilung Bund – Kantone – Gemeinden, in: G. Kocher and W. Oggier (eds.), *Gesundheitswesen Schweiz 2010–2012: Eine aktuelle Übersicht*, Hans Huber, Bern, 4th edition, pp. 133–144.

Kommission für Konjunkturfragen (2006), *Reform des Gesundheitswesens, Jahresbericht 2006*, 385. Mitteilung, Beilage zur Volkswirtschaft, dem Magazin für Wirtschaftspolitik, 1–2006. (http://www.seco.admin.ch/dokumentation/publikation/02640/02644/index.html?lang=de (8 July 2011).)

Lenz, M.J., and M.A. Hochreutener (2001), Das Projekt LORAS und Qualitätssicherung, Teil 3: Einführung der Outcome-Messung im Kanton Zürich, *Zeitschrift für ärztliche Fortbildung und Qualität im Gesundheitswesen* 95, pp. 319–321. (http://shop.elsevier.de/elsevier/journals/files/zaefq/archive/401/9.pdf (8 July 2011).)

Leu, R., F. Rutten, W. Brouwer, Ch. Rütschi and P. Matter (2008), *The Swiss and the Dutch Health Care Systems Compared: A Tale of Two Systems*, Nomos, Baden-Baden.

Leu, R., and M. Schellhorn (2004), The Evolution of Income-Related Inequalities in Health Care Utilization in Switzerland Over Time, IZA Discussion Papers No. 1316, Bonn. (http://ftp.iza.org/dp1316.pdf (8 July 2011)).

Leu, R., and M. Schellhorn (2006), The Evolution of Income-Related Health Inequalities in Switzerland over Time, *CESifo Economic Studies* 52, pp. 666–690.

Linder, W. (2004), Political Culture, in: U. Klöti, P. Knoepfel, et al. (eds.), *Handbook of Swiss Politics*, Neue Zürcher Zeitung Publishing, Zürich, pp. 13–33.

Lunati, D. (2009), La valutazione dell' (in)efficienza produttiva nel settore delle case per anziani in Svizzera: stima econometrica di una frontiera di costo stocastica, *Università della Svizzera italiana* (USI), Ph.D. Thesis.

Mösle, H. (2007), Pflegeheime und Pflegeabteilungen, in: G. Kocher and W. Oggier (eds.), *Gesundheitswesen Schweiz 2007–2009: Eine aktuelle Übersicht*, 3rd edition, Hans Huber, Bern, pp. 251–263.

Oates, W.E. (1972), *Fiscal Federalism*, Harcourt/Brace/Jovanovich, New York.

Oates, W.E. (1999), An Essay on Fiscal Federalism, *Journal of Economic Literature* 37, pp. 1120–1149.

Oates, W.E. (2005), Toward a Second-Generation Theory of Fiscal Federalism, *International Tax and Public Finance* 12, pp. 349–373.

OECD (2006), *OECD Reviews of Health Systems: Switzerland*, OECD, Paris.

Oggier, W. (2010), Kosten und Finanzierung, in: G. Kocher and W. Oggier (eds.), *Gesundheitswesen Schweiz 2010–2012: Eine aktuelle Übersicht*, Hans Huber, Bern, 4th edition, pp. 157–166.

Okma, K., T. Cheng, D. Chinitz, L. Crivelli, M. Lim, H. Maarse and M. Labra (2010), Six Countries, Six Health Reform Models? Health Care Reform in Chile, Israel, Singapore, Switzerland, Taiwan and The Netherlands, *Journal of Comparative Policy Analysis* 12, pp. 75–113.

Paccaud, F., and A. Chiolero (2010), Prävention, Gesundheitsförderung und Public Health, in: G. Kocher and W. Oggier (eds.), *Gesundheitswesen Schweiz 2010–2012: Eine aktuelle Übersicht*, Hans Huber, Bern, 4th edition, pp. 309–319.

Schwappach, D.L.B., M.A. Hochreutner, D. Conen, K. Eichler, A. Blaudszun and C.M. Koeck (2003), *Outcome Measurement in the Canton of Zurich: From Theory to Practice:* Progress report on six years of development, implementation and experience with routine inpatient outcome measurement, Schweizerische Gesellschaft für Gesundheitspolitik, Bern.

Schweizerische Gesellschaft Für Gesundheitspolitik [SGGP] (2010), Prävention: Ungenutzte Potentiale, *Gesundheitspolitische Informationen*, February 2010. (http://www.sggp.ch/gpi/archiv/index.cfm.html (10 August 2011)).

Schweizerische Gesellschaft Für Gesundheitspolitik [SGGP] (2010a), SwissDRG: Chancen und Risiken, *Gesundheitspolitische Informationen*, January 2010. (http://www.sggp.ch/gpi/archiv/index.cfm.html (10 August 2011)).

Schweizerische Gesellschaft Für Gesundheitspolitik [SGGP] (2011), Herausforderung Föderalismus: Fehlende Übersicht im Gesundheits-Dickicht, *Gesundheitspolitische Informationen*, January 2011. (http://www.sggp.ch/gpi/archiv/index.cfm.html (8 July 2011).)

Schweizerische Konferenz der Gesundheitsdirektorinnnen und -direktoren [GDK] (2003), *Vereinbarung zwischen der GDK und der Schweizerischen Eidgenossenschaft zur Nationalen Gesundheits-politik Schweiz.* (http://www.nationalegesundheit.ch/fileadmin/dateien/dialog/   Vereinbarung_zwischen_dem_Bund_und_der_GDK_vom_15.12.2003.pdf (8 July 2011).)

Spycher, S. L. Bayer-Oglesby and S. Cerboni (2007), Stationäre Versorgung und Inanspruchnahme, Ausmass und Ursachen interkantonaler Unterschiede, *Swiss Health Observatory*, Bundesamt für Statistik, Neuchâtel.

Tiebout, Ch.M. (1956), A Pure Theory of Local Expenditures, *Journal of Political Economy* 64 (1956), pp. 416–424.

Vatter, A. (2004), Federalism, in: U. Kloti, P. Knoepfel, et al. (eds.), *Handbook of Swiss Politics*, Neue Zürcher Zeitung Publishing, Zürich, pp. 71–101.

Widmer, W., K. Beck, L. Boos, L. Steinmann and R. Zehnder (2007), *Eigenverantwortung, Wettbewerb und Solidarität: Analyse und Reform der finanziellen Anreize im Gesundheitswesen*, Schweizerische Gesellschaft für Gesundheitspolitik [SGGP], Zürich.

13
Conclusions

Joan Costa-Font and Scott L. Greer

1. Introduction

Health systems throughout Europe often allocate power and resources over health policy to local and regional levels of government. However, rather than a single model of decentralization, we find a heterogeneous array of models that reflect very different political, historical, and policy logics. This book has tried to bring together theoretical and empirical questions about decentralization, examining the implications of various models. This includes whether the state structure is formally federal or unitary, and whether decentralization is down to local, provincial regional or state level. Similarly, decentralization will take different shapes depending on how the health system is funded, given that funding is the ultimate source of legitimacy of public services. This conclusion will use evidence from the book chapters to respond to the three questions articulated at the beginning: what is decentralization, why do countries adopt a decentralized allocation of authority, and what do its effects appear to be?

2. What is decentralization in Europe?

Decentralization of health policy is typically justified in the health economics literature as a means to control public expenditure and pass on the responsibility of a key public service down to subnational governments. Turati in Chapter 3 explain that in the Italian case one of the key arguments for the decentralization of health care was the fact that healthcare expenditure was out of control during the 1980s, with double-digit annual growth rates, and ex-ante funding always inferior to ex-post expenditure.

The jurisdictional unit to which healthcare responsibilities are decentralized differs significantly from country to country. The role of local authorities is especially relevant in Nordic countries and Poland, while in Spain, Italy, and the UK subnational communities are the relevant units of health policymaking.

Tax-funded states tend to decentralize political responsibilities, either through the funding system (e.g. the use of block grants) or through countrywide coordination. Given that tax bases and rates are often centrally determined and collected, they tend to exhibit lower subnational autonomy that impacts on the capacity of the health system to produce diversity, and hence for the intended outcomes of a decentralized health system to be attained. Equalization mechanisms appear in all tax-funded systems, to ensure some levels of equity to healthcare access. Equitable access is part of almost any case for more centralization.

In some cases, we see centralization in Poland and Norway, re-centralization took place as a mechanism of the central government to regain control of the health system. Similar re-centralization appears to be taking place in Germany and France as a device for controlling costs and improving quality.

Social care in every system tends to be a responsibility of local or sometimes regional governments (which never seem to feel sufficiently well funded). The reasons for, and efficiency or equity of, the local government role is rarely explored. Austria is an example where, despite a formally federal structure, fiscal and legal arrangements defy the prescriptions of fiscal federalism with minimal mobility-driven competition, opaque organizations that prevent yardstick competition, and little willingness to adjust the allocation of authority to reap benefits predicted by economists of fiscal federalism.

3. Why does it happen?

The crude functionalist case for decentralization, which identifies it as a response to heterogeneity, does not work on any useful level of abstraction. Managing heterogeneous health systems centrally does not provide incentives for efficient resource allocation, as the chapter on Poland explains. Similarly, bureaucratic modernization and efficiency drives in France (Chapter 10) led to the development of French regional health authorities whose power and close connection to the central government has given them centralizing and homogenizing consequences rather than decentralizing and differentiating ones. Even when complex countries such as Norway decentralize, it seems to be about legitimacy rather than local adaptiveness.

Another important motivation for decentralization is cost-containment. The idea is simple: offload complex, expensive, and inflationary social duties onto regional governments. However, given the reluctance of central states to give up tax powers, partial decentralization led to unintended results in several of our states. Indeed, substate administrative authorities might have incentives to overspend (moral hazard effect) because they expect to be bailed out, and they are aware that they will not bear the blame for their behavior – something that Spanish autonomous communities and German Laender are often accused of exploiting. Hence, decentralization can be, but is by no means always, a solution to soft budget constraints that emerge under centralized healthcare authority. In the worst-case scenario, it can produce soft budget constraint problems that dwarf previous ones.

Another indirect source of decentralization reforms has to do with Europe, and more specifically the need to meet the fiscal stability criteria to share a single currency among those countries that are part of the Eurozone, as is the case for Italy (Chapter 3). Europe can have an influence in a country like Spain (Chapter 4) that democratized its state almost at the same time that it decentralized its health system, and Poland (Chapter 7) where decentralization in the context of the transition from a planned economy implied decentralization and the introduction of competition into the monolithic health system of a communist state. Eurozone membership seems to have been powerful, but often led to giving regional governments either excessively tight or excessively soft budget constraints.

Political transition and the politics of multinational states are extremely powerful arguments where they appear, in Belgium, Spain, and the UK most notably. In each case, the stability and maintenance of the state depended on conceding powers to strong regional governments that reflected component national groups. In Italy, decentralization became a major issue with the collapse of the old republic and the structural change that was brought with the electoral reform in the early 1990s. It led to the emergence of the Northern League's demands for fiscal federalism.

Exploitation of horizontal competition does not seem to be a rationale for decentralization anywhere. Advocates of competitive federalism must be content to find vertical competitive dynamics (if they can), or turn their sights to North America.

Decentralization can be explained as a mechanism to increase transparency of health system governance, including as a means to reduce the level of corruption at the political arena, and to reduce or contain the extent of redistribution at the fiscal level as the Italian and Belgian cases show. However, in either social or private insurance systems, the fragmented nature of the system might actually reduce the transparency of the system.

The territorial or spatial structure of a country as well as its tradition explains that its municipalities play an important role in Nordic countries where local authorities are responsible for providing all (e.g. Finland) or part of its health care. Austria would be another paradigmatic example as more than every second Austrian lives in smaller towns and villages with less than 10,000 residents. In France, regions, including Bretagne and Midi-Pyrénées, struggle to attract enough health professionals to work in the vast rural areas relatively far from cities.

4. What does it do?

As shown in Figure 1.1 (see Introduction), when decentralization encompasses vertical imbalances resulting from a more expansive decentralization of expenditures and political responsibilities, it is likely that decentralization will not lead to cost-containment and a race to the bottom. Instead, the Spanish, Italian, and Polish case studies suggest that levels of debt have mounted after decentralization of health system responsibilities. The latter can be explained by the extent to which constituents can trace accountability, so when the political and fiscal blame are not aligned together incentives to overspend by expanding public debt increases. However, these fiscal imbalances are less common in Nordic countries where typically local authorities can raise taxes and hence can use their fiscal autonomy as a means to increase their resources without drawing on countrywide support.

Decentralization can make the health systems more transparent – to voters, if not necessarily policy analysts. The chapter on Italy shows how decentralization revealed shortcomings in the way that southern regions manage their hospitals and contain pharmaceuticals costs. In the case of Spain, decentralization appears to be allowing some region states to choose to cover sex change, dental care for children, or second specialist opinion while others stay as they are. Switzerland, on the other hand, is a highly fragmented system where federalism does not help to improve the transparency of healthcare delivery.

Evidence suggests that decentralization does not lead to significant diversity in the long run when framework laws and state coordination reduces the extent of variability as it is in the case of Italy, while in the UK lesser central state coordination has allowed different policies to survive. However, as Greer suggests in Chapter 5, having multinational states produces autonomy and democratization and therefore results in divergence.

There is evidence that decentralization promotes some degree of health policy innovation as a means for regional governments in Scotland, Catalonia, and Flanders to justify their existence among its electorate. The same applies to competitive models of federalism, such as in the Swiss healthcare system.

Fiscal decentralization is extremely complex to design. Most country-specific models examined in this book have their own drawbacks, including moral hazard problems, cream-skimming of patients, pressure shifting from one region to the neighboring one, and limited collaboration between different government tiers. In times of austerity, these arrangements can have unexpected and destabilizing effects, as in Spain or the UK.

5. Conclusion

This book asked three simple questions of 14 countries and two academic disciplines. It sought to address some of the gaps in the literature, which range from a lack of precision in reports on individual states to academic theories that are often partial at best. Unsurprisingly, we found that many of the claims made about centralization are true only part of the time: sometimes decentralization makes inequality more visible, as in Spain, and sometimes it makes it less visible, as in Switzerland. Sometimes a change that the World Bank would consider decentralizing, as with the French Regional Health Authorities, is centralizing when examined without definitional blinders. Sometimes decentralization creates hard budgets; sometimes it creates soft ones for governments that have access to bond markets. Norwegians might regard local government as a vehicle for democratic empowerment; Sicilians might not identify their local politicians quite so strongly with democratic responsiveness.

Both political science and economics strongly suggest that the main source of variation in the effects of decentralization lies in the institutional structure of devolution. The most basic lesson to emerge is that there is a profound difference between decentralization to large, elected, general-purpose governments (usually called regions) and to other kinds of governments. The difference is that elected regional governments are strong players with politicians who have and can seek their own distinctive profiles. As a result they can formulate divergent interests and use their political and economic resources to pursue these interests regardless of what the state prefers. Local governments are in every case weaker, sometimes much weaker, and regional organizations without democratic mandates, such as we find in France, are reorganizations of the central state. The result is that regional governments, unlike other kinds of decentralized units, have a capacity to push back against the central government. A conversation about decentralization that elides the difference between an elected Catalan or Scottish government, and the appointed officials of a French ARS or a local government, is one that denies political realities and the actual degree of centralization.

Beyond this difference, which affects the extent and use of regional powers and the consequent level of spending and policy divergence, the lesson was that few generalizations hold well because of the complexity of politics, institutions, powers, and finances in each country. This has a signal lesson: theorists and advocates of decentralization need to be much more careful about what they recommend. An observer who expects German federalism to make the Laender powerful actors in health policy, or French decentralization to produce territorial divergence, is inattentive to politics and institutional details and will be accordingly surprised.

That is a negative lesson: apparently deductive theories usually apply to few cases and are often biased by the country that the author knows best. The positive lesson is that there is a great deal of scope for the study of territorial politics and health policy. The variability of territorial authority over health systems, the scale of centralizing and decentralizing changes, and the universal agreement that they matter are unmatched by general agreement on how to define or study them. Where policy prescription fails due to complexity, scholarship is all the more required.

Index